P9-API-719

IBM PC Assembler Language and Programming

IBM PC Assembler Language and Programming

PETER ABEL
British Columbia
Institute of Technology

Prentice-Hall, Inc.
Englewood Cliffs, New Jersey 07632

Library of Congress Cataloging-in-Publication Data

Abel, Peter, (date)
IBM PC assembler language and programming.

Includes index.
1. IBM Personal Computer—Programming.
2. Assembler language (Computer program language)
I. Title.
QA76.8.I2594A236 1987 005.265 86-17007
ISBN 0-13-448143-7

Editorial/production and interior design: Laura L. Cleveland
Cover design: Wanda Lubelska
Manufacturing buyer: Rhett Conklin

Printed in the United States of America

10 9 8 7 6

ISBN 0-13-448143-7 025

Prentice-Hall International (UK) Limited, *London*
Prentice-Hall of Australia Pty. Limited, *Sydney*
Prentice-Hall Canada Inc., *Toronto*
Prentice-Hall Hispanoamericana, S.A., *Mexico*
Prentice-Hall of India Private Limited, *New Delhi*
Prentice-Hall of Japan, Inc., *Tokyo*
Prentice-Hall of Southeast Asia Pte. Ltd., *Singapore*
Editora Prentice-Hall do Brasil, Ltda., *Rio de Janeiro*

Contents

3 ASSEMBLY LANGUAGE REQUIREMENTS

4 ASSEMBLING AND EXECUTING A PROGRAM

5 DATA DEFINITION

6 COM PROGRAM FILES

7 PROGRAM LOGIC AND ORGANIZATION

8 SCREEN PROCESSING I: BASIC FEATURES

24 ASSEMBLER PSEUDO-OP REFERENCE

25 INSTRUCTION REFERENCE

APPENDIXES

Preface

The microprocessor had its origin in the 1960s when research designers devised the integrated circuit (IC). They combined various electronic components into a single component on a silicon "chip." The manufacturers set this tiny chip into a device resembling a centipede and connected it into a functioning system. In the early 1970s, the Intel 8008 chip in a computer terminal ushered in the first generation of microprocessors.

By 1974, the 8008 evolved into a second generation microprocessor, the 8080, with general-purpose use. Its success prompted other companies to manufacture 8080 or similar processors.

In 1978, Intel produced the third generation 8086 processor, which provided some compatibility with the 8080 and significantly advanced the design. Intel developed a variation of the 8086 to provide a slightly simpler design and compatibility with current input/output devices—the 8088 processor, which IBM selected in 1981 for its announced personal computer.

An enhanced version of the 8088 is the 80188, and enhanced versions of the 8086 are the 80186, 80286, and 80386, which provide additional operations and processing power. The 80286 supports IBM's powerful AT computer, introduced in 1984. You may see these processors referred to as iAPX 86, iAPX 88, iAPX 186, iAPX 286, and, iAPX 386, where iAPX means Intel Advanced Processor Architecture.

The spread of microcomputers has also caused a renewed interest in assembler language for two major reasons. First, a program written in assembler language requires considerably less memory space and execution time. Second, a knowledge of assembler language and its resulting machine code provides an understanding of machine architecture that no "high-level" language can possibly provide. Although most software specialists develop new applications in high-level languages such as Pascal and C, which are easier to write, the most powerful and efficient software is wholly or partially written in assembler language.

High-level languages were designed to eliminate the technicalities of a particular computer. An assembler language, however, is designed for a specific computer or, perhaps more accurately, for a specific processor. As a consequence, in order to write a program in assembler language for your own computer, you have to know something about its architecture, and this book supplies all the necessary basic material. Among the material and knowledge required for this topic are the following:

- Access to an IBM personal computer or equivalent compatible microcomputer with a minimum of 64K memory and one diskette drive. Nice to have but not essential would be additional memory and a second diskette or hard disk drive.
- Familiarity with the IBM Guide to Operations manual.
- A diskette containing the assembler language translator, preferably, but not necessarily, a recent version.
- A copy of PC-DOS or MS-DOS operating system, preferably a recent version.

The following are not required for this topic:

- Mastery of programming language. Although such knowledge may help you grasp some programming concepts more readily, it is by no means essential.
- Prior knowledge of electronics or circuitry. This book provides the necessary information about PC architecture that you require for assembler programming.

Operating Systems

The purpose of an operating system is to allow a user to instruct a computer as to what action to take (such as execute a particular program) and to provide means to store (catalog) and to access information on disk.

The major operating system for the PC and its compatibles is MS-DOS from Microsoft, known as PC-DOS on the IBM PC. Among the enhancements, version 2.0 provided support for hard disk, version 3.0 provided support for the AT, and version 4.0 facilitates multiple users. A discussion of a major operating system for professionals, UNIX and its spinoff XENIX, is outside the scope of this book.

The Approach to Take

This book is intended as both a tutorial and a permanent reference. To make the most effective use of your investment in a microcomputer and software, work through each chapter carefully and reread any material that is not immediately clear. Key in the example programs, convert them to executable "modules," and execute them. Work through the exercises at the end of each chapter.

The first eight chapters furnish the foundation material for the book and for the assembler language. After these chapters, you can begin with Chapters 9, 11, 12, 14, 15, 19, 20, or 21. Related chapters are 8 through 10, 12 and 13, and 15 through 18. Chapters 22 through 25 are intended as reference.

When you have completed this book, you will be able to:

- Understand the hardware of the personal computer.
- Understand machine language code and hexadecimal format.
- Understand the steps involved in assembly, link, and execute.
- Write programs in assembler language to handle the screen, perform arithmetic, convert between ASCII and binary formats, perform table searches and sorts, and perform disk input and output.
- Trace machine execution as an aid in debugging.
- Write your own macro instructions.
- Link together separate programs.

Learning assembler language and getting your programs to work is an exciting experience. For the time and effort invested, the rewards are sure to be great.

Acknowledgments

The author is grateful for the assistance and cooperation of all those who contributed suggestions and reviews.

CHAPTER 1

Introduction to the IBM Personal Computer Family

Objective: To explain features of microcomputer hardware and program organization.

INTRODUCTION

Writing assembler programs requires knowledge of the organization of a computer system. The fundamental building blocks of a computer are the bit and the byte. These supply the means by which a computer can represent data and instructions in memory.

A program in machine code consists of different segments for defining data and for machine instructions and a segment named the *stack* that contains stored addresses. To handle arithmetic, data movement, and addressing, the computer has a number of registers. This chapter covers all this material so that you can get going right away in Chapter 2 on your first machine language program.

BITS AND BYTES

A computer stores data and programs temporarily in main memory for execution. This is the memory that people mean when they claim that their computer has, for example, 512K of memory. The computer also has a number of registers that it uses for temporary calculations.

The smallest unit of data in a computer is a *bit*. A bit may be magnetized as off so that its value is zero, or as on so that its value is one. A single bit doesn't provide much information, but it is surprising what a bunch of them can do.

A group of nine bits represents a *byte*, eight bits for data and one bit for "parity." The eight bits provide the basis for binary arithmetic and for representing characters such as the letter A and the symbol *. Eight bits provide for 256 different combinations of on/off conditions, from all off (00000000) through all on (11111111). For example, a representation of the on and off bits for the letter A is 01000001 and for the asterisk is 00101010 (you don't have to memorize such facts). Each byte has a unique memory address beginning with zero, the lowest.

Parity requires that the "on" bits for a byte are always an odd number. The parity bit for the letter A would be on and for the asterisk would be off. When an instruction references a byte in storage, the computer checks its parity. If parity is even, a bit is assumed to be "lost" and the system displays an error message. A parity error may be a result of a hardware fault or it may be nonrecurring; either way, it is a rare event.

You may have wondered how a computer "knows" that a bit value 01000001 represents the letter A. When you key in an A on the keyboard, the system accepts a signal from that particular key into a byte in memory that sets the bits to 01000001. You can move this byte about in memory as you will, and that particular value when sent to the screen or printer generates the letter A.

For reference purposes, the bits in a byte are numbered 0 to 7 from right to left as shown for the letter A here:

```
Bit number:   7 6 5 4 3 2 1 0
Bit contents: 0 1 0 0 0 0 0 1
```

The number 2^{10} equals 1024, which happens to be the value K, for kilobytes. For example, a computer with 512K memory has 512 × 1024, or 524,288 bytes.

Since the processor in the PC and compatibles uses 16-bit architecture, it can access 16-bit values in both memory and its registers. A 16-bit (two-byte) field is known as a *word.* The bits in a word are numbered 0 through 15 from right to left as shown for the letters PC here:

```
Bit number:   15 14 13 12 11 10 9 8 | 7 6 5 4 3 2 1 0
Bit contents:  0  1  0  1  0  0 0 0 | 0 1 0 0 0 0 1 1
```

ASCII CODE

For purposes of standardization, microcomputers have adopted the ASCII (American National Standard Code for Information Interchange) code. For that reason only, the combination of bits 01000001 means the letter A. A standard code facilitates transfer of data between different computer devices. The 8-bit extended ASCII code that the PC uses provides 256 characters, including symbols for foreign alphabets. Appendix A supplies a list of the ASCII characters, and Chapter 8 shows how to display most of the 256 characters on a screen.

BINARY NUMBERS

Because a computer can distinguish only between 0-bit and 1-bit conditions, it works in a base-2 numbering system known as binary. In fact, a bit derives its name from "binary digit."

A collection of binary digits (bits) can represent any value. The value of a binary number is based on the relative position of each bit and the presence of 1-bits. The following eight-bit number contains all 1-bits:

Position value:	128	64	32	16	8	4	2	1
On-bit:	1	1	1	1	1	1	1	1

The rightmost bit assumes the value 1, the next digit to the left assumes 2, the next assumes 4, and so forth. The total of the 1-bits in this case is 1 + 2 + 4 + . . . + 128, or 255 (or 2^8–1).

For the binary number 01000001, the 1-bits represent the values 1 plus 64, or 65. But wait . . . isn't 01000001 the letter A? Indeed it is. Here's the part that you have to get clear. Bits 01000001 can represent either the number 65 or the letter A:

- If a program defines a data item for arithmetic purposes, then 01000001 represents a binary number equivalent to the decimal number 65.
- If a program defines a data item (one or more adjacent bytes) meant to be descriptive such as a heading, then 01000001 represents a letter, also known as "string" data.

When you start programming, you will find this distinction clearer, because you define the purpose of each data item.

A binary number is not limited to only eight bits. In fact, since the PC's 8088 processor uses 16-bit architecture, it handles 16-bit numbers automatically. 2^{16} minus 1 provides values up to 65,535, and a little creative programming permits numbers up to 32 bits (2^{32}–1 is 4,294,967,295), or more.

Binary Arithmetic

A microcomputer performs arithmetic only in binary format. This being the case, an assembler programmer has to be familiar with binary format and binary addition:

$$0 + 0 = 0$$
$$1 + 0 = 1$$
$$1 + 1 = 10$$
$$1 + 1 + 1 = 11$$

Note the carry of a 1-bit in the last two operations. Now, let's add 01000001 and 00101010. The letter A and an asterisk? No, the number 65 and the number 42:

Binary	*Decimal*
01000001	65
00101010	42
01101011	107

Check that the binary sum 01101011 is actually 107. Let's try another one:

Binary	*Decimal*
00111100	60
00110101	53
01110001	113

Negative Numbers

The preceding binary numbers are all positive values because the leftmost bit contains zero. A negative binary number contains a 1-bit in its leftmost position, but is expressed in *two's complement notation.* That is, to represent a binary number as negative, reverse the bits and add 1. Let's use 01000001 as an example:

Number 65:	01000001	
Reverse bits:	10111110	
Add 1:	10111111	(equals −65)

If you add up the 1-bit values for 10111111, you won't get 65. In fact, a binary number is known to be negative if its leftmost bit is 1. To determine the absolute value of a negative binary number, simply repeat the previous operation: reverse the bits and add 1:

Binary value:	10111111	
Reverse bits:	01000000	
Add 1:	01000001	(equals +65)

The sum of +65 and –65 should be zero. Let's try it:

```
   01000001  (+65)
   10111111  (-65)
(1)00000000
```

The eight-bit value is all zeros. The carry of the 1-bit on the left is lost. However, if there is a carry into the sign bit and a carry out, the result is correct.

Binary subtraction is a simple matter: Reverse the sign of the number being subtracted and add the two numbers. Let's subtract 42 from 65. The binary representation for 42 is 00101010 and its two's complement is 11010110:

```
   65       01000001
+(-42)      11010110
   23    (1)00010111
```

The result, 23, is correct. Once again, there was a carry into the sign bit and a carry out.

If the justification for two's complement notation isn't immediately clear, consider the following proposition: What value would you have to add to binary 00000001 to make it equal to 00000000? In terms of decimal numbers, the answer would be –1. For binary, try 11111111, as follows:

```
           00000001
           11111111
Result: (1)00000000
```

Ignoring the carry (1), you can see that the binary number 11111111 is equivalent to decimal –1, and accordingly

```
    0    00000000
-(+1)   -00000001
   -1    11111111
```

You can also see a pattern form as the binary numbers decrease in value:

```
+3  00000011
+2  00000010
+1  00000001
 0  00000000
-1  11111111
-2  11111110
-3  11111101
```

In fact, the 0-bits in a negative binary number indicate its value: Treat the positional value of each 0-bit as if it were a 1-bit, sum the values, and add 1.

You'll find this material on binary arithmetic and negative numbers particularly relevant when you get to Chapters 12 and 13 on arithmetic.

HEXADECIMAL REPRESENTATION

Imagine that you are viewing the contents of bytes in memory, as you'll be doing in the next chapter. You want to know the contents of four adjacent bytes (two words) that contain a binary value. Since four bytes involves 32 bits, the computer designers have developed a shorthand method of representing binary data. The method divides each byte in half and expresses the value of each half-byte. Consider the following four bytes:

Binary:	0101	1001	0011	0101	1011	1001	1100	1110
Decimal:	5	9	3	5	11	9	12	14

Since there are still some numbers that require two digits, let's extend the numbering system so that 10 = A, 11 = B, 12 = C, 13 = D, 14 = E, and 15 = F. Here's the shorthand number that represents the contents of the bytes just given:

59 35 B9 CE

The numbering system involves the "digits" 0 through F, and since there are 16 such digits it is known as hexadecimal representation. Figure 1-1 provides the binary, decimal, and hexadecimal values of the numbers 0 through 15.

Assembler language makes considerable use of hexadecimal format. Listings of an assembled program show in hexadecimal all addresses, machine code instructions, and the contents of constants. Also, for debugging you will use the DOS DEBUG program, which similarly displays addresses and contents of bytes in hexadecimal format.

Once you have worked with hexadecimal (or hex) format a while, you get quite used to it. Following are some simple examples of hex arithmetic. Keep in mind that the number following hex F is hex 10, which is decimal value 16.

```
 6    5    F    F    10    FF
 4    8    1    F    10     1
 A    D   10   1E    20   100
```

Binary	*Decimal*	*Hexadecimal*	*Binary*	*Decimal*	*Hexadecimal*
0000	0	0	1000	8	8
0001	1	1	1001	9	9
0010	2	2	1010	10	A
0011	3	3	1011	11	B
0100	4	4	1100	12	C
0101	5	5	1101	13	D
0110	6	6	1110	14	E
0111	7	7	1111	15	F

Figure 1-1 Binary, Decimal, and Hexadecimal Representation.

Note also that hex 20 equals decimal 32, hex 100 is decimal 256, and hex 1000 is decimal 4096.

This text normally indicates a hexadecimal number, for example, as hex 4B, a binary number as binary 01001011, and a decimal number as 75—the absence of a description assumes a decimal number. An occasional exception occurs where the base is obvious from its context. To indicate a hex number in an assembler program, code an "H" immediately after the number, as 25H (decimal value 37). A hex number always begins with a decimal digit 0-9; thus, B8H becomes OB8H.

Appendix B explains how to convert a hex number to decimal and vice versa. Now let's examine some features of the PC processor that you need to understand for Chapter 2.

SEGMENTS

A *segment* is an area that begins on a *paragraph boundary,* that is, at any location evenly divisible by 16. Although a segment may be located anywhere in memory and may be up to 64K bytes in size, it requires only as much space as necessary for execution. The three main segments are:

1. *Code Segment.* The code segment contains the machine instructions that are to execute. Typically the first executable instruction is at the start of this segment, and the operating system links to this location for program execution. The code segment (CS) register addresses this segment.

2. *Data Segment.* The data segment contains defined data, constants, and work areas that a program requires. The data segment (DS) register addresses this segment.
3. *Stack Segment.* In simple terms, the stack contains return addresses both for your program to return to the operating system and for any of your own "called" subroutines to return to your main program. The stack segment (SS) register addresses this segment.

One other segment register, the *extra segment* (ES) register, has specialized uses. Figure 1-2 provides a graphic view of the SS, DS, and CS registers, although the registers and segments are not necessarily in this sequence. The three segment registers contain the starting address of each segment, and each segment begins at a paragraph boundary.

Within a program, all memory locations are relative to the start of a segment. All such locations are expressed as an *offset,* or displacement, from the start of a segment. A two-byte (16-bit) offset can range from hex 0000 through hex FFFF, or zero through 65,535. *To reference any memory address in a program, the computer combines the address in a segment register with an offset.* For example, the first byte of the code segment is at offset 00, the second byte is at offset 01, and so forth through to offset 65535.

As an example of addressing, assume that the data segment register contains hex 045F and an instruction references a location within the

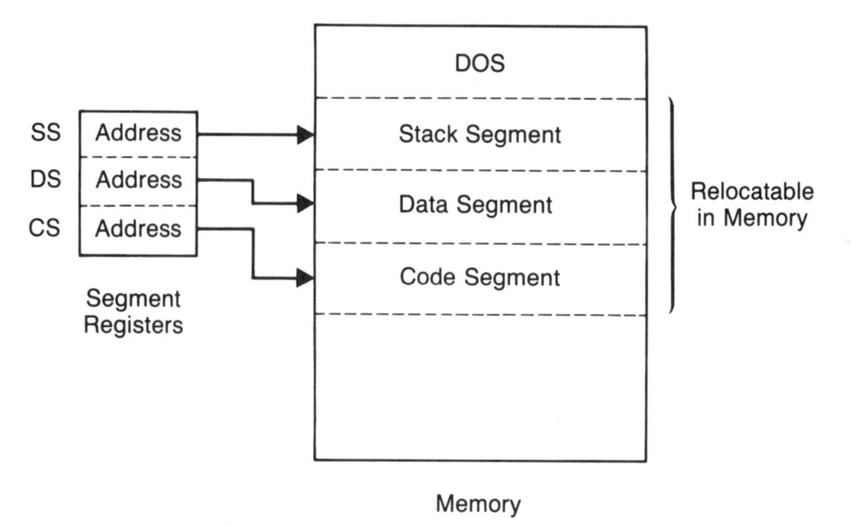

Figure 1-2 Segments and Registers.

data segment with an offset of 0032. Although the data segment contains 045F, it references location 045F0, on a paragraph boundary. The actual memory location referenced is therefore the following:

DS address:	045F0
Offset:	0032
Actual address:	04622

How do the 8086/8088 processors address one million bytes of memory? A register provides 16 bits. Since a segment address is always on a paragraph boundary, the rightmost four bits of the address are zero. Now, hex FFF0 would allow addressing up to 65,520 (plus an offset). But the designers decided that there is no purpose allowing space for bits that are always zero. An address is therefore stored in a segment register as hex nnnn and the computer assumes that there are four more rightmost zero bits (one hex digit), as hex nnnn0. Now, hex FFFF0 allows addressing up to 1,048,560 bytes. If you are uncertain, decode each hex F as binary 1111, allow for the 0-bits, and add up the values for the 1-bits.

The 80286 processor uses 24 bits for addressing, so that FFFFF0 allows addressing up to 16 million bytes, and the 80386 can address up to four billion.

REGISTERS

The 8086/8088 processors have 14 registers that are used to control the instruction being executed, to handle addressing of memory, and to provide arithmetic capability. Each register is one word (16 bits) in length and is addressable by name. Each bit is conventionally numbered from left to right, as

15 14 13 12 11 10 9 8 7 6 5 4 3 2 1 0

The 80286 and 80386 have a number of additional registers, some of which exceed 16 bits; they need not concern us here.

Segment Registers: CS, DS, SS, and ES

Each segment register provides for addressing a 64K area of memory, known as the *current segment.* As discussed earlier, a segment aligns on a paragraph boundary and its address in a segment register assumes four 0-bits to the right.

1. *CS Register.* The code segment register contains the initial address of the code segment. This address plus the offset value in the instruction pointer (IP) indicates the address of an instruction to be fetched for execution. For normal programming purposes you need not reference the CS.
2. *DS Register.* The data segment register contains the initial address of the data segment. In simple terms, this address plus an offset value in an instruction causes a reference to a specific location in the data segment.
3. *SS Register.* The stack segment register contains the initial address of the stack segment.
4. *ES Register.* Some string operations use the extra segment register to handle memory addressing. In this context, the ES register is associated with the DI register. If the ES is required, an assembler program must initialize it.

General Purpose Registers: AX, BX, CX, and DX

For assembler programming, the general purpose registers are the workhorses. They are unique in that you can address them as one word or as a one-byte portion. The leftmost byte is the "high" portion and the rightmost byte is the "low" portion. For example, the CX register consists of a CH and a CL portion, and you can reference any of the three names. The following three assembler instructions move zeros to the CX, CH, and CL registers, respectively:

```
MOV   CX,00
MOV   CH,00
MOV   CL,00
```

1. *AX Register.* The AX register is known as the *primary accumulator* and is used for all input/output operations, some "string" operations, and some arithmetic operations. For example, multiply, divide, and translate instructions assume use of the AX. Some instructions generate more efficient code if they reference the AX.

   AX: | AH | AL |

2. *BX Register.* The BX register is known as the *base register* since it is the only general purpose register that can be used as an "index" to extend addressing. Another common purpose is for computations.

BX: | BH | BL |

3. *CX Register.* The CX register is known as the *count register.* It is required for controlling the number of times a loop is repeated and contains the value by which bits are shifted left or right. The CX is also used for computations.

CX: | CH | CL |

4. *DX Register.* The DX register is known as the *data register.* Some input/output operations require its use, and multiply and divide operations that involve large values assume the DX and AX pair.

DX: | DH | DL |

Any of these general purpose registers may be used for addition and subtraction of either 8-bit or 16-bit values.

Pointer Registers: SP and BP

The pointer registers, SP and BP, permit the system to access data in the stack segment. They may also be used (rarely) for addition and subtraction.

1. *SP Register.* The stack pointer permits implementation of a stack in memory, used for temporary storage of addresses and sometimes data. This register is associated with the SS register for addressing the stack.
2. *BP Register.* The base pointer facilitates referencing of "parameters" (data and addresses passed via the stack).

Index Registers: SI and DI

Both index registers are available for extended addressing and for use in addition and subtraction.

1. *SI Register.* This register is known as the *source index* and is required for some string (character) operations. In this context, the SI is associated with the DS register.
2. *DI Register.* This register is known as the *destination index* and is also required for some string operations. In this context, the DI is associated with the ES register.

Instruction Pointer Register: IP

The IP register contains the offset address of the instruction that is to execute. You would not normally reference this register in a program, but you can change its value when using the DOS DEBUG program to test a program.

Flag Register

Nine of the 16 bits of the flag register are active and indicate the current status of the machine and the results of execution. Many instructions involving comparisons and arithmetic change the status of the flags. Briefly, the flag bits are the following:

Flag	*Purpose*
O (Overflow)	Indicates overflow of a high-order bit following arithmetic.
D (Direction)	Designates left or right direction for moving or comparing "string" data (data in memory that exceeds one word).
I (Interrupt)	Indicates if an interrupt is disabled.
T (Trap)	Permits operation of the CPU in single-step mode. The DOS DEBUG program, for example, sets the trap flag so that you can step through execution one instruction at a time to examine the effect on registers and memory.
S (Sign)	Contains resulting sign of arithmetic operation (0 = plus and 1 = minus).
Z (Zero)	Indicates result of arithmetic or compare operation (0 = nonzero and 1 = zero result).
A (Auxiliary carry)	Contains a carry out of bit 3 on 8-bit data, for specialized arithmetic.
P (Parity)	Indicates parity of low-order 8-bit data operation (1 = even and 0 = odd number).
C (Carry)	Contains carries from high-order (leftmost) bit following an arithmetic operation, and contents of last bit of a shift or rotate.

The flags that are most relevant to assembler programming are O, S, Z, and C for comparisons and arithmetic, and D for direction of string operations. Later chapters contain more detail about the flag register.

PC ARCHITECTURE

The main hardware elements of the PC are a system unit, a keyboard, a display screen, disk drives, printer, and various options for asynchronous communications and game control. The system unit contains a system board, power supply, and expansion slots for optional boards. Features of the system board are the following:

- An Intel microprocessor.
- 40K bytes of read-only memory (ROM).
- Up to 512 bytes of read/write memory (RAM), depending on model.
- An enhanced version of the BASIC interpreter.

Expansion slots provide for connecting display screens, diskette drives, communications channel, additional memory boards, and games.

The keyboard contains its own microprocessor. It performs self-testing when the power is turned on, keyboard scanning, key debounce, and buffering up to 20 key scan codes.

The brain of the PC and its relations is a microprocessor that performs all processing of instructions and data. The 8088 processor uses 16-bit registers that can process two bytes at a time. The 8088 is like an 8086 but with one difference: The 8088 is limited to 8-bit (instead of 16-bit) buses, which provide transfers of data between the processor, memory, and external devices. This limit means a cost in data transfer time with a gain in simplicity of design. The 80286 and 80386 are advanced versions of the 8086.

The processor is partitioned into two logical units: an execution unit (EU) and a bus interface unit (BIU), as illustrated in Figure 1-3. The role of the EU is to execute instructions whereas the BIU provides instructions and data to the EU. The EU contains an arithmetic and logic unit (ALU), a control unit (CU), and ten registers. These features provide for instruction execution, arithmetic computation, and logic (comparison for high, low, and equal).

The three sections of the BIU, bus control unit, instruction queue, and segment registers, control three important functions. First, the BIU controls the buses that transfer data to the EU, to memory, and to external input/output devices. Second, the four segment registers control up to one million bytes of memory addressing.

The third function of the BIU is instruction access. Since all program instructions are in memory, the BIU must access instructions from memory into an instruction queue. Because the queue is four or more bytes in size, depending on the processor, the BIU is able to look ahead

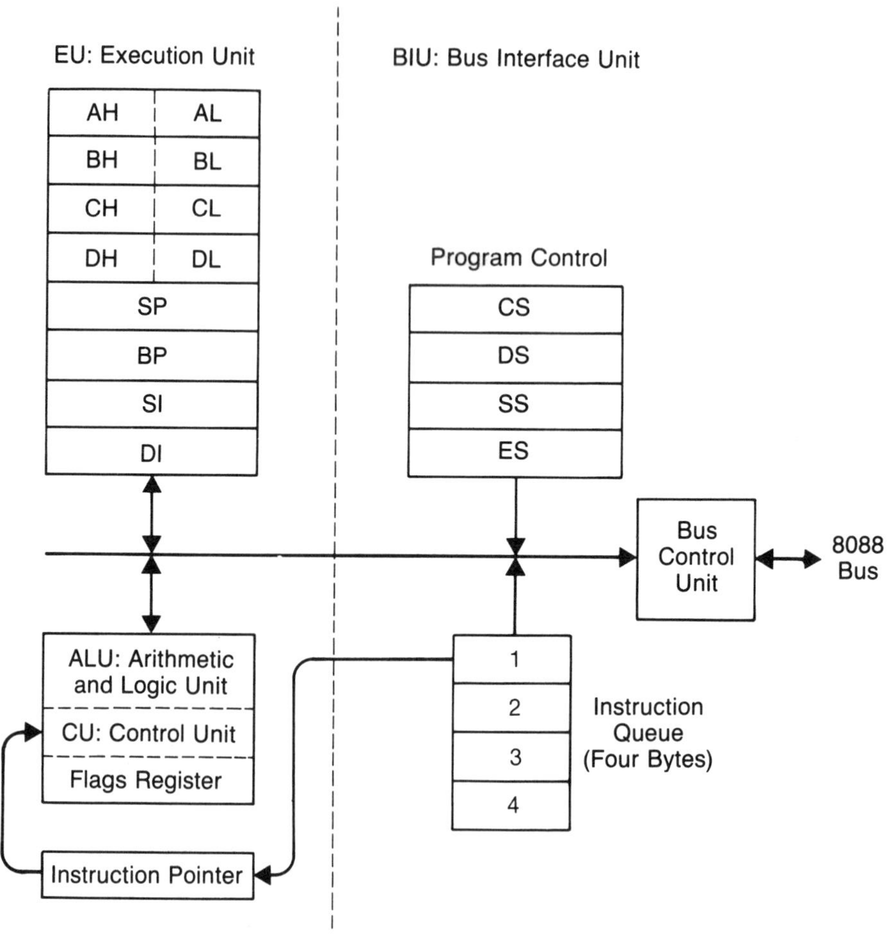

Figure 1-3 8088 Execution Unit and Bus Interface Unit.

and prefetch instructions so that there is always a queue of instructions ready to execute.

The EU and BIU work in parallel, with the BIU keeping one step ahead. The EU notifies the BIU if it needs access to data in memory or an I/O device. Also, the EU requests machine instructions from the BIU instruction queue. The top instruction is the currently executable one, and while the EU is occupied executing an instruction, the BIU fetches another instruction from memory. This fetching overlaps with execution and speeds up processing.

Memory

A typical microcomputer contains two types of internal memory. The first type is ROM, an acronym for read-only memory. A ROM is a special memory chip that (as the name suggests) can only be read. Since data in a sense is permanently "burned into" the memory chip, it cannot be altered.

One main purpose of ROM is to handle start-up procedures; when you switch on the power, ROM performs various check-outs and loads into RAM (main memory) any data from a system diskette (such as DOS). For programming purposes, one feature of ROM is important, the Basic Input/Output System (BIOS), covered in later chapters. (*Basic* here means the conventional word, not the programming language.) ROM also handles the BASIC interpreter, and patterns for graphics characters.

The type of memory that concerns a programmer is RAM, which stands for random access memory, and which would be better named read-write memory. In effect, RAM memory is available as a "worksheet" for temporary storage of a program and its data area for execution.

Since the contents of RAM are lost when you turn off the power, you need separate external storage for keeping programs and data. If you have the DOS diskette inserted or hard disk installed, when you turn on the power, ROM causes the DOS program to load into RAM. (Only the main part of DOS loads, not the entire set of DOS programs.) You then reply to the DOS prompt for the date and can request DOS to perform actions. One action could be to load a program from a disk into RAM. Since DOS does not occupy all of RAM, there is (usually) space for your program as well. Your program executes in RAM and normally produces output on the screen, printer, or disk. When finished, you may load another program into RAM; although this action overwrites the previous program, the previous one is preserved on disk.

Memory Allocation. The fact that a segment can be up to 64K in size and that there are four kinds of segments suggests that the amount of available RAM memory is 4 × 64K, or 256K. But there may be any number of segments; in order to address another segment, it is only necessary to change the address in a segment register.

RAM comprises the first three quarters of memory, and ROM comprises the last one quarter. According to the physical memory map of the PC in Figure 1-4, the first 256K is RAM memory on the system board. Since one area in RAM is reserved for the video displays, you have 640K available for your own use, at least under current versions of DOS. ROM begins at address 768K and handles input/output devices, such as a hard disk controller. ROM beginning at 960K controls the computer's

Start Address		*Purpose*
Dec	Hex	
zero	0	256K of RAM memory on system board
256K	40000	384K RAM memory expansion in I/O channel
640K	A0000	128K graphics/display video buffer (RAM)
768K	C0000	192K memory expansion area (ROM)
960K	F0000	64K base system ROM

Figure 1-4 Physical Memory Map.

basic functions, such as power-on self-test, dot patterns for graphics, and the diskette self-loader.

All further discussions of RAM use the general term *memory.*

Addressing. Memory locations are numbered consecutively from 00, the lowest memory location. The processor accesses bytes or words in memory. Consider the decimal number 1025. The hex representation of this value, 0401, requires two bytes, or one word, of memory. It consists of a high-order portion ("most significant byte"), 04, and a low-order portion ("least significant byte"), 01. The system stores the bytes in a word in memory in *reverse sequence:* the low-order portion in the low memory address and the high-order portion in the high memory address. Assume that the processor has stored hex 0401 from a register into memory locations 5612 and 5613 as follows:

```
                |01|04|
                  |  |
  location 5612,     location 5613,
least significant byte   most significant byte
```

The processor expects numeric data in memory to be in reverse byte sequence and processes it accordingly. Although this feature is entirely automatic, you have to keep alert to this fact when programming and debugging assembler programs.

KEY POINTS TO REMEMBER

- A single character of memory is a byte, comprised of eight data bits and one parity bit. Two adjacent bytes comprise a word.
- The value K equals 1024 bytes.
- The heart of the PC is a microprocessor that can access bytes or words.
- The representation of character data is ASCII format.
- The computer distinguishes only between bits that are 0 (off) and 1 (on) and performs arithmetic only in binary format.
- The value of a binary number is determined by the placement of 1-bits. Thus, binary 1111 equals $2^3 + 2^2 + 2^1 + 2^0$, or 15.
- A negative binary number is represented by two's complement notation: Reverse the bits of its positive representation and add 1.
- Hexadecimal format is an important shorthand notation for representing groups of four bits. The hex digits 0-9 and A-F represent binary 0000 through 1111.
- Programs consist of segments: a stack segment for maintaining return addresses, a data segment for defined data and work areas, and a code segment for executable instructions. All locations in a program are expressed as an offset relative to the start of a segment.
- The registers control instruction execution, addressing, arithmetic, and execution status.
- The two types of internal memory are ROM (read-only memory) and RAM (random access memory).
- The processor stores numeric data in words in memory in reverse byte sequence.

QUESTIONS

1.1. Provide the ASCII bit configuration for the following one-byte characters. Use Appendix A as a guide: (a) P, (b) p, (c) #, (d) 5.

1-2. Provide the binary bit configuration for the following numbers: (a) 5, (b) 13, (c) 21, (d) 27.

1-3. Add the following binary numbers:

(a)	(b)	(c)
00010101	00111110	00011111
00001101	00101001	00000001

1-4. Determine the two's complement for the following binary numbers: (a) 00010011, (b) 00111100, (c) 00111001.

1-5. Determine the positive value of the following negative binary numbers: (a) 11001000, (b) 10111101, (c) 10000000.

1-6. Determine the hex representation for the following: (a) ASCII letter Q, (b) ASCII number 7, (c) binary 01011101, (d) binary 01110111.

1-7. Add the following hex numbers:

(a) 23A6	(b) 51FD	(c) 7779	(d) EABE
0022	3	887	26C4

1-8. Determine the hex representation for the following decimal numbers. Refer to Appendix B for the conversion method. You could also check your result by converting the hex to binary and adding up the 1-bits. (a) 19, (b) 33, (c) 89, (d) 255, (e) 4095, (f) 63,398.

1-9. What are the three kinds of segments, their maximum size, and the address boundary on which they begin?

1-10. What registers can you use for the following purposes: (a) addition and subtraction, (b) counting for looping, (c) multiply and divide, (d) addressing segments, (e) indication of a zero result, (f) address of instruction that is to execute?

1-11. What are the two main kinds of memory on the PC and what is their main purpose?

CHAPTER 2

Machine Execution

Objective: To introduce machine language and the entering and execution of a program in memory.

INTRODUCTION

The basis of this chapter is the use of a DOS program named DEBUG that allows you to view memory, to enter programs, and to trace their execution. The chapter describes how you can enter these programs directly into memory in the code segment area and provides an explanation of each execution step.

The initial exercise has you inspect the contents of particular locations in memory. The first program example uses "immediate" data defined within the instructions for loading into registers and performing arithmetic. The second program example uses data defined separately in the data segment. Tracing these instructions through machine execution provides insight into the operation of a computer and the role of the registers.

You can start right in with no prior knowledge of assembler language or even of programming. All you need is an IBM PC or equivalent micro and a disk containing the DOS operating system.

GETTING STARTED

On startup, diskette users have to insert the DOS diskette in drive A (on the left). If the power is off, turn it on; if the power is already on, press and hold down Ctrl and Alt together, and press Del.

When the working portion of DOS loads into memory, it responds with a *prompt* that asks for the date and time, and then indicates the default disk drive, normally A for diskette and C for hard disk. If this is not the case, change the default by pressing the drive letter, a colon, and the Return key. This is the normal procedure whenever you enter an exercise from this book.

VIEWING MEMORY LOCATIONS

In this first exercise, you use the DOS DEBUG program to view the contents of selected memory locations. To initiate the program, key in DEBUG and press Return. DEBUG should load from disk into memory. When fully loaded, DEBUG's prompt, hyphen (-), appears on the screen, and DEBUG is ready to accept your commands. The only command with which this exercise is concerned is D, for dump.

1. *Memory Size.* The first step is to examine the amount of memory that DOS thinks you have installed. Depending on computer model, the value is based on switches set internally, and may indicate less memory than is actually installed. The value is in memory locations hex 413 and 414, which you can view from DEBUG by means of a two-part address:

   - 400 is the segment address, that you type as 40 (the last zero is assumed), and
   - 13 is the offset from the segment address. Key in the following exactly as you see it:

   D 40:13 [and press Return]

   The first two bytes displayed should be memory size in kilobytes and in hexadecimal, with the bytes in reverse sequence. Some examples showing hex reversed, hex corrected, and the decimal equivalent follow:

Hex Reversed	*Hex Corrected*	*Decimal(K)*
80 00	00 80	128
00 01	01 00	256
80 01	01 80	384
00 02	02 00	512
80 02	02 80	640

2. *Serial Number.* A serial number for your computer is embedded in ROM at location hex FE000. To see it, type in:

   D FE00:0 [and press Return]

   A 7-digit number followed by a copyright date should display on the screen.

3. *ROM BIOS Date.* The date of your ROM BIOS begins at hex location FFFF5, recorded as mm/dd/yy. Type

D FFFF:05 [and press Return]

Knowing this date is sometimes useful to determine a computer's age and model.

Now that you know how to use the display operation, you can set an address to any valid location to view the contents. You can also step through memory simply by pressing D repeatedly—DEBUG displays locations continuing from the last operation.

When you've completed your inspection, press Q (for quit) and the Return key to exit from DEBUG. Let's now use DEBUG to enter programs directly into memory and trace their execution.

MACHINE LANGUAGE EXAMPLE: IMMEDIATE DATA

The purpose of this example is to illustrate a simple machine language program, how it would appear in main storage, and the effect of its execution. The following program steps are in hexadecimal format:

Instruction	*Explanation*
B82301	Move the hex value 0123 to the AX.
052500	Add the hex value 0025 to the AX.
8BD8	Move the contents of the AX to the BX.
03D8	Add the contents of AX to BX.
8BCB	Move the contents of BX to CX.
2BC8	Subtract the contents of AX from CX.
2BC0	Subtract the contents of AX from AX (clear AX).
90	No operation (do nothing).
CB	Return to DOS.

You may have noticed that machine instructions vary in length: one, two, or three bytes. Also, machine instructions appear in memory one immediately following the other. Program execution begins with the first instruction and steps through each instruction one after another. Do not at this point expect to make much sense of the machine code. For example, in one case a MOV is hex B8 and in another case the MOV is hex 8B.

You can enter this program directly into memory and execute it one instruction at a time. At the same time, you can view the contents of the registers after each instruction. Begin this exercise just as you did for the previous one—key in the command DEBUG and press Return. When DEBUG has fully loaded, its prompt, a hyphen (-) displays. To print this exercise, turn on your printer and press Ctrl and PrtSc together.

To enter the machine language program directly, key in the following command, including the blanks where indicated:

```
E CS:100 B8 23 01 05 25 00  [press Return]
```

The command E stands for Enter. CS:100 indicates the memory address where the instructions are to be entered—hex 100 (256) bytes following the start of the code segment (the normal starting address for machine code under DEBUG). The E command causes each pair of hexadecimal digits to enter a byte in memory, from CS:100 through CS:105.

The next Enter command is

```
E CS:106 8B D8 03 D8 8B CB  [Return]
```

which enters six bytes starting at CS:106 through 107, 108, 109, 10A, and 10B. The last Enter command

```
E CS:10C 2B C8 2B C0 90 CB  [Return]
```

enters six bytes starting at CS:10C through 10D, 10E, 10F, 110, and 111. Double-check that you have keyed in the correct values. If not, you can simply repeat any command that is incorrect.

Now it's just a simple matter of executing these instructions. Figure 2-1 shows all the steps including the E commands. Your screen should display similar results as you enter each DEBUG command.

Key in the command R, followed by Return in order to view the contents of the registers and flags. At this moment DEBUG shows the contents of the registers in hexadecimal format, for example as

AX=0000, BX=0000, ...

Because of differences in DOS versions, the register contents on your screen may not be identical to those shown in Figure 2-1. The IP (instruction pointer) register displays IP=0100 indicating that instruction execution is to begin 100 bytes past the start of the code segment. (That is why you used E CS:100 to enter the start of the program.)

The flags register in Figure 2-1 shows the following flag setting:

NV UP DI PL NZ NA PO NC

```
D>DEBUG
-E CS:100 B8 23 01 05 25 00
-E CS:106 8B D8 03 D8 8B CB
-E CS:10C 2B C8 2B C0 90 CB
-R
AX=0000  BX=0000  CX=0000  DX=0000  SP=FFEE  BP=0000  SI=0000  DI=0000
DS=13C6  ES=13C6  SS=13C6  CS=13C6  IP=0100   NV UP EI PL NZ NA PO NC
13C6:0100 B82301        MOV     AX,0123
-T

AX=0123  BX=0000  CX=0000  DX=0000  SP=FFEE  BP=0000  SI=0000  DI=0000
DS=13C6  ES=13C6  SS=13C6  CS=13C6  IP=0103   NV UP EI PL NZ NA PO NC
13C6:0103 052500        ADD     AX,0025
-T

AX=0148  BX=0000  CX=0000  DX=0000  SP=FFEE  BP=0000  SI=0000  DI=0000
DS=13C6  ES=13C6  SS=13C6  CS=13C6  IP=0106   NV UP EI PL NZ NA PE NC
13C6:0106 8BD8          MOV     BX,AX
-T

AX=0148  BX=0148  CX=0000  DX=0000  SP=FFEE  BP=0000  SI=0000  DI=0000
DS=13C6  ES=13C6  SS=13C6  CS=13C6  IP=0108   NV UP EI PL NZ NA PE NC
13C6:0108 03D8          ADD     BX,AX
-T

AX=0148  BX=0290  CX=0000  DX=0000  SP=FFEE  BP=0000  SI=0000  DI=0000
DS=13C6  ES=13C6  SS=13C6  CS=13C6  IP=010A   NV UP EI PL NZ AC PE NC
13C6:010A 8BCB          MOV     CX,BX
-T

AX=0148  BX=0290  CX=0290  DX=0000  SP=FFEE  BP=0000  SI=0000  DI=0000
DS=13C6  ES=13C6  SS=13C6  CS=13C6  IP=010C   NV UP EI PL NZ AC PE NC
13C6:010C 2BC8          SUB     CX,AX
-T

AX=0148  BX=0290  CX=0148  DX=0000  SP=FFEE  BP=0000  SI=0000  DI=0000
DS=13C6  ES=13C6  SS=13C6  CS=13C6  IP=010E   NV UP EI PL NZ AC PE NC
13C6:010E 2BC0          SUB     AX,AX
-T

AX=0000  BX=0290  CX=0148  DX=0000  SP=FFEE  BP=0000  SI=0000  DI=0000
DS=13C6  ES=13C6  SS=13C6  CS=13C6  IP=0110   NV UP EI PL ZR NA PE NC
13C6:0110 90            NOP
-T

AX=0000  BX=0290  CX=0148  DX=0000  SP=FFEE  BP=0000  SI=0000  DI=0000
DS=13C6  ES=13C6  SS=13C6  CS=13C6  IP=0111   NV UP EI PL ZR NA PE NC
13C6:0111 CB            RETF
-
```

Figure 2-1 Trace of Machine Instructions.

These settings mean, respectively, no overflow, up (right) direction, disable interrupt, plus sign, nonzero, no auxiliary carry, parity odd, and no carry. At this time, none of these flags is important.

The R command also displays at offset 0100 the first instruction to be executed. Note that in Figure 2-1 the CS register contains CS=13C6 (yours may differ) and the instruction is the following:

```
13C6:0100  B82301    MOV AX,0123
```

- CS=13C6 means that the start of the code segment is at location 13C6, or rather, 13C60. The value 13C6:0100 means 100 (hex) bytes following the CS address 13C6.
- B82301 is the machine address that you entered at CS:100.
- MOV AX,0123 is the symbolic assembler instruction for the machine code. This is the result of an "unassembly" operation, which DEBUG displays so that you may more easily interpret the machine instruction. In later chapters, you code assembler instructions exclusively. This assembler instruction means, in effect, Move the immediate value 0123 into the AX register.

At this point, the MOV instruction has not executed. For this purpose, key in T (for trace) and press Return. DEBUG now displays the contents of the registers, the flags, and the next instruction that is to execute. Note that the AX register now contains 0123. The machine code was B8 (Move to AX register) followed by 2301. The operation moves the 23 to the low half (AL) of the AX register and the 01 to the high half (AH) of the AX register:

AX: |01|23|

The contents of the IP register is 0103 to indicate the location in the code segment of the next instruction to be executed:

```
13C6:0103  052500  ADD  AX,0025
```

To execute this instruction, enter another T. The instruction adds 25 to the low half (AL) of the AX register and 00 to the high half (AH) of the AX, in effect adding 0025 to the AX. AX now contains 0148, and IP contains 0106 for the next instruction to be executed.

Key in another T command. The instruction moves the contents of the AX register to the BX register—note that BX now contains 0148. AX still contains 0148 too because the MOV operation actually copies the data from one location to another.

Now key in a T command to step through each remaining instruction in the program. The next instruction adds the contents of AX to BX, giving 0290 in BX. Then the program moves (copies) the contents of BX into CX, subtracts AX from CX, and subtracts AX from itself. After this last operation, the zero flag is changed from NZ (nonzero) to ZR (zero) to indicate that the result of the last operation was zero (subtracting AX from itself cleared it to zero).

Although you can also press T for the last instructions, NOP and RET, it is not recommended going past this point. To view the machine language program in the code segment, key in D for Dump as follows:

```
D CS:100
```

On an 80-column screen, DEBUG displays 16 bytes (32 hex digits) to the left of each line. To the right is the ASCII representation (if printable) of each byte (pair of hex digits). In the case of machine code, the ASCII representation is meaningless and may be ignored. Later sections discuss the right side of the dump in more detail.

The first line of the dump begins at 00 and represents the contents of locations CS:100 through CS:10F. The second line represents the contents of CS:110 through CS:11F. Although your program ends at CS:111, the Dump command automatically displays eight lines (on an 80-column screen) from CS:100 through CS:170.

If you want to reexecute these instructions, reset the IP register and trace through again. Enter R IP, enter 100, then R, and the required number of T commands, all followed by Return.

Figure 2-2 shows the results of the D CS:100 command. Expect only the machine code from CS:100 through 111 to be identical to your own dump; the bytes that follow could contain anything.

```
-D CS:100
13C6:0100  B8 23 01 05 25 00 8B D8-03 D8 8B CB 2B C8 2B C0   .#..%.......+.+.
13C6:0110  90 CB 8D 46 14 50 51 52-FF 76 28 E8 74 00 8B E5   ...F.PQR.v(.t...
13C6:0120  B8 01 00 50 FF 76 32 FF-76 30 FF 76 2E FF 76 28   ...P.v2.v0.v..v(
13C6:0130  E8 88 15 8B E5 FF 36 18-12 FF 36 16 12 8B 76 28   ......6...6...v(
13C6:0140  FF 74 3A 89 46 06 E8 22-CE 8B E5 30 E4 3D 0A 00   .t:.F.."...0.=..
13C6:0150  75 32 A1 16 12 2D 01 00-8B 1E 18 12 83 DB 00 53   u2...-.........S
13C6:0160  50 8B 76 28 FF 74 3A A3-16 12 89 1E 18 12 E8 FA   P.v(.t:.........
13C6:0170  CD 8B E5 30 E4 3D 0D 00-74 0A 83 06 16 12 01 83   ...0.=..t.......
-Q
```

Figure 2-2 Dump of the Code Segment.

To terminate the DEBUG session, enter Q (for Quit). This operation returns you to DOS, which displays its prompt A> or C>. If you printed the session, press Ctrl/PrtSc again to terminate printing.

MACHINE LANGUAGE EXAMPLE: DEFINED DATA

The previous example used immediate values defined directly within the first two instructions (MOV and ADD). We next illustrate a similar example that defines the two data fields 0123 and 0025 in the data segment. Working through this example should provide insight into how a computer accesses data by means of the DS register and offset addresses.

The present example defines data items containing, respectively, the following:

DS Location	*Hex Value*	*Bytes Occupied*
0000	2301	0 and 1
0002	2500	2 and 3
0004	0000	4 and 5
0006	2A2A2A	6, 7, and 8

Remember that a hex character occupies a half-byte, so that, for example, 23 is stored in byte 0 (the first byte) of the data segment, and 01 is stored in byte 1 (the second byte).

The machine language instructions in the code segment that process these items are the following:

Instruction	*Explanation*
A10000	Move the word (two bytes) beginning at DS location 0000 into the AX register.
03060200	Add the contents of the word (two bytes) beginning at DS location 0002 to the AX register.
A30400	Move the contents of the AX register to the word beginning at DS location 0004.
CB	Return to DOS.

You may have noticed that there are two MOV instructions with different machine codes: A1 and A3. The actual machine code is dependent on the registers that are referenced, the number of bytes (byte or word), the direction of data transfer (from or to a register), and the reference to immediate data or memory.

Once again, you can use DEBUG to enter this program and to watch its execution. When DEBUG signals its hyphen prompt, it is ready for your commands.

First key in the Enter (E) commands for the data segment:

```
E DS:00 23 01 25 00 00 00  [press Return]
E DS:06 2A 2A 2A  [press Return]
```

The first command stores the three words (six bytes) at the start of the data segment, DS:00. Note that you have to enter words with the bytes reversed so that 0123 is 2301 and 0025 is 2500. When a MOV instruction accesses these words into a register, it "unreverses" the bytes so that 2301 becomes 0123 and 2500 becomes 0025.

The second command stores three asterisks (***) so that you can view them later using the Dump (D) command—the asterisks serve no purpose in the data segment. Now key in the instructions in the code segment, once again beginning at CS:100, as follows:

```
E CS:100 A1 00 00 03 06 02 00
E CS:107 A3 04 00 CB
```

These instructions are now found in memory locations CS:100 through CS:10A. You can execute them just as you did earlier. Figure 2-3 shows all the steps including the E commands. Your screen should display similar results, although the CS and DS addresses probably differ. You may want to look at the stored data in the data segment and the instructions in the code segment. Key in the Dump commands respectively:

To view the data segment: `D DS:000 [press Return]`
To view the code segment: `D CS:100 [press Return]`

Compare the contents of both segments to what you keyed in and to Figure 2-3. DS:00 through 08 and CS:100 through 10A should be identical to Figure 2-3.

Now press R to view the contents of the registers and flags and to display the first instruction. The registers contain the same values as at the start of the first example. The displayed instruction is

```
13C6:0100  A10000   MOV AX,[0000]
```

Since the CS register contains 13C6, then CS:0100 contains your first instruction, A10000. DEBUG interprets this instruction as a MOV and has determined that the reference is to the first location [0000] in the data segment. The square brackets are to tell you that this reference is to a

```
>DEBUG
-E DS:000 23 01 25 00 00
-E DS:006 2A 2A 2A
-E CS:100 A1 00 00 03 06 02 00
-E CS:107 A3 04 00 CB
-D DS:0
13C6:0000  23 01 25 00 00 9A 2A 2A-2A F0 F5 02 2C 10 2E 03   #.%...***...,...
13C6:0010  2C 10 BD 02 2C 10 B1 0D-01 03 01 00 02 FF FF FF   ,...,...........
13C6:0020  FF FF FF FF FF FF FF FF-FF FF FF FF EF 0F 64 00   ..............d.
13C6:0030  61 13 14 00 18 00 C7 13-FF FF FF FF 00 00 00 00   a...............
13C6:0040  00 00 00 00 00 00 00 00-00 00 00 00 00 00 00 00   ................
13C6:0050  CD 21 CB 00 00 00 00 00-00 00 00 00 20 20 20      .!...........
13C6:0060  20 20 20 20 20 20 20 20-00 00 00 00 20 20 20           .....
13C6:0070  20 20 20 20 20 20 20 20-00 00 00 00 00 00 00 00      ........
-R
AX=0000  BX=0000  CX=0000  DX=0000  SP=FFEE  BP=0000  SI=0000  DI=0000
DS=13C6  ES=13C6  SS=13C6  CS=13C6  IP=0100   NV UP EI PL NZ NA PO NC
13C6:0100 A10000        MOV     AX,[0000]                     DS:0000=0123
-T

AX=0123  BX=0000  CX=0000  DX=0000  SP=FFEE  BP=0000  SI=0000  DI=0000
DS=13C6  ES=13C6  SS=13C6  CS=13C6  IP=0103   NV UP EI PL NZ NA PO NC
13C6:0103 03060200      ADD     AX,[0002]                     DS:0002=0025
-T

AX=0148  BX=0000  CX=0000  DX=0000  SP=FFEE  BP=0000  SI=0000  DI=0000
DS=13C6  ES=13C6  SS=13C6  CS=13C6  IP=0107   NV UP EI PL NZ NA PE NC
13C6:0107 A30400        MOV     [0004],AX                     DS:0004=9A00
-T

AX=0148  BX=0000  CX=0000  DX=0000  SP=FFEE  BP=0000  SI=0000  DI=0000
DS=13C6  ES=13C6  SS=13C6  CS=13C6  IP=010A   NV UP EI PL NZ NA PE NC
13C6:010A CB            RETF
-D DS:0
13C6:0000  23 01 25 00 48 01 2A 2A-2A F0 F5 02 2C 10 2E 03   #.%.H.***...,...
13C6:0010  2C 10 BD 02 2C 10 B1 0D-01 03 01 00 02 FF FF FF   ,...,...........
13C6:0020  FF FF FF FF FF FF FF FF-FF FF FF FF EF 0F 64 00   ..............d.
13C6:0030  61 13 14 00 18 00 C7 13-FF FF FF FF 00 00 00 00   a...............
13C6:0040  00 00 00 00 00 00 00 00-00 00 00 00 00 00 00 00   ................
13C6:0050  CD 21 CB 00 00 00 00 00-00 00 00 00 20 20 20      .!...........
13C6:0060  20 20 20 20 20 20 20 20-00 00 00 00 20 20 20           .....
13C6:0070  20 20 20 20 20 20 20 20-00 00 00 00 00 00 00 00      ........
-Q
```

Figure 2-3 Trace of Machine Instructions.

memory address and not an immediate value. An immediate value that would move zeros to the AX register would appear as

```
MOV  AX,0000
```

Now key in the DEBUG command T. The instruction MOV AX,[0000] moves the contents of the word at offset zero in the data segment to the AX register. The contents are 2301, which the operation reverses in AX as 0123.

The next instruction is ADD, which you can cause to execute by keying in another T command. The operation adds the contents of the word at DS offset 0002 to the AX register. The result in the AX is now the sum of 0123 and 0025, or 0148.

The next instruction is MOV [0004],AX. Key in a T command for it to execute. The instruction moves the contents of the AX register to the word at DS offset 0004. To view the changed contents of the data segment, key in D DS:00. The first nine bytes are

Value in data segment:	23 01 25 00 48 01 2A 2A 2A
Offset number:	00 01 02 03 04 05 06 07 08

The value of 0148 that was moved from the AX register to offset 04 and 05 is reversed as 4801. Note that these hex values are represented on the right of the screen by their ASCII equivalents. For example, hex 23 generates a number (#) symbol and hex 25 generates a percent (%) symbol. The three hex 2A bytes generate asterisks (*). The left side of the dump shows the actual machine code as it appears in memory. The right side of a dump simply helps you locate alphabetic (string) data more easily.

To view the contents of the code segment, key in D CS:100, just as Figure 2-3 shows. Finally, enter Q (for Quit) to terminate the DEBUG session.

MACHINE ADDRESSING

To access an instruction, the processor determines its address from the contents of the CS register plus the offset in the IP register. For example, assume that the CS contains hex 04AF (actually 04AF0) and the IP contains hex 0023:

CS:	04AF0
IP:	0023
Instruction address:	04B13

Let's say that the instruction beginning at 04B13 is the following:

```
A11200          MOV  AX,[0012]
|
location 04B13
```

Memory location 04B13 contains the first byte of the instruction to be accessed. The processor determines from the operation itself (A1) that the instruction is three bytes long.

To access the data item at offset [0012], the processor determines its location from the contents of the DS register (usually) plus the offset in the instruction operand. If the DS contains hex 04B1 (actually 04B10), then the actual location of the referenced data item is

```
            DS:  04B10
        Offset:   0012
               -------
Address of data: 04B22
```

Let's say that the contents of locations 04B22 and 04B23 are the following:

```
Contents:   24      01
            |       |
Location: 04B22   04B23
```

The processor extracts the 24 at location 04B22 and inserts it into the AL register, and the 01 at location 04B23 into the AH register. The AX now contains 0124. As the processor fetches each byte of the instruction, it increments the IP register so that it contains the offset (0026) for the next instruction. The processor is now ready to execute the next instruction, which it derives once again from the contents of the CS (04AF0) plus the current offset in the IP (0026), in effect 04B16.

Even-Numbered Addresses

The 8086, 80286 and 80386 processors operate more efficiently if an accessed word begins on an even-numbered address. In the previous example, the processor can access the word at 4B22 directly into a register. But if the word begins on an odd-numbered address, the processor performs two accesses. For example, assume that an instruction has to access a word beginning at location 04B23 into the AX register:

```
Memory contents: |xx|24|01|xx|
                        |
       Location:      04B23
```

The processor first accesses the bytes at 4B22 and 4B23 and delivers the byte from 4B23 to the AL register. It then accesses the bytes at 4B24 and 4B25 and delivers the byte from 4B24 to the AH register. The AX now contains 0124.

You don't have to perform any special programming for even or odd locations, nor do you have to know whether an address is odd. The significant points are (1) the accessing operation reverses a word from memory into a register so that it resumes its correct sequence, and (2) if you have a routine that accesses memory repetitively, for efficiency you could define the data to begin at an even location.

For example, since the beginning of the data segment is always an even address, the first data field begins on an even number, and as long as successive data fields are defined as even-numbered words, they all begin on even addresses. For most purposes, however, these processors execute at such rapid speed that you'll never notice the effects of this efficiency.

The assembler has an EVEN pseudo-operation that aligns data and instructions on even memory locations.

MACHINE LANGUAGE EXAMPLE: MEMORY SIZE DETERMINATION

In the first exercise in this chapter, you checked the amount of memory (RAM) that your computer contains. BIOS (basic input/output system) in ROM has a routine that delivers memory size. You can access BIOS through INT instructions, in this case an interrupt 12H. BIOS then returns the value to the AX register in terms of 1K bytes. Load DEBUG into memory and enter the following machine code for INT 12H and RET:

```
E CS:100 CD 12 CB
```

Press R (and Return) to display the registers and the first instruction. The AX contains 0000 and the IP contains 0100; the instruction is INT 12H. Now press T (and Return) repeatedly and see the following BIOS instructions execute (DEBUG shows the symbolic instructions, although it is the machine code that actually executes):

```
STI
PUSH  DS
MOV   AX,0040
MOV   DS,AX
MOV   AX,[0013]
POP   DS
IRET
```

At this point, the AX contains the size of memory in hexadecimal format. Now enter another T command to exit from BIOS and to return to your program. The displayed instruction is RET for the machine code CB that you entered.

SPECIAL DEBUG FEATURES

Under DOS 2.0 and on, you can use DEBUG to enter assembler instructions as well as machine language instructions. You'll find occasions to use both methods.

The A Command

The DEBUG A (Assemble) command tells DEBUG to begin accepting assembler instructions and to convert them into machine language. Initialize the starting address as

```
A 100  [Return]
```

DEBUG displays the value of the code segment and the offset, as xxxx:0100. Type in each instruction followed by the Return key. When you've entered the program, press Return again to exit the A command. Try entering the following program:

```
MOV  AL,25    [Return]
MOV  BL,32    [Return]
ADD  AL,BL    [Return]
RET           [Return]
```

On completion, the screen should display the following:

```
xxxx:0100    MOV AL,25
xxxx:0102    MOV BL,32
xxxx:0104    ADD AL,BL
xxxx:0106    RET
```

At this point, DEBUG is ready to accept another instruction. Just press Return again to terminate the operation.

You can see that DEBUG has determined the starting location of each instruction. But before executing the program, let's examine the generated machine language.

The U Command

DEBUG's U (Unassemble) command displays the machine code for your assembler instructions. You have to tell DEBUG the locations of the first and last instructions that you want to see, in this case, 100 and 106. Key in

```
U 100,106  [and Return]
```

The screen should display

```
xxxx:0100    B025  MOV  AL,25
xxxx:0102    B332  MOV  BL,32
xxxx:0104    00D8  ADD  AL,BL
xxxx:0106    C3    RET
```

Now trace execution of the program. Begin with R to display the registers and the first instruction, and T to trace subsequent instructions.

You can now see how to enter a program in either machine or assembly language. A common use for entering assembler is where you don't know the machine code; a common use for entering machine code is to change values in a program during execution. However, DEBUG is really intended for what its name implies—debugging programs—and most of your efforts will involve use of the assembler program, as discussed in the next chapter.

Saving a Program from Within DEBUG

You may use DEBUG to save a program on disk under two circumstances.

1. You have read a program, modified it, and now want to save it. Follow these steps:
   - Read the program under its name: DEBUG n:filename [Return]
   - Use the D command to view the program and E to enter changes.
   - Write the revised program: W [Return].
2. You have used DEBUG to write a very small program that you now want to save.
   - Request the DEBUG program.
   - Use A (assemble) and E (enter) to create the program.
   - Name the program: N filename.COM [Return]. The program extension must be COM—see Chapter 6 for details of COM files.
   - Since only you know where the program really ends, tell DEBUG the length of the program in bytes. In the preceding example, the last instruction was

     xxxx:0106 C3 RET

The last instruction is one byte, and therefore the program size is 106 (end) minus 100 (start), or 6.

- First request the CX register as R CX [Return].
- DEBUG replies with CX 0000 (zero value).
- You reply with the program length, 6.
- Write the revised program: W [Return].

For both methods, DEBUG displays a message "Writing nnnn bytes." If the number is zero, you have failed to enter the program length; try again.

KEY POINTS TO REMEMBER

DOS DEBUG is a powerful program that is useful for debugging assembler programs. But be careful in its use, especially the Enter (E) command. Entering data at a wrong location or entering incorrect data may cause unpredictable results. You may find your screen filled up with strange characters, have your keyboard lock, or even cause DOS to interrupt DEBUG and reload itself from disk. You are not likely to cause any damage, but you may get a bit of a surprise and may lose data that you entered during the DEBUG session.

If you enter incorrect values in the data segment or code segment, reenter the E command to correct them. However, you may not have noticed the error until after beginning the trace. You can still use E to make the changes, but you may want to begin execution back at the first instruction. No problem—just set the instruction pointer (IP) register to 0100. Key in the R (register) command followed by the designated register:

```
R IP  [Return]
```

DEBUG displays the contents of the IP and waits for an entry. Key in the value 0100 (followed by Return). To check the result, key in an R command (without the IP). DEBUG displays the registers, flags, and the first instruction to be executed. You can now use T to trace through the instruction steps again.

If your program is accumulating totals, you may have to clear to zero some memory locations and registers. But be sure not to change the contents of the CS, DS, SP, and SS registers, all of which have specific purposes.

Read the chapter in the DOS manual on DEBUG. The parts that are relevant at this time are all the introductory material and the following

DEBUG commands: Dump (D), Enter (E), Hexadecimal (H), Name (N), Quit (Q), Register (R), Trace (T), and Write (W). You may want to examine the other DEBUG commands to see what they do.

QUESTIONS

2-1. Determine the machine instruction for each of the following:

(a) Move the hex value 4629 to the AX register.

(b) Add the hex value 036A to the AX register.

2-2. Assume that you have entered the following E command:

```
E CS:100 B8 45 01 05 25 00
```

The hex value 45 was supposed to be 54. Code an E command to correct only the one byte that is incorrect, that is, directly change 45 to 54.

2-3. Assume that you have entered the following E command:

```
E CS:100 B8 04 30 05 00 30 CB
```

(a) What are the three instructions here? (The first program in this chapter gives a clue.)

(b) On executing this program, you discover that the AX register ends up with 6004 instead of 0460. What is the error and how would you correct it?

(c) Having corrected the instructions, you now want to reexecute the program from the first instruction. What two commands are required?

2-4. The following is a machine language program:

```
B0 25 D0 E0 B3 15 F6 E3 CB
```

The program performs the following:

- Moves the hex value 25 to the AL register.
- Shifts the contents of the AL one bit left (the result is 4A).
- Moves the hex value 15 to the BL register.
- Multiplies AL by BL.

Use DEBUG to enter (E) this program beginning at CS:100. Remember that these are hexadecimal values. After entering the program, key in D CS:100 to view it. Then key in R and enough successive T commands to step through the program until reaching RET. What is the final product in the AX register?

2-5. Use DEBUG to enter (E) the following machine language program:

Data: `25 15 00 00`
Machine code: `A0 00 00 D0 E0 F6 26 01 00 A3 02 00 CB`

The program performs the following:

- Moves the contents of the one byte at DS:00 (25) to the AL register.
- Shifts the AL contents one bit left (the result is 4A).
- Multiplies the AL by the one byte contents at DS:01 (15).
- Moves the product from the AX to the word beginning at DS:02.

After entering the program, key in D commands to view the data segment and code segment. Then key in R and enough successive T commands to step through the program until reaching RET. At this point, the AX should contain the product 0612. Key in another D DS:00 and note that the product at DS:02 is stored as 1206.

2-6. For Question 2-5, code the commands that write the program on disk under the name TRIAL.COM.

2-7. Use the DEBUG A command to enter the following instructions:

```
MOV  BX,25
ADD  BX,30
SHL  BX,01
SUB  BX,22
NOP
RET
```

Unassemble and trace execution through to the NOP.

CHAPTER 3

Assembly Language Requirements

Objective: To cover the basic assembler coding requirements and the steps in assembling, linking, and executing a program.

INTRODUCTION

Chapter 2 showed how to key in and execute a machine language program. No doubt you were also very aware of the difficulty in deciphering the machine code even for a small program. It is questionable whether anyone seriously codes in machine language other than patching machine code routines into high-level language programs and software applications. A higher level of coding is at the assembly level in which a programmer uses symbolic instructions in place of machine instructions and descriptive names for data fields and memory locations.

The symbolic instructions that are coded in assembler language are known as the *source program.* To enter them, use DOS EDLIN or any suitable screen editor program. Then use the assembler program to translate the source program into machine code, known as the *object program.* Finally, use the DOS LINK program to complete the machine addressing for the object program, generating an *executable module.*

This chapter explains the requirements for a simple assembler program and takes you through the steps for assembly, link, and execution.

ASSEMBLER COMMENTS

The use of comments throughout a program can improve clarity, especially in assembler where the purpose of a set of instructions is often unclear. A comment always begins with a semicolon(;), and wherever you code it, the assembler assumes that all characters to its right are comments. A comment may contain any printable character, including a blank.

A comment may appear on a line by itself or following an instruction on the same line, as the following two examples illustrate:

```
1.  ;This entire line is a comment
2.          ADD   AX,BX ;Comment on same line as instruction
```

Since a comment appears only on a listing of an assembled source program and generates no machine code, you may include any number of comments without affecting program execution. In this book, assembler instructions are in uppercase letters and comments are in lowercase, only as a convention and to make programs more readable.

CODING FORMAT

The general format for an assembler instruction is the following:

[name] operation [operand(s)]

A name (if any), operation, and operand (if any) are separated by at least one blank or tab character. There is a maximum of 132 characters on a line, although most people prefer to stay within 80 characters because of the screen width. Two examples follow:

```
Name    Op'n  Operand
COUNT   DB    1          ;Name, operation, one operand
        MOV   AX,0       ;Operation, two operands
```

Names

A name in assembler language can use the following characters:

Alphabetic letters:	A through Z and a through z
Digits:	0 through 9
Special characters:	question mark (?)
	period (.) (only first character)
	at (@)
	underline (_)
	dollar ($)

The first character of a name must be an alphabetic letter or a special character. The assembler treats upper and lower case letters the same.

The maximum length is 31 characters. Examples of valid names are COUNT, PAGE25, and $E10. Descriptive, meaningful names are recommended. The names of registers, such as AX, DI, and AL, are reserved for referencing registers. Consequently, in an instruction such as

```
ADD AX,BX
```

the assembler automatically knows that AX and BX refer to registers. However, in an instruction such as

```
MOV REGSAVE,AX
```

the assembler can recognize the name REGSAVE only if you define it in the data segment. Appendix C provides a list of all the assembler reserved words.

Operation

An *operation* tells the assembler what action the statement is to perform. In the data segment, an operation defines a field, work area, or constant. In the code segment, an operation indicates an action such as a move (MOV) or add (ADD).

Operand

Whereas the operation specifies what action to perform, the operand indicates (a) its initial value, if a data item, or (b) where to perform the action, if an instruction. In the following definition of COUNTER in the data segment, the operand indicates that the contents of the defined field is 0:

```
Name    Oper'n  Operand
COUNTR  DB      0         ;Define Byte (DB) with 0 value
```

In an instruction, an operand may contain one, two, or even no entries. Following are three examples:

	Oper'n	Operand	Comment
No operand	RET		;Return
One operand	INC	CX	;Increment CX
Two operands	ADD	AX,12	;Add 12 to AX

The name, operation, and operand need not begin in any specific column. However, consistently starting on the same column for these entries makes a more readable program. Also, the DOS EDLIN editor provides useful tab stops every eight positions.

PSEUDO-OPERATIONS

Assembler supports a number of instructions that enable you to control the way in which a program assembles and lists. These instructions, named pseudo-operations (or pseudo-ops), act only during the assembly of a program and generate no machine-executable code. The most common pseudo-ops are explained in the next sections. Chapter 24 covers all of the pseudo-ops in detail; there is too much information to cover at this point, but you can use that chapter as a reference.

Listing Pseudo-operations: PAGE and TITLE

The assembler provides a number of pseudo-ops to control the format of an assembled listing. Two pseudo-ops that you can use in every program are PAGE and TITLE.

PAGE. At the start of a program you can designate the number of lines that are to list on a page and the maximum number of characters on a line. The pseudo-op for this purpose is PAGE. The following example sets 60 lines per page and 132 characters per line:

```
PAGE  60,132
```

Lines per page may range from 10 to 255, and characters per line may range from 60 to 132. Omission of a PAGE statement causes the assembler to assume PAGE 66,80.

Assume that the line count is set to 60. When the assembled program has listed 60 lines, it ejects the forms to the top of the next page and increments a page count. You may also want to force a page to eject at a specific line, such as at the end of a segment. At the required line, simply code PAGE with no operand. The assembled listing automatically ejects the page on encountering PAGE.

TITLE. You can use the TITLE pseudo-op to cause a title for a program to print at the top of each page, as follows:

```
TITLE text
```

As text, a recommended technique is to use the name of the program as cataloged on disk. For example, if the program is named ASMSORT, code that name plus a descriptive comment, all up to 60 characters in length, as follows:

```
TITLE ASMSORT—Assembler program to sort customer names
```

The assembler also supports a subtitle pseudo-op named SUBTTL that you may find useful for very large programs which contain sub-programs.

SEGMENT Pseudo-Operation

All assembler programs consist of at least one segment, a code segment for executable code. Some programs define a stack segment for stack storage and a data segment for data definitions. The assembler pseudo-op for defining a segment, SEGMENT, has the following format:

```
Name    Operation    Operand
name    SEGMENT      [options]
          .
          .
          .
name    ENDS
```

The segment name must be present, must be unique, and must follow assembler naming conventions. The ENDS statement indicates the end of a segment and contains the same name as the SEGMENT statement. A SEGMENT statement may contain three types of options: alignment, combine, and class.

1. *Alignment type.* This entry indicates the boundary on which the segment is to begin. The typical requirement is PARA for which the segment aligns on a paragraph boundary. The starting address is evenly divisible by 16 as in hex nnn0. Omission of an operand causes the assembler to assume (default to) PARA.
2. *Combine type.* This entry indicates whether to combine with other segments when "linked" after assembly (explained in a later section, Linking the Program). Types are STACK, COMMON, PUBLIC, AT expression, and MEMORY. The STACK SEGMENT is defined as follows:

```
name    SEGMENT    PARA STACK
```

You may use PUBLIC, COMMON, and MEMORY when separately assembled programs are to be combined when linked. Otherwise, a program that is not to be combined with other programs may omit this option.

3. *Class type.* This entry, enclosed in apostrophes, is used to group related segments when linking, as follows:

```
name    SEGMENT  PARA STACK 'Stack'
```

The partial program in Figure 3-1 in a later section illustrates a SEGMENT statement and various options.

PROC Pseudo-Operation

The code segment contains the executable code for a program. This segment also contains one or more procedures, defined with the PROC pseudo-op. A segment that contains only one procedure would appear as follows:

```
segname  SEGMENT  PARA
procname PROC     FAR      One
            .              procedure
            .              within
            .              the
         RET               code
procname ENDP              segment
segname  ENDS
```

The procedure name must be present, must be unique, and must follow assembler naming conventions. The operand FAR indicates to the DOS program loader that this PROC is the entry point for program execution.

The ENDP pseudo-op indicates the end of a procedure and contains the same name as the PROC statement. The RET instruction terminates processing and returns control (in this case) to DOS.

A segment may contain more than one procedure; Chapter 7 covers this condition.

ASSUME Pseudo-Operation

The processor uses the SS register to address the stack, the DS register to address the data segment, and the CS register to address the code segment. You have to tell the assembler the purpose of each segment.

The pseudo-op for this purpose is ASSUME, coded in the code segment as follows:

```
Operation   Operand
ASSUME      SS:stackname,DS:datasegname,CS:codesegname
```

For example, SS:stackname means that the assembler is to associate the name of the stack segment with the SS register. The operands may appear in any sequence. The ES register may also contain an entry; if your program does not use the ES register, you may omit its reference or code ES:NOTHING.

END Pseudo-Operation

As already seen, the ENDS pseudo-op terminates a segment, and the ENDP pseudo-op terminates a procedure. An END pseudo-op terminates the entire program as follows:

```
Operation   Operand
END         [procname]
```

The operand may be blank if the program is not to execute—for example, you may want to assemble only data definitions, or the program is to be linked with another (main) module. For typical programs consisting of one module, the operand contains the name of the PROC that was designated FAR.

MEMORY AND REGISTER REFERENCES

One feature to get clear is the use in instruction operands of names, of names in square brackets, and of numbers. In the following examples, assume that WORDA is defined as a word in memory:

```
MOV AX,BX      ;Move contents of BX to AX
MOV AX,WORDA   ;Move contents of WORDA to AX
MOV AX,[BX]    ;Move contents of memory location specified by BX
MOV AX,25      ;Move value 25 to AX
```

The only new item is the use of square brackets, which you'll use in more advanced chapters.

PROGRAM INITIALIZATION

There are two basic types of executable programs, EXE and COM. We'll develop the requirements for EXE first and leave COM for Chapter 6. DOS has four requirements for initializing an assembler EXE program: (1) Notify the assembler which segments to associate with which segment registers, (2) store in the stack the address that is in the DS when the program begins execution, (3) store in the stack a zero address, and (4) load the DS with the address of the data segment.

Exiting from the program and returning to DOS involve use of the RET instruction. Figure 3-1 illustrates initialization and exit requirements.

1. ASSUME is an assembler pseudo-op that notifies the assembler to associate certain segments with certain segment registers, in this case, CODESG with CS, DATASG with DS, and STACKSG with SS. DATASG and STACKSG are not defined in this example, but would be coded as follows:

   ```
   STACKSG SEGMENT PARA STACK  Stack 'Stack'
   DATASG  SEGMENT PARA 'Data'
   ```

   By associating segments with segment registers, the assembler can determine offset addresses of items within each segment. For example, each instruction in the code segment is a specific length. The first instruction is at offset 0, and if it is one byte long, the second instruction is at offset 2, and so forth.
2. Immediately preceding your executable program in memory is a 256-byte (hex 100) area known as the program segment prefix (PSP). The DOS loader program uses the DS register to establish the starting point of the PSP. Your program has to save this address by "pushing" it onto the stack. Later, RET uses this address to return to DOS.
3. The system requires that the next value on the stack is an address (actually an offset) of zero. For this purpose, the SUB instruction clears the AX to zero by subtracting it from itself, and PUSH stores this value on the stack.
4. The DOS loader program has initialized the correct addresses of the stack in the SS and the code segment in the CS. Since the loader program has used the DS for another purpose, you have to initialize the DS as shown by the two MOV instructions in Figure 3-1. A later section in this chapter, "Example Source Program II," explains the initialization of the DS in detail.

```
        CODESG   SEGMENT PARA 'CODE'
        BEGIN    PROC FAR
1.               ASSUME   CS:CODESG,DS:DATASG,SS:STACKSG
2.               PUSH     DS                    ;Store DS on stack
3.               SUB      AX,AX                 ;Set AX to zero
                 PUSH     AX                    ;Store zero on stack
4.               MOV      AX,DATASG             ;Store address of
                 MOV      DS,AX                 ; DATASG in DS
                 .
                 .
                 .
5.               RET                            ;Return to DOS
        BEGIN    ENDP
        CODESG   ENDS
                 END      BEGIN
```

Figure 3-1 Initialization for EXE Programs.

5. The RET instruction exits from your program and returns to DOS by means of the address that was pushed onto the stack at the start (PUSH DS). Another commonly used exit is the INT 20H instruction.

Now, even if this initialization is not clear at this point, take heart. Every program has virtually identical initialization steps that you can duplicate each time you code a program.

EXAMPLE SOURCE PROGRAM

Figure 3-2 combines the preceding information into a simple assembler source program. The program consists of a stack segment named STACKSG and a code segment named CODESG.

STACKSG contains one entry, DB (Define Byte), that defines 12 copies of the word 'STACKSEG.' Subsequent programs do not define the stack this way, but when you use DEBUG to view the assembled program on the screen, the definition will help you locate the stack.

CODESG contains the executable instructions for the program, although the first statement, ASSUME, generates no executable code. The ASSUME pseudo-op assigns STACKSG to the SS register and CODESG to the CS register. In effect, the statement tells the assembler to use the address in the SS register for addressing STACKSG and the address in the CS register for addressing CODESG. The system loader, when loading

```
         page    60,132
TITLE    EXASM1 (EXE)  Example register operations
;-------------------------------------------------------
STACKSG  SEGMENT PARA STACK 'Stack'
         DB      12 DUP('STACKSEG')
STACKSG  ENDS
;-------------------------------------------------------
CODESG   SEGMENT PARA 'Code'
BEGIN    PROC    FAR
         ASSUME  SS:STACKSG,CS:CODESG,DS:NOTHING
         PUSH    DS               ;Push DS onto stack
         SUB     AX,AX            ;Push zero offset
         PUSH    AX               ;   onto stack

         MOV     AX,0123H         ;Move hex 0123 to AX
         ADD     AX,0025H         ;Add hex 25 to AX
         MOV     BX,AX            ;Move AX to BX
         ADD     BX,AX            ;Add AX to BX
         MOV     CX,BX            ;Move BX to CX
         SUB     CX,AX            ;Subtract AX from CX
         SUB     AX,AX            ;Clear AX to zero
         NOP
         RET                      ;Return to DOS
BEGIN    ENDP                     ;End of procedure

CODESG   ENDS                     ;End of segment
         END     BEGIN            ;End of program
```

Figure 3-2 Assembler Source Program.

a program from disk into memory for execution, sets the actual addresses in the SS and CS registers. Since this program contains no defined data, it has no data segment, and consequently ASSUME need not assign the DS register.

The instructions following ASSUME—PUSH, SUB, and PUSH—are standard operations to initialize the stack with first the current address in the DS register and second a zero address. Since the normal practice is to execute a program from DOS, these instructions facilitate the return to DOS after execution of this program. (You can also execute a program from DEBUG, although normally in special cases.)

The succeeding instructions then perform the same operations as Figure 2-1 in the previous chapter when you used DEBUG.

KEY POINTS TO REMEMBER

- Be sure to code a semicolon before comments.
- Terminate each segment with ENDS, each procedure with ENDP, and the program with END.

- In the ASSUME pseudo-op, associate segment registers with the appropriate segment names.
- For EXE programs (but not COM programs, covered in Chapter 6), provide at least 32 words for stack addressing; follow the convention for initializing the stack with PUSH, SUB, and PUSH; and initialize the DS register with the address of the data segment.

QUESTIONS

3-1. What commands cause the assembler to print a heading at the top of a page of the listing and to eject to a new page?

3-2. Determine which of the following names are valid: (a) PC_AT, (b) $50, (c) @$_Z, (d) 34B7, (e) AX.

3-3. What is the purpose of each of the three segments described in this chapter?

3-4. What particular END statements are concerned with terminating (a) a program, (b) a procedure, (c) a segment?

3-5. Distinguish between a pseudo-operation and an instruction.

3-6. Distinguish between the purpose of RET and END.

3-7. Given the names CDSEG, DATSEG, and STKSEG for the code segment, data segment, and stack, respectively, code the ASSUME.

3-8. Code the three instructions to initialize the stack with the address in the DS and a zero address.

CHAPTER 4

Assembling and Executing a Program

Objective: To cover the steps in assembling, linking, and executing a program.

INTRODUCTION

This chapter explains how to key in an assembler source program and how to assemble, link, and execute it. Another feature covered is the generation of cross-reference lists as a debugging aid.

KEYING IN A PROGRAM

Figure 3-2 illustrated only source code for a program that was keyed in under an editor. Now is the time to use the DOS EDLIN or an equivalent editor to key in this program. If you have never used EDLIN, now is a good time to perform the exercises in the DOS manual. To activate EDLIN, insert the DOS diskette in disk drive A and a formatted diskette in drive B—you can use CHKDSK B: to make sure that it has space for this program. Users of hard disk should substitute drive C in the following examples. To key in the source program EXASM1, key in the command

```
EDLIN B:EXASM1.ASM [followed by Return]
```

DOS loads EDLIN into memory, and displays a message "New file" and a prompt "*_." Enter an I command to insert lines, and key in each assembler instruction just the way you see it. Although the spacing is not important to the assembler, a program is more readable if you keep the name, operation, operand, and comments aligned. EDLIN has tab stops at every eight positions to facilitate aligning.

Once you have entered the program, scan the code to ensure its accuracy. Then key in E (and Return) to terminate EDLIN. You can check that the program is cataloged on disk by keying in:

```
      DIR B:              (for all files)
or    DIR B:EXASM1.ASM    (for one file)
```

If you expect to key in a large amount of program code, a good investment is a full-screen editor. For a printout of the program, turn on your printer and adjust the paper. Request the DOS program PRINT (DOS 2.0 and on). DOS loads the program into memory and copies the text onto the printer:

```
PRINT B:EXASM1.ASM [Return]
```

As it stands, EXASM1.ASM does not execute—you must first assemble and link it. The next section depicts a list of the same program after assembly and explains the steps for assembling and listing.

PREPARING A PROGRAM FOR EXECUTION

After keying in your source program onto disk under EXASM1.ASM, you still have two major steps before you can execute it. You must first *assemble* and then *link* it. Users of BASIC are used to keying in a source program and executing it directly; however, assembly and compiler languages require steps for translation and linking.

The assembly step involves translation of source code to machine object code and generates an OBJ (object) file, or module. You have already seen examples of machine code in Chapter 2 and examples of source code in this chapter.

The OBJ module is almost—but not quite—in executable form. The link edit step involves converting the OBJ module to an EXE (executable) module containing machine code. The LINK program on the DOS disk performs the following:

1. Completes any addresses that the assembler has left empty in the OBJ module. You will see such addresses, which the assembler lists in object code as ---- R, in many subsequent programs.
2. Combines, if requested, more than one separately assembled module into one executable program, such as two or more assembler programs or an assembler program with a program written in a high-level language such as Pascal or BASIC.

3. Initializes the EXE module with instructions for loading it for execution.

Once you have linked an OBJ module (one or more) into an EXE module, you may execute the EXE module any number of times. But whenever you need to make a change in the EXE module, you must correct the source program, assemble it into another OBJ module, and link the OBJ module into an EXE module. Even if initially these steps are not entirely clear, you will find that with only a little experience, the steps eventually become automatic. Note: You may convert certain types of EXE programs to very efficient COM programs. The preceding examples, however, are not suitable for this purpose. See Chapter 6 for details.

ASSEMBLING A PROGRAM

In order to execute an assembler source program, you first assemble and then link it. The diskette that is included in the assembler package contains two versions of the assembler. ASM.EXE is a smaller version with some minor features omitted; MASM.EXE has all the features. If size of memory permits, use the MASM version—check the assembler manual for details.

To assemble, insert the assembler diskette in drive A and your program diskette containing EXASM1.ASM in drive B. Users of hard disk can assume drive C in place of the drive numbers in the examples. The simplest approach is to key in the command MASM (or ASM), which causes the assembler program to load from disk into memory. The screen displays:

```
source filename [.ASM]:
object filename [filename.OBJ]:
source listing [NUL.LST]:
cross-reference [NUL.CRF]:
```

The cursor is placed at the end of the first line, ready for you to enter the name of the file. Type the drive (if it's not the default) and the file name, as B:EXASM1. Do not type the extension ASM—the assembler assumes it.

The second prompt assumes the same file name (you could change it). If necessary, enter the drive number, B:.

The third prompt assumes that you do not want a listing of the assembled program. To get one on drive B, type B: and press Return.

The last prompt assumes that you do not want a cross-reference listing. To get one on drive B, type B: and press Return.

For the last three prompts, just press Return if you want to accept the default. Here's an example of prompts and replies in which the assembler is to produce OBJ, LST, and CRF files. Enter the replies just as shown, except that your disk drive may differ.

```
source filename [.ASM]:B:EXASM1 [Return]
object filename [filename.OBJ]:B: [Return]
source listing [NUL.LST]:B: [Return]
cross-reference [NUL.CRF]:B: [Return]
```

You always enter the name of the source file and you usually request an OBJ file—it's required for linking a program into executable form. You'll probably often request LST files, especially when you want to examine generated machine code. A CRF file is useful for very large programs where you want to see which instructions reference which data items. Also, the entry causes the assembler to generate line numbers on the LST file to which the CRF file refers.

Appendix D, "Assembler and Link Options," lists options for assembler versions 1.0 and 2.0.

The assembler converts your source statements into machine code and displays on the screen any errors. Typical errors include a name that violates naming conventions, an operation that is spelled incorrectly (such as MOVE instead of MOV), and an operand containing a name that is not defined. The ASM version lists only an error code that is explained in the Assembler manual, whereas the MASM version lists both code and explanation. There are in total about 100 error messages.

The assembler attempts to correct some errors, but in any event you should reload the editor, correct the source program (EXASM1.ASM), and reassemble.

Figure 4-1 provides a listing of the assembled program that the assembler wrote on disk under the name EXASM1.LST.

Note at the top of the listing how the assembler has acted on the PAGE and TITLE pseudo-ops. None of the pseudo-ops, including SEGMENT, PROC, ASSUME, and END, generates machine code.

The listing shows not only the original source code but also to the left the translated machine code in hexadecimal format. At the extreme left are the hex addresses of the data fields and the instructions.

The stack segment "begins" at location 0000. Actually, it loads into memory according to an address that will be in the SS register and is offset zero bytes from that address. The SEGMENT pseudo-op causes alignment of an address divisible by 16 and notifies the assembler that this is a stack—the statement itself generates no machine code. The DB instruction, also aligned at location 0000, contains 12 copies of the word 'STACKSEG'; the machine code is indicated by hex OC (decimal value 12)

```
                                   page    60,132
                           TITLE   EXASM1 (EXE)  Example register operations
                           ;--------------------------------------------------
0000                       STACKSG SEGMENT PARA STACK 'Stack'
0000    0C [                       DB      12 DUP('STACKSEG')
             53 54 41 43
             4B 53 45 47
                         ]

0060                       STACKSG ENDS
                           ;--------------------------------------------------
0000                       CODESG  SEGMENT PARA 'Code'
0000                       BEGIN   PROC    FAR
                                   ASSUME  SS:STACKSG,CS:CODESG,DS:NOTHING
0000    1E                         PUSH    DS               ;Push DS onto stack
0001    2B C0                      SUB     AX,AX            ;Push zero offset
0003    50                         PUSH    AX               ;   onto stack

0004    B8 0123                    MOV     AX,0123H         ;Move hex 0123 to AX
0007    05 0025                    ADD     AX,0025H         ;Add hex 25 to AX
000A    8B D8                      MOV     BX,AX            ;Move AX to BX
000C    03 D8                      ADD     BX,AX            ;Add AX to BX
000E    8B CB                      MOV     CX,BX            ;Move BX to CX
0010    2B C8                      SUB     CX,AX            ;Subtract AX from CX
0012    2B C0                      SUB     AX,AX            ;Clear AX to zero
0014    90                         NOP
0015    CB                         RET                      ;Return to DOS
0016                        BEGIN  ENDP                     ;End of procedure

0016                       CODESG  ENDS                     ;End of segment
                                   END     BEGIN            ;End of program
```

```
Segments and Groups:
            N a m e          Size    Align   Combine Class
CODESG . . . . . . . . . . . 0016    PARA    NONE    'CODE'
STACKSG. . . . . . . . . . . 0060    PARA    STACK   'STACK'

Symbols:
            N a m e          Type    Value   Attr
BEGIN. . . . . . . . . . . . F PROC  0000    CODESG  Length =0016
```

Figure 4-1 Assembled Program.

and the hex representation of the ASCII characters. (You can use DEBUG later to view the results in memory.) The stack segment ends at address hex 0060, which is the eqivalent of decimal value 96 (12 × 8).

The code segment also "begins" at location 0000. It loads into memory according to an address that will be in the CS register and is offset zero bytes from that address. Since ASSUME is a pseudo-op (a message to the assembler), the first instruction to generate actual machine code is PUSH DS, a one-byte instruction (1E) at offset location zero. The next instruction SUB AX,AX generates a two-byte machine code (2B C0) beginning at offset location 0001. The blank space between the two bytes is for readability only. In this example, machine instructions range from one to three bytes in length.

The last statement, END, contains the operand BEGIN, which relates to the name of the PROC at offset 0000. This is the location in the code segment where the program loader is to begin execution.

You can print the assembled program EXASM1.LST, which has a print width of 132 positions because of the PAGE entry. Many printers can compress the print line—turn on the printer and key in the DOS command

```
MODE LPT1:132,6
```

Symbol Table

Following the program listing is a *symbol table.* The first part is a table of any segments and groups defined in the program along with their size in bytes, their alignment, and their combine class. The second part is a table of symbols—the names of data fields in the data segment (there are none in this example) and the names applied to instructions in the code segment (only one in this example). To cause the assembler to omit this table, code a /N parameter following the MASM command, as MASM/N.

Two-Pass Assembler

The assembler makes two passes through the symbolic program. One of the main reasons is because of forward references—an instruction may reference a label but the assembler has not yet encountered its definition.

During pass 1, the assembler reads the entire symbolic program and constructs a symbol table of names and labels used in the program, that is, names of data fields and program labels and their relative location in the program. Pass 1 determines the amount of code to be generated but does not generate object code as such.

During pass 2, the assembler uses the symbol table that it constructed in pass 1. Now that it knows the length and relative positions of each data field and instruction, it can generate the object code for each instruction. It then produces, if requested, the various files for OBJ, LST, and CRF.

LINKING A PROGRAM

Once a program is free of error messages, the next step is to link the object module. EXASM1.OBJ contains only machine code, all in hex format. Because a program can load almost anywhere in memory for execution, the assembler may not have completed all the machine addresses. Also, there may be other (sub)programs to combine with this one. The function of LINK is to complete address references and to combine (if required) any other programs.

To link an assembled program from diskette, insert the DOS diskette in drive A and the program diskette in drive B. Hard disk users can load LINK directly from drive C. Key in the command LINK followed by Return. Once loaded into memory, the linker issues a series of prompts (like MASM) to which you are to reply:

Link Prompt	*Reply*	*Action*
`Object Modules [.OBJ]:`	`B:EXASM1`	`Links EXASM1.OBJ`
`Run File [EXASM1.EXE]:`	`B:`	`Creates EXASM1.EXE`
`List File [NUL.MAP]:`	`CON`	`Creates EXASM1.MAP`
`Libraries [.LIB]:`	`[Return]`	`Defaults`

The first prompt asks for the name of the object module that is to be linked and defaults to OBJ if the extension is omitted.

The second prompt requests the name of the file that is to execute (run) and allows a default to the filename A:EXASM1.EXE. The reply requests that LINK produce the file on drive B. The practice of supplying the same filename will simplify keeping track of all your programs.

The third prompt tells you that LINK defaults the "List File" under the name NUL.MAP (that is, no map). The MAP file contains a map of the names and sizes of segments and any errors that LINK has found. A typical error is failure to define a stack segment. The reply CON tells LINK to display the map on the screen instead of writing it on disk. Replying CON saves disk space and allows you to view the map immediately for errors. For this example, the MAP file contains the following:

Start	*Stop*	*Length*	*Name*
`00000H`	`00015H`	`0016H`	`CODESG`
`00020H`	`0007FH`	`0060H`	`STACKSG`

The reply to the fourth prompt is to press Return, which tells LINK to default the remaining option. The DOS manual contains a description of the libraries option.

At this stage the only error that you are likely to encounter is entering wrong filenames. The solution is to restart with the LINK command. Appendix D supplies a number of LINK options.

EXECUTING A PROGRAM

Having assembled and linked the program, you can now (at last!) execute it. Figure 4-2 provides a chart of commands and steps involved in assembling, linking, and executing the program named EXASM1. If the EXE file is in drive B, you could cause execution by entering:

```
B:EXASM1.EXE   or   B:EXASM1
```

DOS assumes that the file extension is EXE (or COM) and loads the file for execution. However, since this program produces no visible output, run it under DEBUG and step through with trace commands. Key in the following, including the extension EXE:

```
DEBUG B:EXASM1.EXE
```

DOS then loads DEBUG, which in turn loads the EXE program module. Once ready, DEBUG displays a hyphen (-) as a prompt. To view the stack segment, key in

```
D SS:0
```

This area is recognizable because of the 12 duplicated constants, STACKSEG. To view the code segment, key in

```
D CS:0
```

Compare the machine code to the assembled listing:

```
1E2BC050B823010525008BD803 ...
```

The immediate operands shown on the listing as 0123 and 0025 are actually in memory as, respectively, 2301 and 2500. In this case, the assembled listing does not accurately show the machine code. All two-byte (word) addresses and immediate operands are stored in machine code with the bytes reversed.

Key in R to view the registers, and step through program execution with successive T (Trace) commands. Note the effect of the two PUSH instructions on the stack—the end (technically the top) of the stack now contains the contents of the DS register and the zero address.

As you step through the program, take note of the contents of the registers. When you reach the RET instruction, you can use Q (QUIT) to terminate DEBUG.

Use the DOS DIR command to check the files on your program disk:

```
DIR B:EXASM1.*
```

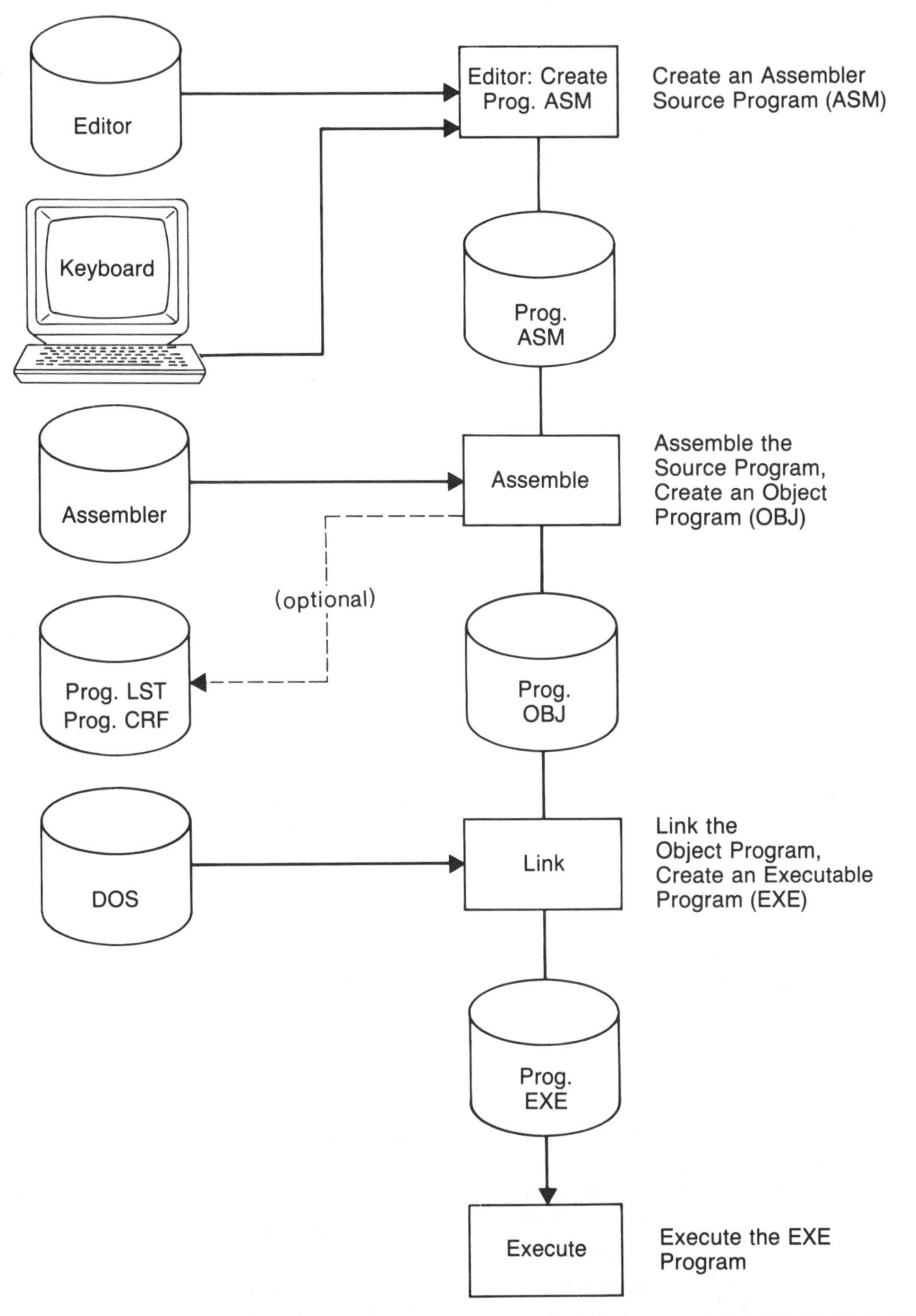

Figure 4-2 Steps in Assembly, Link, and Execute.

DIR displays the following filenames: EXASM1.BAK (if you used EDLIN to change EXASM1.ASM), EXASM1.ASM, EXASM1.OBJ, EXASM1.LST, EXASM1.EXE, and EXASM1.CRF. The sequence of these files may vary depending on what your disk already contains.

No doubt you realize that writing a number of programs causes a shortage of disk space. It's a good idea to use the DOS command CHKDSK regularly to check the remaining space. You can use the DOS ERASE (or DEL) command to erase OBJ, CRF, BAK, and LST files as follows:

```
ERASE B:EXASM1.OBJ,  ...
```

You need the ASM file in case of further changes and the EXE file to execute the program.

The next section introduces defined data and the data segment. A later section, "Cross-Reference File," describes the cross-reference table.

EXAMPLE SOURCE PROGRAM

The program in Figure 4-1 is unique in that it contains no defined data. Virtually all programs contain defined constants, work areas for arithmetic computations, and areas for accepting input and writing output.

In Chapter 2, Figure 2-3, you studied a machine language program with two defined fields. In this chapter, Figure 4-3 portrays the same program, this time written in assembler source language and, for brevity, already assembled. The program introduces several new features.

The stack segment contains a DW (Define Word) pseudo-op that defines 32 words, each generating an undefined value designated by (?). This definition of 32 words is a more realistic size for the stack because a large program may require many "interrupts" for input/output and "calls" to subprograms, all involving use of the stack. Further, the only reason that Figure 3-2 defined a duplicated constant, 'STACKSEG,' was to help you locate the stack during the DEBUG session.

Suggestion: Define at least a size of 32 words for the stack. If the size is too small, neither the assembler nor the linker will warn you, and the program may "crash" in a most unpredictable way.

Figure 4-3 defines a data segment named DATASG in the example and beginning at offset location 0000. The segment contains three defined values all in DW (Define Word) format. FLDA defines a word (two bytes) with the decimal value 250, which the assembler has translated to hex 00FA (shown on the left).

FLDB defines a word with the decimal value 125, which the assembler has translated to hex 007D. The actual storage values of these

```
                               page 60,132
                       TITLE   EXASM2 (EXE)  Move and add operations
                       ; ---------------------------------------------
 0000                  STACKSG SEGMENT PARA STACK 'Stack'
 0000   20 [                   DW      32 DUP(?)
            ????
                ]

 0040                  STACKSG ENDS
                       ; ---------------------------------------------
 0000                  DATASG  SEGMENT PARA 'Data'
 0000   00FA           FLDA    DW      250
 0002   007D           FLDB    DW      125
 0004   ????           FLDC    DW      ?
 0006                  DATASG  ENDS
                       ; ---------------------------------------------
 0000                  CODESG  SEGMENT PARA 'Code'
 0000                  BEGIN   PROC    FAR
                               ASSUME  CS:CODESG,DS:DATASG,SS:STACKSG,ES:NOTHING
 0000   1E                     PUSH    DS            ;Push DS onto stack
 0001   2B C0                  SUB     AX,AX         ;Push zero offset
 0003   50                     PUSH    AX            ;  onto stack
 0004   B8 ---- R              MOV     AX,DATASG     ;Set up address of DATASG
 0007   8E D8                  MOV     DS,AX         ;  in DS register

 0009   A1 0000 R              MOV     AX,FLDA       ;Move 0250 to AX
 000C   03 06 0002 R           ADD     AX,FLDB       ;Add  0125 to AX
 0010   A3 0004 R              MOV     FLDC,AX       ;Store sum in FLDC
 0013   CB                     RET                   ;Return to DOS
 0014                   BEGIN  ENDP
 0014                  CODESG  ENDS
                               END     BEGIN
```

```
Segments and Groups:
                N a m e          Size   Align   Combine Class
CODESG . . . . . . . . . . . . . 0014   PARA    NONE    'CODE'
DATASG . . . . . . . . . . . . . 0006   PARA    NONE    'DATA'
STACKSG. . . . . . . . . . . . . 0040   PARA    STACK   'STACK'

Symbols:
                N a m e          Type   Value   Attr
BEGIN. . . . . . . . . . . . . . F PROC 0000    CODESG  Length =0014
FLDA . . . . . . . . . . . . . . L WORD         0000    DATASG
FLDB . . . . . . . . . . . . . . L WORD         0002    DATASG
FLDC . . . . . . . . . . . . . . L WORD         0004    DATASG
```

Figure 4-3 Assembled Program with Data Segment.

two constants are, respectively, FA00 and 7D00, which you can check with DEBUG.

FLDC defines a word with an unknown constant signified by (?).

The code segment, named CODESG in the example, contains new features concerned with the data segment. First, the ASSUME pseudo-op now relates DATASG to the DS register. This program does not require the ES register, but some programmers define its use for standardization.

Second, following the PUSH, SUB, and PUSH instructions that initialize the stack are two instructions that establish addressability for the data segment:

```
0004  B8 ---- R        MOV  AX,DATASG
0007  8E D8            MOV  DS,AX
```

The first MOV instruction "stores" DATASG in the AX register. Now, an instruction cannot actually store a segment in a register—it is trying to load the address of DATASG. Note the machine code to the left:

```
B8 ---- R
```

The four hyphens mean that the assembler cannot determine the address of DATASG; this is determined only when the object program is linked and loaded for execution. Since the program loader may locate a program anywhere in memory, the assembler leaves the address open and indicates the fact with an R; the linker is to replace (or relocate) the incomplete address with the actual one.

The second MOV instruction then moves the contents of the AX register to the DS register. The program now has an ASSUME that relates the DS with the data segment and instructions that initialize DS with the offset address of DATASG.

You may have two questions about this business. First, why not use one instruction to initialize the DS as

```
MOV DS,DATASG    ?
```

There is no valid instruction for a direct move from memory to the DS. Consequently, you have to code two instructions to initialize the DS.

Second, why does the program initialize the DS but not the SS or CS registers? The loader program automatically initializes the SS and CS when it loads a program for execution, but it is your responsibility to initialize the DS, and the ES if required.

While all this business may seem unduly involved, at this point you really don't have to understand it. All subsequent programs in this text use the same standard initialization of the stack and the data segment. You simply have to reproduce this code for each of your programs. Indeed, you may want to store a skeleton program on disk, and for each new program, COPY it into a file with its correct name, and use your editor to complete the additional instructions.

As an exercise, use your editor to create the program in Figure 4-3, assemble it, and link it. Then use DEBUG to view the code segment, the data segment, the registers, and the trace of execution.

CROSS-REFERENCE FILE

The assembler produces an optional symbol table (CRF) that you can use to produce a cross-reference listing of a program's labels, symbols, and variables. To request this file, reply to the fourth assembler prompt, assuming that the file is to be on disk B:

```
cross-reference [NUL.CRF]:B: [Return]
```

You still have to convert the resulting CRF file to a proper sorted cross-reference. A program on the assembler disk performs this function. After a successful assembly, enter the command CREF. The screen displays two prompts:

```
Cref filename [.CRF]:
List filename [cross-ref.REF]:
```

For the first prompt, enter the name of the CRF file, such as B:EXASM1. For the second prompt, you can enter the drive number only and accept the default file name. This choice causes CRF to write a cross-reference file named EXASM1.REF on drive B.

Use the DOS PRINT command to print a cross-reference file. Appendix D provides a number of CREF options.

Figure 4-4 contains the cross-reference for the program in Figure 4-3. The entries are in alphabetic sequence followed by the line number

```
          EXASM2  (EXE)  Move and add operations

Symbol Cross Reference          (# is definition)        Cref-1

BEGIN. . . . . . . . . . . . . .     18#     30      32

CODE . . . . . . . . . . . . . .     17
CODESG . . . . . . . . . . . . .     17#     19      31

DATA . . . . . . . . . . . . . .     11
DATASG . . . . . . . . . . . . .     11#     15      19      23

FLDA . . . . . . . . . . . . . .     12#     26
FLDB . . . . . . . . . . . . . .     13#     27
FLDC . . . . . . . . . . . . . .     14#     28

STACK. . . . . . . . . . . . . .      4
STACKSG. . . . . . . . . . . . .      4#      9      19

10 Symbols
```

Figure 4-4 Cross-Reference Table.

in the source program where it is defined and referenced. Names of segments and data items are in alphabetic sequence. The first number to the right shown as n# displays the line number where the symbol is defined in the LST program. Numbers to its right are the lines where the symbol is referenced. For example, CODESEG is defined in line 17, and is referenced in lines 19 and 32.

KEY POINTS TO REMEMBER

- The assembler converts a source program to an OBJ file and LINK converts an OBJ file to an executable EXE file.
- Double-check each command and prompt reply for (M)ASM, LINK, and CREF before pressing Return. Be especially careful of designating drive number.
- The CREF program produces a useful cross-reference listing.
- Delete unnecessary files from your program disks. Use CHKDSK regularly to check for available space. Also back up your program disks regularly: keep the original diskette as your backup and the newly copied one for subsequent programming.

QUESTIONS

4-1. Code the MASM command and replies to prompts to assemble a program named TEMPY.ASM with files LST, OBJ, and CRF. Assume that the program diskette is on drive B.

4-2. Code the commands for TEMPY from Question 1 for the following: (a) Execution through DEBUG, (b) Direct execution from DOS.

4-3. Give the purpose of each of the following files: (a) file.BAK, (b) file.ASM, (c) file.LST, (d) file.CRF, (e) file.OBJ, (f) file.EXE, (g) file.MAP.

4-4. Code the two instructions to initialize the DS register. Assume that the name of the data segment is DATSEG.

4-5. Write an assembler program for the following:

- Move hex 30 (immediate value) to the AL register.
- Shift the AL contents one bit left (SHL).
- Move hex 18 (immediate value) to the BL register.
- Multiply AL by BL (code MUL BL).

Remember the RET. The program does not need to define or initialize a data segment. Remember to COPY a skeleton program and use your editor to develop the program. Assemble and link. Use DEBUG to check the code segment, registers, and the trace.

4-6. Revise the program in Question 4-5 as follows:

- Define a one-byte item (DB) named FLDA containing hex 28 and another named FLDB containing hex 14.
- Define a two-byte item (DW) named FLDC with no constant.
- Move the contents of FLDA to the AL register and shift left one bit.
- Multiply the AL by FLDB (MUL FLDB).
- Move the product in the AX to FLDC.

This program requires a data segment. Assemble, link, and use DEBUG to test.

CHAPTER 5

Data Definition

Objective: To provide the methods of defining constants and work areas in an assembler program.

INTRODUCTION

The purpose of the data segment is for defining constants, work areas, and input/output areas. The assembler permits definition of items in various lengths according to the pseudo-operation that defines data: for example, DB defines a byte and DW defines a word. A data item may contain an undefined value or it may contain a constant defined either as a character string or as a numeric value.

Another way of defining a constant is directly within an instruction operand, as an immediate value, such as

```
MOV   AL,20H
```

In this case, the hex number 20 becomes part of the machine object code. An immediate value is restricted to one byte or one word, but where it can be used, it is more efficient than the use of a defined constant.

DATA DEFINITION PSEUDO-OPERATION

The assembler provides two ways to define data, first by means of its length and second by means of its contents. The general format for data definition is the following:

```
[name]  Dn   expression
```

- The name of a data item is optional (as indicated by the square brackets), but if the program references the item, it does so by means of a name. The section "Coding Format" in Chapter 3 provides the rules of names.

- The pseudo-ops that define data items are DB (byte), DW (word), DD (doubleword), DQ (quadword), and DT (tenbytes).
- The expression operand may contain either a constant expression such as

```
FLD1  DB  25
```

or a question mark to indicate an uninitialized item, as

```
FLDB  DB  ?
```

An expression may contain multiple constants separated by commas and limited only by the length of a line as follows:

```
FLD3  DB  11,  12,  13,  14,  15,  16, ...
```

The assembler defines these constants in adjacent bytes. A reference to FLD3 is to the first constant, 11, and a reference to FLD3+1 is to the second constant, 12. (You could think of FLD3 as FLD3+0.) For example, the instruction

```
MOV  AL,FLD3+3
```

loads the value 14 (hex 0E) into the AL register. The expression also permits duplication of constants of the general form

```
[name]  Dn  repeat-count DUP(expression) ...
```

The following three examples illustrate duplication:

```
DW  10 DUP(?)          ;Ten words, uninitialized
DB  5 DUP(14)          ;Five bytes containing hex 0E
DB  3 DUP(4 DUP(8))    ;Generates twelve 8s
```

The third example first generates four copies of the digit 8 (8888), then duplicates that value three times, giving twelve 8s in all.

An expression may contain a character string or a numeric constant.

Character Strings

A character string is used for descriptive data such as people's names and page titles. The string is contained within single quotes as 'PC' or within double quotes as "PC." The assembler stores character strings in object code as normal ASCII format.

Only DB format defines a character string that exceeds two characters and stores them in normal left-to-right sequence. Consequently, DB is the only sensible format for defining character data. Figure 5-1 gives some examples.

Numeric Constants

Numeric constants are used for arithmetic values and for memory addresses. The constant is not stored within quotes. The assembler converts all numeric constants to hexadecimal and stores the bytes in

```
                                  page    60,132
                         TITLE    EXDEF  (EXE)  Define assembler pseudo-ops
0000                     DATASG   SEGMENT PARA 'Data'

                         ;                Define Byte - DB:
                         ;                ----------------
0000 ??                  FLD1DB   DB      ?                    ;Uninitialized
0001 50 65 72 73 6F 6E   FLD2DB   DB      'Personal Computer' ;Char. string
     61 6C 20 43 6F 6D
     70 75 74 65 72
0012 20                  FLD3DB   DB      32                   ;Decimal constant
0013 20                  FLD4DB   DB      20H                  ;Hex constant
0014 59                  FLD5DB   DB      01011001B            ;Binary constant
0015 01 4A 41 4E 02 46   FLD6DB   DB      01,'JAN',02,'FEB',03,'MAR' ;Table
     45 42 03 4D 41 52
0021 33 32 36 35 34      FLD7DB   DB      '32654'              ;Numbers as chars
0026    0A [ 00 ]        FLD8DB   DB      10 DUP(0)            ;Ten zeros

                         ;                Define Word - DW:
                         ;                ----------------
0030 FFF0                FLD1DW   DW      0FFF0H               ;Hex constant
0032 0059                FLD2DW   DW      01011001B            ;Binary constant
0034 0021 R              FLD3DW   DW      FLD7DB               ;Address constant
0036 0003 0004 0007      FLD4DW   DW      3,4,7,8,9            ;Five constants
     0008 0009
0040    05 [ 0000 ]      FLD5DW   DW      5 DUP(0)             ;Five zeros

                         ;                Define Doubleword - DD:
                         ;                ----------------------
004A ????????            FLD1DD   DD      ?                    ;Uninitialized
004E 43 50 00 00         FLD2DD   DD      'PC'                 ;Character string
0052 3C 7F 00 00         FLD3DD   DD      32572                ;Decimal value
0056 11 00 00 00         FLD4DD   DD      FLD3DB - FLD2DB      ;Diff betw address
005A 0E 00 00 00 31 00   FLD5DD   DD      14,49                ;Two constants
     00 00
                         ;                Define Quadword - DQ:
                         ;                --------------------
0062 ????????????????    FLD1DQ   DQ      ?                    ;Uninitialized
006A 47 4D 00 00 00 00   FLD2DQ   DQ      04D47H               ;Hex constant
     00 00
```

Figure 5-1 Definitions of Character Strings and Numeric Values.

```
0072 3C 7F 00 00 00 00  FLD3DQ  DQ     32572         ;Decimal constant
     00 00
                        ;              Define Tenbytes - DT:
                        ;              --------------------
007A ?????????????????? FLD1DT  DT     ?             ;Uninitialized
     ??
0084 43 50 00 00 00 00  FLD2DT  DT     'PC'          ;Character string
     00 00 00 00

008E                    DATASG  ENDS
                                END
```

```
Segments and Groups:
               N a m e                Size   Align  Combine Class
DATASG . . . . . . . . . . . . .      008E   PARA   NONE    'DATA'

Symbols:
               N a m e          Type  Value  Attr
FLD1DB . . . . . . . . . . . . L BYTE  0000   DATASG
FLD1DD . . . . . . . . . . . . L DWORD 004A   DATASG
FLD1DQ . . . . . . . . . . . . L QWORD 0062   DATASG
FLD1DT . . . . . . . . . . . . L TBYTE 007A   DATASG
FLD1DW . . . . . . . . . . . . L WORD  0030   DATASG
FLD2DB . . . . . . . . . . . . L BYTE  0001   DATASG
FLD2DD . . . . . . . . . . . . L DWORD 004E   DATASG
FLD2DQ . . . . . . . . . . . . L QWORD 006A   DATASG
FLD2DT . . . . . . . . . . . . L TBYTE 0084   DATASG
FLD2DW . . . . . . . . . . . . L WORD  0032   DATASG
FLD3DB . . . . . . . . . . . . L BYTE  0012   DATASG
FLD3DD . . . . . . . . . . . . L DWORD 0052   DATASG
FLD3DQ . . . . . . . . . . . . L QWORD 0072   DATASG
FLD3DW . . . . . . . . . . . . L WORD  0034   DATASG
FLD4DB . . . . . . . . . . . . L BYTE  0013   DATASG
FLD4DD . . . . . . . . . . . . L DWORD 0056   DATASG
FLD4DW . . . . . . . . . . . . L WORD  0036   DATASG
FLD5DB . . . . . . . . . . . . L BYTE  0014   DATASG
FLD5DD . . . . . . . . . . . . L DWORD 005A   DATASG
FLD5DW . . . . . . . . . . . . L WORD  0040   DATASG  Length =0005
FLD6DB . . . . . . . . . . . . L BYTE  0015   DATASG
FLD7DB . . . . . . . . . . . . L BYTE  0021   DATASG
FLD8DB . . . . . . . . . . . . L BYTE  0026   DATASG  Length =000A
```

Figure 5-1 ***(continued)***

object code in reverse sequence—right to left. Following are the various numeric formats.

Decimal. Decimal format permits the decimal digits 0 through 9 optionally followed by the letter D, as 125 or 125D. Although the assembler allows decimal format as a coding convenience, it converts it to hex object code. Consequently, decimal 125 becomes hex 7D.

Hexadecimal. Hex format permits the hex digits 0 through F followed by the letter H. Since the assembler expects that a reference beginning with a letter is a symbolic name, the first digit of a hex constant must be 0 to 9. Examples are 2EH and 0FFFH, which the assembler stores respectively as 2E and FF0F—the bytes in the second example are stored in reverse sequence.

Binary. Binary format permits the binary digits 0 and 1 followed by the letter B. The normal use for binary format is to clearly distinguish the bit values for the Boolean instructions AND, OR, XOR, and TEST. Decimal 12, hex C, and binary 1100B all generate the same value: hex 0C or binary 00001100 depending on how you view the contents of the byte.

Octal. This specialized format permits the octal digits 0 through 7 followed by the letter Q or O, such as 253Q. Octal is rarely used today.

Decimal Scientific (Floating Point) and Hex Real. These formats are supported only by MASM.

Be sure to distinguish between the effect of character and numeric constants. A character constant defined as DB '12' represents ASCII characters and generates hex 3132. A numeric constant defined as DB 12 represents a binary number and generates hex 0C.

Figure 5-1 illustrates the preceding data pseudo-ops with various character strings and numeric constants. The data segment has been assembled in order to show the generated object code on the left.

DEFINE BYTE (DB)

Of the various pseudo-ops that define data items, one of the most useful is DB (Define Byte). A DB character expression may contain a string of any length up to the end of a line. For examples, see FLD2DB and FLD7DB in Figure 5-1. Note that the constant FLD2DB contains the character string 'Personal Computer.' The object code shows the ASCII character for each byte; hex 20 represents a blank character.

A DB numeric expression may contain one or more one-byte constants. This maximum of one byte means two hex digits. The largest positive hex number is 7F; all "higher" numbers 80 through FF represent negative values. In terms of decimal numbers, the limits are +127 and -128.

In Figure 5-1, numeric constants are FLD3DB, FLD4DB, FLD5DB, and FLD8DB. FLD6DB depicts a mixture of numeric and string constants suitable for a table.

DEFINE WORD (DW)

The DW pseudo-op defines items that are one word (two bytes) in length. A DW character expression is limited to two characters, which the assembler reverses in object code such that 'PC' becomes 'CP.' For defining character strings, DW is of limited use.

A DW numeric expression may contain one or more one-word constants. This maximum of two bytes means four hex digits. The largest positive hex number is 7FFF; all "higher" numbers 8000 through FFFF represent negative values. In terms of decimal numbers, the limits are +32,767 and –32,768.

In Figure 5-1, FLD1DW and FLD2DW define numeric constants. FLD3DW defines the operand as an address—in this case as the offset address of FLD7DB. The generated object code is 0021 (the R to the right means relocatable), and a check above in the figure shows that the offset address of FLD7DB is indeed 0021.

FLD4DW defines a table of five numeric constants. Note that the object code for each constant is one word (two bytes).

For DW, DD, and DQ formats, the assembler converts the constant to hex object code but stores it in reverse sequence. Consequently, the decimal value 12345 converts to hex 3039 but is stored as 3930.

DEFINE DOUBLEWORD (DD)

The DD pseudo-op defines items that are two words (four bytes) in length. A numeric expression may contain one or more constants, each with a maximum of four bytes (eight hex digits). The largest positive hex number is 7FFFFFFF; all "higher" numbers 80000000 through FFFFFFFF represent negative values. In terms of decimal numbers, these maximums are +2,147,483,647 and –2,147,483,648.

In Figure 5-1, FLD3DD defines a numeric constant. FLD4DD generates the numeric difference between two defined addresses; in this case, the result is the length of FLD2DB. FLD5DD defines two numeric constants.

The assembler converts all DD numeric constants to hex but stores the object code in reverse sequence. Consequently, the decimal value 12345 converts to 00003039 but is stored as 39300000.

A DD character expression is limited to two characters. The assembler reverses the characters and left-adjusts them in the four-byte doubleword, as shown by FLD2DD in object code.

DEFINE QUADWORD (DQ)

The DQ pseudo-op defines items that are four words (eight bytes) in length. A numeric expression may contain one or more constants, each with a maximum of eight bytes or 16 hex digits. The largest positive hex number is 7 followed by 15 Fs. As an indication of the magnitude of this number, hex 1 followed by 15 0s equals the following decimal number:

1,152,921,504,606,846,976

In Figure 5-1, FLD2DQ and FLD3DQ illustrate numeric values. The assembler converts all DQ numeric constants to hex but stores the object code in reverse sequence as for DD and DW.

The assembler handles DQ character strings like DD and DW.

DEFINE TENBYTES (DT)

The DT pseudo-op defines data items that are ten bytes long. Its purpose appears to be related to "packed decimal" numeric values (discussed in Chapter 13). Note that DT generates different constants depending on assembler version; check your assembler manual for its practice.

Figure 5-1 supplies examples of DT for an uninitialized item and for a two-character constant.

The program in Figure 5-1 contains only a data segment. Although the assembler generated no error messages, LINK MAP displayed "Warning: No STACK Segment" and LINK displayed "There were 1 errors detected." Despite the warning, you can still use DEBUG to view the object code, as shown in Figure 5-2.

The right side of the dump clearly shows the alphabetic data such as "Personal Computer."

IMMEDIATE OPERANDS

Figure 2-1 in Chapter 2 illustrated the use of immediate operands. The instruction

```
MOV   AX,0123H
```

moves the immediate constant hex 0123 to the AX register. The three-byte object code for this instruction is B82301, where B8 means "move an immediate value to the AX register," and the following two bytes

```
D:\ D>DEBUG D:EXDEF.EXE
-D
1421:0000  00 50 65 72 73 6F 6E 61-6C 20 43 6F 6D 70 75 74   .Personal Comput
1421:0010  65 72 20 20 59 01 4A 41-4E 02 46 45 42 03 4D 41   er  Y.JAN.FEB.MA
1421:0020  52 33 32 36 35 34 00 00-00 00 00 00 00 00 00 00   R32654..........
1421:0030  F0 FF 59 00 21 00 03 00-04 00 07 00 08 00 09 00   ..Y.!...........
1421:0040  00 00 00 00 00 00 00 00-00 00 00 00 00 00 43 50   ..............CP
1421:0050  00 00 3C 7F 00 00 11 00-00 00 0E 00 00 00 31 00   ..<...........1.
1421:0060  00 00 00 00 00 00 00 00-00 00 47 4D 00 00 00 00   ..........GM....
1421:0070  00 00 3C 7F 00 00 00 00-00 00 00 00 00 00 00 00   ..<.............
-D
1421:0080  00 00 00 00 43 50 00 00-00 00 00 00 00 00 33 33   ....CP........33
1421:0090  3E 36 33 33 73 00 00 00-0A 0E 00 00 3E 63 63 30   >633s.......>cc0
1421:00A0  1C 06 63 63 3E 00 00 00-0A 0E 00 00 FF DB 99 18   ..cc>...........
1421:00B0  18 18 18 18 3C 00 00 00-0A 0E 00 00 63 63 63 63   ....<.......cccc
1421:00C0  63 63 63 63 3E 00 00 00-0A 0E 00 00 C3 C3 C3 C3   cccc>...........
1421:00D0  C3 C3 66 3C 18 00 00 00-0A 0E 00 00 C3 C3 C3 C3   ..f<............
1421:00E0  DB DB FF 66 66 00 00 00-0A 0E 00 00 C3 C3 66 3C   ...ff.........f<
1421:00F0  18 3C 66 C3 C3 00 00 00-0A 0E 00 00 C3 C3 C3 66   .<f............f
-Q
```

Figure 5-2 Dump of the Data Segment.

contain the value itself. Many instructions provide for two operands; the first operand may be a register or memory location, and the second operand may be an immediate constant.

The use of an immediate operand is more efficient than defining a numeric constant in the data segment and referencing it in the operand of the MOV, for example, as

Data segment: `AMT1 DW 0123H`
Code segment: `MOV AX,AMT1`

Length of Immediate Operands

The length of an immediate constant is subject to the length of the first operand. For example, the following immediate operand is two bytes but the AL register is only one byte:

```
MOV   AL,0123H   (invalid)
```

However, if an immediate operand is shorter than a receiving operand, as

```
ADD   AX,25H   (valid)
```

the assembler expands the immediate operand to two bytes, 0025, and stores the object code as 2500.

Immediate Formats

An immediate constant may be hex, such as 0123H; decimal, such as 291 (which the assembler converts to hex 0123); or binary, such as 100100011B (which converts to hex 0123).

Instructions that allow immediate operands are the following, listed by class:

Move and compare:	`MOV, CMP.`
Arithmetic:	`ADC, ADD, SBB, SUB.`
Shift:	`RCL, RCR, ROL, ROR, SHL, SAR, SHR.`
Logical:	`AND, OR, TEST, XOR.`

Figure 5-3 provides examples of valid immediate operands using these instructions. Later chapters explain arithmetic carry operations, shift, and logical instructions. Since the example is not intended for execution, it omits defining a stack and initializing segment registers.

To process items longer than two bytes, you may have to code a loop (Chapter 7) or use a string operation (Chapter 11).

EQU PSEUDO-OPERATION

The EQU pseudo-op does not define a data item. Instead, it defines a value that can be used to substitute in other instructions. Assume the following EQU instruction coded in the data segment:

```
TIMES   EQU   10
```

The name, in this case TIMES, may be any acceptable assembler name. Now whenever the word TIMES appears in an instruction or another pseudo-op, the assembler substitutes the value 10. For example, the assembler converts the pseudo-op

```
      FIELDA  DB  TIMES DUP(?)
to    FIELDA  DB  10 DUP(?)
```

An equated operand may also appear in an instruction, as in the following:

```
COUNTR  EQU  05
        ...
        MOV   CX,COUNTR
```

```
                                 page    60,132
                         TITLE   EXIMM  (EXE)  Example immediate operands
                         ;       (Coded for assembly, NOT for execution)
0000                     DATASG  SEGMENT PARA 'Data'
0000 ??                  FLD1    DB      ?
0001 ????                FLD2    DW      ?
0003                     DATASG  ENDS

0000                     CODESG  SEGMENT PARA 'Code'
0000                     BEGIN   PROC    FAR
                                 ASSUME  CS:CODESG,DS:DATASG

                         ;               Move & Compare Operations:
                         ;               --------------------------
0000 BB 0113                     MOV     BX,275          ;Move
0003 3C 19                       CMP     AL,19H          ;Compare

                         ;               Arithmetic Operations:
                         ;               ----------------------
0005 14 05                       ADC     AL,5            ;Add with carry
0007 80 C7 0C                    ADD     BH,12           ;Add
000A 1C 05                       SBB     AL,5            ;Sub with borrow
000C 80 2E 0000 R 05             SUB     FLD1,5          ;Subtract

                         ;               Rotate & Shift (1 bit only):
                         ;               ----------------------------
0011 D0 D3                       RCL     BL,1            ;Rotate left/carry
0013 D0 DC                       RCR     AH,1            ;Rotate right/carry
0015 D1 06 0001 R                ROL     FLD2,1          ;Rotate left
0019 D0 C8                       ROR     AL,1            ;Rotate right
001B D1 E1                       SAL     CX,1            ;Shift left
001D D1 FB                       SAR     BX,1            ;Shift arith right
001F D0 2E 0000 R                SHR     FLD1,1          ;Shift right

                         ;               Logical Operations:
                         ;               -------------------
0023 24 2C                       AND     AL,00101100B    ;AND register
0025 80 CF 2A                    OR      BH,2AH          ;OR register
0028 F6 C3 7A                    TEST    BL,7AH          ;TEST register
002B 80 36 0000 R 23             OR      FLD1,23H        ;XOR storage
0030                     BEGIN   ENDP
0030                     CODESG  ENDS
                                 END
```

Figure 5-3 Immediate Operations.

The assembler replaces COUNTR in the MOV instruction with the value 05, making the operand an immediate value as if it were coded as

```
MOV   CX,05     ;Assembler substitutes 05
```

The advantage of EQU is that many instructions may use the value defined by COUNTR. If the value has to be changed, you need change only one instruction—the EQU. Needless to say, you can use an equated value only where a substitution makes sense to the assembler. You can also equate symbolic names:

```
1.  TP   EQU  TOTALPAY
2.  MPY  EQU  MUL
```

The first example assumes that the program has defined TOTALPAY in the data segment. For any instruction that contains the operand TP, the assembler replaces it with the address of TOTALPAY. The second example enables a program to use the word MPY in place of the regular symbolic instruction MUL.

KEY POINTS TO REMEMBER

- Keep names of data items unique and descriptive. For example, an item for an employee's wage could be named EMPWAGE.
- Use DB to define character strings since this format permits strings longer than two bytes and converts them to normal left-to-right sequence.
- Be careful to distinguish between a decimal and a hex value. For example, consider the effect of adding decimal 25 and of adding hex 25:

```
ADD  AX,25   ;Adds 25
ADD  AX,25H  ;Adds 37
```

- Remember that DW, DD, and DQ store a numeric value in object code with the bytes in reverse sequence.
- Use DB items for processing a half register (AL, AH, BL, etc.) and DW for processing a full register (AX, BX, CX, etc.). Numeric items defined as DD and DQ require special handling.
- Match immediate operands to the size of a register: a one-byte constant with a one-byte register (AL, BH) and a one-word constant with a one-word register (AX, BX).

QUESTIONS

5-1. What are the lengths in bytes of the following data pseudo-ops: (a) DW, (b) DD, (c) DT, (d) DB, (e) DQ?

5-2. Define a character string named TITLE1 containing the constant RGB Electronics.

5-3. Define the following numeric values in data items named, respectively, FLDA through FLDE:

   (a) A four-byte item containing the hex equivalent to decimal 115.
   (b) A one-byte item containing the hex equivalent to decimal 25.
   (c) A two-byte item containing an undefined value.
   (d) A one-byte item containing the binary equivalent to decimal 25.
   (e) A DW containing the consecutive values 16, 19, 20, 27, 30.

5-4. Show the generated hex object code for (a) DB '26' and (b) DB 26.

5-5. Determine the assembled hex object code for (a) DB 26H, (b) DW 2645H, (c) DD 25733AH, (d) DQ 25733AH.

5-6. Code the following instructions with immediate operands:

   (a) Store 320 in the AX.
   (b) Compare FLDB to zero.
   (c) Add hex 40 to BX.
   (d) Subtract hex 40 from CX.
   (e) Shift FLDB one bit left.
   (f) Shift the CH one bit right.

5-7. Key in and assemble the data items and instructions for Questions 5-2, 5-3, and 5-6. You don't require a stack or a LINK step unless you use DEBUG to check the assembled code. Print the LST listing when the assembly is free of error messages. Remember MODE LPT1:132,6 to set printer width.

CHAPTER 6

COM Program Files

Objective: To explain the purpose and uses of COM files and how to prepare an assembler program for that format.

INTRODUCTION

Up to now, you have written, assembled, and executed programs in EXE format. LINK automatically generates a particular format for an EXE file, preceded by a special header block that is at least 512 bytes long. (Chapter 22 provides details of header blocks.)

You can also generate a COM file for execution. One example of a commonly used COM file is COMMAND.COM. A DOS program named EXE2BIN.COM converts EXE files to COM files. Actually, it converts to a BIN (binary) file; the program name means "convert EXE-to-BIN," but you can rename your output file COM.

DIFFERENCES BETWEEN EXE AND COM PROGRAM FILES

Although you use EXE2BIN to convert an EXE file to a COM file, there are some significant differences in the way you create a file that is to execute as EXE and one that is to execute as COM.

Program Size. An EXE program may be virtually any size, whereas a COM file is restricted to one segment and a maximum of 64K. A COM file is always smaller that its original EXE file; one reason is that the 512-byte header block that precedes an EXE file on disk is not present on a COM file.

Stack Segment. An EXE program defines a stack segment, whereas a COM program automatically generates a stack. Thus, when you write an assembler program that is to be converted to a COM file, you omit the stack.

Data Segment. An EXE program usually defines a data segment, and initializes the DS register with its address. A COM program must define its data within the code segment. As you'll see, there are simple ways to handle this situation.

Initialization. An EXE program pushes a zero word on the stack and initializes the DS register. Since a COM program has neither a stack nor a data segment, it omits these steps. When a COM program initializes, all segment registers contain the address of the program segment prefix (PSP), a 256-byte (hex 100) block that DOS inserts immediately preceding a COM and EXE program in memory. Because addressing begins at an offset of hex 100 bytes from the beginning of the PSP, code an ORG pseudo-op immediately following the Code SEGMENT statement, as ORG 100H.

Conversion. For both EXE and COM programs, you assemble and produce an OBJ file, and link the OBJ file to produce an EXE file. If you originally wrote the program to run as an EXE file, you can now execute it. If you originally wrote the program to run as a COM file, the linker produces a message:

```
Warning: No STACK Segment
```

You may safely ignore this message, since there is supposed to be no defined stack. Use EXE2BIN to convert the EXE file to COM. Assuming that EXE2BIN is in drive A and a linked file named CALC.EXE is in drive B, type

```
EXE2BIN B:CALC,B:CALC.COM
```

Since the first operand of the command always references an EXE file, do not code the EXE extension. The second operand could be a name other than CALC.COM. If you omit the extension, EXE2BIN assumes a BIN extension, which you would have to subsequently rename as COM. When conversion is complete, you can delete the OBJ and EXE files.

If you have a source program already written in EXE format, you can use an editor to convert the instructions to a form suitable for a COM file.

EXAMPLE COM PROGRAM FILE

The program in Figure 6-1, named EXCOM1, is the same as the one in Figure 4-3 revised to conform to COM requirements. Note the following changes in this COM program:

- There is no stack or data segment.
- An ASSUME statement tells the assembler to begin offsets from the start of the code segment. The CS register also contains this address, which is also that of the PSP. The ORG pseudo-op, however, causes the program to reside hex 100 bytes from this point, past the PSP.
- ORG 100H sets an offset address for the start of execution. The program loader stores this in the instruction pointer.
- A JMP instruction transfers control of execution around the defined data.

The steps to convert and execute this program are:

```
MASM [reply to prompts the usual way]
LINK [reply to prompts the usual way]
EXE2BIN B:EXCOM1,B:EXCOM1.COM
DEL B:EXCOM1.OBJ,B:EXCOM1.EXE (Delete OBJ and EXE modules)
```

The size of the EXE and COM programs is 788 bytes and 20 bytes, respectively. Because of the efficiency of COM files, you may be wise to write all small programs for COM format. Type DEBUG B:EXCOM1.COM to trace execution up to (but not including) the RET instruction.

Some programmers code data items following the instructions, so that no initial JMP instruction is required. Coding data items first speeds up the assembly, and is the method the assembler manual suggests.

```
        page 60,132
TITLE   EXCOM1  COM program to move and add
CODESG  SEGMENT PARA 'Code'
        ASSUME  CS:CODESG,DS:CODESG,SS:CODESG,ES:CODESG
        ORG     100H            ;Start at end of PSP
BEGIN:  JMP     MAIN            ;Jump past data
; ---------------------------------------------------------
FLDA    DW      250             ;Data definitions
FLDB    DW      125
FLDC    DW      ?
; ---------------------------------------------------------
MAIN    PROC    NEAR
        MOV     AX,FLDA         ;Move 0250 to AX
        ADD     AX,FLDB         ;Add  0125 to AX
        MOV     FLDC,AX         ;Store sum in FLDC
        RET                     ;Return to DOS
MAIN    ENDP
CODESG  ENDS
        END     BEGIN
```

Figure 6-1 Example COM Program.

THE COM STACK

For a COM file, DOS automatically defines a stack and sets the same common segment address in all four segment registers. If the 64K segment for the program is large enough, DOS sets the SP register to an address at the end of the segment, hex FFFE, as the top of the stack. If the 64K segment does not contain enough space for a stack, DOS sets the stack at the end of memory. For both cases, DOS then pushes a zero word onto the stack.

Where your program is large or memory is restricted, you may have to take care in pushing words onto the stack. The DIR command indicates the size of a file, and will give you a good idea as to the space available for a stack.

In general, the smaller programs in this book are COM, and should be clear from their format.

DEBUGGING TIPS

Omission of only one COM requirement may cause a program to fail. If EXE2BIN finds an error, it simply notifies you that it cannot convert the file, but does not provide a reason. Check the SEGMENT, ASSUME, and END statements. If you omit ORG 100H, the program incorrectly references data in the program segment prefix, with unpredictable results.

If you run a COM program under DEBUG, use D CS:100 to view the data and instructions. Do not follow the RET through termination; instead, use DEBUG's Q command. Some programmers use INT 20H instead of RET.

An attempt to execute the EXE module of a program written as COM will fail.

KEY POINTS TO REMEMBER

- A COM file is restricted to 64K.
- A COM file is smaller than its original EXE file.
- A program written to run as a COM file does not contain a stack or data segment, nor does it initialize the DS register.
- A program written to run as a COM file uses ORG 100H immediately following the Code SEGMENT statement in order to set the offset

address to the beginning of execution following the program segment prefix.

- The EXE2BIN program converts an EXE file to a COM file, provided you code a COM extension.
- DOS defines a stack for a COM program, either at the end of the program or, if insufficient space, at the end of memory.

QUESTIONS

6-1. What is the maximum size of a COM file?

6-2. What are the segments that you can define in a program to be converted to a COM file?

6-3. How does a COM file handle the fact that you do not define a stack?

6-4. A program has been converted to a file named SAMPLE.EXE. Provide the command to convert it to a COM file.

6-5. Revise the program in Question 4-6 for COM format, convert it, and execute it under DEBUG.

CHAPTER 7

Program Logic and Organization

Objective: To cover the requirements for program control (looping and jumping), for logical comparisons, and for program organization.

INTRODUCTION

Up to this chapter, program examples have executed in a straight line, with one instruction sequentially following another. Seldom, however, is a programmable problem that simple. Most programs consist of a number of *loops* in which a series of steps repeats until reaching a specific requirement and various tests to determine which of several actions to take. A common requirement is to test if a program is to terminate execution.

These requirements involve a transfer of control to the address of an instruction that does not immediately follow the one currently executing. A transfer of control may be forward to execute a new series of steps or backward to reexecute the same steps.

Certain instructions can transfer control outside the normal sequential steps by causing an offset value to be added to the instruction pointer. Following are the four classes of transfer operations, all covered in this chapter:

Unconditional Jump:	JMP
Looping:	LOOP
Conditional Jump:	Jnnn (high, low, equal)
Call a procedure:	CALL

Note that there are three types of addresses: SHORT, NEAR, and FAR. SHORT addressing is involved with looping, conditional jumps, and some unconditional jumps. NEAR and FAR addressing involves the CALL instruction, and unconditional jumps that don't qualify as SHORT. All types affect the IP register; FAR also affects the CS register.

THE JMP INSTRUCTION

One commonly used instruction for transferring control is the jump (JMP) instruction. A jump is *unconditional* since the operation transfers control under all circumstances.

The COM program in Figure 7-1 uses a JMP instruction. The AX, BX, and CX registers are initialized to the value of 1 and loop performs the following:

Add 1 to AX

Add AX to BX

Double the value in CX

The effect of repeating the loop causes AX to increase as 1, 2, 3, 4, . . .; BX to increase according to the sum of the digits 1, 3, 6, 10, . . .; and CX to double as 1, 2, 4, 8, . . . The beginning of the loop has a label, in this case, A20:—the colon indicates that the label is inside a procedure (BEGIN in this case) in the code segment. The end of the loop contains the instruction

```
JMP   A20
```

to indicate that control is to transfer to the instruction labeled A20. Note that an address label in an instruction operand does not have a colon. Also, since this loop has no exit, processing is endless—usually not a good idea.

```
                         page 60,132
                  TITLE  EXJUMP (COM)  Illustration of JMP for looping
0000              CODESG SEGMENT PARA 'Code'
                         ASSUME  CS:CODESG,DS:CODESG,SS:CODESG
0100                     ORG     100H

0100              MAIN   PROC    NEAR
0100  B8 0001            MOV     AX,01          ;Init'ze AX,
0103  BB 0001            MOV     BX,01          ;        BX, &
0106  B9 0001            MOV     CX,01          ;        CX to 01
0109              A20:
0109  05 0001            ADD     AX,01          ;Add 01 to AX
010C  03 D8              ADD     BX,AX          ;Add AX to BX
010E  D1 E1              SHL     CX,1           ;Double CX
0110  EB F7              JMP     A20            ;Jump to A20 instr'n
0112             MAIN    ENDP
0112             CODESG  ENDS
                         END     MAIN
```

Figure 7-1 Use of the JMP Instruction.

You can code a label either on a line with an instruction as

```
A20:   ADD  AX,01
```

or on a separate line as

```
A20:
       ADD  AX,01
```

In both cases, the address of A20 references the first byte of the ADD instruction. Technically, the colon in A20: gives the label the NEAR attribute. Watch out—omission of the colon is a common error. In this example, A20 is -9 bytes from the JMP. You can confirm this distance by examining the object code for the JMP: EBF7. EB is the machine code for a near JMP and F7 is a negative offset value for -9. The JMP operation adds the F7 to the instruction pointer (IP), which contains the offset 0112 of the instruction following the JMP:

	Dec	Hex	
Instruction pointer:	274	112	
JMP offset:	-9	F7	(two's complement)
Transfer address:	265	109	

The jump address calculates as hex 109, and a check of the program listing for the offset address of A20 shows 0109. Conversely, the operand for a forward JMP is a positive value.

A JMP operation within -128 to +127 bytes is a SHORT jump. The assembler generates a one-byte operand whose limits are hex 00 to FF. A JMP that exceeds this limit becomes a FAR jump for which the assembler generates a different machine code and a 2-byte operand. On its first pass through a source program, the assembler generates the length of each instruction. However, a JMP instruction may be either two or three bytes long. If the assembler has already encountered the designated operand (a backward jump), as

```
A50:
       . . .
       JMP  A50
```

then it generates a 2-byte instruction. If the assembler has not encountered the designated operand (a forward jump), as

```
       JMP  A90
       . . .
A90:
```

then it doesn't know if this is a NEAR or FAR jump, but automatically generates a 3-byte instruction. However, you can use a SHORT operator to force a SHORT jump and a 2-byte instruction, as

```
        JMP   SHORT A90
        . . .
A90:
```

As a useful experience, key in the program, and assemble, link, and convert it to COM format. No data definitions are required, since immediate operands generate all the data. Use DEBUG to trace the COM module for a number of iterations. Once AX contains 08, BX and CX will be incremented to hex 24 (decimal 36) and hex 80 (decimal 128), respectively. Use DEBUG's Q command to exit.

THE LOOP INSTRUCTION

The JMP instruction in Figure 7-1 causes an endless loop. But a routine is more likely to loop a specified number of times or until a particular value is reached. The LOOP instruction, which serves this purpose, requires an initial value in the CX register. For each iteration, LOOP automatically deducts 1 from the CX; if CX is nonzero, control jumps to the operand address, and if zero, control drops through to the following instruction.

The program in Figure 7-2 illustrates use of LOOP and performs the same operation as Figure 7-1 except it terminates after ten loops. A MOV instruction initializes CX with the value 10. Since LOOP uses the CX, this program now uses DX in place of CX for doubling the initial value 1. The LOOP instruction replaces JMP A20, and for efficiency INC AX (increment the AX by 1) replaces ADD AX,01.

Just as for JMP, the operand contains the distance from the end of the LOOP instruction to the address of A20, which is added to the instruction pointer. *For LOOP, this distance must be within –128 to +127 bytes.* For an operation that exceeds this limit, the assembler issues a message "relative jump out of range."

It is recommended that you modify your copy of Figure 7-1 for these changes and assemble, link, and convert it to COM. Use DEBUG to trace the entire ten loops. Once CX is reduced to zero, the contents of AX, BX, and DX are, respectively, hex 000B, 0042, and 0400. Use DEBUG's Q command to exit.

Two variations of the LOOP instruction are LOOPE (or LOOPZ) and LOOPNE (or LOOPNZ). Both operations decrement the CX by 1. LOOPE transfers to the operand address if the CX is not zero and the zero

```
                          page 60,132
                    TITLE EXLOOP (COM)  Illustration of LOOP
0000                CODESG SEGMENT PARA 'Code'
                          ASSUME  CS:CODESG,DS:CODESG,SS:CODESG
0100                      ORG     100H

0100                BEGIN PROC    NEAR
0100   B8 0001            MOV     AX,01        ;Init'ze AX,
0103   BB 0001            MOV     BX,01        ;      BX, &
0106   BA 0001            MOV     DX,01        ;      DX to 01
0109   B9 000A            MOV     CX,10        ;Init'ze no. of loops
010C               A20:
010C   40                 INC     AX           ;Add 01 to AX
010D   03 D8              ADD     BX,AX        ;Add AX to BX
010F   D1 E2              SHL     DX,1         ;Double DX
0111   E2 F9              LOOP    A20          ;Decr CX, loop if nonzero
0113   C3                 RET                  ;Terminate
0114               BEGIN  ENDP
0114               CODESG ENDS
                          END     BEGIN
```

Figure 7-2 Use of the LOOP Instruction.

condition is set (ZF = 1). LOOPNE transfers if the CX is not zero and the nonzero condition is set (ZF = 0).

FLAGS REGISTER

The remaining material in this chapter requires a more detailed knowledge of the flags register. This register contains 16 bits that various instructions set to indicate the status of an operation. In all cases, a flag remains set until another instruction changes it. The flags register contains the following nine used bits (an asterisk indicates an unused bit), which the following sections explain from right to left:

Bit no.:	15	14	13	12	11	10	9	8	7	6	5	4	3	2	1	0
Flag:	*	*	*	*	O	D	I	T	S	Z	*	A	*	P	*	C

CF (Carry Flag). Contains "carries" (0 or 1) from the high-order bit following arithmetic operations and some shift and rotate operations (Chapter 12).

PF (Parity Flag). A check of the low-order eight bits of data operations. An odd number of data bits sets the flag to 0 and an even number to 1—not to be confused with the parity bit and seldom of concern for conventional programming.

AF (Auxiliary Carry Flag). Set to 1 if arithmetic causes a carry out of bit 3 (fourth from the right) of a register one-byte operation. This flag is concerned with arithmetic on ASCII and packed-decimal fields (Chapter 13).

ZF (Zero Flag). Set as a result of arithmetic or compare operations. Unexpectedly, a nonzero result sets it to 0 and a zero result sets it to 1. However, the setting, if not apparently correct, is logically correct: 0 means no (the result is not equal to zero) and 1 means yes (the result equals zero). JE and JZ test this flag.

SF (Sign Flag). Set according to the sign (high-order or leftmost bit) after an arithmetic operation: positive sets to 0 and negative sets to 1. JG and JL instructions test this flag.

TF (Trap Flag). You have already set this flag when you entered the T command in DEBUG. When set, the trap flag causes the processor to execute in single-step mode, that is, one instruction at a time under user control.

IF (Interrupt Flag). When 0 all interrupts are disabled, and when 1 all interrupts are enabled.

DF (Direction Flag). Used by string operations to determine the direction of data transfer. When 0 the operation increments the SI and DI registers causing left-to-right data transfer; when 1 the operation decrements the SI and DI causing right-to-left data transfer (Chapter 11).

OF (Overflow Flag). Indicates a carry into and out of the high-order (leftmost) sign bit following a signed arithmetic operation (Chapter 12).

As an example, the CMP instruction compares two operands and affects the AF, CF, OF, PF, SF, and ZF flags. However, you do not have to test these flags individually. The following tests if the BX register contains a zero value:

```
        CMP  BX,00            ;Compare BX to zero
        JZ   B50              ;Jump if zero to B50
         .  (action if nonzero)
         .
B50:     ...                  ;Jump point if BX zero
```

If the BX contains zero, CMP sets the ZF to 1 and may or may not change other flags. The JZ (Jump if Zero) instruction tests only the ZF flag. Since ZF contains 1 (meaning a zero condition), JZ transfers control (jumps) to the address indicated by operand B50.

CONDITIONAL JUMP INSTRUCTIONS

An earlier example explains how the LOOP instruction decrements and tests the CX register; if nonzero, the instruction transfers control to the operand address. In effect, the transfer occurs depending on a certain condition. The assembler supports a wide variety of *conditional jump* instructions that transfer control depending on settings in the flags register. For example, you can compare two fields and then jump according to flag values.

You could replace the LOOP instruction in Figure 7-2 with two instructions, one that decrements CX and the other that performs a conditional jump:

Use of LOOP	*Use of Conditional Jump*
`LOOP   A20`	`DEC   CX`
	`JNZ   A20`

The DEC and JNZ perform exactly what LOOP does: Decrement the CX by 1 and jump to A20 if CX is nonzero. DEC also sets the zero flag in the flags register either to zero or nonzero. JNZ then tests the setting of the zero flag. In this example, LOOP, although it has limited uses, is more efficient than the two instructions DEC and JNZ.

Just as for JMP and LOOP, the operand contains the distance from the end of the JNZ instruction to the address of A20, which is added to the instruction pointer. *This distance must be within –128 to +127 bytes.* For an operation that exceeds this limit, the assembler issues a message "relative jump out of range."

Signed and Unsigned Data

Distinguishing the purpose of conditional jumps should clarify their use. The type of data on which you are performing comparisons or arithmetic can determine which instruction to use: unsigned or signed. An *unsigned* data item treats all bits as data bits; typical examples are character strings such as names and addresses and numeric values such as customer numbers. A *signed* data item treats the leftmost bit as a sign, where 0 is positive and 1 is negative. Many numeric values may be either positive or negative.

As an example, assume that the AX contains 11000110 and the BX contains 00010110. The instruction

```
CMP   AX,BX
```

compares the contents of the AX to the BX. As unsigned data, the AX value is larger; as signed data, the AX value is smaller.

Jumps Based on Unsigned Data

Symbol	*Description*	*Flags Tested*
JE/JZ	Jump Equal or Jump Zero	ZF
JNE/JNZ	Jump Not Equal or Jump Not Zero	ZF
JA/JNBE	Jump Above or Jump Not Below/Equal	CF, ZF
JAE/JNB	Jump Above/Equal or Jump Not Below	CF
JB/JNAE	Jump Below or Jump Not Above/Equal	CF
JBE/JNA	Jump Below/Equal or Jump Not Above	CF, AF

You can express each test in one of two symbolic codes. For example, JB and JNAE generate the same object code, but, for example, positive test JB is easier to understand than negative test JNAE.

Jumps Based on Signed Data

Symbol	*Description*	*Flags Tested*
JE/JZ	Jump Equal or Jump Zero	ZF
JNE/JNZ	Jump Not Equal or Jump Not Zero	ZF
JG/JNLE	Jump Greater or Jump Not Less/Equal	ZF, SF, OF
JGE/JNL	Jump Greater/Equal or Jump Not Less	SF, OF
JL/JNGE	Jump Less or Jump Not Greater/Equal	SF, OF
JLE/JNG	Jump Less/Equal or Jump Not Greater	ZF, SF, OF

The jumps for testing equal/zero (JE/JZ) and for not equal/zero (JNE/JNZ) are included in both lists for unsigned and signed data. An equal/zero condition occurs regardless of the presence of a sign.

Special Arithmetic Tests

Symbol	*Description*	*Flags Tested*
JS	Jump Sign (negative)	SF
JNS	Jump No Sign (positive)	SF
JC	Jump Carry (same as JB)	CF
JNC	Jump No Carry	CF
JO	Jump Overflow	OF
JNO	Jump No Overflow	OF
JP/JPE	Jump Parity Even	PF
JNP/JP	Jump Parity Odd	PF

One other conditional jump, JCXZ, tests if the contents of the CX register is zero. This instruction need not be placed immediately following an arithmetic or compare operation. One use for JCXZ could be at the start of a loop to ensure that the CX actually contains a nonzero value.

Now, don't expect to memorize these instructions. For unsigned data, remember that a jump is equal, above, or below. For signed data, remember that a jump is equal, greater, or less. The jumps for testing the carry, overflow, and parity flags have unique purposes. The assembler translates symbolic to object code regardless of which instruction you use, but, for example, JAE and JGE, although apparently similar, do not test the same flags.

CALL AND PROCEDURES

Up to this point, code segments have consisted of only one procedure, coded as follows:

```
BEGIN   PROC   FAR
          .
          .
BEGIN   ENDP
```

The FAR operand informs the system that this address is the entry point for program execution, whereas the ENDP pseudo-op defines the end of the procedure. A code segment, however, may contain any number of procedures all distinguished by PROC and ENDP. A typical organization could appear as shown in Figure 7-3.

Note the following features in Figure 7-3:

- The PROC pseudo-ops for B10 and C10 contain the operand NEAR to indicate that these procedures are within the current code segment. Since omission of the operand causes the assembler to default to NEAR, many subsequent examples omit this operand.
- Each procedure has a unique name and contains its own ENDP for termination.
- To transfer control, the procedure BEGIN contains two CALL instructions: CALL B10 and CALL C10. The effect of executing the first CALL is that program control transfers to the procedure B10 and begins its execution. Reaching the RET instruction then causes control to return to the instruction immediately following CALL B10. The second CALL performs similarly—it transfers control to C10, executes its instructions, and returns by means of the RET.

```
CODESG  SEGMENT  PARA

BEGIN   PROC     FAR
          .
          .
        CALL     B10
        CALL     C10
        RET
BEGIN   ENDP

B10     PROC     NEAR
          .
          .
        RET
B10     ENDP

C10     PROC     NEAR
          .
          .
        RET
C10     ENDP

CODESG  ENDS
        END      BEGIN
```

Figure 7-3 Called Procedures.

- RET always returns to the original calling routine. BEGIN calls B10 and C10, which therefore return to BEGIN. At the start of program execution, DOS "called" BEGIN, and BEGIN's RET instruction returns control to DOS. If B10 did not end with a RET instruction, instructions would execute through B10 and drop directly into C10. In fact, if C10 did not contain a RET, the program would execute past the end of C10 into whatever instructions happen to be there (if any), with unpredictable results.

The use of procedures can better enable you to organize a program into logical routines that contain related logic. Also, operands for a CALL do not have to be within -128 and +127 bytes.

Technically, you can transfer control to a NEAR procedure by means of a jump instruction or even by normal in-line code. But for normal purposes, use CALL to transfer control to a procedure, and use RET to terminate its execution.

STACK SEGMENT

Up to this point, the only operations involving the stack have been the two PUSH instructions at the start of the code segment that facilitate return to DOS when an EXE program terminates. Consequently, these programs needed to define only a very small stack. However, CALL automatically pushes onto the stack the offset address of the instruction that immediately follows the CALL. In the called procedure, the RET instruction uses this address for returning to the calling procedure and automatically pops the stack.

In simple terms, an instruction that pushes onto the stack moves a one-word address or value onto the stack. An instruction that pops the stack (usually) accesses the previously pushed word. Both operations change the offset address in the SP (stack pointer) register for the next word. Because of this feature, you must ensure that a RET matches its original CALL. Also, a called procedure can CALL another procedure which in turn can CALL yet another procedure. The stack must be large enough to contain the pushed addresses. All this turns out to be easier than it first appears, and a stack definition of 32 words is ample for most of our purposes.

Certain instructions—PUSH, PUSHF, CALL, INT, and INTO—save a return address or the contents of the flags register by pushing them onto the stack. Other instructions—POP, POPF, RET, and IRET—return the address or flags by popping them off the stack.

On entry to an EXE program, the system sets the following register values:

DS and ES: Address of the program segment prefix, a 256-byte (hex 100) area that precedes your executable program module in memory.

CS: Address of the entry point to your program, the first executable instruction.

IP: Zero.

SS: Address of the stack segment.

SP: Offset to the top of the stack. For example, if you define the stack with 32 words (64 bytes) as

```
DW  32 DUP(?)
```

the SP contains 64, or hex 40.

Let's trace the simple EXE program in Figure 7-4 through execution. In practice, called procedures would contain any number of instructions.

The current available location for pushing or popping is the "top" of the stack. The first PUSH decrements the SP by 2 and stores the DS (containing 049F in this example) at the top of the stack, at 4B00 + 3E. The second PUSH decrements the SP by 2 and stores the AX containing 0000 on the stack at 4B00 + 3C. CALL B10 decrements the SP and stores the offset address of the following instruction (0007) in the stack at 4B00 + 3A. CALL C10 decrements the SP and stores the offset address of the following instruction (000B) in the stack at 4B00 + 38.

On return from C10, the RET instruction pops the address (000B) from the stack at 4B00 + 38, inserts it in the IP, and increments the SP by 2. There is now an automatic return to offset 000B in the code segment, in B10.

The RET at the end of procedure B10 pops the address (0007) from the stack at 4B00 + 3A, inserts it into the IP, and increments the SP by

```
                              TITLE   CALLPROC (EXE) Calling procedures

0000                          STACKSG SEGMENT PARA STACK 'Stack'
0000      20 [  ???? ]                DW      32 DUP(?)
0040                          STACKSG ENDS

0000                          CODESG  SEGMENT PARA 'Code'
0000                          BEGIN   PROC    FAR
                                      ASSUME  CS:CODESG,SS:STACKSG
0000  1E                              PUSH    DS
0001  2B C0                           SUB     AX,AX
0003  50                              PUSH    AX
0004  E8 0008 R                       CALL    B10       ;Call B10
                              ;       ...
0007  CB                              RET               ;Terminate
0008                          BEGIN   ENDP
                                      ;--------------------------
0008                          B10     PROC
0008  E8 000C R                       CALL    C10       ;Call C10
                              ;       ...
000B  C3                              RET               ;Return to
000C                          B10     ENDP              ;  caller
                              ;----------------------------------
000C                          C10     PROC
                              ;       ...
000C  C3                              RET               ;Return to
000D                          C10     ENDP              ;  caller
                              ;----------------------------------
000D                          CODESG  ENDS
                                      END     BEGIN
```

Figure 7-4 Effect of Execution on the Stack.

2. There is now an automatic return to offset 0007 in the code segment. At 0007, the program terminates its execution with a FAR return.

The following shows the effect on the stack as each instruction executes. You could also use DEBUG to trace this program. The example shows only locations 0034 through 003F and the contents of the SP:

Operation	*Stack*						*SP*
On entry, initially:	xxxx	xxxx	xxxx	xxxx	xxxx	xxxx	0040
PUSH DS (push 049F)	xxxx	xxxx	xxxx	xxxx	xxxx	9F04	003E
PUSH AX (push 0000)	xxxx	xxxx	xxxx	xxxx	0000	9F04	003C
CALL B10 (push 0007)	xxxx	xxxx	xxxx	0700	0000	9F40	003A
CALL C10 (push 000B)	xxxx	xxxx	0B00	0700	0000	9F40	0038
RET (pop 000B)	xxxx	xxxx	xxxx	0700	0000	9F40	003A
RET (pop 0007)	xxxx	xxxx	xxxx	xxxx	0000	9F40	003C
Stack offset:	0034	0036	0038	003A	003C	003E	

Note two points. First, words in memory contain the bytes in reverse sequence, such that 0007 becomes 0700. Second, if you use DEBUG to view the stack, it stores other values including the contents of the IP for its own purposes.

PROGRAM: EXTENDED MOVE OPERATIONS

Previous programs moved immediate data into a register, moved data from defined memory to a register, moved register contents to memory, and moved the contents of one register to another. In all cases, data length was limited to one or two bytes, and no operation moved data from one memory area directly to another memory area. It is possible to move data that exceeds two bytes, and this section explains this process. It is also possible to use string instructions to move data from one memory area directly to another, a process covered in Chapter 11.

In the EXE program in Figure 7-5, the data segment contains three nine-byte fields defined as NAME1, NAME2, and NAME3. The object of the program is to move NAME1 to NAME2 and to move NAME2 to NAME3. Since these fields are each nine bytes long, more than a simple MOV instruction is required. The program contains a number of new features.

The procedure BEGIN initializes the segment registers and then calls B10MOVE and C10MOVE. B10MOVE moves the contents of NAME1 to NAME2. Since the operation moves one byte at a time, the routine begins with the leftmost byte of NAME1 and loops to move the second byte, the third byte, and so on, as follows:

```
        page    65,132
TITLE   EXMOVE  (EXE)  Extended move operations
;---------------------------------------------------------
STACKSG SEGMENT PARA STACK 'Stack'
        DW      32 DUP(?)
STACKSG ENDS
;---------------------------------------------------------
DATASG  SEGMENT PARA 'Data'
NAME1   DB      'ABCDEFGHI'
NAME2   DB      'JKLMNOPQR'
NAME3   DB      'STUVWXYZ*'
DATASG  ENDS
;---------------------------------------------------------
CODESG  SEGMENT PARA 'Code'
BEGIN   PROC    FAR
        ASSUME  CS:CODESG,DS:DATASG,SS:STACKSG,ES:DATASG
        PUSH    DS
        SUB     AX,AX
        PUSH    AX
        MOV     AX,DATASG
        MOV     DS,AX
        MOV     ES,AX
        CALL    B10MOVE          ;Call jump routine
        CALL    C10MOVE          ;Call loop routine
        RET                      ;Terminate processing
BEGIN   ENDP

;       Extended Move using Jump-on-Condition:
;       -------------------------------------
B10MOVE PROC
        LEA     SI,NAME1         ;Init'ze address of NAME1
        LEA     DI,NAME2         ;   & NAME2
        MOV     CX,09            ;Init'ze to move 9 chars
B20:
        MOV     AL,[SI]          ;Move from NAME1
        MOV     [DI],AL          ;Move to NAME2
        INC     SI               ;Incr next char in NAME1
        INC     DI               ;Incr next pos'n in NAME2
        DEC     CX               ;Decr loop count
        JNZ     B20              ;Count not zero? Yes, loop
        RET                      ;If count = 0, return to
B10MOVE ENDP                     ;  caller

;       Extended Move using LOOP:
;       ------------------------
C10MOVE PROC
        LEA     SI,NAME2         ;Init'ze address of NAME2
        LEA     DI,NAME3         ;   & NAME3
        MOV     CX,09            ;Init'ze to move 9 chars
C20:
        MOV     AL,[SI]          ;Move from NAME2
        MOV     [DI],AL          ;Move to NAME3
        INC     DI               ;Incr next char of NAME2
        INC     SI               ;Incr next pos'n of NAME3
        LOOP    C20              ;Decr count, loop nonzero
        RET                      ;If count = 0, return to
C10MOVE ENDP                     ;  caller
CODESG  ENDS
        END     BEGIN
```

Figure 7-5 Extended Move Operations.

```
NAME1:  A  B  C  D  E  F  G  H  I
        |  |  |  |  |  |  |  |  |
NAME2:  J  K  L  M  N  O  P  Q  R
```

Because the routine has to step through NAME1 and NAME2, it initializes the CX register to 9 and uses the index registers, SI and DI. Two LEA instructions load the offset addresses of NAME1 and NAME2 into the SI and DI registers as follows:

```
LEA   SI,NAME1       ;Load offset addresses
LEA   DI,NAME2       ;  of NAME1 and NAME2
```

A looping routine uses the addresses in the SI and DI registers to move the first byte of NAME1 to the first byte of NAME2. The square brackets around SI and DI in the MOV operands mean that the instruction is to use the address in that register for accessing the memory location. Thus,

```
MOV   AL,[SI]
```

means: Use the address in SI (which is NAME1) to move the referenced byte to the AL register. And the instruction

```
MOV   [DI],AL
```

means: Move the contents of the AL to the address referenced by DI (which is NAME2).

The next instructions increment the SI and DI registers. If CX is nonzero, the routine loops back to B20. And since SI and DI have been incremented by 1, the next MOV references NAME1+1 and NAME2+1. The loop continues in this fashion until it has moved NAME1+8 to NAME2+8.

The procedure C10MOVE is similar to B10MOVE with two exceptions: it moves NAME2 to NAME3 and uses LOOP instead of DEC/JNZ.

Suggestion: Key in the program, and then assemble, link, and trace it using DEBUG. Note the effect on the registers, the instruction pointer, and the stack. Use D DS:0 to view the changes to NAME2 and NAME3.

BOOLEAN OPERATIONS: AND, OR, XOR, TEST, NOT

Boolean logic is important in circuitry design and has a parallel in programming logic. The programming instructions for Boolean logic are AND, OR, XOR, and TEST. These instructions are useful in clearing and setting bits and in handling ASCII data for arithmetic purposes (Chapter 13). All of these instructions process one byte or one word in a register or in memory. They match the bits of the two referenced operands and set the CF, OF, PF, SF, and ZF flags (AF is undefined).

AND: If the matched bits are both 1, the result is 1; all other conditions result in 0.

OR: If either of the matched bits is 1, the result is 1; if both are 0, the result is 0.

XOR: If one matched bit is 0 and the other 1, the result is 1; if the matched bits are the same (both 0 or both 1), the result is 0.

TEST: Acts like AND—sets the flags but does not change the bits.

The first operand references one byte or word in a register or memory and is the only value that is changed. The following AND, OR, and XOR instructions use the same bit values:

	AND	OR	XOR
	0101	0101	0101
	0011	0011	0011
Result:	0001	0111	0110

For the following unrelated examples, assume that the AL contains 1100 0101 and the BH contains 0101 1100:

```
1.  AND   AL,BH          ;Sets AL to 0100 0100
2.  OR    BH,AL          ;Sets BH to 1101 1101
3.  XOR   AL,AL          ;Sets AL to 0000 0000
4.  AND   AL,00          ;Sets AL to 0000 0000
5.  AND   AL,0FH         ;Sets AL to 0000 0101
6.  OR    CL,CL          ;Sets SF and ZF
```

Examples 3 and 4 provide ways of clearing a register to zero. Example 5 zeros the left four bits of the AL. Although the use of CMP may be clearer, you can use OR for the following purposes:

```
1.      OR CX,CX       ;Test if CX is zero
        JZ ...         ;Jump if zero
2.      OR CX,CX       ;Test sign in CX
        JS ...         ;Jump if negative
```

TEST acts like AND but only sets flags. Following are some examples:

```
1.      TEST  BL,11110000B   ;Any of leftmost bits
        JNZ   ...            ;  in BL nonzero?
```

```
2.          TEST   AL,00000001B     ;Does the AL contain
            JNZ    ...              ;  an odd number?
3.          TEST   DX,0FFH          ;Does the DX contain
            JZ     ...              ;  a zero value?
```

Another related instruction, NOT, simply reverses the bits in a byte or word in a register or memory—0s become 1s and 1s become 0s. For example, if the AL contains 1100 0101, then the instruction NOT AL changes the AL to 0011 1010. Flags are unaffected. NOT is not the same as NEG, which changes a value from positive to negative and vice versa by reversing the bits and adding 1 (see "Negative Numbers" in Chapter 1).

PROGRAM: CHANGING LOWERCASE TO UPPERCASE

There are various reasons for converting between uppercase and lowercase letters. For example, you may have received a data file created by a micro that processes only uppercase letters. Or a program has to allow users to enter commands either as uppercase or lowercase (such as YES or yes) and converts to uppercase for testing it. Uppercase letters A through Z are hex 41 through 5A, and lowercase letters a through z are hex 61 through 7A. The only difference is that bit 5 is 0 for uppercase and 1 for lowercase, as the following shows:

Bit:	76543210	*Bit:*	76543210
Letter A:	01000001	*Letter a:*	01100001
Letter Z:	01011010	*Letter z:*	01111010

The COM program in Figure 7-6 converts the contents of a data item, TITLEX, from lowercase to uppercase, beginning at TITLEX+1. The program initializes the BX with the address of TITLEX+1 and uses the address to move each character starting at TITLEX+1 to the AH. If the value is between hex 61 and 7A, an AND instruction sets bit 5 to 0:

```
AND   AH,11011111B
```

All characters other than a through z remain unchanged. The routine then moves the changed character back to TITLEX, increments the BX for the next character, and loops.

Used this way, the BX register acts as an index register for addressing memory locations. The SI and DI may also be used for this purpose.

```
                                TITLE   CASE     (COM)  Change lowercase to uppercase
0000                            CODESG  SEGMENT  PARA 'CODE'
                                        ASSUME   CS:CODESG,DS:CODESG,SS:CODESG
0100                                    ORG      100H
0100  EB 1C 90                  BEGIN:  JMP      MAIN
                                ; ------------------------------------------
0103  43 68 61 6E 67 65         TITLEX  DB       'Change to uppercase letters'
      20 74 6F 20 75 70
      70 65 72 63 61 73
      65 20 6C 65 74 74
      65 72 73
                                ; ------------------------------------------
011E                            MAIN    PROC     NEAR
011E  8D 1E 0104 R                      LEA      BX,TITLEX+1    ;1st char to change
0122  B9 001F                           MOV      CX,31          ;No. chars to change
0125                            B20:
0125  8A 27                             MOV      AH,[BX]        ;Char from TITLEX
0127  80 FC 61                          CMP      AH,61H         ;Is it
012A  72 0A                             JB       B30            ;  lower
012C  80 FC 7A                          CMP      AH,7AH         ;  case
012F  77 05                             JA       B30            ;  letter?
0131  80 E4 DF                          AND      AH,11011111B   ;Yes - convert
0134  88 27                             MOV      [BX],AH        ;Restore in TITLEX
0136                            B30:
0136  43                                INC      BX             ;Set for next char
0137  E2 EC                             LOOP     B20            ;Loop 31 times
0139  C3                                RET
013A                            MAIN    ENDP
013A                            CODESG  ENDS
                                        END      BEGIN
```

Figure 7-6 Changing Lowercase to Uppercase.

SHIFTING AND ROTATING

The shift and rotate instructions, which are part of the computer's "logical" capability, have the following features:

- Reference a byte or a word.
- Reference a register or memory.
- Shift/rotate left or right.
- Shift/rotate up to 8 bits if a byte and up to 16 bits if a word.
- Shift/rotate logically (unsigned) or arithmetically (signed).

A shift value of 1 can be coded as an immediate operand; a value greater than 1 must be contained in the CL register.

Shifting

A bit that is shifted off enters the CF flag. The shift instructions are the following:

```
SHR  ;Shift unsigned right
SHL  ;Shift unsigned left
SAR  ;Shift arithmetic right
SAL  ;Shift arithmetic left
```

The following related instructions illustrate SHR:

```
MOV  CL,03        ;    AX:
MOV  AX,10110111B ; 10110111
SHR  AX,1         ; 01011011   ;Shift right 1
SHR  AX,CL        ; 00001011   ;Shift right 3
```

The first SHR shifts the contents of the AX one bit to the right. The shifted 1-bit now resides in the CF flag and a 0-bit is filled to the left in the AX. The second SHR shifts the AX three more bits. The CF flag contains successively 1, 1, then 0, and three 0-bits are filled to the left in the AX.

Notice the effect of using SAR for arithmetic shifts:

```
MOV  CL,03        ;    AX:
MOV  AX,10110111B ; 10110111
SAR  AX,1         ; 11011011   ;Shift right 1
SAR  AX,CL        ; 11111011   ;Shift right 3
```

SAR differs from SHR in one important way: SAR uses the sign bit to fill leftmost vacated bits. In this way, positive and negative values retain their sign. In the above example, the sign is a 1-bit.

Left shifts always fill 0-bits to the right. As a result, SHL and SAL are identical.

Left shift is especially useful for doubling values and right shift for halving values, and both are significantly faster than multiply and divide. Halving odd numbers such as 5 and 7 generates a smaller value (2 and 3, respectively) and sets the CF flag to 1. Also, if you have to shift two bits, coding two shift instructions is more efficient than storing 2 in the CL and coding one shift.

One use for the JC (Jump if Carry) instruction is to test the bit shifted into the CF flag.

Rotating

For rotate instructions, the bit that is shifted off rotates to fill the vacated bit position. The rotate instructions are the following:

```
ROR        ;Rotate right
ROL        ;Rotate left
RCR        ;Rotate with carry right
RCL        ;Rotate with carry left
```

The following related instructions illustrate ROR:

```
MOV  CL,03          ;     BX:
MOV  BX,10110111B   ; 10110111
ROR  BX,1           ; 11011011    ;Rotate right 1
ROR  BX,CL          ; 01111011    ;Rotate right 3
```

The first ROR rotates the rightmost 1-bit of the BX to the leftmost vacated position. The second ROR rotates the three rightmost bits.

RCR and RCL cause the CF flag to participate. The shifted off bit moves into the CF, and the CF bit moves into the vacated bit position.

Here's an example that uses both shift and rotate. Consider a 32-bit value of which the leftmost 16 bits are in the DX and the rightmost 16 bits are in the AX, as DX:AX. Instructions to "multiply" the value by two could be:

```
SHL AX,1   ;Multiply DX:AX pair
RCL DX,1   ; by 2
```

The SHL shifts all bits to the left, and the leftmost bit shifts into the CF flag. The RCL shifts the DX left and inserts the bit from the CF into the rightmost vacated bit.

PROGRAM ORGANIZATION

The following are typical steps in writing an assembler program:

1. Have a clear idea of the problem that the program is to solve.
2. Sketch your ideas in general terms and plan the overall logic. For example, if a problem is to test multibyte move operations such as in Figure 7-5, start by defining the fields to be moved. Then plan the strategy for the instructions: routines for initialization, for using a conditional jump, and for using a LOOP. The following, which shows

the main logic, is pseudo-code that many programmers use to plan a program:

```
Initialize stack and segment registers
Call Jump routine
Call Loop routine
Return
```

Jump routine could be planned as

```
        Initialize registers for count, addresses of names
Jump1:  Move one character of name
        Increment for next characters of names
        Decrement count: If nonzero, Jump1
                         If zero, Return
```

Loop routine could be sketched in a similar way.

3. Organize the program into logical units, such that related routines follow one another. A procedure that is about 25 lines (the size of the screen) is easier to debug.
4. Use example programs as a guide. Attempts to memorize all the technical material and code "off the top of the head" often result in even more program bugs.
5. Use comments to clarify what a procedure is supposed to accomplish, what arithmetic and comparison operations are performing, and what a seldom-used instruction is doing. (A good example of the latter is the XLAT instruction, which has no operands.)
6. For keying in the program, use a cataloged skeleton program that you can copy into a newly named file.

The remaining programs in this text make considerable use of the LEA instruction, the SI and DI index registers, and called procedures. Having covered the basics of assembler, you are now in a position for more advanced and realistic programming.

KEY POINTS TO REMEMBER

- Labels such as B20: within procedures require colons to indicate a NEAR label. Omission of the colon causes an assembly error.
- Labels for conditional jump and LOOP instructions must be within -128 to +127 bytes. The operand generates one byte of object code. Hex 01 to 7F covers the range from decimal +1 to +127, and hex FF to 80 covers the range from -1 to -128. Since machine instruc-

tions vary in length from one to four bytes, the limit is not obvious, but about two screens full of source code is a practical guide.

- For using LOOP, initialize the CX with a positive number. LOOP checks for only a zero value, so if CX is negative, the program will continue looping.
- When an instruction sets a flag, the flag remains set until another instruction changes it. For example, you could perform an arithmetic operation that sets flags and if the operation is immediately followed by MOV instructions, the flags remain unchanged. However, to minimize bugs, code a conditional jump instruction immediately following the instruction that set the flag.
- Select an appropriate conditional jump instruction depending on whether the operation processes signed or unsigned data.
- Always CALL a procedure, and always include RET for returning. A called procedure may call other procedures, and if you follow the conventions, RET causes the correct address in the stack to pop. The only examples in this book that jump to a procedure are at the beginning of COM programs.
- Be careful when using indexed operands. Consider the following moves:

```
MOV   AX,SI
MOV   AX,[SI]
```

  The first MOV moves the contents of the SI register. The second MOV uses the offset address in the SI to access a word in memory.
- Use shift instructions to double or halve values, but be sure to select the appropriate instruction for unsigned and signed data.

QUESTIONS

7-1. What is the maximum number of bytes that a near JMP, a LOOP, and a conditional jump instruction may jump? What characteristic of the machine code operand causes this limit?

7-2. A JMP instruction begins at hex location 0624. Determine the transfer address based on the following hex object code for the JMP operand: (a) 27, (b) 6B, (c) C6.

7-3. Code a routine using LOOP that calculates the Fibonacci series: 1, 1, 2, 3, 5, 8, 13, . . . (each number is the sum of the preceding two numbers). Set the limit for 12 loops. Assemble, link, and use DEBUG to trace.

7-4. Assume that AX and BX contain signed data and that CX and DX contain unsigned data. Determine the CMP (where necessary) and conditional jump instructions for the following:

(a) Does the DX value exceed the CX?
(b) Does the BX value exceed the AX?
(c) Does the CX contain zero?
(d) Was there an overflow?
(e) Is the BX equal to or smaller than the AX?
(f) Is the DX equal to or smaller than the CX?

7-5. In the following, what flags are affected and what would they contain?

(a) An overflow occurred.
(b) A result is negative.
(c) A result is zero.
(d) Processing is in single-step mode.
(e) A string data transfer is to be right to left.

7-6. Refer to Figure 7-4. What would be the effect on program execution if the procedure BEGIN did not contain a RET?

7-7. What is the difference between coding a PROC operand with FAR and with NEAR?

7-8. What are the ways in which a program can begin executing a procedure?

7-9. In an EXE program, A10 calls B10, B10 calls C10, and C10 calls D10. Other than the initial return address to DOS, how many addresses does the stack contain?

7-10. Assume that the BL contains 1110 0011 and that a location named BOONO contains 0111 1001. Determine the effect on the BL for the following: (a) XOR BL,BOONO; (b) AND BL,BOONO; (c) OR BL,BOONO; (d) XOR BL,11111111B; (e) AND BL,00000000B.

7-11. Revise the program in Figure 7-6 as follows: (a) Define the contents of TITLEX as uppercase letters; (b) Convert uppercase to lowercase.

7-12. Assume that the DX contains 10111001 10111001 and the CL contains 03. Determine the contents of the DX after the following unrelated instructions: (a) SHR DX,1; (b) SHR DX,CL; (c) SHL DX,CL; (d) SHL DL,1; (e) ROR DX,CL; (f) ROR DL,CL; (g) SAL DH,1.

7-13. Use shift, move, and add instructions to multiply the contents of the AX by 10.

7-14. An example routine at the end of the section "Shifting and Rounding" multiplies the DX:AX by 2. Revise the routine to (a) multiply by 4, (b) divide by 4, (c) multiply the 48 bits in the DX:AX:BX by 2.

CHAPTER 8

Screen Processing I: Basic Features

Objective: To cover the requirments for displaying information on a screen and accepting input from a keyboard.

INTRODUCTION

Up to this point, programs have defined data within an instruction operand (immediate data) or initialized in the data area. The number of practical applications for programs that process only defined data is few indeed. Most programs require input data from a keyboard, disk, or modem, and provide answers in a useful format on a screen, printer, or disk. Data for screen and keyboard is in ASCII format.

The INT (Interrupt) instruction performs input and output. There are various requirements for telling the system whether processing is to be input or output, and on what device. This chapter covers basic requirements for displaying information on a screen and for accepting input from a keyboard.

You can perform all required screen/keyboard operations by the use of an INT 10H instruction that transfers control directly to BIOS. However, to facilitate some of the more complex operations, there is a higher level of interrupt, INT 21H, that first transfers control to DOS. For example, input from a keyboard may require a count of characters entered, a check against a maximum number of characters, and a check for the return character. The DOS INT 21H operation handles much of this additional processing and then transfers automatically to BIOS.

The material in this chapter is suitable for both monochrome (black and white, BW) and color video monitors. Chapters 9 and 10 cover more advanced screen handling features and the use of color.

THE INTERRUPT INSTRUCTION: INT

The INT instruction interrupts processing, transfers to DOS or to BIOS for specified action, and returns to the program to continue processing. Most often, an interrupt is to perform an input or output operation. All interrupts require a trail for exiting from your program and for returning. For this purpose, INT performs the following:

- Decrements the stack pointer by 2 and pushes the flags register onto the stack.
- Clears the TF and IF flags.
- Decrements the stack pointer by 2 and pushes the CS register onto the stack.
- Decrements the stack pointer by 2 and pushes the instruction pointer onto the stack.
- Causes the required operation to be performed.
- Pops the registers off the stack and returns to the instruction following the INT.

This process is entirely automatic, and your only concern is to define a stack segment large enough for the necessary pushing and popping.

The two types of interrupts that this chapter covers are BIOS operation INT 10H for screen and keyboard processing and DOS operation INT 21H for displaying output and accepting input. For the latter, operations use what are known as function calls to request an action. Depending on requirements, examples use both INT 10H and INT 21H.

SETTING THE CURSOR

The screen is a grid of addressable locations at any one of which the cursor can be set. A typical video monitor, for example, has 25 rows (numbered 0 to 24) and 80 columns (numbered 0 to 79). Some examples of cursor locations follow:

	Decimal Format		*Hex Format*	
Location	*Row*	*Column*	*Row*	*Column*
Upper left corner	00	00	00	00
Upper right corner	00	79	00	4F
Center of screen	12	39/40	0C	27/28
Lower left corner	24	00	18	00
Lower right corner	24	79	18	4F

Features of the INT 10H instruction include setting the cursor at any location and clearing the screen. The following sets the cursor to row 05 and column 12:

```
MOV   AH,02   ;Request set cursor
MOV   BH,00   ;Screen #0
MOV   DH,05   ;Row 05
MOV   DL,12   ;Column 12
INT   10H     ;Interrupt -- exit to BIOS
```

The value 02 in the AH notifies INT 10H to set the cursor. Row and column must be in the DX register, and screen (or "page") number, normally 0, is in the BH. The contents of the other registers is not important. To set row and column, you could also use one MOV instruction with an immediate hex value as

```
MOV DX,050CH      ;Row 5, column 12
```

CLEARING THE SCREEN

Prompts and commands stay on the screen until overwritten or scrolled off. When your program starts executing, you may want the screen cleared. You can clear beginning at any location and ending at any higher numbered location. Insert the starting row/column in the DX, the value 07 in the BH, and 0600H in the AX. The following clears the entire screen:

```
MOV   AX,0600H      ;AH 06 (scroll), AL 00 (full screen)
MOV   BH,07         ;Normal attribute (black & white)
MOV   CX,0000       ;Upper left row/col
MOV   DX,184FH      ;Lower right row/col
INT   10H           ;Interrupt -- exit to BIOS
```

The value 06 in the AH notifies INT 10H to scroll. This operation scrolls a full screen to blank; the next chapter describes scrolling in more detail. If you mistakenly set the lower right location higher than hex 184F, the operation wraps around the screen and clears some locations twice. Although the action causes no harm on mono screens, it may cause a serious error on some color monitors.

SCREEN AND KEYBOARD OPERATIONS: ORIGINAL DOS

A program often has to display messages indicating completion or errors detected and prompts to a user requesting data or action to take. We'll first examine the methods for original DOS versions, and later examine the extended method introduced by DOS 2.0. The original DOS operations work under all versions, although the DOS manual recommends use of the extended operations for new development. The display operation for original DOS is a little more involved, but keyboard input is easier to use because of its built-in checks.

DISPLAYING ON THE SCREEN: ORIGINAL DOS

Displaying under original DOS requires defining a prompt message in the data area, setting the AH register to 09 (a DOS function call), and issuing a DOS INT 21H instruction. The operation recognizes the end of a message by a dollar sign ($) delimiter, as shown next:

```
NAMPRMP    DB      'Customer name? ','$'
           .
           .
           MOV     AH,09              ;Request display
           LEA     DX,NAMPRMP         ;Load address of prompt
           INT     21H                ;DOS interrupt
```

You can code a dollar sign delimiter immediately following the prompt as just shown, inside the prompt as 'Customer name?$', or on the next line as DB '$'. The effect, however, is that you can't use this operation to display a $ character on the screen. Also, if you omit the dollar sign at the end of the display string, the operation displays characters from memory until it finds one—if any.

The LEA instruction loads the address of NAMPRMP in the DX to enable DOS to locate the information that is to display. For the actual memory address, LEA loads the offset address of NAMPRMP, and DOS uses the address in the DS register plus the DX (DS:DX).

PROGRAM: DISPLAYING THE ASCII CHARACTER SET

Most of the 256 ASCII characters are represented by a symbol that can display on a video screen. Hex 00 and FF have no symbol and display as blank, although the true ASCII blank character is hex 20.

The COM program in Figure 8-1 displays the entire range of ASCII characters. The program calls three procedures: B10CLR, C10SET, and D10DISP. B10CLR clears the screen and C10SET initializes the cursor to 00,00. D10DISP displays the contents of CTR, which is initialized to hex 00 and is successively incremented for each display until reaching hex FF.

```
        page 60,132
TITLE   ALLASC (COM)  Display ASCII characters 00-FF
CODESG  SEGMENT PARA 'Code'
        ASSUME  CS:CODESG,DS:CODESG,SS:CODESG,ES:NOTHING
        ORG     100H
BEGIN:  JMP     SHORT MAIN
CTR     DB      00,'$'

;               Main procedure:
;               --------------
MAIN    PROC    NEAR
        CALL    B10CLR          ;Clear screen
        CALL    C10SET          ;Set cursor
        CALL    D10DISP         ;Display chars
        RET
MAIN    ENDP
;               Clear screen:
;               ------------
B10CLR  PROC
        MOV     AX,0600H
        MOV     BH,07
        MOV     CX,0000         ;Upper left location
        MOV     DX,184FH        ;Lower right location
        INT     10H
        RET
B10CLR  ENDP
;               Set cursor to 00,00:
;               -------------------
C10SET  PROC
        MOV     AH,02
        MOV     BH,00
        MOV     DX,0000
        INT     10H
        RET
C10SET  ENDP
;               Display ASCII characters:
;               ------------------------
D10DISP PROC
        MOV     CX,256          ;Init'ze for 256 iterations
        LEA     DX,CTR          ;Init'ze address of count
D20:
        MOV     AH,09           ;Display ASCII char
        INT     21H
        INC     CTR             ;Increment count
        LOOP    D20             ;Decr CX, loop if nonzero
        RET                     ;Terminate
D10DISP ENDP

CODESG  ENDS
        END     BEGIN
```

Figure 8-1 Displaying the ASCII Character Set.

A problem is that the dollar symbol does not display and the characters between hex 08 and hex 0D, which are special "forms control characters" for backspacing and so forth, cause the cursor to move. Suggestion: Reproduce the program as it stands, assemble it, link it, and convert it to a COM file. To run, enter its name, such as B:ASCII.COM.

The first displayed line begins with a blank character (hex 00), two "happy faces" (hex 01 and 02), and then a heart, a diamond, and a club (hex 03, 04, and 05). Hex 07 causes the speaker to sound. Hex 06 would have been a spade but the control characters hex 08 through 0D erased it. In fact, hex 0D caused a "carriage return" to the start of the next line. The musical note is hex 0E. The characters above hex 7F include graphics symbols.

You can change the program to bypass the control characters. The following instructions bypass all characters between hex 08 and 0D; you may want to experiment with bypassing only, say, hex 08 (backspace) and 0D (carriage return).

```
            CMP   CTR,08H         ;Lower than 08?
            JB    D30             ;Yes -- accept
            CMP   CTR,0DH         ;Lower/equal 0D?
            JBE   D40             ;Yes -- bypass
D30:
            MOV   AH,40H          ;Display < 08
            ...                   ;    and > 0D
            INT   21H
D40:
            INC   CTR
```

ACCEPTING INPUT FROM THE KEYBOARD: ORIGINAL DOS

The procedure to accept data from a keyboard is similar to that for displaying output. For input using original DOS, the input area requires a *parameter list* containing specified fields that the INT operation is to process. First, the interrupt needs to know the maximum length of the input reply. The purpose is to warn users who key in a reply that is too long; the operation sounds the speaker and does not accept additional characters. Second, the operation returns the length in bytes of the actual reply into the parameter list.

The following defines a parameter list for an input area. LABEL is a pseudo-op with the type attribute of BYTE. The first byte is your limit for the maximum length of input. Since this is a one-byte field, the maximum is hex FF, or 255. The second byte is for DOS to store the actual number of characters entered. The third byte begins a field that is to contain the typed characters.

```
NAMEPAR   LABEL     BYTE              ;Start of parameter list:
MAXLEN    DB        20                ;  Max length of input
ACTLEN    DB        ?                 ;  Actual length
NAMEFLD   DB        20 DUP('  ')  ;   Chars entered from keyboard
```

In the parameter list, since the LABEL pseudo-op takes no space, NAMEPAR and MAXLEN refer to the same memory location. MASM can also use the STRUC pseudo-op to define a parameter list as a structure. However, since references to names defined within a structure require special addressing, our discussion delays this topic until Chapter 24, "Assembler Pseudo-op Reference."

To request input, use DOS function call 10 (hex 0AH) in the AH, load the address of the parameter list (NAMEPAR in the example) into the DX, and issue INT 21H as follows:

```
MOV   AH,0AH                 ;Request input function
LEA   DX,NAMEPAR             ;Load address of para list
INT   21H                    ;DOS interrupt
```

The INT operation waits for a user to enter characters and checks that the number entered does not exceed the maximum in the parameter list (20 in the example). The user presses the return key (hex 0D) to signal the end of an entry. This character also enters the input field (NAMEFLD in the examples). If you key in a name such as BROWN (Return), the parameter list appears as follows:

```
decimal:    |20 | 5 | B | R | O | W | N | # |   |   |   |   | ...
hex:        |14 |05 |42 |52 |4F |57 |4E |0D |20 |20 |20 |20 | ...
```

The operation delivers the length of the input name, 05, into the second byte of the parameter list, named ACTLEN in the example. The return character is at NAMEFLD+5. The # symbol here is to indicate this character because hex 0D has no printable symbol. Since the maximum length of 20 includes the hex 0D, the actual name may be only 19 characters long.

PROGRAM: ACCEPTING AND DISPLAYING NAMES

The EXE program in Figure 8-2 requests that a user enter a name, then displays the name on the center of the screen and sounds the speaker. The program continues accepting and displaying names until the user presses Return as a reply to a prompt. Consider a user entering the name TED SMITH:

```
        page    60,132
TITLE   CTRNAME (EXE)  Accept names & center on screen
;----------------------------------------------------------
STACKSG SEGMENT PARA STACK 'Stack'
        DW      32 DUP(?)
STACKSG ENDS
;----------------------------------------------------------
DATASG  SEGMENT PARA 'Data'
NAMEPAR LABEL   BYTE                ;Name parameter list:
MAXNLEN DB      20                  ;  max. length of name
NAMELEN DB      ?                   ;  no. chars entered
NAMEFLD DB      20 DUP(' '),'$'     ;  name, & delimiter
                                    ;  for displaying
PROMPT  DB      'Name? ', '$'
DATASG  ENDS
;----------------------------------------------------------
CODESG  SEGMENT PARA 'Code'
BEGIN   PROC    FAR
        ASSUME  CS:CODESG,DS:DATASG,SS:STACKSG,ES:DATASG
        PUSH    DS
        SUB     AX,AX
        PUSH    AX
        MOV     AX,DATASG
        MOV     DS,AX
        MOV     ES,AX
        CALL    Q10CLR              ;Clear screen
A20LOOP:
        MOV     DX,0000             ;Set cursor to 00,00
        CALL    Q20CURS
        CALL    B10PRMP             ;Display prompt
        CALL    D10INPT             ;Provide for input of name
        CALL    Q10CLR              ;Clear screen
        CMP     NAMELEN,00          ;Name entered?
        JE      A30                 ;  no --  exit
        CALL    E10CODE             ;Set bell & '$'
        CALL    F10CENT             ;Center & display name
        JMP     A20LOOP
A30:
        RET                         ;Return to DOS
BEGIN   ENDP
;               Display prompt:
;               --------------
B10PRMP PROC    NEAR
        MOV     AH,09               ;Request display
        LEA     DX,PROMPT
        INT     21H
        RET
B10PRMP ENDP
;               Accept input of name:
;               --------------------
D10INPT PROC    NEAR
        MOV     AH,0AH              ;Request input
        LEA     DX,NAMEPAR
        INT     21H
        RET
D10INPT ENDP
```

Figure 8-2 Accepting and Displaying Names

```
;               Set bell & '$' delimiter:
;               -----------------------
E10CODE PROC    NEAR
        MOV     BH,00               ;Replace return char (0D)
        MOV     BL,NAMELEN          ; with bell (07)
        MOV     NAMEFLD[BX],07
        MOV     NAMEFLD[BX+1],'$'  ;Set display delimiter
        RET
E10CODE ENDP
;               Center & display name:
;               ---------------------
F10CENT PROC    NEAR
        MOV     DL,NAMELEN          ;Locate center column:
        SHR     DL,1                ;  divide length by 2,
        NEG     DL                  ;  reverse sign,
        ADD     DL,40               ;  add 40
        MOV     DH,12               ;Center row
        CALL    Q20CURS             ;Set cursor
        MOV     AH,09
        LEA     DX,NAMEFLD          ;Display name
        INT     21H
        RET
F10CENT ENDP
;               Clear screen:
;               ------------
Q10CLR  PROC    NEAR
        MOV     AX,0600H            ;Request scroll screen
        MOV     BH,30               ;Color (07 for BW)
        MOV     CX,0000             ;From 00,00
        MOV     DX,184FH            ;To 24,79
        INT     10H                 ;Call BIOS
        RET
Q10CLR  ENDP
;               Set cursor row/col:
;               ------------------
Q20CURS PROC    NEAR                ;DX set on entry
        MOV     AH,02               ;Request set cursor
        MOV     BH,00               ;Page #0
        INT     10H                 ;Call BIOS
        RET
Q20CURS ENDP

CODESG  ENDS
        END     BEGIN
```

Figure 8-2 ***(continued)***

1. Divide the length 09 by 2 = 4, and
2. Subtract this value from 40 = 36

In E10CENT, the SHR instruction shifts the length 09 one bit to the right, effectively dividing it by 2. Bits 00001001 become 00000100. The NEG instruction reverses the sign, changing +4 to –4. ADD adds the value 40, giving the starting position for the column, 36, in the DL register. With the cursor set at row 12, column 36, the name appears on the screen as follows:

```
Row 12:     TED SMITH
            |   |
Column:    36   40
```

Note the instruction in E10CODE that inserts the bell (07) character in the input area immediately following the name:

```
MOV   NAMEFLD[BX],07
```

The preceding instruction set the BX with the length. The effect of this MOV is to combine the length in the BX with the address of NAMEFLD and to move the 07 to this address. Thus, for a length of 05, the instruction inserts 07 at NAMEFLD+05 (replacing the return character) following the name. The last instruction in E10CODE inserts a '$' delimiter following the 07 so that when F10CENT displays the name, the speaker also sounds.

Entering Only the Return Character

If you key in a name that exceeds the maximum in a parameter list, the speaker sounds and the operation accepts only the return character. But if you key in only Return, the operation accepts it and inserts a length of zero in the parameter list, as follows:

Parameter list (hex): |14|00|0D| ...

To signify end of input data on a prompt for name, a user can simply press Return. If the length is zero, the program determines that input is ended.

Clearing the Return Character

You can use an input value for various purposes, such as printing on reports, storing in a table, or writing on disk. For these purposes, you may have to replace the return character (hex 0D) somewhere in NAMEFLD with a blank (hex 20). The field containing the actual length, NAMELEN, provides its relative position. If NAMELEN contains 05, then this position is NAMEFLD+5. You can move this length into the BX register for indexing the address of NAMEFLD as follows:

```
MOV   BH,00              ;Set BX
MOV   BL,NAMELEN         ;  to 00 05
MOV   NAMEFLD[BX],20H    ;Clear ret char to blank
```

The third MOV instruction moves a blank (hex 20) to the address specified in the first operand: the address of NAMEFLD plus the contents of BX, in effect, NAMEFLD+5.

Clearing the Input Area

Entered characters replace the previous contents in an input area, and remain there until other characters replace them. Assume the following successive input:

```
   Input                   NAMEPAR (hex)
1.  BROWN       |14|05|42|52|4F|57|4E|0D|20|20|20| ... |20|
2.  HAMILTON    |14|08|48|41|4D|49|4C|54|4F|4E|0D| ... |20|
3.  ADAMS       |14|05|41|44|41|4D|53|0D|45|5A|0D| ... |20|
```

The name HAMILTON replaces the shorter name BROWN. But because the name ADAMS is shorter than HAMILTON, it replaces HAMIL and the return character replaces the T. The remaining letters, ON, still follow ADAMS. A useful practice is to clear NAMEFLD prior to prompting for a name as follows:

```
       MOV   CX,20              ;Init'ze for 20 loops
       MOV   SI,0000            ;Start position for name
B30:
       MOV   NAMEFLD[SI],20H    ;One blank to name
       INC   SI                 ;Incr for next char
       LOOP  B30                ;20 times
```

Instead of the SI register, you could use DI or BX. A more efficient method that moves a word of two blanks requires only ten loops. However, because NAMEFLD is defined as DB (byte), you would have to override its length with a WORD and PTR (pointer) operand as the following indicates:

```
       MOV   CX,10                ;Init'ze for 10 loops
       LEA   SI,NAMEFLD           ;Init'ze start of name
B30:
       MOV   WORD PTR[SI],2020H   ;Two blanks to name
       INC   SI                   ;Incr 2 positions
       INC   SI                   ;  in name
       LOOP  B30                  ;Loop 10 times
```

Interpret the MOV at B30 as: Move a blank word to where the address in the SI register points. This example uses LEA to initialize and uses a slightly different method for the MOV at B30 because you cannot code an instruction such as

```
MOV WORD PTR[NAMEFLD],2020H    ;Invalid
```

Clearing the input area solves the problem of short names being followed by previous data. A more efficient practice is to clear only positions to the right of an entered name.

SCREEN AND KEYBOARD OPERATIONS: EXTENDED DOS

We'll now examine the extended method introduced by DOS 2.0, which is more in the UNIX style. If you use a version of DOS prior to 2.0, you won't be able to execute the programs in this section. The extended method involves a *file handle* that you set in the BX register when requesting an I/O operation. The following standard file handles are always available:

0 Input, normally keyboard (CON)
1 Output, normally display (CON)
2 Error output, display (CON)
3 Auxiliary device (AUX)
4 Printer (LPT1 or PRN)

The DOS interrupt is INT 21H, and the required function call is requested in the AH register: hex 3F for input and hex 40 for output. Set the CX with the number of bytes to read or display, and load the DX with the address of the input or output area.

A successful operation clears the carry flag and inserts in the AX the number of characters actually entered or displayed. An unsuccessful operation sets the CF flag and inserts an error code (6 in this case) in the AX. Since the AX could contain either a length or an error code, the only way to determine an error condition is to test the CF flag, although keyboard and display errors would presumably be rare. You also use file handles in a similar way to process disk files, where error conditions are more common.

You can use these function calls to redirect input and output to other devices, although we won't concern ourselves with this feature here.

DISPLAYING ON THE SCREEN: EXTENDED DOS

The following instructions illustrate the use of the extended DOS function required to request display:

```
DISAREA DB 20 DUP('  ')    ;Display area
        . . .
        MOV AH,40H         ;Request display
        MOV BX,01          ;File handle for output
        MOV CX,20          ;Maximum 20 characters
        LEA DX,DISAREA     ;Display area
        INT 21H            ;Call DOS
```

LEA loads the address of DISAREA in the DX to enable DOS to locate the information that is to display. A successful operation clears the carry flag (which you may test) and sets the AX with the number of characters displayed. An unsuccessful operation could occur because of an invalid handle. The operation sets the CF flag and inserts an error code (6 in this case) in the AX. Since the AX could contain either a length or an error code, the only way to determine an error condition is to test the CF flag.

Exercise: Displaying on the Screen

Let's use DEBUG to examine the internal effects of an interrupt. Load DEBUG, and when its prompt appears, type A 100 in order to begin entering assembler instructions (but not the numbers) at location 100. Remember that DEBUG assumes that all numbers entered are hexadecimal.

```
100 MOV  AH,40
102 MOV  BX,01
105 MOV  CX,xx    (Insert length of your name)
108 MOV  DX,10E
10B INT  21
10D RET
10E DB   'Your name'
```

The program sets the AH to request display and sets the hex value 10F in the DX—the location of the DB containing your name, at the end of the program.

When you have keyed in the instructions, press Return again. Try the U command (U 100,10D) to unassemble the program and R and then repeat T commands to trace execution. When DEBUG executes INT 21H, it traces through BIOS, so on reaching 10B, use the GO command (G 10D) to execute directly through to the next instruction. Your name should display on the screen. Use the Q command to return to DOS.

ACCEPTING INPUT FROM THE KEYBOARD: EXTENDED DOS

The following illustrates use of the extended DOS function to request keyboard input:

```
INAREA DB 20 DUP(' ')      ;Input area
       ...
       MOV AH,3FH          ;Request input
       MOV BX,00           ;File handle for keyboard
       MOV CX,20           ;Maximum 20 characters
       LEA DX,INAREA       ;Input area
       INT 21H             ;Call DOS
```

LEA loads the offset address of INAREA in the DX. The INT operation waits for the user to enter characters, but does not check if the number of characters exceeds the maximum in the CX register (20 in the example). Pressing the return key (hex 0D) signals the end of an entry. For example, entering the characters "PC Users Group" causes the following in INAREA:

PC Users Group, hex 0D, hex 0A

The entered characters are immediately followed by a carriage return (hex 0D), which you entered, and a line feed (hex 0A), which you did not enter. Because of this feature, the maximum number and the length of the input area should provide for an additional two characters. If you enter fewer characters than the maximum, the locations in memory following the entered characters still contain the previous contents.

A successful operation clears the CF flag (which you may test) and sets the AX with the number of characters delivered. In the preceding example, this length is 14, plus 2 for the return and line feed, or 16. Accordingly, a program can determine the actual number of characters entered. Although this feature is trivial for YES and NO type of replies, it is useful for replies with variable length such as names.

An unsuccessful operation could occur because of an invalid handle. The operation sets the CF flag and inserts an error code (6 in this case) in the AX. Since the AX could contain either a length or an error code, the only way to determine an error condition is to test the CF flag.

If you key in a name that exceeds the maximum in the CX register, the operation accepts all characters. Consider a situation in which the CX contains 08 and a user enters the characters "PC Exchange." The operation sets the first eight characters in the input area as "PC Excha" with no return and line feed following, and sets the AX with a length of 08. The next INT operation does not accept a name directly from the keyboard, because it still has the rest of the previous string in its buffer. It delivers "nge" followed by the return and line feed to the input area and sets the AX to 05. Both operations are "normal" and the CF flag is cleared.

First INT:	PC Excha	AX = 08
Second INT:	nge, OD, OA	AX = 05

A program can tell that a user has keyed in a valid number of characters if (a) the number returned in the AX is less than the number in the CX or (b) the number returned is equal and the last two characters in the input area are OD and OA.

The built-in checks of original DOS function call 0AH for keyboard input offer a far more powerful operation and, at least at the time of this writing, that operation is the preferred choice.

Exercise: Entering Data

Here's an exercise in which you can view the effect of entering data while in DEBUG. The program allows you to enter up to 12 characters, including return and line feed. Load DEBUG, and when the prompt appears, type A 100 to begin entering assembler instructions at location 100. Remember that DEBUG assumes that numbers entered are hexadecimal.

```
100 MOV AH,3F
102 MOV BX,00
105 MOV CX,0C
108 MOV DX,10F
10B INT 21
10D JMP 100
10F DB' '
```

The program sets the AH and BX to request keyboard input, inserts the maximum length in the CX, and sets hex 10F in the DX—the location of the DB at the end of the program. The entered characters appear beginning at location hex 10F.

When you key in the instructions, press Return again. Try the U command (U 100,108) to unassemble the program. Use R then repeated T commands to trace execution of the four MOV instructions. When at location 10B, use G 10D to execute through the interrupt (don't follow it through BIOS). DEBUG stops to let you enter characters, and is followed by Return. Check the contents of the AX register, the carry flag, and use D 10F to display the entered characters in memory. You can continue looping indefinitely. Enter Q to terminate any time.

USE OF CARRIAGE RETURN, LINE FEED, AND TAB FOR DISPLAY

One way to make displays more efficient is to use the carriage return, line feed, and tab characters. You can code them in ASCII or hex, as:

	ASCII	*Hex*
CR	13	0DH
LF	10	0AH
TAB	09	09H

Use these characters where you display or accept input for advancing the cursor automatically to the start of the next row, either for original or extended DOS. Example:

```
MESSAGE DB   09,'PC Users Group Annual Report', 13, 10
        ...
        MOV  AH,40H           ;Request display
        MOV  BX,01            ;Handle
        MOV  CX,31            ;Length
        LEA  DX,MESSAG1       ;Message
        INT  21H              ;Call DOS
```

The use of EQU to define the operations makes a program more readable:

```
CR            EQU  13          or EQU     0DH
LF            EQU  10          or EQU     0AH
TAB           EQU  09          or EQU     09H
MESSAGE       DB   TAB, 'PC Users Group Annual Report', CR, LF
```

KEY POINTS TO REMEMBER

- INT 10H is the instruction that links to BIOS for keyboard and display operations. INT 21H is a special DOS operation that handles some of the complexity of input/output.
- Be consistent in using hex notation. For example, INT 21 is not the same as INT 21H.

- Be careful to enter the correct values in the AX, BX, CX, and DX registers depending on the operation.
- When using INT 21H for original DOS, define a delimiter ($) immediately following the display area. Be careful when clearing the field not to clear the delimiter as well. A missing delimiter can cause spectacular effects on a screen.
- For input under original DOS, define a parameter list carefully. The INT 21H operation expects the first byte to contain a maximum value and automatically inserts an actual value in the second byte.
- For extended DOS function call to display, set the AH with hex 40 and use handle 01 in the BX.
- For extended DOS function call to read, set the AH with hex 3F and use handle 00 in the BX. Entries are followed in the input area by a return and a form feed character. The operation does not check for entries that exceed the maximum.

QUESTIONS

8-1. What is the hex value for the bottom rightmost location on a 40-column screen?

8-2. Code the instructions to set the cursor to row 12, column 8.

8-3. Code the instructions to clear the screen beginning at row 12, column 0, through row 22, column 79.

8-4. Code data items and instructions to display a message "What is the date (mm/dd/yy)?." Follow the message with a beep sound. Use (a) original DOS function calls and (b) extended DOS function calls and file handles.

8-5. Code data items and instructions to accept data from the keyboard according to the format in Question 8-4. Use (a) original DOS function calls and (b) extended DOS function calls and file handles.

8-6. What are the standard file handles for keyboard input, normal screen display, and printer?

8-7. Key in the program in Figure 8-2 with the following changes then assemble, link, and test: (a) Instead of row 12, center at row 15. (b) Instead of clearing the entire screen, clear only rows 0 through 15.

8-8. Revise Figure 8-2 for use with extended DOS function calls for input and display. Assemble, link, and test.

CHAPTER 9

Screen Processing II: Advanced Features

Objective: To cover more advanced features of screen handling, including scrolling, reverse video, blinking, and the use of scan codes for keyboard input.

INTRODUCTION

Chapter 8 introduced the basic features concerned with screen handling and keyboard input. This chapter provides more advanced features related to scrolling the screen and setting an attribute byte for underlining, blinking, and high intensity. The material in the first section on BIOS interrupt 10 is suitable for both monochrome and color displays. Other advanced features include the use of the keyboard scan code to determine the actual key or key combination pressed.

Monochrome Display

The monochrome display supports 4K bytes of memory (display buffer) starting at address hex B0000. This memory provides for:

- 2K bytes of 25 rows and 80 columns of characters.
- 2K bytes for each screen character for an attribute that specifies reverse video, blinking, high intensity, and underlining.

Color/Graphics Display

The standard color/graphics display supports 16K bytes of memory (display buffer) starting at address hex B8000. This display can operate in either color or BW and has modes for *text* display (normal ASCII characters) and for *graphics.* The display buffer provides for screen "pages" numbered 0 through 3 for an 80-column screen and 0 through 7 for a 40-column screen. The default page number is 0, but you may format any of the pages in memory. The next chapter covers color video and graphics in detail.

ATTRIBUTE BYTE

The attribute byte for both monochrome and color in text (not graphics) mode determines the characteristics of each displayed character. The attribute provides the following features:

		Background				*Foreground*		
Attribute:	BL	R	G	B	I	R	G	B
Bit no.:	7	6	5	4	3	2	1	0

The letters RGB each represent a bit position that stand for red, green, and blue for a color monitor. Bit 7 (BL) sets blinking, and bit 3 (I) sets high intensity. On a monochrome monitor, the foreground is green or amber and the background is black, although this chapter refers to the display as black and white (BW).

To modify these attributes, you may combine them as follows:

Function	*Background*	*Foreground*
	RGB	RGB
Nondisplay (black on black)	000	000
Underline (not for color)	000	001
Normal video: white on black	000	111
Reverse video: black on white	111	000

Color monitors do not provide underlining; instead, setting the underline bit selects the blue color as foreground, thereby displaying blue on black. Following are some typical attributes based on the above background, foreground, blinking, and intensity bits:

Binary	*Hex*	*Effect*
0000 0000	00	No display (for passwords?)
0000 0111	07	White on black, normal
1000 0111	87	White on black, blinking
0000 1111	0F	White on black, intense
0111 0000	70	Black on white, reverse
1111 0000	F0	Black on white, reverse blinking

These attributes are valid for text display in both monochrome and color. The next chapter explains how to select specific colors. You can generate a screen attribute through INT 10H instructions with the BL containing the required attribute and the AH containing either 06 (scroll up), 07 (scroll down), 08 (read attribute/character), or 09 (display attribute/character). When a program sets an attribute, it remains set until another operation changes it. If you set the attribute to hex 00, the character doesn't display at all.

BIOS INTERRUPT 10H

INT 10H facilitates full screen handling. Insert in the AH register a code that determines the function of the interrupt. The operation preserves the contents of the BX, CX, DX, DI, SI, and BP registers. The following sections describe each function.

AH = 00: Set Mode. Use this operation to switch between text and graphics on a color monitor. Use INT 10H to set the mode for the currently executing program. Setting mode also clears the screen. Set the AH to 00 and set the AL as follows:

00	40 x 25 BW text
01	40 x 25 standard 16-color text
02	80 x 25 BW text
03	80 x 25 standard 16-color text
04	320 x 200 standard 4-color graphics
05	320 x 200 BW graphics
06	640 x 200 BW graphics
07	80 x 25 BW (standard monochrome)
08 - 0A	Formats for the PCjr
0D	320 x 200 16-color graphics (EGA)
0E	640 x 200 16-color graphics (EGA)
0F	640 x 350 BW graphics (EGA)
10	640 x 350 64-color graphics (EGA)

EGA means *enhanced graphics adapter.* The following example sets the video mode for standard color text:

```
MOV   AH,00      ;Request set mode
MOV   AL,03      ;80 x 25 standard color text
INT   10H        ;Call BIOS
```

If you write software for unknown video monitors, you can use BIOS INT 11H to determine the device attached to the system; the operation returns a value to the AX, with bits 5 and 4 indicating video mode:

01	40x25 BW using a color adapter
10	80x25 BW using a color adapter
11	80x25 BW using a BW adapter

Test the AX for the type of monitor, and then set the mode.

AH = 01: Set Cursor Size. The cursor is not part of the ASCII character set. The computer maintains its own hardware for its control, and there are special INT operations for its use. The normal cursor symbol is similar to an underline or break character. Use INT 10H to adjust its size vertically: set the CH (bits 4-0) for the top ("start scan line") and the CL (bits 4-0) for the bottom ("end scan line"). You can adjust the size between the top and bottom, 0/13 for monochrome and enhanced graphics, and 0/7 for most color monitors. For example, to enlarge the cursor from its top to its bottom position:

```
MOV  AH,01      ;Request set cursor size
MOV  CH,00      ;Start scan line
MOV  CL,13      ;End scan line (mono)
INT  10H        ;Call BIOS
```

The cursor now blinks as a solid rectangle. You can adjust its size anywhere between these bounds, such as 04/08, 03/10, and so forth. The cursor remains at this type until another operation changes it. Using 12/13 (mono) or 6/7 (color) resets the cursor to normal.

AH = 02: Set Cursor Position. This operation sets the cursor anywhere on a screen according to row and column coordinates. Page number is normally 0, but for 80-column mode can be 0 through 3. Set the AH to 02, the BH to page number, and the DX to row/column:

```
MOV  AH,02      ;Request move cursor
MOV  BH,00      ;Page #0
MOV  DH,row     ;Row
MOV  DL,col     ;Column
INT  10H        ;Call BIOS
```

AH = 03: Read Current Cursor Location. A program can determine the present row, column, and size of the cursor as follows:

```
MOV   AH,03        ;Request cursor location
MOV   BH,00        ;Set page #0 (normal)
INT   10H          ;Call BIOS
```

On return, DH contains the row, the DL contains the column, the CH contains the starting scan line, and the CL contains the ending scan line.

AH = 04: Read Light Pen Position. Use this operation with graphics to determine the position of a light pen.

AH = 05: Select an Active Page. For color text modes 0 through 3, set a new page. In 40-column mode, pages may be 0 through 7; in 80-column mode, 0 through 3.

```
MOV   AH,05        ;Request active page
MOV   AL,page#     ;Page no.
INT   10H          ;Call BIOS
```

AH = 06: Scroll Up Screen. When a program displays down the screen past the bottom, the next line wraps around to start at the top. But even if the interrupt operation specifies column 0, the new lines are indented, and succeeding lines may be badly skewed. The solution is to "scroll" the screen.

Earlier you used code 06 to clear the screen. For text mode, setting the AL to 00 causes a scroll up of the entire screen, effectively clearing it to blank. Inserting a nonzero value in the AL causes that number of lines to scroll up. Top lines scroll off and blank lines appear at the bottom. The following instructions scroll up the entire screen one line:

```
MOV   AX,0601H         ;Scroll up one line
MOV   BH,07            ;Normal BW attribute
MOV   CX,0000          ;From 00,00
MOV   DX,184FH         ;  to 24,79 (full screen)
INT   10H              ;Call BIOS
```

To scroll any number of lines, simply insert the value in the AL. The BH contains the attribute for normal or reverse video, blinking, setting colors, and so forth. The CX and DX registers permit scrolling any portion of the screen. Here's a standard approach to scrolling:

1. Define an item named ROW, initialized to 0, for setting the row location of the cursor.

2. Display a line and advance the cursor to the next line.
3. Test if ROW is near the bottom of the screen (CMP ROW,22).
4. If yes, increment ROW (INC ROW) and exit.
5. If no, scroll one line and use ROW to reset the cursor.

AH = 07: Scroll Down Screen. For text mode, scrolling down the screen causes the bottom lines to scroll off and blank lines to appear at the top. Set the AH to 07 and set the other registers just as for code 06, scroll up.

AH = 08: Read Attribute/Character at Current Cursor Position. Use the following instructions to read both character and attribute from the display area in either text or graphics mode:

```
MOV  AH,08       ;Request read attrib/char
MOV  BH,00       ;Page #0  (for text mode)
INT  10H         ;Call BIOS
```

The operation returns the character in the AL and its attribute in the AH. In graphics mode, the operation returns hex 00 for a non-ASCII character. Since this operation reads one character at a time, you have to code a loop to read successive characters.

AH = 09: Display Attribute/Character at Current Cursor Position. Here's a fun operation to display characters in text or graphics mode with blinking, reverse video, and all that, as follows:

```
MOV  AH,09            ;Request display
MOV  AL,char-to-display
MOV  BH,page#         ;Page # (for text mode)
MOV  BL,attribute     ;Attribute or color
MOV  CX,repetition    ;No. of repeated chars.
INT  10H              ;Call BIOS
```

The entry in the AL is a single character that is to display any number of times. The value in the CX determines the number of times to repetitively display the character in the AL. Displaying different characters requires a loop. The operation does not advance the cursor. The following example displays five blinking hearts with reverse video:

```
MOV  AH,09            ;Request display
MOV  AL,03H           ;Heart
MOV  BH,00            ;Page #0 (for text mode)
```

```
MOV   BL,0F0H          ;Blink reverse video
MOV   CX,05            ;Five times
INT   10H              ;Call BIOS
```

In text but not graphics mode, characters automatically display from one line to the next. To display a prompt or message, code a routine that sets the CX to 01 and loops to move one character at a time from memory into the AL. But since the CX is occupied, you can't use the LOOP instruction. Also, when displaying each character, you have to advance the cursor to the next column (code 02).

For graphics mode, use the BL for defining the foreground color. If bit 7 is 0, the defined color replaces present pixel colors; if bit 7 is 1, the defined color is combined (XORed) with them.

AH = 0A: Display a Character at Current Cursor Position. The only difference between code 0A and 09 is that code 0A does not set the attribute.

```
MOV   AH,0AH           ;Request display
MOV   AL,char          ;Character to display
MOV   BH,page#         ;Page # (for text mode)
MOV   CX,repetition    ;No. of repeated chars.
INT   10H              ;Call BIOS
```

For most display purposes, DOS interrupt 21H is more convenient.

AH = 0E: Write Teletype. This operation lets you use a monitor as a simple terminal. Set the AH to hex 0E, the character to display in the AL, the foreground color (graphics mode) in the BL, and the page number (text mode) in the BH. Bell (07H), backspace (08H), line feed (0AH), and return (0DH) act as commands for screen formatting. The operation automatically advances the cursor, wraps characters onto the next line, scrolls the screen, and maintains the present screen attributes.

AH = 0F: Get Current Video Mode. This operation returns the mode (see code AH = 00) in the AL, the characters per line in the AH (20, 40, or 80), and the page in the BH.

AH = 13: Display Character String (AT only). This operation allows AT users to display strings with options of setting attributes and moving the cursor.

```
MOV AH,13H       ;Request display
MOV AL,service   ;0, 1, 2, or 3
```

```
MOV BH,page#      ;
LEA BP,address    ;Address of string in ES:BP
MOV CX,length     ;Length of string
MOV DX,screen     ;Starting location on screen
INT 10H           ;Call BIOS
```

The four services are:

0 Use attribute and do not advance cursor.
1 Use attribute and advance cursor.
2 Display character first, then attribute, and do not advance cursor.
3 Display character first, then attribute, and advance cursor.

PROGRAM: BLINKING, REVERSE VIDEO, AND SCROLLING

The program in Figure 9-1 accepts names from the keyboard and displays them on the screen. This program, however, displays the prompt with reverse video, accepts the name normally, and displays the name at column 40 on the same row with blinking and reverse video. Following is the format:

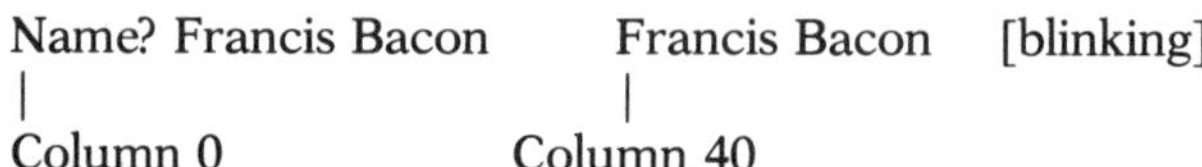

To control cursor placement, the program defines ROW for incrementing the row and COL for moving the cursor horizontally when displaying the prompt and name. (INT 10H does not automatically advance the cursor.) The program displays down the screen until it reaches row 20, and then it begins scrolling up one line for each additional prompt.

For input, the procedure D10INPT uses DOS operation INT 21H. To substitute with BIOS INT 10H:

1. Initialize a counter for the address of the input name and a counter for name length.
2. Execute INT 10H with 08 in the AH and 00 in the BH. The operation returns each character to the AL.
3. If the AL does not contain the return character and the counter is at its maximum, sound the speaker and exit.

4. Move the AL to the name field.
5. If the AL contains the return character, exit.
6. Increment the counter and the address of the name field.
7. Advance the cursor one column.
8. Loop back to point 2.

At the end of the loop, the name field contains the name and return character, and the counter contains the number of characters entered.

EXTENDED ASCII CHARACTERS

An inspection of the ASCII characters 128—255 (hex 80—FF) reveals a number of special characters that are useful for displaying prompts, menus, and logos, coupled with the screen display attribute. For example, use these characters to draw a rectangle with solid lines:

Hex	*Character*
DA	Top left corner angle
BF	Top right corner angle
C0	Bottom left corner angle
D9	Bottom right corner angle
C4	Solid horizontal line
B3	Solid vertical line

The following code uses INT 10H to draw a solid horizontal line 25 positions long:

```
MOV  AH,09              ;Request display
MOV  AL,0C4H            ;Solid line
MOV  BH,00              ;Page #0
MOV  BL,0FH             ;Intense attribute
MOV  CX,25              ;25 repetitions
INT  10H                ;Call BIOS
```

Remember that the cursor does not advance. Drawing a vertical line involves a loop that advances the cursor down one line and displays the hex B3 character. The "dots on" characters for shaded areas can also be useful:

```
        page    60,132
TITLE   NMSCROLL (EXE) Reverse video, blinking, scrolling
; ---------------------------------------------------------
STACKSG SEGMENT PARA STACK 'Stack'
        DW      32 DUP(?)
STACKSG ENDS
; ---------------------------------------------------------
DATASG  SEGMENT PARA 'Data'
NAMEPAR LABEL   BYTE                ;Name parameter list:
MAXNLEN DB      20                  ;  max. length of name
ACTNLEN DB      ?                   ;  no. chars entered
NAMEFLD DB      20 DUP(' ')         ;  name

COL     DB      00
COUNT   DB      ?
PROMPT  DB      'Name? '
ROW     DB      00
DATASG  ENDS
; ---------------------------------------------------------
CODESG  SEGMENT PARA 'Code'
BEGIN   PROC    FAR
        ASSUME  CS:CODESG,DS:DATASG,SS:STACKSG,ES:DATASG
        PUSH    DS
        SUB     AX,AX
        PUSH    AX
        MOV     AX,DATASG
        MOV     DS,AX
        MOV     ES,AX
        MOV     AX,0600H
        CALL    Q10CLR              ;Clear screen
A20LOOP:
        MOV     COL,00              ;Set column to 0
        CALL    Q20CURS
        CALL    B10PRMP             ;Display prompt
        CALL    D10INPT             ;Provide for input of name
        CMP     ACTNLEN,00          ;No name? (indicates end)
        JNE     A30
        MOV     AX,0600H
        CALL    Q10CLR              ;If so, clear screen,
        RET                         ;  terminate
A30:
        CALL    E10NAME             ;Display name
        JMP     A20LOOP
BEGIN   ENDP
;               Display prompt:
;               --------------
B10PRMP PROC    NEAR
        LEA     SI,PROMPT           ;Set address of prompt
        MOV     COUNT,05
B20:
        MOV     BL,70H              ;Reverse video
        CALL    F10DISP             ;Display routine
        INC     SI                  ;Next char in name
        INC     COL                 ;Next column
        CALL    Q20CURS
        DEC     COUNT               ;Countdown
        JNZ     B20                 ;Loop n times
        RET
B10PRMP ENDP
```

Figure 9-1 Blinking, Reverse Video, and Scrolling.

```
;                Accept input of name:
;                --------------------
D10INPT PROC     NEAR
        MOV      AH,0AH
        LEA      DX,NAMEPAR
        INT      21H
        RET
D10INPT ENDP
;                Display name with blinking reverse video:
;                ----------------------------------------
E10NAME PROC     NEAR
        LEA      SI,NAMEFLD         ;Initialize name
        MOV      COL,40             ;Set screen column
E20:
        CALL     Q20CURS            ;Set cursor
        MOV      BL,0F0H            ;Blink reverse video
        CALL     F10DISP            ;Display routine
        INC      SI                 ;Next character in name
        INC      COL                ;Next screen column
        DEC      ACTNLEN            ;Countdown name length
        JNZ      E20                ;Loop n times
        CMP      ROW,20             ;Near bottom screen?
        JAE      E30                ;  no
        INC      ROW
        RET
E30:    MOV      AX,0601H           ;  yes --
        CALL     Q10CLR             ;  clear screen
        RET
E10NAME ENDP
;                Display character:
;                ----------------
F10DISP PROC     NEAR               ;BL (attribute) set on entry
        MOV      AH,09              ;Request display
        MOV      AL,[SI]            ;Get name character
        MOV      BH,00              ;Page#
        MOV      CX,01              ;One character
        INT      10H                ;Call BIOS
        RET
F10DISP ENDP
;                Clear screen:
;                ------------
Q10CLR  PROC     NEAR               ;AX set on entry
        MOV      BH,07              ;Normal BW
        MOV      CX,0000
        MOV      DX,184FH
        INT      10H                ;Call BIOS
        RET
Q10CLR  ENDP
;                Set cursor row/col:
;                ------------------
Q20CURS PROC     NEAR
        MOV      AH,02
        MOV      BH,00
        MOV      DH,ROW
        MOV      DL,COL
        INT      10H
        RET
Q20CURS ENDP
CODESG  ENDS
        END      BEGIN
```

Figure 9-1 ***(continued)***

Hex	*Character*
B0	One-quarter dots on (light)
B1	One-half dots on (medium)
B2	Three-quarter dots on (dark)

You can derive many good ideas from examining the displays of professionally designed software, or let your imagination dream up some original ideas.

OTHER DOS INPUT/OUTPUT OPERATIONS

Following are other DOS function calls that you may find useful. Insert the code in the AH and request INT 21H.

AH = 01: Keyboard Input with Echo. The operation returns one of two actions. If the AL is nonzero, it represents a standard ASCII character, such as a letter or number. Zero in the AL means that the user has pressed a special function key such as Home, F1, or PgUp. To get the scan code, immediately repeat the function call—see "Extended Function Keys" in a later section. The operation responds to a Ctrl/Break request.

AH = 02: Display Character. Place in the DL the character that is to display at the current cursor position. Tab, return, and line feed act normally.

AH = 07: Direct Keyboard Input without Echo. This operation works like function call 01 with two differences: The entered character does not display ("echo") on the screen and the operation does not respond to a Ctrl/Break request.

AH = 08: Keyboard Input without Echo. This operation works like function call 01 with one difference: The entered character does not display ("echo") on the screen.

AH = 0B: Check Keyboard Status. The operation returns hex FF in the AL if an input character is available, otherwise it returns 00. This service is related to function calls 01, 07, and 08, which do not wait for keyboard input.

BIOS INT 16H FOR KEYBOARD INPUT

BIOS INT 16H, a specialized operation, provides the following three keyboard input commands according to a code in the AH.

AH = 00: Read a character. The operation reads into the AL the next ASCII character entered from the keyboard and sets the scan code in the AH. (The next section covers scan codes.) If the character entered is a special key such as Home or F1, the AL is set to 00. The operation does not automatically echo the character to the screen.

AH = 01: Determine if a character is available. The operation clears the zero flag (ZF = 0) to indicate that a character is available for reading; the next character and scan code to be read are in the AL and AH, respectively, and the entry remains in the buffer.

AH = 02: Return the current shift status. The operation returns the status of keyboard shift from location hex 417 in memory into the AL:

Bit	*Bit*
7 Insert state is active	3 Alt/shift pressed
6 Caps lock state toggled	2 Ctrl/shift pressed
5 Numeric lock state toggled	1 Left shift pressed
4 Scroll lock state toggled	0 Right shift pressed

EXTENDED FUNCTION KEYS

The keyboard provides three basic types of keys:

1. *Characters* such as letters A through Z, numbers 0 through 9, %, $, #, and so forth.
2. *Extended function keys* such as Home, End, Backspace, Arrows, Return, Del, Ins, PgUp, PgDn, and the program function keys.
3. *Control keys* for Alt, Ctrl, and Shift that work in association with other keys.

An extended function key requests an action rather than delivers a character. There is nothing in the design of the keys that compels them to perform a specific action. As programmer, you determine, for example, that pressing the Home key is to set the cursor at the top left corner of the screen, or that pressing the End key sets the cursor at the end of text on the screen. You could as easily program them to perform a wholly unrelated operation.

Each key has a designated scan code numbered from 1 (Esc) through 83 (Del), or hex 01 through 53. By means of these scan codes, a program may determine the source of any keystroke. For example, a request for input of one character from the keyboard involves 00 in the AH register and issuing interrupt 16H, as follows:

```
MOV   AH,00   ;Request input from keyboard
INT   16H     ;Call BIOS
```

The operation replies in one of two ways, depending on whether you press a character key or an extended function key. For a character such as the letter A, the keyboard sends the computer two items of information:

1. The ASCII character A (hex 41) in the AL.
2. The scan code for the letter A, hex 1E, in the AH.

If you press an extended function key such as Ins, the keyboard also delivers two items of information:

1. Zero in the AL register.
2. The scan code for Ins, hex 52, in the AH.

Thus, after an INT 16H instruction, you can test the AL. If zero, the request is for an extended function code; if nonzero, the operation has delivered a character. The following tests for an extended function:

```
MOV  AH,00   ;Request input
INT  16H     ;Call BIOS
CMP  AL,00   ;Extended function?
JZ   exit    ;Yes -- exit
```

Scan Codes

Figure 9-2 provides scan codes for some common extended functions.

The keyboard contains two keys for such characters as *, +, and –. Pressing the asterisk key, for example, sets the character code hex 2A in the AL and one of two scan codes in the AH, depending on which key was pressed: hex 09 if the asterisk above the number 8, or hex 29 if the asterisk on the PrtSc key.

The following logic tests the scan code for an asterisk:

```
CMP  AL,2AH  ;Asterisk?
JNE  EXIT1   ;No -- exit
CMP  AH,09H  ;Which scan code?
JE   EXIT2
```

Extended Function	*Scan Code*
Alt/A through Alt/Z	1E — 2C
F1 through F10	3B — 44
Home	47
Up arrow	48
PgUp	49
Left arrow	4B
Right arrow	4D
End	4F
Down arrow	50
PgDn	51
Ins	52
Del	53

Figure 9-2 Common Scan Codes.

Let's set the cursor to row 0, column 0 if a user presses the Home key, scan code 47:

```
MOV  AH,00    ;Request input
INT  16H      ;
CMP  AL,00    ;Extended function?
JNE  EXIT1    ;No -- exit
CMP  AH,47H   ;Scan code for Home?
JNE  EXIT2    ;No -- exit
MOV  AH,02    ;
MOV  BH,00    ;Set cursor
MOV  DX,00    ; to 0,0
INT  10H      ;Call BIOS
```

Function keys F1 through F10 generate scan codes hex 3B through hex 44, respectively. The following tests for function key F10:

```
CMP  AH,44H  ;Function key F10?
JE   EXIT1   ;Yes
```

At EXIT1, the program could perform any required action.

A complete list of scan codes is available in the BASIC manual. The IBM PC Technical Reference manual contains full details for all scan codes as well as the use of the Alt, Ctrl, and Shift keys.

KEY POINTS TO REMEMBER

- Monochrome display supports 4K bytes of memory, 2K of which are available for characters and 2K for an attribute for each character.
- Color display supports 16K bytes and can operate in color or BW. You can process in either text mode for normal character display or in graphics mode.
- The attribute byte is available for both monochrome display and for color display in text mode. The attribute provides for blinking, reverse video, and high intensity. For color text, the RGB bits enable you to select colors but no underlining.
- BIOS INT 10H provides the interrupt for full screen processing such as setting mode, setting the cursor location, scrolling the screen, reading from the keyboard, and writing characters.
- If your program displays down the screen, scroll up before it reaches the bottom.
- When using the attribute for blinking and reverse video, watch out for resetting it to normal.
- For INT 10H operations that read and display, remember to advance the cursor.
- BIOS INT 16H provides for accepting extended functions.
- An extended function key requests an action rather than delivers a character.
- Each key on the keyboard has a designated scan code numbered from 1 (Esc) through 83 (Del), or hex 01 through 53.
- Pressing a character key causes the keyboard to deliver the character to the AL and the key's scan code to the AH.
- Pressing an extended function key causes the keyboard to deliver zero to the AL and the key's scan code to the AH.

QUESTIONS

9-1. Provide the screen attributes for the following: (a) blinking underline, (b) normal intensity, (c) reverse video intensity.

9-2. Code the following routines: (a) Set the mode for 80-column BW; (b) Set the cursor type for start line 5 and end line 12; (c) Scroll up the screen 10 lines; (d) Display ten blinking "dots" with one-half dots on (hex B1).

9-3. Provide the scan codes for the following extended functions: (a) up arrow, (b) function key F3, (c) Home, (d) PgUp.

9-4. Use DEBUG to examine the effects on the AX register for entered keystrokes. To request entry of assembler statements, type A 100 (Return), and enter the following instructions:

```
MOV  AH,00
INT  16H
JMP  100
```

Use U 100,104 to unassemble the program and use G 104 to get DEBUG to execute through the INT. Execution stops, waiting for your input. Press any key and examine the AH register. Continue entering G 104 and press keys for a variety of keys. Press Q when ready to quit.

9-5. Code the instructions to enter a keystroke; if the key is PgDn, set the cursor to row 24, column 0.

CHAPTER 10

Screen Processing III: Color/Graphics

Objective: To cover advanced features concerned with video color and graphics.

INTRODUCTION

This chapter introduces the use of color for both text (normal character display) and for graphics. The three common types of video monitors used to display color graphics, in order of increasing cost and quality, are as follows:

1. An unmodified color television is the common home TV set that many people use with their computer.
2. A composite video monitor accepts a combined color signal without the radio frequency modulation used for transmission over the airwaves and provides a superior image.
3. An RGB monitor accepts input signals that are sent to three separate electron guns—red, green, and blue, for each of the primary additive colors. Although more expensive, an RGB monitor provides a better quality image.

The standard color/graphics monitor adapter (CGA) supports 16K bytes of color display memory beginning at address hex B8000, with 8K available for the characters and 8K for their attributes. When operating in 80 × 25 format, the adapter can store four pages (0—3) of display screen, each 4K bytes in size; when operating in 40 × 25 format, it can store eight pages (0—7), each 2K bytes in size. The default page number is 0, at the beginning of display memory, but you may format any page in memory, and then display one page while formatting another page internally.

The enhanced graphics adapter (EGA) provides for significantly better resolution than the standard color adapter (CGA) and in many ways is compatible. Resolutions include 320×200, 640×200, and 640×350.

The color adapters have two basic modes of operation: text (or alphanumeric) and graphics, with additional modes possible between these basic modes. The default mode is text. See Chapter 9 on setting mode (AH=00) under the section "BIOS Interrupt 10H." Use BIOS interrupt INT 10H to set graphics mode or to return to text mode, as the following two examples show:

```
MOV   AH,00   ;Set mode        MOV   AH,00   ;Set mode
MOV   AL,03   ;Color text      MOV   AL,04   ;Medium graphics
INT   10H                      INT   10H
```

TEXT (ALPHANUMERIC) MODE

Text mode is for normal processing of letters and numbers on the screen. Processing is similar for both BW and color, except that color does not support the underline attribute. Text mode provides access to the same 256 extended ASCII character set as the monochrome adapter. Each character can be one of 16 colors, and its background can be one of eight colors. You can also select one of 16 colors for the border.

Colors

The three basic colors are red, green, and blue. You can combine these to form a total of eight colors (including black and white), and can set high intensity for a total of 16 colors:

	I R G B		I R G B
black	0 0 0 0	gray	1 0 0 0
blue	0 0 0 1	light blue	1 0 0 1
green	0 0 1 0	light green	1 0 1 0
cyan	0 0 1 1	light cyan	1 0 1 1
red	0 1 0 0	light red	1 1 0 0
magenta	0 1 0 1	light magenta	1 1 0 1
brown	0 1 1 0	yellow	1 1 1 0
white	0 1 1 1	high-intensity white	1 1 1 1

Foreground (the actual displayed character) can consist of all 16 colors. Background to a displayed character can consist of only the first eight colors. Note that if foreground and background are the same color, the displayed character is invisible. You can also use the attribute byte to cause a foreground character to blink.

Attribute Byte

Text mode involves use of the attribute byte discussed in Chapter 9. In the following picture of the attribute byte, RGB means, respectively, red, green, and blue, BL means blinking, and I means high intensity:

	Background				*Foreground*			
Attribute:	BL	R	G	B	I	R	G	B
Bit no.:	7	6	5	4	3	2	1	0

Blinking and intensity apply to foreground. The following are some typical attributes:

Bit:	7	6	5	4	3	2	1	0	
	BL	R	G	B	I	R	G	B	Hex
Black on black	0	0	0	0	0	0	0	0	00
Blue on black	0	0	0	0	0	0	0	1	01
Red on blue	0	0	0	1	0	1	0	0	14
Cyan on green	0	0	1	0	0	0	1	1	23
Light magenta on white	0	1	1	1	1	1	0	1	7D
Gray on green, blinking	1	0	1	0	1	0	0	0	A8

Use the attribute byte the same way as was shown for a BW monitor. However, you may want to use INT 11H to test the type of monitor. For BW, use 07 to set normal attribute. For color, use any of the color combinations just given. The color stays set until another operation changes it. The following INT 10H operations can set color: AH=06, AH=07, and AH=09. For example, to display five asterisks as light green on magenta, blinking:

```
MOV  AH,09     ;Request display
MOV  AL,'*'    ;Asterisk
MOV  BH,00     ;Page #0
MOV  BL,0DAH   ;Color attribute
MOV  CX,05     ;Five times
INT  10H       ;Call BIOS
```

GRAPHICS MODE

Graphics mode uses pixels (picture elements, or pels) to generate color patterns. The color/graphics adapter (CGA) has three resolutions:

1. Low resolution, not supported by ROM, provides a display of 100 rows of 160 pixels (that is, four bits per pixel). Each can consist of the standard 16 colors as described in the preceding section, "Colors." Producing this mode involves direct addressing of the Motorola 6845 CRT Controller. The two ports are hex 3D4 and 3D5.
2. Medium resolution for standard color graphics provides 200 rows of 320 pixels. Each byte represents four pixels (that is, two bits per pixel).
3. High resolution provides 200 rows of 640 pixels. Since it requires the full 16K bytes of color/graphics storage, high resolution graphics can support only BW. Each byte represents eight pixels (that is, one bit per pixel) providing for 0 (black) and 1 (white).

Note that for graphics mode, ROM contains dot patterns for only the first (bottom) 128 characters. INT 1FH provides access to a 1K area in memory that defines the top 128 characters, eight bytes per character. The mapping of graphics bytes to video scan lines is the same for both medium- and high-resolution graphics.

MEDIUM RESOLUTION MODE

Under medium resolution, each byte represents four pixels, numbered 0 through 3, as follows:

```
byte:  |C1 C0|C1 C0|C1 C0|C1 C0|
pixel:    0     1     2     3
```

At any given time there are four available colors numbered 0 through 3. The limitation of four colors is because a two-bit pixel provides four bit combinations: 00, 01, 10, and 11. You can choose pixel 00 for any one of the 16 available colors for background, and choose pixel 01, 10, and 11 for any one of two three-color palettes:

C1	*C0*	*Palette 0*	*Palette 1*
0	0	background	background
0	1	green	cyan
1	0	red	magenta
1	1	brown	white

Use INT 10H to select a color palette and the background. Thus, if you choose background color yellow and palette 0 just given, available colors are yellow, green, red, and brown. A byte consisting of the pixel value 10101010 would display as all red. If you choose background color blue and palette 1, available colors are blue, cyan, magenta, and white. A byte consisting of pixel value 00011011 displays blue, cyan, magenta, and white.

BIOS Interrupt 10H for Graphics

For graphics, use INT 10H (AH = 00) first to set graphics mode. Subsequently, use INT 10H (AH = 11) to set the color palette and display a graphics character. A code in the AH register determines the operation.

AH = 00: Set Mode. Zero in the AH and 04 in the AL sets standard color graphics mode:

```
MOV   AH,00   ;Set mode for
MOV   AL,04   ;   320 × 200 resolution
INT   10H
```

Setting graphics mode causes the cursor to disappear. See Chapter 9 for other details of setting mode.

AH = 0BH: Set Color Palette. The BH value determines the purpose of the BL register:

BH = 00 Select the background and border color according to the BL, which contains the background color (1 of 16, hex 0-F).

BH = 01 Select the palette according to the BL, which contains the palette (0 or 1). The following provides an example:

```
MOV   AH,0BH   ;Request color
MOV   BH,01    ;Select palette
MOV   BL,00    ;   #0 (green, red, brown)
INT   10H      ;Call BIOS
```

If you want to keep the same palette, you need set it only once. But once you change palette, the whole screen changes to that color combination. If you use code 0BH while in text mode, the value set for color 0 for the palette determines the border color.

AH = 0CH: Write Pixel Dot. Use code 0C in the AH to display a selected color (background and palette). Assuming 320 × 200 resolution, for the vertical value load the DX in the range 0 through 199; for the horizontal value load the CX in the range 0 through 319. The AL contains the color (0-3) of the pixel.

```
MOV  AH,0CH       ;Request write dot
MOV  AL,color     ;Color of pixel
MOV  CX,column    ;Horizontal position
MOV  DX,row       ;Vertical position
INT  10H          ;Call BIOS
```

AH = 0DH: Read Pixel Dot. This operation reads a dot to determine its color value. Set the DX for row (0 through 199), the CX for column (0

```
TITLE   GRAPHIX (COM)  Example color/graphics program
CODESG  SEGMENT PARA 'Code'
        ASSUME  CS:CODESG,DS:CODESG,SS:CODESG
        ORG     100H

MAIN    PROC    NEAR
        MOV     AH,00               ;Set graphics mode
        MOV     AL,0DH              ;  for EGA (CGA = 04)
        INT     10H

        MOV     AH,0BH              ;Set color palette
        MOV     BH,00               ;Background
        MOV     BL,02               ;Green
        INT     10H

        MOV     BX,00               ;Set initial color,
        MOV     CX,00               ;  column,
        MOV     DX,00               ;  & row
A50:
        MOV     AH,0CH              ;Write pixel dot
        MOV     AL,BL               ;Set color
        INT     10H                 ;BX, CX, & DX are preserved
        INC     CX                  ;Increment column
        CMP     CX,320              ;Column at 320?
        JNE     A50                 ;  no -- loop
        MOV     CX,00               ;  yes - reset column
        INC     BL                  ;Change color
        INC     DX                  ;Increment row
        CMP     DX,40               ;Row at 40?
        JNE     A50                 ;  no  - loop
        RET                         ;  yes - terminate
MAIN    ENDP
CODESG  ENDS
        END     MAIN
```

Figure 10-1 Color/Graphics Display.

through 319), and the AH to hex 0D. The operation returns the pixel color to the AL.

PROGRAM: SET GRAPHICS MODE AND DISPLAY COLOR

The program in Figure 10-1 uses INT 10H to set graphics mode, to select background color green, and to write pixel dots for 40 rows and 320 columns. This program increments the color for each row, and since only the rightmost three bits are used, the colors repeat after every seven rows.

The program leaves the display in graphics mode. Restore text mode either by means of the DOS MODE command (MODE CO80) or by your own COM program that simply uses INT 10H to set text mode.

KEY POINTS TO REMEMBER

- The 16K memory for color display permits storing additional "pages" or "screens." There are four pages for 80-column screens and eight pages for 40-column screens.
- Graphics mode provides for low resolution (not supported by ROM), medium resolution (for normal color graphics), and high resolution (for BW graphics).
- A pixel (picture element) consists of a specified number of bits depending on the graphics adapter and the resolution (low, medium, or high).
- Under medium-resolution graphics on the color/graphics adapter (CGA), you can select four colors of which one is any of the 16 available colors and the other three are from a color palette.

QUESTIONS

10-1. Under text mode, how many colors are available for background and for foreground on the standard color adapter (CGA)?

10-2. Provide the attribute bytes in binary for the following: (a) magenta on light cyan, (b) brown on yellow, (c) red on gray, blinking.

10-3. Explain the reason for the number of colors available under low-, medium-, and high-resolution graphics.

10-4. Code the instructions for displaying five diamond characters in text mode with light green on magenta.

10-5. Code the instructions to set graphics mode for (a) 320 × 200 resolution on the CGA and (b) 640 × 200 on the EGA.

10-6. Code the instructions for selecting background color blue in graphics mode.

10-7. Code the instructions to read a dot from row 12, column 13 in graphics mode.

10-8. Revise Figure 10-1 for the following: (a) graphics mode for your own monitor; (b) background color red; (c) row beginning at 10 and ending at 30; (d) column beginning at 20 and ending at 300.

CHAPTER 11

String Instructions

Objective: To explain the special string instructions used to process character data.

INTRODUCTION

Instructions to this point have handled only one byte or one word at a time. It is often necessary, however, to move or compare data fields that exceed one word. For example, you may want to compare descriptions or names in order to sort them into ascending sequence. Items of this format are known as *string data* and may be either character or numeric. For processing string data, the assembler provides five string instructions:

MOVS	Moves one byte or one word from one location to another location in memory.
LODS	Loads from memory one byte into the AL or one word into the AX register.
STOS	Stores the AL or AX registers into memory.
CMPS	Compares two memory locations of one byte or one word.
SCAS	Compares the contents of the AL or AX to a memory location.

An associated instruction, the REP prefix, causes the string instructions just given to perform repetitively through a specified string length.

FEATURES OF STRING OPERATIONS

You can code a string instruction to specify repetitive processing of one byte or one word at a time. For example, you could select a byte instruction for a string with an odd number of bytes and a word instruction for an even number of bytes. The following indicates the registers implied for each string instruction and the one-byte and one-word versions. Assume that DI and SI contain valid addresses:

Instruction	*Implied Operands*	*Byte*	*Word*
MOVS	DI,SI	MOVSB	MOVSW
LODS	AL,SI or AX,SI	LODSB	LODSW
STOS	DI,AL or DI,AX	STOSB	STOSW
CMPS	SI,DI	CMPSB	CMPSW
SCAS	DI,AL or DI,AX	SCASB	SCASW

For example, you code operands for MOVS, but omit them for MOVSB and MOVSW. These instructions assume that the DI and SI contain offset addresses that reference memory (use LEA for this purpose). The SI register is normally associated with the DS (data segment) register, as DS:SI. The DI register is always associated with the ES (extra segment) register, as ES:DI. *Consequently, MOVS, STOS, CMPS, and SCAS require that you initialize the ES register, usually with the address in the DS register.*

REP: REPEAT STRING PREFIX

Although string instructions reference only one byte or one word, the REP prefix provides for repeated execution. Code REP immediately before a string instruction, such as REP MOVSB. For REP, you have to insert an initial value in the CX register. It executes the string instruction, decrements the CX, and repeats this operation until CX is zero. In this way, you can handle strings of virtually any length.

The direction flag determines the direction of a repeated operation:

- For left to right, use CLD to set the DF flag to 0.
- For right to left, use STD to set the DF flag to 1.

The following example moves the 20 bytes of STRING1 to STRING2. Assume that both the DS and ES are initialized with the address of the data segment.

```
STRING1   DB   20 DUP('*')
STRING2   DB   20 DUP(' ')

          ...
          CLD             ;Clear DF flag
          MOV  CX,20      ;Init'ze for 20 bytes
          LEA  DI,STRING2 ;Init'ze receiving name
```

```
LEA  SI,STRING1 ;Init'ze sending address
REP MOVSB       ;Move STRING1 to STRING2
```

Following execution, CMPS and SCAS also set status flags so that the operation can terminate immediately on finding a specified condition. The variations of REP for this purpose are the following:

REP	Repeat the operation until CX equals zero.
REPZ or REPE	Repeat the operation while the ZF (Zero) flag indicates equal/zero. Terminate when the ZF indicates not equal/zero or CX equals zero.
REPNE or REPNZ	Repeat the operation while the ZF flag indicates not equal/zero. Terminate when the ZF indicates equal/zero or CX equals zero.

For the 8086, 80286, and 80386 processors, which handle a word at a time, it is more efficient to use string word operations where possible.

MOVS: MOVE STRING

Earlier, Figure 7-5 illustrated moving a nine-byte field. The operation involved three instructions for initialization and five for looping. MOVS combined with a REP prefix and a length in the CX can move any number of characters more efficiently.

For the receiving string, the segment register is the ES and the offset register is the DI. For the sending string, the segment register is the DS and the offset register is the SI. As a result, at the start of the program, initialize the ES register along with the DS register, and prior to executing the MOVS, use LEA to initialize the DI and SI registers. Depending on the DF flag, MOVS increments or decrements the DI and SI registers by 1 for a byte and by 2 for a word.

The instructions equivalent to REP MOVSB are:

```
         JCXZ     LABEL2
LABEL1:  MOV      AL,[SI]
         MOV      [DI],AL
         INC/DEC  DI        ;Increment or decrement
         INC/DEC  SI        ;Increment or decrement
         LOOP     LABEL1
LABEL2:  ...
```

In Figure 11-1, the procedure C10MVSB uses MOVSB to move a ten-byte field, NAME1, one byte at a time to NAME2. The first instruction, CLD, clears the direction flag to zero so that the operation will process left to right. The DF flag is normally zero at the start of execution, but CLD is coded here as a wise precaution.

The two LEA instructions load the SI and DI registers respectively with the offset addresses of NAME1 and NAME2. Since earlier instructions initialized the DS and ES registers with the address of DATASG, the segment/offset addresses are correct for ES:DI and DS:SI. (A COM program would have automatically initialized these registers.) A MOV instruction initializes CX with 10 (the length of NAME1 and NAME2). The instruction REP MOVSB now performs the following:

- Moves the leftmost byte of NAME1 (addressed by ES:DI) to the leftmost byte of NAME2 (addressed by DS:SI).
- Increments DI and SI by 1 for the next bytes to the right.
- Decrements CX by 1.
- Repeats this operation, ten loops in all, until CX becomes zero.

Because the DF flag is zero and MOVSB increments DI and SI, each iteration processes one byte farther to the right, as NAME1+1 to NAME2+1, and so on. If the DF flag is 1, MOVSB would decrement DI and SI, causing processing from right to left. But in that case, you would have to initialize the SI and DI registers with NAME1+9 and NAME2+9, respectively.

The next procedure in Figure 11-1, D10MVSW, uses MOVSW to move a word at a time. Since MOVSW increments the DI and SI registers by 2, the operation requires only five loops. For processing right to left, initialize the SI with NAME1+8 and the DI with NAME2+8.

LODS: LOAD STRING

LODS loads the AL with a byte or the AX with a word from memory. The memory address is subject to the DS:SI registers (although you can override the SI.) Depending on the DF flag, the operation also increments or decrements the SI register.

Since one LODS operation fills the register, there is no practical use for the REP prefix. For normal purposes, a simple MOV instruction is adequate. But MOV generates three bytes of machine code whereas LODS generates only one, although it requires you to initialize the SI register. You could use LODS where you want to step through a string one byte or word at a time examining successively for a particular value.

The instructions equivalent to LODSB are:

```
MOV   AL,[SI]
INC   SI
```

In Figure 11-1, the procedure E10LODS depicts the LODSW instruction. The example processes only one word and inserts the first byte of NAME1 (containing As) in the AL register and the second byte in the AH (that is, reversed), so that the AX contains sA.

STOS: STORE STRING

STOS "stores" the contents of the AL or AX register into a byte or word in memory. The memory address is always subject to the ES:DI registers. Depending on the DF flag, STOS also increments or decrements the DI register, by 1 for a byte and by 2 for a word.

A practical use of STOS with a REP prefix is to initialize a data area to any specified value, such as clearing a display area to blank. The length (bytes or words) is in the AX. The instructions equivalent to REP STOSB are:

```
          JCXZ     LABEL2
LABEL1:   MOV      [DI],AL
          INC/DEC  DI          ;Increment or decrement
          LOOP     LABEL1
LABEL2:   ...
```

In Figure 11-1, the procedure F10STOS depicts the STOSW instruction. The operation repeatedly stores hex 2020 (blanks) five times through NAME3. The operation stores the AL in the first byte and the AH in the next byte (that is, reversed). On termination, the DI register contains the address of NAME3+10.

CMPS: COMPARE STRING

CMPS compares the contents of one memory location (addressed by DS:SI) to another memory location (addressed by ES:DI). Depending on the DF flag, CMPS also increments or decrements the SI and DI registers, by 1 for a byte and by 2 for a word. CMPS sets the AF, CF, OF, PF, SF, and ZF flags. When combined with a REP prefix and a length in the CX, CMPS can successively compare any number of bytes or words.

```
        page 60,132
TITLE   STRING (EXE)  Tests of string operations
; -----------------------------------------------
STACKSG SEGMENT PARA STACK 'Stack'
        DW      32 DUP(?)
STACKSG ENDS
; -----------------------------------------------
DATASG  SEGMENT PARA 'Data'
NAME1   DB      'Assemblers'    ;Data items
NAME2   DB      10 DUP(' ')
NAME3   DB      10 DUP(' ')
DATASG  ENDS
; -----------------------------------------------
CODESG  SEGMENT PARA 'Code'
BEGIN   PROC    FAR             ;Main procedure
        ASSUME  CS:CODESG,DS:DATASG,SS:STACKSG,ES:DATASG
        PUSH    DS
        SUB     AX,AX
        PUSH    AX
        MOV     AX,DATASG
        MOV     DS,AX
        MOV     ES,AX
        CALL    C10MVSB         ;MVSB subroutine
        CALL    D10MVSW         ;MVSW subroutine
        CALL    E10LODS         ;LODS subroutine
        CALL    F10STOS         ;STOS subroutine
        CALL    G10CMPS         ;CMPS subroutine
        CALL    H10SCAS         ;SCAS subroutine
        RET
BEGIN   ENDP
;               Use of MOVSB:
;               ------------
C10MVSB PROC    NEAR
        CLD
        LEA     SI,NAME1
        LEA     DI,NAME2
        MOV     CX,10           ;Move 10 bytes,
        REP MOVSB               ;  NAME1 to NAME2
        RET
C10MVSB ENDP
;               Use of MOVSW:
;               ------------
D10MVSW PROC    NEAR
        CLD
        LEA     SI,NAME2
        LEA     DI,NAME3
        MOV     CX,05           ;Move 5 words,
        REP MOVSW               ;  NAME2 to NAME3
        RET
D10MVSW ENDP
;               Use of LODSW:
;               ------------
E10LODS PROC    NEAR
        CLD
        LEA     SI,NAME1        ;Load 1st word of NAME1
        LODSW                   ;  into AX reg.
        RET
E10LODS ENDP
```

Figure 11-1 Use of String Operations.

```
;                Use of STOSW:
;                ------------
F10STOS PROC     NEAR
        CLD
        LEA      DI,NAME3
        MOV      CX,05
        MOV      AX,2020H          ;Move blanks
        REP STOSW                  ;  to NAME3
        RET
F10STOS ENDP
;                Use of CMPSB:
;                ------------
G10CMPS PROC     NEAR
        CLD
        MOV      CX,10
        LEA      SI,NAME1
        LEA      DI,NAME2
        REPE CMPSB                 ;Compare NAME1:NAME2
        JNE      G20               ;Not equal?
        MOV      BH,01

G20:    MOV      CX,10
        LEA      SI,NAME2
        LEA      DI,NAME3
        REPE CMPSB                 ;Compare NAME2:NAME3
        JE       G30               ;If equal, exit
        MOV      BL,02
G30:    RET
G10CMPS ENDP

;       Use of SCASB:
;       ------------
H10SCAS PROC     NEAR
        CLD
        MOV      CX,10
        LEA      DI,NAME1
        MOV      AL,'m'            ;Scan NAME1
        REPNE SCASB                ;  for 'm'
        JNE      H20               ;If not found, exit
        MOV      AH,03
H20:    RET
H10SCAS ENDP

CODESG  ENDS
        END      BEGIN
```

Figure 11-1 ***(continued)***

Consider the comparison of two strings containing JEAN and JOAN. A comparison from left to right one byte at a time causes the following:

J : J Equal
E : O Unequal (E is low)
A : A Equal
N : N Equal

A comparison of the entire four bytes ends with a comparison of N to N: equal/zero. Now since the two names are not "equal," the operation should terminate as soon as it finds an unequal condition. For this purpose, REP has a variation, REPE, which repeats the operation as long as the comparison is equal, or until the CX register equals zero. The coding for repeated one-byte compares is as follows:

```
REPE CMPSB
```

In Figure 11-1, the procedure G10CMPS consists of two examples that use CMPSB. The first example compares NAME1 to NAME2. Earlier, MOVSB moved the contents of NAME1 to NAME2. Therefore, the CMPSB operation continues for the entire ten bytes and results in an equal/zero condition: the SF flag is 0 (positive) and the ZF flag is 1 (for zero).

The second example compares NAME2 to NAME3. Earlier, STOSW stored blanks in NAME3. Therefore, the CMPSB operation terminates after comparing the first byte and results in a high/unequal condition: the SF flag is 0 (positive) and the ZF flag is 0 (for nonzero).

The first example results in equal/zero and moves 01 to the BH register. The second example results in unequal and moves 02 to the BL register. If you use DEBUG to trace the instructions, at the end of G10CMPS the BX register should contain 0102.

Warning! These examples use CMPSB to compare one byte at a time. If you use CMPSW to compare a word at a time, then initialize CX to 5. But that's not the problem. When comparing words, CMPSW reverses the bytes. For example, let's compare the name SAMUEL to ARNOLD. For the initial comparison of words, instead of comparing SA to AR, the operation compares AS to RA. So, instead of higher, the result is lower—and incorrect. CMPSW works correctly only if the compared strings contain *numeric* data defined as DW, DD, or DQ.

SCAS: SCAN STRING

SCAS differs slightly from CMPS because it scans a string for a specified byte or word value. SCAS compares the contents of a memory location (addressed by ES:DI) to the AL or AX register. Depending on the DF flag, SCAS also increments or decrements the DI register, by 1 for a byte and by 2 for a word. SCAS sets the AF, CF, OF, PF, SF, and ZF flags. When combined with the REP prefix and a length in the CX, SCAS can scan any string length.

SCAS would be particularly useful for a text-editing application where the program has to scan for punctuation such as periods, commas, and blanks.

In Figure 11-1, the procedure H10SCAS scans NAME1 for the lowercase letter m. Since the SCASB operation is to continue scanning while the comparison is not equal or until the CX is zero, the REP prefix is REPNE:

```
REPNE SCASB
```

Since NAME1 contains "Assemblers," SCASB finds an equal on the fifth compare. If you use DEBUG to trace the instructions, at the end of H10SCAS you will see that the AH register contains 03 to indicate that an "m" was found. The REP SCASB operation has also decremented the CX from 10 to 06.

SCASW scans for a word in memory that matches the word in the AX register. If you used LODSW or MOV to transfer a word into the AX register, the first byte will be in the AL and the second byte in the AH. Since SCAS compares the bytes in reversed sequence, the operation works correctly.

SCAN AND REPLACE

You may also want to replace a specific character with another character, for example, to clear editing characters such as paragraph and end-of-page symbols from a document. The following partial program scans STRING for an ampersand (&) and replaces it with a blank. If SCASB locates an ampersand, it terminates the operation. In this example there is an ampersand at STRING+8, where the blank is to be inserted. The SCASB operation will have incremented the DI register to STRING+9. Decrementing DI by 1 provides the correct address for the blank replacement character.

```
STRLEN    EQU    15                   ;Length of STRING
STRING    DB     'The time&is now'
          . . .
          CLD
          MOV    AL,'&'               ;Search character
          MOV    CX,STRLEN            ;Length of STRING
          LEA    DI,STRING            ;Address of STRING
          REPNE  SCASB                ;Scan
          JNZ    K20                  ;Found?
          DEC    DI                   ;Yes -- adjust address
          MOV    BYTE PTR[DI],20H     ;Replace with blank
K20:      RET
```

ALTERNATE CODING

If you code explicitly with a byte or word instruction such as MOVSB or MOVSW, the assembler assumes the correct length and does not require operands. For instructions such as MOVS, which do not indicate byte or word, you must indicate the length in the operands. For example, if FLDA and FLDB are defined as byte (DB), then the instruction

```
REP MOVS FLDA,FLDB
```

implies a repeated move of the byte beginning at FLDB to the byte beginning at FLDA. You could also code the instruction as

```
REP MOVS ES:BYTE PTR[DI],DS:[SI]
```

However, you must still load the DI and SI registers with the addresses of FLDA and FLDB.

DUPLICATING A PATTERN

The STOS instruction is useful for setting an area according to a specific byte or word value. For repeating a pattern that exceeds a word, you can use the MOVS instruction with a minor modification. Let's say that you want to set a display line to the following pattern:

```
***---***---***---***---***--- . . .
```

Rather than define the entire pattern repetitively, you need only define the first six bytes. Code the pattern immediately before the display line; the required coding is as follows:

```
PATTERN DB      '***---'
DISAREA DB      42 DUP(?)
        .
        .
        CLD
        MOV     CX,21
        LEA     DI,DISAREA
        LEA     SI,PATTERN
        REP MOVSW
```

On execution, the MOVSW operation moves the first word of PATTERN (**) to the first word of DISAREA, and then moves the second (*-) and third (--) words:

At this point the DI contains the address of DISAREA+6, and the SI contains the address of PATTERN+6, which is also the address of DISAREA. The operation now automatically duplicates the pattern by moving the first word of DISAREA to DISAREA+6, DISAREA+2 to DISAREA+8, DISAREA+4 to DISAREA+10, and so forth. Eventually the pattern is duplicated through to the end of DISAREA:

You can use this technique to duplicate any pattern any number of times. The pattern must be located immediately before the receiving field.

PROGRAM: RIGHT-ADJUSTING ON THE SCREEN

The COM program in Figure 11-2 illustrates most of the material described in this chapter. The procedures perform the following:

B10INPT Accepts names up to 30 characters in length at the top of the screen.

D10SCAS Uses SCASB to scan the name and bypasses any input containing an asterisk.

E10RGHT Uses MOVSB to right-adjust the names to the right of the screen, one under the other. The length in ACTNLEN in the input parameter list is used to calculate the rightmost character of a name, as follows:

```
       JEROME KERN
OSCAR HAMMERSTEIN
   RICHARD ROGERS
```

F10CLNM Uses STOSW to clear the name in memory.

KEY POINTS TO REMEMBER

- For the string instructions MOVS, STOS, CMPS, and SCAS, be sure to initialize the ES register.
- Clear (CLD) or set (STD) the direction flag depending on the direction of processing.

```
         page    60,132
TITLE    EXRIGHT (COM)  Right-adjust displayed names
CODESG   SEGMENT PARA 'Code'
         ASSUME  CS:CODESG,DS:CODESG,SS:CODESG,ES:CODESG
         ORG     100H
BEGIN:   JMP     SHORT MAIN
;------------------------------------------------------
NAMEPAR LABEL    BYTE              ;Name parameter list
MAXNLEN DB       31                ;Max. length
ACTNLEN DB       ?                 ;No. chars entered
NAMEFLD DB       31 DUP(' ')       ;Name

PROMPT  DB       'Name?', '$'
NAMEDSP DB       31 DUP(' '), 13, 10, '$'
ROW     DB       00
;------------------------------------------------------
MAIN     PROC    NEAR              ;Main procedure
         MOV     AX,0600H
         CALL    Q10SCR            ;Clear screen
         SUB     DX,DX             ;Set cursor 00,00
         CALL    Q20CURS
A10LOOP:
         CALL    B10INPT           ;Provide for input of name
         TEST    ACTNLEN,0FFH      ;No name? (indicates end)
         JZ      A90               ; yes - exit
         CALL    D10SCAS           ;Scan for asterisk
         CMP     AL,'*'            ;Found?
         JE      A10LOOP           ; yes - bypass
         CALL    E10RGHT           ;Right-adjust name
         CALL    F10CLNM           ;Clear name
         JMP     A10LOOP
A90:     RET
MAIN     ENDP
;                Prompt for input:
;                -----------------
B10INPT PROC
         MOV     AH,09
         LEA     DX,PROMPT         ;Display prompt
         INT     21H
         MOV     AH,0AH
         LEA     DX,NAMEPAR        ;Accept input
         INT     21H
         RET
B10INPT ENDP
;                Scan name for asterisk:
;                -----------------------
D10SCAS PROC
         CLD
         MOV     AL,'*'
         MOV     CX,30             ;Set 30-byte scan
         LEA     DI,NAMEFLD
         REPNE SCASB               ;Asterisk found?
         JE      D20               ; yes - exit
         MOV     AL,20H            ; no  - clear * in AL
D20:     RET
D10SCAS ENDP
```

Figure 11-2 Right-Adjusting on the Screen.

```
;               Right-adjust & display name:
;               ---------------------------
E10RGHT PROC
        STD
        SUB     CH,CH
        MOV     CL,ACTNLEN        ;Length in CX for REP
        LEA     SI,NAMEFLD        ;Calc rightmost
        ADD     SI,CX             ;  position
        DEC     SI                ;  of input name
        LEA     DI,NAMEDSP+30     ;Right pos'n of display name
        REP MOVSB                 ;Move string right to left
        MOV     DH,ROW
        MOV     DL,48
        CALL    Q20CURS           ;Set cursor
        MOV     AH,09
        LEA     DX,NAMEDSP        ;Display name
        INT     21H
        CMP     ROW,20            ;Bottom of screen?
        JAE     E20               ;  no --
        INC     ROW               ;  increment row
        JMP     E90
E20:
        MOV     AX,0601H          ;  yes --
        CALL    Q10SCR            ;  scroll &
        MOV     DH,ROW            ;  set cursor
        MOV     DL,00
        CALL    Q20CURS
E90:    RET
E10RGHT ENDP
;               Clear name:
;               ----------
F10CLNM PROC
        CLD
        MOV     AX,2020H
        MOV     CX,15             ;Clear 15 words
        LEA     DI,NAMEDSP
        REP STOSW
        RET
F10CLNM ENDP
;               Scroll screen:
;               -------------
Q10SCR  PROC                      ;AX set on entry
        MOV     BH,30             ;Color (07 for BW)
        MOV     CX,00
        MOV     DX,184FH
        INT     10H
        RET
Q10SCR  ENDP
;               Set cursor row/col:
;               ------------------
Q20CURS PROC                      ;DX set on entry
        MOV     AH,02
        SUB     BH,BH
        INT     10H
        RET
Q20CURS ENDP
CODESG  ENDS
        END     BEGIN
```

Figure 11-2 ***(continued)***

- Double-check initialization of the DI and SI registers. For example, MOVS implies operands DI,SI, whereas CMPS implies operands SI,DI.
- Initialize the CX register according to the number of bytes or number of words being processed.
- For normal processing, use REP with MOVS and STOS, and use a modified REP (REPE or REPNE) with CMPS and SCAS.
- Watch out for CMPSW and SCASW, which reverse the bytes in compared words.
- Where you want to process right to left, watch out for addressing beginning at the rightmost byte of a field. If the field is NAME1 and is ten bytes long, then for processing bytes, the load address for LEA is NAME+9. For processing words, however, the load address for LEA is NAME+8 because the string operation initially accesses NAME+8 and NAME+9.

QUESTIONS

11-1. The chapter gives the instructions equivalent to (a) MOVSB, (b) LODSB, and (c) STOSB, each with a REP prefix. For each case, provide equivalent code for processing words.

11-2. Key in, assemble, and link the program in Figure 11-1. Be sure to initialize the ES register. Change the MOVSB and MOVSW operations to move from right to left. Also, change H10SCAS to scan NAME1 for the word "mb." Use DEBUG to trace through the procedures and note the contents of the data segment and registers.

11-3. Assume the following data definitions:

```
DATASG  SEGMENT PARA
        CONAME  DB     'SPACE EXPLORERS INC.'
        PRLINE  DB     20 DUP(' ')
```

Use string operations to code the following related questions:
(a) Move CONAME to PRLINE left to right.
(b) Move CONAME to PRLINE right to left.
(c) Load the third and fourth bytes of CONAME into the AX.
(d) Store the AX beginning at PRLINE+5.
(e) Compare CONAME to PRLINE (they will be unequal).
(f) Scan CONAME for a blank character and if found move it to the BH.

11-4. Revise H10SCAS in Figure 11-1 so that the operation scans NAME1 for "er." A check of NAME1 discloses that the characters "er" do not appear as a word, as shown by the following: /As/se/mb/le/rs/. Two possible solutions are:
   (a) Use SCASW twice. The first SCASW begins at NAME1 and the second SCASW begins at NAME1+1.
   (b) Use SCASB and on finding an "e" compare the following byte for an "r."

11-5. Define a field containing hex 03, hex 04, hex 05, and hex B4. Duplicate this field 20 times and display the result.

CHAPTER 12

Arithmetic I: Processing Binary Data

Objective: To cover the requirements for addition, subtraction, multiplication, and division of binary data.

INTRODUCTION

Although we are accustomed to decimal (base 10) arithmetic, a microcomputer performs only binary (base 2) arithmetic. Further, because of the limitations of 16-bit registers, large values require special treatment.

This chapter covers addition, subtraction, multiplication, and division and the use of unsigned and signed data. The chapter also provides many examples and warnings of various pitfalls for the unwary traveler in the realm of the microprocessor. Chapter 13 proceeds with special requirements involved with converting between binary and ASCII data formats.

ADDITION AND SUBTRACTION

The instructions ADD and SUB process designated bytes and words that contain binary data. A computer performs subtraction by means of two's complement methodology: reverse the bits of operand 2, add 1, and add to operand 1. Other than this latter step, the processing of ADD and SUB are identical.

Figure 12-1 furnishes examples of ADD and SUB, which process a byte or a word. The procedure B10ADD uses ADD to process bytes and the procedure C10SUB uses SUB to process words. The examples depict all five possibilities:

Add/sub register to register

Add/sub memory to register

```
        page 60,132
TITLE   EXADD (COM)  Example ADD and SUB operations
CODESG  SEGMENT PARA 'Code'
        ASSUME  CS:CODESG,DS:CODESG,SS:CODESG
        ORG     100H
BEGIN:  JMP     SHORT MAIN
; -----------------------------------------------------
BYTEA   DB      64H             ;Data items
BYTEB   DB      40H
BYTEC   DB      16H
WORDA   DW      4000H
WORDB   DW      2000H
WORDC   DW      1000H
; -----------------------------------------------------
MAIN    PROC    NEAR            ;Main procedure:
        CALL    B10ADD          ;Call ADD routine
        CALL    C10SUB          ;Call SUB routine
        RET
MAIN    ENDP
;               Examples of ADD bytes:
;               ---------------------
B10ADD  PROC
        MOV     AL,BYTEA
        MOV     BL,BYTEB
        ADD     AL,BL           ;Reg-to-reg
        ADD     AL,BYTEC        ;Memory-to-reg
        ADD     BYTEA,BL        ;Register-to-memory
        ADD     BL,10H          ;Immediate-to-reg
        ADD     BYTEA,25H       ;Immediate-to-memory
        RET
B10ADD  ENDP
;               Examples of SUB words:
;               ---------------------
C10SUB  PROC
        MOV     AX,WORDA
        MOV     BX,WORDB
        SUB     AX,BX           ;Reg-from-reg
        SUB     AX,WORDC        ;Memory-from-reg
        SUB     WORDA,BX        ;Reg-from-memory
        SUB     BX,1000H        ;Immediate-from-reg
        SUB     WORDA,256H      ;Immediate-from-memory
        RET
C10SUB  ENDP

CODESG  ENDS
        END     BEGIN
```

Figure 12-1 Examples of ADD and SUB.

Add/sub register to memory

Add/sub immediate to register

Add/sub immediate to memory

Since there is no direct memory-to-memory operation, use a register to handle this situation. The following example adds WORDA to WORDB, both assumed to be DW:

```
MOV    AX,WORDA
ADD    AX,WORDB
MOV    WORDB,AX
```

Overflows

Be alert for overflows in arithmetic operations. A byte provides for only a sign bit plus seven data bits, from -128 to +127. Consequently, an arithmetic operation can easily exceed the capacity of a one-byte register. For example, a sum in the AL register that exceeds its capacity does not automatically overflow into the AH register. Assume that the AL register contains hex 60. The effect of

```
ADD    AL,20H
```

generates a sum of hex 80 in the AL. But the operation also sets the overflow flag to overflow and the sign flag to negative. The reason? Hex 80, or binary 10000000, is a negative number. Instead of +128, the sum is -128. Since the problem is that the AL register is too small, the sum should be in the AX register. In the following example, the CBW (Convert Byte to Word) instruction extends the hex 60 in the AL into hex 0060 in the AX by propagating the sign bit (0) through the AH. ADD generates the correct result in the AX: hex 0080, or +128:

```
CBW              ;Extend AL to AH
ADD    AX,20H    ;Add to AX
```

But even a full word allows only for a sign bit plus 15 data bits, from -32,768 to +32,767. Our next step examines how to handle numbers that exceed this maximum.

Multiword Addition

A maximum of +32,767 in a register restricts a computer's ability to handle arithmetic. Let's examine two ways to perform multiword arithmetic. The first is very simple and specific, the second more sophisticated and general.

In Figure 12-2, D10DWD illustrates a simple way of adding one pair of words (WORD1A and WORD1B) to a second pair (WORD2A and WORD2B) and storing the sum in a third pair (WORD3A and WORD3B) The operation first adds the rightmost words:

```
         page 60,132
TITLE    EXDBADD (COM)  Example ADD doublewords
CODESG   SEGMENT PARA 'Code'
         ASSUME  CS:CODESG,DS:CODESG,SS:CODESG
         ORG     100H
BEGIN:   JMP     SHORT MAIN
; -----------------------------------------------
WORD1A   DW      0123H            ;Data items
WORD1B   DW      0BC62H
WORD2A   DW      0012H
WORD2B   DW      553AH
WORD3A   DW      ?
WORD3B   DW      ?
; -----------------------------------------------
MAIN     PROC    NEAR             ;Main procedure
         CALL    D10DWD           ;Call 1st ADD
         CALL    E10DWD           ;Call 2nd ADD
         RET
MAIN     ENDP
;                Example of ADD doublewords:
;                --------------------------
D10DWD   PROC
         MOV     AX,WORD1B        ;Add rightmost word
         ADD     AX,WORD2B
         MOV     WORD3B,AX
         MOV     AX,WORD1A        ;Add leftmost word
         ADC     AX,WORD2A        ;  with carry
         MOV     WORD3A,AX
         RET
D10DWD   ENDP
;                Generalized add operation:
;                -------------------------
E10DWD   PROC
         CLC                      ;Clear carry flag
         MOV     CX,02            ;Set loop count
         LEA     SI,WORD1B        ;Leftmost word of DWORD1
         LEA     DI,WORD2B        ;Leftmost word of DWORD2
         LEA     BX,WORD3B        ;Leftmost word of sum
E20:
         MOV     AX,[SI]          ;Move word to AX
         ADC     AX,[DI]          ;Add with carry to AX
         MOV     [BX],AX          ;Store word
         DEC     SI               ;Adjust addresses for
         DEC     SI               ;  next word to left
         DEC     DI
         DEC     DI
         DEC     BX
         DEC     BX
         LOOP    E20              ;Repeat for next word
         RET
E10DWD   ENDP

CODESG   ENDS
         END     BEGIN
```

Figure 12-2 Multiword Addition.

```
WORD1B        BC62
WORD2B        553A
Total        1119C
```

The sum, hex 1119C, exceeds the capacity of the AX register. The overflow digit sets the carry flag to 1. Next, the example adds the word at the left, but in this case using ADC (Add With Carry) instead of ADD. The instruction adds the two values, and if the CF flag is already set, adds 1 to the sum:

```
WORD1A        0123
WORD2A        0012
Plus carry       1
Total         0136
```

By using DEBUG to trace the arithmetic, you can see the sum 0136 in the AX, and the reversed values 3601 stored in WORD3A and 9C11 in WORD3B.

In Figure 12-2, E10DWD provides an approach to adding values of any length. The example begins with the rightmost words of the fields to be added. The first loop adds the rightmost words and the second loop adds the leftmost words. Since the second loop is to process the words to the left, the addresses in the SI, DI, and BX registers must be decremented by 2. Two DEC instructions perform this operation for each register. Note that the instruction

SUB reg,02

would clear the carry flag and would cause an incorrect answer.

Because of the loop, there is only one add instruction, ADC. At the start, a CLC (Clear Carry) instruction ensures that the carry flag is initially clear. To make this method work, ensure that (1) the words are defined adjacent to each other, (2) processing is from right to left, and (3) the CX is initialized to the number of words to be added.

For multiword subtraction, the instruction equivalent to ADC is SBB (Subtract With Borrow). Simply replace ADC with SBB in the E10DWD procedure.

UNSIGNED AND SIGNED DATA

Some numeric fields are *unsigned*; examples include a customer number and a memory address. Some numeric fields are supposed to be always positive; examples include rate of pay, day of the month, and the value of pi. Other numeric fields are *signed* because the contents may be positive or negative. Examples include customer balance owing (which could be negative if overpaid) and an algebraic number.

For unsigned data, all bits are intended to be data bits. Instead of +32,767, a register could contain +65,535. For signed data, the leftmost bit is a sign bit. The ADD and SUB instructions do not distinguish between unsigned and signed data, and indeed simply add and subtract the bits. In the following addition of two binary numbers, the top number contains a 1-bit to the left. For unsigned data, the bits represent 249, but for signed data the bits represent -7:

	Unsigned	*Signed*
11111001	249	-7
00000010	2	+2
11111011	251	-5

The result of adding in binary is the same for both unsigned and signed. However, the bits in the unsigned field represent +251 whereas the bits in the signed field represent -5. In effect, the contents of a field mean whatever you want.

A *carry* occurs where there is a carry into the sign bit. An *overflow* occurs where a carry into the sign bit does not carry out, or a carry out has no carry in. Where a carry occurs on unsigned data, the result is invalid:

	Unsigned	*Signed*	*CF*	*OF*
11111100	252	-4		
00000101	5	+5		
00000001	1 (invalid)	1	1	0

Where an overflow occurs on signed data, the result is invalid:

	Unsigned	*Signed*	*CF*	*OF*
01111001	121	+121		
00001011	11	+11		
10000100	132	-124 (invalid)	0	1

And an add operation may cause both a carry and an overflow:

	Unsigned	*Signed*	*CF*	*OF*
11110110	246	-10		
10001001	137	-119		
01111111	127 (invalid)	+127 (invalid)	1	1

MULTIPLICATION

For multiplication, the MUL instruction handles unsigned data and the IMUL (Integer Multiplication) instruction handles signed data. As programmer, you have control over the format of data that you process and the responsibility of selecting the appropriate instruction. The two basic multiplication operations are the following:

Byte Times Byte. The multiplicand is in the AL register and the multiplier is a byte in memory or a register. After multiplication, the product is in the AX register. The operation ignores and erases any data that is already in the AH.

```
        | AH | AL     |          | AX      |
Before: |    | Mult'd |   After: | Product |
```

Word Times Word. The multiplicand is in the AX register and the multiplier is a word in memory or a register. After multiplication, the product is a doubleword that requires two registers: The high order (leftmost) portion is in the DX and the low order (rightmost) portion is in the AX. The operation ignores and erases any data that is already in the DX.

```
        | AX           |         | DX           | | AX          |
Before: | Multiplicand |  After: | High product | | Low product |
```

The operand of MUL and IMUL references only the multiplier. Assume the following instruction:

```
MUL   MULTR
```

If MULTR is defined as DB, the operation assumes AL times byte. If MULTR is defined as DW, the operation assumes AX times word. When the multiplier is in a register, the length of the register determines the type of operation, as shown next:

```
MUL CL  ;1-byte multiplier: multiplicand in AL, product in AX
MUL BX  ;1-word multiplier: multiplicand in AX, product in DX:AX
```

Unsigned Multiplication: MUL

The MUL (Multiplication) instruction multiplies unsigned data. In Figure 12-3, C10MUL gives three examples of multiplication: byte times byte, word times word, and word times byte. The first MUL example multiplies hex 80 (128) and hex 40 (64). The product in the AX is hex 2000 (8,192).

```
        page    60,132
TITLE   EXMULT (COM)  Example MUL & IMUL operations
CODESG  SEGMENT PARA 'Code'
        ASSUME  CS:CODESG,DS:CODESG,SS:CODESG
        ORG     100H
BEGIN:  JMP     SHORT MAIN
; ------------------------------------------------
BYTE1   DB      80H
BYTE2   DB      40H
WORD1   DW      8000H
WORD2   DW      2000H
; ------------------------------------------------
MAIN    PROC    NEAR              ;Main procedure
        CALL    C10MUL            ;Call MUL  routine
        CALL    D10IMUL           ;Call IMUL routine
        RET
MAIN    ENDP
;               Examples of MUL:
;               ---------------
C10MUL  PROC
        MOV     AL,BYTE1          ;Byte x byte
        MUL     BYTE2             ;  product in AX

        MOV     AX,WORD1          ;Word x word
        MUL     WORD2             ;  product in DX:AX

        MOV     AL,BYTE1          ;Byte x word
        SUB     AH,AH             ;  extend multiplicand in AH
        MUL     WORD1             ;  product in DX:AX
        RET
C10MUL  ENDP
;               Examples of IMUL:
;               ----------------
D10IMUL PROC
        MOV     AL,BYTE1          ;Byte x byte
        IMUL    BYTE2             ;  product in AX

        MOV     AX,WORD1          ;Word x word
        IMUL    WORD2             ;  product in DX:AX

        MOV     AL,BYTE1          ;Byte x word
        CBW                       ;  extend multiplicand in AH
        IMUL    WORD1             ;  product in DX:AX
        RET
D10IMUL ENDP

CODESG  ENDS
        END     BEGIN
```

Figure 12-3 Unsigned and Signed Multiplication.

The second MUL example generates hex 1000 0000 in the DX:AX registers.

The third MUL example involves word times byte and requires extending BYTE1 to a word. Since the values are supposed to be unsigned, the example assumes that leftmost bits in the AH register are to be zero. (The problem with using CBW is that the leftmost bit of the AL could be 0 or 1.) The product in the DX:AX is hex 0040 0000.

Signed Multiplication: IMUL

The IMUL (Integer Multiplication) instruction multiplies signed data. In Figure 12-3, D10IMUL uses the same three examples as C10MUL, replacing MUL with IMUL.

The first IMUL example multiplies hex 80 (a negative number) by hex 40 (a positive number). The product in the AX register is hex E000. Using the same data, MUL generated a product of hex 2000, so you can see the difference in using MUL and IMUL. MUL treats hex 80 as +128, whereas IMUL treats hex 80 as -128. The product of -128 times +64 is -8,192, which equals hex E000. (Try converting hex E000 to bits, reverse the bits, add 1, and add up the bit values.)

The second IMUL example multiplies hex 8000 (a negative value) times hex 2000 (a positive value). The product in the DX:AX is hex F000 0000 and is the negative of the product that MUL generated.

The third IMUL example extends BYTE1 to a word in the AX. Since the values are supposed to be signed, the example uses CBW to extend the leftmost sign bit into the AH register: hex 80 in the AL becomes hex FF80 in the AX. Since the multiplier, WORD1, is also negative, the product should be positive. And indeed it is: hex 0040 0000 in the DX:AX—the same result as MUL, which assumed it was multiplying two positive numbers.

In effect, if the multiplicand and multiplier have the same sign bit, MUL and IMUL generate the same result. But if the multiplicand and multiplier have different sign bits, MUL produces a positive product and IMUL produces a negative product.

You may find it worthwhile to use DEBUG to trace these examples.

Efficiency. If you multiply by a power of 2 (2, 4, 8, etc.), it is more efficient to shift left the required number of bits. A shift greater than 1 requires the shift value in the CL register. In the following examples, assume that the multiplicand is in the AL or AX:

```
Multiply by 2: SHL  AL,1
Multiply by 8: MOV  CL,3
               SHL  AX,CL
```

Multiword Multiplication

Conventional multiplication involves multiplying byte by byte or word by word. As already seen, the maximum signed value in a word is +32,767.

Multiplying larger values involves some additional steps. The approach is to multiply each word separately and to add each product to a sum. Consider the following multiplication in decimal format:

```
 1365
  ×12
 ----
 2730
 1365
 ----
16380
```

What if decimal arithmetic could multiply only two-digit numbers? You could multiply the 13 and the 65 by 12 separately, as follows:

```
 13      65
×12     ×12
---     ---
 26     130
 13      65
---     ---
156     780
```

Next, add the two products; but remember, since the 13 is at the 100s position, its product is actually 15600:

```
15600
 +780
-----
16380
```

An assembler program uses the same basic technique, except that the data consists of words (four digits) in hexadecimal format.

Doubleword by Word. E10XMUL in Figure 12-4 multiplies a doubleword by a word. The multiplicand, MULTCND, consists of two words contain-

```
TITLE    EXDWMUL - Multiplication of doublewords
CODESG   SEGMENT PARA 'Code'
         ASSUME  CS:CODESG,DS:CODESG,SS:CODESG
         ORG     100H
BEGIN:   JMP     SHORT MAIN
; -----------------------------------------------
MULTCND  DW      3206H            ;Data items
         DW      2521H
MULTPLR  DW      6400H
         DW      0A26H
PRODUCT  DW      0
         DW      0
         DW      0
         DW      0
```

Figure 12-4 Multiword Multiplication.

```
; ----------------------------------------------
MAIN     PROC    NEAR              ;Main procedure
         CALL    E10XMUL           ;Call 1st mult
         CALL    Z10ZERO           ;Clear product
         CALL    F10XMUL           ;Call 2nd mult
         RET
MAIN     ENDP
;                Doubleword x word:
;                -----------------
E10XMUL  PROC
         MOV     AX,MULTCND+2      ;Multiply right word
         MUL     MULTPLR           ; of multiplicand
         MOV     PRODUCT+4,AX      ;Store product
         MOV     PRODUCT+2,DX

         MOV     AX,MULTCND        ;Multiply left word
         MUL     MULTPLR           ; of multiplicand
         ADD     PRODUCT+2,AX      ;Add to stored product
         ADC     PRODUCT,DX
         RET
E10XMUL  ENDP
;                Doubleword x doubleword:
;                -----------------------
F10XMUL  PROC
         MOV     AX,MULTCND+2      ;Multiplicand word-2
         MUL     MULTPLR+2         ; x multiplier word-2
         MOV     PRODUCT+6,AX      ;Store product
         MOV     PRODUCT+4,DX

         MOV     AX,MULTCND+2      ;Multiplicand word-2
         MUL     MULTPLR           ; x multiplier word-1
         ADD     PRODUCT+4,AX      ;Add to stored product
         ADC     PRODUCT+2,DX
         ADC     PRODUCT,00        ;Add any carry

         MOV     AX,MULTCND        ;Multiplicand word-1
         MUL     MULTPLR+2         ; x multiplier word-2
         ADD     PRODUCT+4,AX      ;Add to stored product
         ADC     PRODUCT+2,DX
         ADC     PRODUCT,00        ;Add any carry
         MOV     AX,MULTCND        ;Multiplicand word-1
         MUL     MULTPLR           ; x multiplier word-1
         ADD     PRODUCT+2,AX      ;Add to product
         ADC     PRODUCT,DX
         RET
F10XMUL  ENDP
;                Clear product area:
;                ------------------
Z10ZERO  PROC
         MOV     PRODUCT,0000
         MOV     PRODUCT+2,0000
         MOV     PRODUCT+4,0000
         MOV     PRODUCT+6,0000
         RET
Z10ZERO  ENDP

CODESG   ENDS
         END     BEGIN
```

Figure 12-4 ***(continued)***

ing, respectively, hex 3206 and 2521. The reason for defining two DWs instead of a DD is to facilitate addressing for MOV instructions that move words to the AX register. The multiplier, MULTPLR, contains hex 6400. The field for the generated product, PRODUCT, provides for three words. The first MUL operation multiplies MULTPLR and the right word of MULTCND; the product is hex 0E80 E400, stored in PRODUCT+2 and PRODUCT+4. The second MUL multiplies MULTPLR and the left word of MULTCND; the product is hex 138A 5800. The routine adds the two products as follows:

```
Product 1:    0000 0E80 E400
Product 2:    138A 5800
              ______________
Total:        138A 6680 E400
```

Since the first ADD may cause a carry, the second add is ADC (Add with Carry). Because of the reversed storage method of the 8086/8088 processors, PRODUCT will actually contain 8A13 8066 00E4. The routine requires that the first word of PRODUCT initially contains zero.

Doubleword by Doubleword. Multiplying two doublewords involves the following four multiply operations:

Multiplicand		*Multiplier*
word 2	×	word 2
word 2	×	word 1
word 1	×	word 2
word 1	×	word 1

You add each product in the DX and AX to the appropriate word in the final product. In Figure 12-4, F10XMUL gives an example. MULTCND contains hex 3206 2521, MULTPLR contains hex 6400 0A26, and PRODUCT provides for four words.

Although the logic is similar to multiplying doubleword by word, this problem requires an additional feature. Following the ADD/ADC pair is another ADC that adds 0 to PRODUCT. The first ADC itself could cause a carry, which subsequent instructions would clear. The second ADC, therefore, adds 0 if there is no carry and adds 1 if there is a carry. The final ADD/ADC pair does not require an additional ADC; since PRODUCT is large enough for the final generated answer, there is no carry.

The final product is 138A 687C 8E5C CCE6, stored in PRODUCT with the bytes reversed. Try using DEBUG to trace this example.

SHIFTING THE DX:AX REGISTERS

The following routines could be useful for shifting a product in the DX:AX registers to the left or right. You could contrive a more efficient method, but these examples are generalized for any number of loops (and shifts) in the CX. Note that shifting off a 1-bit sets the carry flag.

```
                Shift Left 4 Bits
        MOV   CX,04            ;Init'ze 4 loops
C20:    SHL   DX,1             ;Shift DX
        SHL   AX,1             ;Shift AX
        ADC   DX,00            ;Add AX carry, if any
        LOOP  C20              ;Repeat
                Shift Right 4 Bits
        MOV   CX,04            ;Init'ze 4 loops
D20:    SHR   AX,1             ;Shift AX
        SHR   DX,1             ;Shift DX
        JNC   D30              ;If DX carry,
        OR    AH,10000000B     ;  insert 1-bit in AH
D30:    LOOP  D20              ;Repeat
```

Following is a more efficient method for left shifting that does not require looping. This example stores a shift factor in the CL register. The example is specific to a 4-bit shift but could be adapted to other shifts.

```
MOV    CL,04        ;Set shift
SHL    DX,CL        ;Shift DX left 4 bits
MOV    BL,AH        ;Store AH in BL
SHL    AX,CL        ;Shift AX left 4 bits
SHR    BL,CL        ;Shift BL right 4 bits
OR     DL,BL        ;Insert BL 4 bits in DL
```

DIVISION

For division, the DIV instruction handles unsigned data and the IDIV instruction handles signed data. You are responsible for selecting the appropriate instruction. The two basic divide operations are the following:

Byte Into Word. The dividend is in the AX and the divisor is a byte in a register or in memory. After division, the remainder is in the AH and the quotient is in the AL. Since a one-byte quotient is very small—a maximum of +255 (hex FF) if unsigned and +127 (hex 7F) if signed—this operation is of limited use.

```
          |    AX    |             |   AH    |   AL   |
*Before:* | Dividend |     *After:* | Rmnder | Quot't |
```

Word Into Doubleword. The dividend is in the DX:AX pair and the divisor is a word in a register or memory. After division, the remainder is in the DX and the quotient is in the AX. The quotient of one word allows a maximum of +32,767 (hex FFFF) if unsigned and +16,383 (hex 7FFF) if signed.

```
         |    DX     | |    AX    |          |   DX    | |    AX    |
Before:  | High div'd| | Low div'd|  After:  | Rmnder  | | Quotient |
```

The operand of DIV and IDIV references the divisor. Assume the following instruction:

```
DIV  DIVISOR
```

If DIVISOR is defined as DB, the operation assumes byte into word. If DIVISOR is defined as DW, the operation assumes word into doubleword.

If you divide 13 by 3, the result is $4\frac{1}{3}$. The quotient is 4 and the true remainder is 1. Note that a hand calculator (and a BASIC program for that matter) would deliver a quotient of 4.333. . . . The value consists of an integer portion (4) and a fractional portion (.333). The values 1/3 and .333 are fractions, whereas the 1 is a remainder.

Unsigned Division: DIV

The DIV instruction divides unsigned data. In Figure 12-5, D10DIV gives four examples: byte into word, byte into byte, word into doubleword, and word into word. The first DIV example divides hex 2000 (8092) by hex 80 (128). The remainder in the AH is 00 and the quotient in the AL is hex 40 (64).

The second DIV example requires extending BYTE1 to a word. Since the value is supposed to be unsigned, the example assumes that leftmost bits in the AH register are to be zero. The remainder in the AH is hex 12 and the quotient in the AL is hex 05.

The third DIV example generates a remainder in the DX of hex 1000 and a quotient in the AX of hex 0080.

The fourth DIV requires extending WORD1 to a doubleword in the DX register. After the divide, the remainder in the DX is hex 0000 and the quotient in the AX is hex 0002.

```
        page    60,132
TITLE   EXDIV (COM)  Examples of DIV & IDIV operations
CODESG  SEGMENT PARA 'Code'
        ASSUME  CS:CODESG,DS:CODESG,SS:CODESG
        ORG     100H
BEGIN:  JMP     SHORT MAIN
; -----------------------------------------------
BYTE1   DB      80H               ;Data items
BYTE3   DB      16H
WORD1   DW      2000H
WORD2   DW      0010H
WORD3   DW      1000H
; -----------------------------------------------
MAIN    PROC    NEAR              ;Main procedure
        CALL    D10DIV            ;Call DIV  routine
        CALL    E10IDIV           ;Call IDIV routine
        RET
MAIN    ENDP
;               Examples of DIV:
;               ----------------
D10DIV  PROC
        MOV     AX,WORD1          ;Word / byte
        DIV     BYTE1             ;  rmdr:quot in AH:AL
        MOV     AL,BYTE1          ;Byte / byte
        SUB     AH,AH             ;  extend dividend in AH
        DIV     BYTE3             ;  rmdr:quot in AH:AL

        MOV     DX,WORD2          ;Doubleword / word
        MOV     AX,WORD3          ;  dividend in DX:AX
        DIV     WORD1             ;  rmdr:quot in DX:AX
        MOV     AX,WORD1          ;Word / word
        SUB     DX,DX             ;  extend dividend in DX
        DIV     WORD3             ;  rmdr:quot in DX:AX
        RET
D10DIV  ENDP
;               Examples of IDIV:
;               -----------------
E10IDIV PROC
        MOV     AX,WORD1          ;Word / byte
        IDIV    BYTE1             ;  rmdr:quot in AH:AL
        MOV     AL,BYTE1          ;Byte / byte
        CBW                       ;  extend dividend in AH
        IDIV    BYTE3             ;  rmdr:quot in AH:AL

        MOV     DX,WORD2          ;Doubleword / word
        MOV     AX,WORD3          ;  dividend in DX:AX
        IDIV    WORD1             ;  rmdr:quot in DX:AX
        MOV     AX,WORD1          ;Word / word
        CWD                       ;  extend dividend in DX
        IDIV    WORD3             ;  rmdr:quot in DX:AX
        RET
E10IDIV ENDP

CODESG  ENDS
        END     BEGIN
```

Figure 12-5 Unsigned and Signed Division.

Signed Division: IDIV

The IDIV (Integer Divide) instruction divides signed data. In Figure 12-5, E10IDIV uses the same four examples as D10DIV, replacing DIV with IDIV. The first IDIV example divides hex 2000 (positive) by hex 80 (negative). The remainder in the AH is hex 00 and the quotient in the AL is hex C0 (–64). DIV using the same data caused a quotient of +64.

The results in hex of the remaining three IDIV examples are as follows:

IDIV Example	*Remainder*	*Quotient*
2	EE (-18)	FB (-5)
3	1000 (4096)	0080 (128)
4	0000	0002

Only Example 4 produces the same answer as DIV. In effect, if the dividend and divisor have the same sign bit, DIV and IDIV generate the same result. But if the dividend and divisor have different sign bits, DIV generates a positive quotient and IDIV generates a negative quotient.

You may find it worthwhile to use DEBUG to trace these examples.

Efficiency. If you divide by a power of 2 (2, 4, etc.), it is more efficient simply to shift right the required number of bits. In the following examples, assume that the dividend is in the AX:

```
Divide by 2: SHR  AX,1
Divide by 8: MOV  CL,3
             SHR  AX,CL
```

Overflows and Interrupts

It is remarkably easy to cause an overflow using DIV and especially IDIV. An interrupt occurs, and, at least with the system used for testing these programs, the results are unpredictable. The operation assumes that the quotient is significantly smaller than the original dividend. Dividing by zero always causes an interrupt. But dividing by 1 generates a quotient that is the same as the dividend and could easily cause an interrupt.

One rule you can apply is as follows: If the divisor is a *byte,* its contents must be less than the left byte (AH) of the dividend; if the divisor is a *word,* its contents must be less than the left word (DX) of the dividend. Here's an illustration using a divisor of 1, although other values could serve:

Divide operation:	Dividend:	Divisor:	Quotient:
Word by byte:	0123	01	(1)23
Doubleword by word:	0001 4026	0001	(1)4026

In both cases, the quotient exceeds its available space. You may be wise to include a test prior to a DIV or IDIV operation. In the first example following, assume that DIVBYTE is a one-byte divisor and that the dividend is already in the AX. In the second example, DIVWORD is a one-word divisor and the dividend is in the DX:AX.

Word by Byte	*Doubleword by Word*
`CMP AH,DIVBYTE`	`CMP AX,DIVWORD`
`JNB overflow-rtne`	`JNB overflow-rtne`
`DIV DIVBYTE`	`DIV DIVWORD`

For IDIV, the logic should account for the fact that either dividend or divisor could be negative. Since the absolute value of the divisor must be smaller, you could use the NEG instruction to temporarily set negative values to positive.

Division by Subtraction

If a quotient is too large for the divisor, you could perform successive subtraction. That is, subtract the divisor from the dividend, increment a quotient value by 1, and continue subtracting until the dividend is less than the divisor. In the following example, the dividend is in the AX, the divisor is in the BX, and the quotient is developed in the CX:

```
        SUB  CX,CX      ;Clear quotient
C20:    CMP  AX,BX      ;If dividend < divisor,
        JB   C30        ; then exit
        SUB  AX,BX      ;Subtract div'r from div'd
        INC  CX         ;Add 1 to quotient
        JMP  C20        ;Repeat
C30:    RET             ;Quotient in CX, rmdr in AX
```

At the end of the routine, the CX contains the quotient and the AX contains the remainder. The example is intentionally primitive to demonstrate the technique. If the quotient is in the DX:AX, make the following two additions:

1. At C20, compare AX to BX only if DX is zero.
2. After the SUB instruction, insert SBB DX,00.

Note: A very large quotient and a small divisor may cause thousands of loops.

REVERSING THE SIGN

The NEG (negate) instruction reverses the sign of a binary value, from positive to negative, and vice versa. In effect, NEG reverses the bits, just like NOT, and then adds 1. Examples:

```
NEG   AX
NEG   BL
NEG   BINAMT   (byte or word in memory)
```

Reversing the sign of a 32-bit (or larger) value involves more steps. Assume that the DX:AX pair contains a 32-bit binary number. Because NEG cannot act on the DX:AX pair concurrently, its use causes incorrect results. The following instructions make use of NOT:

```
NOT  DX    ;Flip bits
NOT  AX    ;Flip bits
ADD  AX,1  ;Add 1 to AX
ADC  DX,0  ;Add carry to DX
```

One minor problem remains: It is all very well to perform arithmetic on binary data that the program itself defines. However, data that enters a program from a disk file may already be in binary format, but data entered from a terminal is in ASCII format. Although ASCII data is fine for displaying and printing, it requires special adjusting for arithmetic. But that's a topic for the next chapter.

INTEL 8087 AND 80287 NUMERIC DATA PROCESSORS

The system board contains an empty socket reserved for an Intel 8087 (or 80287) Numeric Data Processor. The 8087 coprocessor operates in conjunction with an 8088, and the 80286 coprocessor operates in conjunction with an 80286. Each coprocessor has its own instruction set and floating-point hardware for performing such operations as exponentiation, logarithmic, and trigonometric functions. The coprocessor contains eight 80-bit floating-point registers that can represent numeric values up to 10 to the 400th power. Its mathematical processing is rated at about 100 times faster than a regular processor.

The processor requests a specific operation and delivers numeric data to the coprocessor, which performs the operation and returns the result. For assembling, use the /E or /R parameter, as MASM /R.

KEY POINTS TO REMEMBER

- Watch out especially when using one-byte accumulators. The maximum signed values are +127 and -128.
- For multiword addition, use ADC to account for any carry from a previous ADD. If the operation is performed in a loop, use CLC to initialize the carry flag to zero.
- Select MUL or DIV for unsigned data and IMUL and IDIV for signed data.
- For division, be especially careful of overflows. If a zero divisor is a possibility, be sure to test for the condition. Also, the divisor must be greater than the contents of the AH (if a byte) or the DX (if a word).
- For multiplying or dividing by powers of 2, use shifting for efficiency. For right shifts, use SHR for unsigned fields and SAR for signed fields. For left shifts, SHL and SAL act identically.
- Be alert for assembler defaults. For example, if FACTOR is defined as DB, then MUL FACTOR assumes the multiplicand is the AL, and DIV FACTOR assumes the dividend is the AX. If FACTOR is a DW, then MUL FACTOR assumes the multiplicand is the AX, and DIV FACTOR assumes the dividend is the DX:AX.

QUESTIONS

Questions refer to the following data:

```
DATAX    DW 0148H
         DW 2316H
DATAY    DW 0237H
         DW 4052H
```

12-1. Code the instructions to add the following: (a) The word DATAX to the word DATAY; (b) The doubleword beginning at DATAX to the doubleword at DATAY.

12-2. Explain the effect of the following instructions:

```
STC
MOV    BX,DATAX
ADC    BX,DATAY
```

12-3. Code the instructions to multiply (MUL) the following: (a) The contents of the word DATAX by the word DATAY; (b) The doubleword beginning at DATAX by the word DATAY.

12-4. Other than zero, what divisors cause an overflow error?

12-5. Code the instructions to divide (DIV) the following: (a) The contents of the word DATAX by 23; (b) The doubleword beginning at DATAX by the word DATAY.

12-6. Refer to the section "Shifting the DX:AX Registers." The second part contains a more efficient method of shifting left four bits. Revise the example for a right shift of four bits.

CHAPTER 13

Arithmetic II: Processing ASCII and BCD Data

Objective: To examine ASCII and BCD data formats and to cover conversions between these formats and binary.

INTRODUCTION

For efficiency, a computer performs arithmetic in binary format. As seen in Chapter 12, this format causes no major problems as long as the program itself defines the data. For many purposes, new data enters a program from a keyboard as ASCII characters, in base-10 format. Similarly, the display of answers on a screen is in ASCII. As an example, the number 23 in binary is 00010111, or hex 17; in ASCII, each character requires a full byte, and the ASCII number 25 internally is hex 3235.

The purpose of this chapter is to cover the techniques of converting ASCII data into binary in order to perform arithmetic, and converting the binary results back into ASCII for viewing. The program at the end of this chapter combines most of the material from Chapters 1 through 12.

If you have programmed in a high-level language such as BASIC or Pascal, you are used to the compiler accounting for decimal positions. However, a computer does not recognize a decimal point in an arithmetic field. In fact, since a binary value has no provision for inserting a decimal (or binal) point, you as programmer have to fully account for its placement.

ASCII FORMAT

Since data that you enter through a keyboard is in ASCII format, the representation in memory of an entered alphabetic value such as SAM is hex 53414D, and the representation of a numeric value such as 1234 is hex 31323334. For most purposes, the format of an alphabetic entry such as a person's name or an item description remains unchanged in a program. But performing arithmetic on the numeric value hex 31323334 involves special treatment.

Now, it is possible to perform arithmetic directly on ASCII numbers using the following assembler instructions:

AAA (ASCII Adjust for Addition)
AAD (ASCII Adjust for Division)
AAM (ASCII Adjust for Multiplication)
AAS (ASCII Adjust for Subtraction)

These instructions are coded without operands and automatically adjust the AX register. The adjust occurs because an ASCII value represents a so-called unpacked base-10 number whereas a computer performs base-2 arithmetic.

ASCII Addition

Consider the effect of adding the ASCII numbers 8 and 4:

```
hex 38
    34
hex 6C
```

The sum hex 6C is neither a correct ASCII nor binary value. However, ignore the leftmost 6 and add 6 to the rightmost hex C: hex C plus 6 = hex 12—the correct answer in terms of decimal numbers. Well, that's a little oversimplified, but it does indicate the way in which AAA performs an adjustment.

As an example, assume that the AX contains hex 0038 and the BX contains hex 0034. The 38 and 34 represent two ASCII bytes that are to be added. Addition and adjustment are as follows:

```
ADD  AL,BL ;Add hex 34 to 38
AAA        ;Adjust for ASCII add
```

The AAA instruction checks the rightmost hex digit (four bits) of the AL register. If the digit is between A and F or the AF flag is 1, the operation adds 6 to the AL register, adds 1 to the AH register, and sets the AF and CF flags to 1. In all cases, AAA clears to zero the leftmost hex digit of the AL. The result of the above in the AX is:

```
After the ADD:  006C
After the AAA:  0102
```

To restore the ASCII representation, simply insert 3s in the leftmost hex digits as follows:

```
OR    AX,3030H        ;Result now 3132
```

All that is very well for adding one-byte numbers. Addition of multibyte ASCII numbers requires a loop that processes from right to left (low order to high order) and accounts for carries. The example in Figure 13-1 adds two three-byte ASCII numbers into a four-byte sum. Note the following points:

- The routine uses ADC for addition because any add may cause a carry that should be added to the next (left) byte. A CLC initializes the CF flag to zero.

```
TITLE   ASCADD (COM)  Add ASCII numbers
CODESG  SEGMENT PARA 'Code'
        ASSUME  CS:CODESG,DS:CODESG,SS:CODESG
        ORG     100H
BEGIN:  JMP     SHORT MAIN
; -----------------------------------------
ASC1    DB      '578'           ;Data items
ASC2    DB      '694'
ASC3    DB      '0000'
; -----------------------------------------
MAIN    PROC    NEAR
        CLC
        LEA     SI,ASC1+2       ;Init'ze ASCII numbers
        LEA     DI,ASC2+2
        LEA     BX,ASC3+3
        MOV     CX,03           ;Init'ze 3 loops
A20:
        MOV     AH,00           ;Clear AH
        MOV     AL,[SI]         ;Load ASCII byte
        ADC     AL,[DI]         ;Add (with carry)
        AAA                     ;Adjust for ASCII
        MOV     [BX],AL         ;Store sum
        DEC     SI
        DEC     DI
        DEC     BX
        LOOP    A20             ;Loop 3 times
        MOV     [BX],AH         ;At end, store carry
        RET
MAIN    ENDP
CODESG  ENDS
        END     BEGIN
```

Figure 13-1 ASCII Addition.

- A MOV instruction clears the AH on each loop because each AAA may add 1 to the AH. ADC, however, accounts for any carry. Note that the use of XOR or SUB to clear the AH would change the CF flag.
- When looping is complete, the routine moves the AH (containing either 00 or 01) to the leftmost byte of the sum.
- At the end, the sum is 01020702. The routine did not use OR after AAA to insert leftmost 3s because OR sets the CF flag and changes the effect for the ADC instructions. One solution to save the flag settings is to push (PUSHF) the flags register, execute the OR, and then pop (POPF) the flags to restore them:

```
ADC     AL,[DI] ;Add with carry
AAA             ;Adjust for ASCII
PUSHF           ;Save flags
OR      AL,30H  ;Insert ASCII 3
POPF            ;Restore flags
MOV     [BX],AL ;Store sum
```

The instructions LAHF (Load AH with Flags) and SAHF (Store AH in Flag Register) could replace PUSHF and POPF, respectively. LAHF loads the AH with the SF, ZF, AF, PF, and CF flags; SAHF stores the AH contents back into the specific flags. This example, however, already uses the AH for arithmetic overflows. Another solution to insert ASCII 3s is to loop through the sum in memory and OR each byte with hex 30.

ASCII Subtraction

The AAS (ASCII Adjust for Subtraction) instruction works in a similar fashion to AAA. The AAS instruction checks the rightmost hex digit (four bits) of the AL. If the digit is between A and F or the AF flag is 1, the operation subtracts 6 from the AL, subtracts 1 from the AH, and sets the AF and CF flags. For all cases, AAS clears to zero the leftmost hex digit of the AL.

In the following two examples, assume that ASC1 contains hex 38 and ASC2 contains hex 34:

```
Example 1:                 AX     AF
     MOV  AL,ASC1        ;0038
     SUB  AL,ASC2        ;0004     0
     AAS                 ;0004     0
```

```
Example 2:                    AX     AF
        MOV   AL,ASC2      ;0034
        SUB   AL,ASC1      ;00FC      1
        AAS                ;FF06      1
```

In Example 1, AAS does not need to make an adjustment. In Example 2, since the rightmost digit is hex C, AAS subtracts 6 from the AL, 1 from the AH, and sets the AF and CF flags. The answer, which should be -4, is hex FF06, its 10s complement.

ASCII Multiplication

The AAM (ASCII Adjust for Multiplication) instruction corrects the result of multiplying ASCII data in the AX register. However, leftmost hex digits must first be cleared of 3s and accordingly the data is not true ASCII (the IBM manual uses the term *unpacked decimal*). For example, the ASCII number 31323334 as unpacked decimal is 01020304. Further, because the adjustment is only one byte at a time, you can multiply only one-byte fields and have to code the operation as a loop.

AAM divides the AL by 10 (hex 0A) and stores the quotient in the AH and the remainder in the AL. For example, suppose the AL contains hex 35 and the CL contains hex 39. The following multiplies the contents of the AL by the CL and converts the result to ASCII format:

```
                                                    AX:
AND    CL,0FH      ;Convert CL to 09
AND    AL,0FH      ;Convert AL to 05               0005
MUL    CL          ;Mult AL by CL                  002D
AAM                ;Convert to unpacked dec        0405
OR     AX,3030H    ;Convert to ASCII               3435
```

The MUL operation generates 45 (hex 002D) in the AX. AAM then divides this value by 10, generating a quotient of 04 in the AH and a remainder of 05 in the AL. The OR instruction then converts the unpacked decimal value to ASCII format.

Figure 13-2 depicts multiplying a four-byte multiplicand by a one-byte multiplier. Since AAM can accommodate only one-byte operations, the routine steps through the multiplicand one byte at a time, from right to left. The final product is 0108090105.

If a multiplier is greater than one byte, you have to provide for yet another loop that steps through the multiplier. It may be simpler to convert the ASCII data to binary format—see the later section, "Conversion of ASCII to Binary Format."

```
TITLE   ASCMUL (COM)  Multiply ASCII numbers
CODESG  SEGMENT PARA 'Code'
        ASSUME  CS:CODESG,DS:CODESG,SS:CODESG
        ORG     100H
BEGIN:  JMP     MAIN
;---------------------------------------------
MULTCND DB      '3783'            ;Data items
MULTPLR DB      '5'
PRODUCT DB      5 DUP(0)
;---------------------------------------------
MAIN    PROC    NEAR
        MOV     CX,04             ;Init'ze 4 loops
        LEA     SI,MULTCND+3
        LEA     DI,PRODUCT+4
        AND     MULTPLR,0FH       ;Clear ASCII 3
A20:
        MOV     AL,[SI]           ;Load ASCII char (or LODSB)
        AND     AL,0FH            ;Clear ASCII 3
        MUL     MULTPLR           ;Multiply
        AAM                       ;Adjust for ASCII
        ADD     AL,[DI]           ;Add to
        AAA                       ;  stored
        MOV     [DI],AL           ;  product
        DEC     DI
        MOV     [DI],AH           ;Store product carry
        DEC     SI
        LOOP    A20               ;Loop 4 times
        RET
MAIN    ENDP
CODESG  ENDS
        END     BEGIN
```

Figure 13-2 ASCII Multiplication.

ASCII Division

The AAD (ASCII Adjust for Division) instruction provides a correction of an ASCII dividend prior to dividing. However, you must first clear the leftmost 3s from the ASCII bytes to create "unpacked decimal." AAD allows for a two-byte dividend in the AX. Assume that the AX contains the ASCII value 3238 and the divisor, 37, is in the CL. The following performs the adjustment and the division:

```
                                         AX
AND  CL,0FH       ;Convert to unpacked
AND  AX,0F0FH     ;Convert to unpacked   0208
AAD               ;Convert to binary     001C
DIV  CL           ;Divide by 7           0004
```

The AAD operation multiplies the AH by 10 (hex 0A), adds the product 20 (hex 14) to the AL, and clears the AH. The result, 001C, is the hex representation of decimal 28. The divisor can be only a single byte containing 01 to 09.

Figure 13-3 allows for dividing a one-byte divisor into a four-byte dividend. The routine steps through the dividend from left to right. The remainders stay in the AH register so that AAD will adjust it in the AL. The final quotient is 00090204 and the remainder in the AH is 02.

If the divisor is greater than one byte, you have to provide for yet another loop to step through the divisor. Better yet, see the later section, "Conversion of ASCII to Binary Format."

BINARY CODED DECIMAL (BCD) FORMAT

In the preceding example of ASCII division, the quotient was 00090204. If you were to compress this value keeping only the right digit of each byte, the value would be 0924. This latter value is known as *binary coded decimal* (BCD) format (also known as *packed*) and contains only the decimal digits 0 through 9. The BCD length is one-half the ASCII length.

```
TITLE   ASCDIV (COM)  Divide ASCII numbers
CODESG  SEGMENT PARA 'Code'
        ASSUME  CS:CODESG,DS:CODESG,SS:CODESG
        ORG     100H
BEGIN:  JMP     SHORT MAIN
;-----------------------------------------------
DIVDND  DB      '3698'              ;Data items
DIVSOR  DB      '4'
QUOTNT  DB      4 DUP(0)
;-----------------------------------------------
MAIN    PROC    NEAR
        MOV     CX,04               ;Init'ze 4 loops
        SUB     AH,AH               ;Clear left byte of dividend
        AND     DIVSOR,0FH          ;Clear divisor of ASCII 3
        LEA     SI,DIVDND
        LEA     DI,QUOTNT
A20:
        MOV     AL,[SI]             ;Load ASCII byte (or LODSB)
        AND     AL,0FH              ;Clear ASCII 3
        AAD                         ;Adjust for divide
        DIV     DIVSOR              ;Divide
        MOV     [DI],AL             ;Store quotient
        INC     SI
        INC     DI
        LOOP    A20                 ;Loop 4 times
        RET
MAIN    ENDP
CODESG  ENDS
        END     BEGIN
```

Figure 13-3 ASCII Division.

Note, however, that the decimal number 0924 is in base 10; converted to base 16 (hexadecimal) it would appear as hex 039C.

You can perform addition and subtraction on BCD data. For this purpose, there are two adjustment instructions:

```
DAA (Decimal Adjustment for Addition)
DAS (Decimal Adjustment for Subtraction)
```

Once again, you have to process the fields one byte at a time. The example program in Figure 13-4 converts two ASCII numbers to BCD format and adds them. The procedure B10CONV converts ASCII to BCD. Processing, which is from right to left, could just as easily be left to right. Also, processing words is easier than bytes because you need two ASCII bytes to generate one BCD byte. The use of words requires an even number of bytes in the ASCII field.

The procedure C10ADD adds the BCD numbers. The final total is 127263.

CONVERSION OF ASCII TO BINARY FORMAT

Performing arithmetic in ASCII or BCD formats is suitable only for short fields. For most arithmetic purposes, it is more practical to convert into binary format. In fact, it is easier to convert from ASCII directly to binary rather than convert from ASCII to BCD to binary.

The conversion method is based on the fact that an ASCII number is in base 10 and the computer performs arithmetic only in base 2. The procedure is as follows:

1. Start with the rightmost byte of the ASCII number and process from right to left.
2. Strip the 3s from the left hex digit of the ASCII bytes.
3. Multiply the ASCII digits progressively by 1, then 10, then 100 (hex 1, A, 64), and so forth, and sum the products.

For example, assume conversion of the ASCII number 1234:

	Decimal	*Hexadecimal*
4 × 1 =	4	4
3 × 10 =	30	1E
2 × 100 =	200	C8
1 × 1000 =	1000	3E8
Total:		04D2

```
TITLE    BCDADD (COM)  Convert ASCII nos to BCD and add
CODESG   SEGMENT PARA 'Code'
         ASSUME  CS:CODESG,DS:CODESG,SS:CODESG
         ORG     100H
BEGIN:   JMP     SHORT MAIN
;-------------------------------------------------
ASC1     DB      '057836'
ASC2     DB      '069427'
BCD1     DB      '000'
BCD2     DB      '000'
BCD3     DB      4 DUP(0)
;-------------------------------------------------
MAIN     PROC    NEAR
         LEA     SI,ASC1+4        ;Init'ze for ASC1
         LEA     DI,BCD1+2
         CALL    B10CONV          ;Call convert routine
         LEA     SI,ASC2+4        ;Init'ze for ASC2
         LEA     DI,BCD2+2
         CALL    B10CONV          ;Call convert routine
         CALL    C10ADD           ;Call add routine
         RET
MAIN     ENDP
;                Convert ASCII to BCD:
;                --------------------
B10CONV  PROC
         MOV     CL,04            ;Shift factor
         MOV     DX,03            ;No. of words to convert
B20:
         MOV     AX,[SI]          ;Get ASCII pair (or LODSW)
         XCHG    AH,AL
         SHL     AL,CL            ;Shift off
         SHL     AX,CL            ;  ASCII 3's
         MOV     [DI],AH          ;Store BCD digits
         DEC     SI
         DEC     SI
         DEC     DI
         DEC     DX
         JNZ     B20
         RET
B10CONV  ENDP
;                Add BCD numbers:
;                ---------------
C10ADD   PROC
         XOR     AH,AH            ;Clear AH
         LEA     SI,BCD1+2        ;Init'ze
         LEA     DI,BCD2+2        ; BCD
         LEA     BX,BCD3+3        ; addresses
         MOV     CX,03            ;3 byte fields
         CLC
C20:
         MOV     AL,[SI]          ;Get BCD1 (or LODSB)
         ADC     AL,[DI]          ;Add BCD2
         DAA                      ;Decimal adjust
         MOV     [BX],AL          ;Store in BCD3
         DEC     SI
         DEC     DI
         DEC     BX
         LOOP    C20              ;Loop 3 times
         RET
C10ADD   ENDP
CODESG   ENDS
         END     BEGIN
```

Figure 13-4 BCD Conversion and Arithmetic.

Try checking that hex 04D2 really equals decimal 1234. In Figure 13-5, B10ASBI converts ASCII number 1234 to binary. The example assumes that the length of the ASCII number, 4, is stored in ASCLEN. For initialization, the address of the ASCII field, ASCVAL-1, is in the SI register and the length is in the BX. The instruction at B20 that moves the ASCII byte to the AL is

```
MOV  AL,[SI+BX]
```

which uses the address of ASCVAL–1 plus the contents of the BX (4), or ASCVAL+3 (initially the rightmost byte of ASCVAL). Each iteration of the loop decrements BX by 1 and references the next byte to the left. For this addressing you can use BX but not CX, and consequently you cannot use the LOOP instruction. Also, each iteration multiplies MULT10 by 10 giving a multiplier of 1, 10, 100, and so forth. The routine is coded for clarity; for efficiency, the multiplier could be stored in the SI or DI register.

CONVERSION OF BINARY TO ASCII FORMAT

In order to print or display an arithmetic result, you have to convert it into ASCII format. The operation involves reversing the previous step: Instead of multiplying, simply divide the binary number by 10 (hex 0A) successively until the result is less than 10. The remainders, which can be only 0 through 9, generate the ASCII number. As an example, let's convert hex 4D2 back into decimal format:

	Quotient	*Remainder*
A | 4D2	7B	4
A | 7B	C	3
A | C	1	2

Since the quotient, 1, is now less than hex A, the operation is complete. The remainders along with the last quotient form the ASCII result, from right to left, as 1234. All that remains is to store these digits in memory with ASCII 3s, as 31323334.

In Figure 13-5, C10BIAS converts binary hex 4D2 (as calculated in B10ASBI) to ASCII 1234. You may find it useful if not downright entertaining to reproduce this program and trace its execution step by step.

```
TITLE   EXCONV (COM)  Conversion of ASCII & binary formats
CODESG  SEGMENT PARA 'Code'
        ASSUME  CS:CODESG,DS:CODESG,SS:CODESG
        ORG     100H
BEGIN:  JMP     SHORT MAIN
; ------------------------------------------------------
ASCVAL  DB      '1234'          ;Data items
BINVAL  DW      0
ASCLEN  DW      4
MULT10  DW      1
; ------------------------------------------------------
MAIN    PROC    NEAR            ;Main procedure
        CALL    B10ASBI         ;Call convert ASCII
        CALL    C10BIAS         ;Call convert binary
        RET
MAIN    ENDP
;               Convert ASCII to binary:
;               ----------------------
B10ASBI PROC
        MOV     CX,10           ;Mult factor
        LEA     SI,ASCVAL-1     ;Address of ASCVAL
        MOV     BX,ASCLEN       ;Length of ASCVAL
B20:
        MOV     AL,[SI+BX]      ;Select ASCII char.
        AND     AX,000FH        ;Remove 3-zone
        MUL     MULT10          ;Multiply by 10 factor
        ADD     BINVAL,AX       ;Add to binary
        MOV     AX,MULT10       ;Calculate next
        MUL     CX              ;  10 factor
        MOV     MULT10,AX
        DEC     BX              ;Last ASCII char?
        JNZ     B20             ;  no - continue
        RET
B10ASBI ENDP
;               Convert binary to ASCII:
;               ----------------------
C10BIAS PROC
        MOV     CX,0010         ;Divide factor
        LEA     SI,ASCVAL+3     ;Address of ASCVAL
        MOV     AX,BINVAL       ;Get binary field
C20:
        CMP     AX,0010         ;Value < 10?
        JB      C30             ;  yes - exit
        XOR     DX,DX           ;Clear upper quotient
        DIV     CX              ;Divide by 10
        OR      DL,30H
        MOV     [SI],DL         ;Store ASCII char.
        DEC     SI
        JMP     C20
C30:
        OR      AL,30H          ;Store last quotient
        MOV     [SI],AL         ;  as ASCII char.
        RET
C10BIAS ENDP

CODESG  ENDS
        END     BEGIN
```

Figure 13-5 Conversion of ASCII and Binary Formats.

SHIFTING AND ROUNDING

Consider rounding a product to two decimal places. If the product is 12.345, then add 5 to the unwanted decimal position and shift right one digit as follows:

Product:	12.345
Add 5:	+5
Rounded product:	12.350 = 12.35

If the product is 12.3455, add 50 and shift two digits, and if the product is 12.34555, add 500 and shift three digits:

12.3455	12.34555
+50	+500
12.3505 = 12.35	12.35055 = 12.35

Further, a number with six decimal places requires adding 5000 and shifting four digits, and so forth. Now, since data representation on the computer is binary, 12.345 appears as hex 3039. Adding 5 to 3039 gives 303E, or 12350 in decimal format. So far, so good. But *shifting* one binary digit results in hex 181F, or 6175—indeed, the shift simply halves the value. What we require is a shift that is *equivalent* to shifting right one decimal digit. You can accomplish this shift by dividing by 10, or hex A:

Hex 303E divided by hex A = 4D3, or decimal 1235

Conversion of hex 4D3 to an ASCII number gives 1235. Now just insert a decimal point in the correct position, 12.35, and you can display a rounded and shifted value.

In this fashion you can round and shift any binary number. For three decimal places, add 5 and divide by 10; for four decimal places, add 50 and divide by 100. Perhaps you have noticed a pattern: The rounding factor (5, 50, 500, etc.) is always one-half of the value of the shift factor (10, 100, 1000, etc.).

Of course, a "decimal point" in a binary number is implied and is not normally present.

PROGRAM: CONVERTING HOURS AND RATE FOR CALCULATING WAGE

The program in Figure 13-6 allows users to enter hours worked and rate of pay for employees and displays the calculated wage. For brevity, the program omits some error checking. The procedures are as follows:

B10INPT Accepts hours and rate of pay from the terminal. These values may contain a decimal point.

D10HOUR Initializes conversion of ASCII hours to binary.

E10RATE Initializes conversion of ASCII rate to binary.

F10MULT Performs the multiplication, rounding, and shifting. A wage with zero, one, or two decimal places does not require rounding or shifting. A limitation of this procedure is that it allows up to only six decimal places in wage, although that is certainly more than would normally be required.

G10WAGE Inserts the decimal point, determines the right position to begin storing ASCII characters, and converts the binary wage to ASCII.

K10DISP Clears leading zeros to blank and displays the wage.

M10ASBI Converts ASCII to binary (a common routine for hours and for rate) and determines the number of decimal places in the entered value.

```
TITLE   SCREMP (EXE)  Enter hours & rate, display wage
; -------------------------------------------------------
STACKSG SEGMENT PARA STACK 'Stack'
        DW      32 DUP(?)
STACKSG ENDS
; -------------------------------------------------------
DATASG  SEGMENT PARA 'Data'
HRSPAR  LABEL   BYTE                ;Hours parameter list:
MAXHLEN DB      6                   ;----- --------- ----
ACTHLEN DB      ?
HRSFLD  DB      6 DUP(?)

RATEPAR LABEL   BYTE                ;Rate parameter list:
MAXRLEN DB      6                   ;---- --------- ----
ACTRLEN DB      ?
RATEFLD DB      6 DUP(?)

MESSG1  DB      'Hours worked? ','$'
MESSG2  DB      'Rate of pay?  ','$'
MESSG3  DB      'Wage = '
ASCWAGE DB      10 DUP(30H), 13, 10, '$'
ADJUST  DW      ?
ASCHRS  DB      0
ASCRATE DB      0
BINVAL  DW      00
BINHRS  DW      00
BINRATE DW      00
COL     DB      00
DECIND  DB      00
MULT10  DW      01
NODEC   DW      00
ROW     DB      00
SHIFT   DW      ?
TENWD   DW      10
DATASG  ENDS
; -------------------------------------------------------
```

Figure 13-6 Displaying Employee Wages.

```
CODESG  SEGMENT PARA 'Code'
BEGIN   PROC    FAR
        ASSUME  CS:CODESG,DS:DATASG,SS:STACKSG,ES:DATASG
        PUSH    DS
        SUB     AX,AX
        PUSH    AX
        MOV     AX,DATASG
        MOV     DS,AX
        MOV     ES,AX
        MOV     AX,0600H
        CALL    Q10SCR          ;Clear screen
        CALL    Q20CURS         ;Set cursor
A20LOOP:
        CALL    B10INPT         ;Accept hours & rate
        CMP     ACTHLEN,00      ;End of input?
        JE      A30
        CALL    D10HOUR         ;Convert hours to binary
        CALL    E10RATE         ;Convert rate to binary
        CALL    F10MULT         ;Calc wage, round
        CALL    G10WAGE         ;Convert wage to ASCII
        CALL    K10DISP         ;Display wage
        JMP     A20LOOP
A30:
        MOV     AX,0600H
        CALL    Q10SCR          ;Clear screen
        RET                     ;Exit program
BEGIN   ENDP
;               Input hours & rate:
;               ------------------
B10INPT PROC
        LEA     DX,MESSG1       ;Prompt for hours
        MOV     AH,09
        INT     21H
        LEA     DX,HRSPAR       ;Accept hours
        MOV     AH,0AH
        INT     21H
        CMP     ACTHLEN,00      ;No hours? (indicates end)
        JNE     B20
        RET                     ;If so, return to A20LOOP
B20:
        MOV     COL,25          ;Set column
        CALL    Q20CURS
        LEA     DX,MESSG2       ;Prompt for rate
        MOV     AH,09
        INT     21H
        LEA     DX,RATEPAR      ;Accept rate
        MOV     AH,0AH
        INT     21H
        RET
B10INPT ENDP
;               Process hours:
;               -------------
D10HOUR PROC
        MOV     NODEC,00
        MOV     CL,ACTHLEN
        SUB     CH,CH
        LEA     SI,HRSFLD-1     ;Set right pos'n
        ADD     SI,CX           ;  of hours
```

Figure 13-6 (Continued)

```
        CALL    M10ASBI         ;Convert to binary
        MOV     AX,BINVAL
        MOV     BINHRS,AX
        RET
D10HOUR ENDP
;               Process rate:
;               ------------
E10RATE PROC
        MOV     CL,ACTRLEN
        SUB     CH,CH
        LEA     SI,RATEFLD-1    ;Set right pos'n
        ADD     SI,CX           ; of rate
        CALL    M10ASBI         ;Convert to binary
        MOV     AX,BINVAL
        MOV     BINRATE,AX
        RET
E10RATE ENDP
;               Multiply, round, & shift:
;               ------------------------
F10MULT PROC
        MOV     CX,05
        LEA     DI,ASCWAGE      ;Set ASCII wage
        MOV     AX,3030H        ; to 30's
        CLD
        REP STOSW

        MOV     SHIFT,10
        MOV     ADJUST,00
        MOV     CX,NODEC
        CMP     CL,06           ;If more than 6
        JA      F40             ; decimals, error
        DEC     CX
        DEC     CX
        JLE     F30             ;Bypass if 0, 1, 2 decs
        MOV     NODEC,02
        MOV     AX,01
F20:
        MUL     TENWD           ;Calculate shift factor
        LOOP    F20

        MOV     SHIFT,AX
        SHR     AX,1            ;Calculate round value
        MOV     ADJUST,AX
F30:
        MOV     AX,BINHRS
        MUL     BINRATE         ;Calculate wage
        ADD     AX,ADJUST       ;Round wage
        ADC     DX,00
        CMP     DX,SHIFT        ;Product too large
        JB      F50             ; for DIV?
F40:
        SUB     AX,AX
        JMP     F70
F50:
        CMP     ADJUST,00       ;No shift required?
        JZ      F80
        DIV     SHIFT           ;Shift wage
F70:    SUB     DX,DX           ;Clear remainder
```

Figure 13-6 (Continued)

```
F80:     RET
F10MULT ENDP
;                 Convert to ASCII:
;                 ----------------
G10WAGE PROC
         LEA      SI,ASCWAGE+7      ;Set decimal pt.
         MOV      BYTE PTR[SI],'.'
         ADD      SI,NODEC          ;Set right start pos'n
G30:
         CMP      BYTE PTR[SI],'.'
         JNE      G35               ;Bypass if at dec pos'n
         DEC      SI
G35:
         CMP      DX,00             ;If DX:AX < 10,
         JNZ      G40
         CMP      AX,0010           ; operation finished
         JB       G50
G40:
         DIV      TENWD             ;Remainder is ASCII digit
         OR       DL,30H
         MOV      [SI],DL           ;Store ASCII character
         DEC      SI
         SUB      DX,DX             ;Clear remainder
         JMP      G30
G50:
         OR       AL,30H            ;Store last ASCII
         MOV      [SI],AL           ; character
         RET
G10WAGE ENDP
;                 Display wage:
;                 ------------
K10DISP PROC
         MOV      COL,50            ;Set column
         CALL     Q20CURS
         MOV      CX,09
         LEA      SI,ASCWAGE
K20:                                ;Clear leading zeros
         CMP      BYTE PTR[SI],30H
         JNE      K30               ; to blanks
         MOV      BYTE PTR[SI],20H
         INC      SI
         LOOP     K20
K30:
         LEA      DX,MESSG3         ;Display
         MOV      AH,09
         INT      21H
         CMP      ROW,20            ;Bottom of screen?
         JAE      K80
         INC      ROW               ; no -- increment row
         JMP      K90
K80:
         MOV      AX,0601H          ; yes --
         CALL     Q10SCR            ; scroll &
         MOV      COL,00            ; set cursor
         CALL     Q20CURS
K90:     RET
K10DISP ENDP
;                 Convert ASCII to binary:
```

Figure 13-6 (Continued)

```
;               -----------------------
M10ASBI PROC
        MOV     MULT10,0001
        MOV     BINVAL,00
        MOV     DECIND,00
        SUB     BX,BX
M20:
        MOV     AL,[SI]          ;Get ASCII character
        CMP     AL,'.'           ;Bypass if dec pt.
        JNE     M40
        MOV     DECIND,01
        JMP     M90
M40:
        AND     AX,000FH
        MUL     MULT10           ;Multiply by factor
        ADD     BINVAL,AX        ;Add to binary
        MOV     AX,MULT10        ;Calculate next
        MUL     TENWD            ;  factor x 10
        MOV     MULT10,AX
        CMP     DECIND,00        ;Reached decimal pt?
        JNZ     M90
        INC     BX               ;  yes - add to count
M90:
        DEC     SI
        LOOP    M20

        CMP     DECIND,00        ;End of loop
        JZ      M100             ;Any decimal pt?
        ADD     NODEC,BX         ;  yes - add to total
M100:   RET
M10ASBI ENDP
;               Scroll screen:
;               -------------
Q10SCR  PROC    NEAR             ;AX set on entry
        MOV     BH,30            ;Color (07 for BW)
        SUB     CX,CX
        MOV     DX,184FH
        INT     10H
        RET
Q10SCR  ENDP
;               Set cursor:
;               ----------
Q20CURS PROC    NEAR
        MOV     AH,02
        SUB     BH,BH
        MOV     DH,ROW
        MOV     DL,COL
        INT     10H
        RET
Q20CURS ENDP

CODESG  ENDS
        END     BEGIN
```

Figure 13-6 (Continued)

Limitations. One limitation in the program in Figure 13-6 is that it allows only a total of six decimal places. Another limitation is the magnitude of the wage itself and the fact that shifting involves dividing by a multiple of 10 and converting to ASCII involves dividing by 10. If hours and rate contain a total that exceeds six decimal places or if the wage exceeds about 655,350, the program clears the wage to zero. In practice, a program would print a warning message or would contain subroutines to overcome these limitations.

Error Checking. A program designed for users other than the programmer not only should produce warning messages, but also should validate hours and rate. The only valid characters are numbers 0 through 9 and one decimal point. For any other character, the program should display a message and return to the input prompt. A useful instruction for validating is XLAT, which Chapter 14 covers.

Test your program thoroughly for all possible conditions: zero value, extreme high and low values, and negative values.

Negative Values

Some applications involve negative amounts, especially for reversing and correcting entries. You could allow a minus sign following a value, such as 12.34–, or preceding the value, such as –12.34. The program could check for a minus sign during conversion to binary. You may want to leave the binary number as positive and simply set an indicator to record the fact that the amount is negative. When the arithmetic is complete, the program, if required, can insert a minus sign in the ASCII field.

If you want the binary number to be negative, convert the ASCII input to binary as usual. See "Reversing the Sign" in Chapter 12 for changing the sign of a binary field. And watch out for using IMUL and IDIV to handle signed data. For rounding, subtract 5 instead of add 5.

KEY POINTS TO REMEMBER

- An ASCII field requires one byte for each character. If the field contains only digits 0 through 9, then converting the high-order ASCII 3s to 0s causes the field to contain "unpacked decimal." Compressing the digits to two digits per byte causes the field to contain "packed decimal."
- After an ASCII add, adjust the answer with AAA; after an ASCII subtract adjust the answer with AAS.

- Before an ASCII multiplication, convert the multiplicand and multiplier to "unpacked decimal" by clearing the leftmost hex 3s. After the multiplication adjust the product with AAM.
- Before an ASCII divide, (1) convert the dividend and divisor to "unpacked decimal" by clearing the leftmost hex 3s, and (2) adjust the dividend with AAD.
- For most arithmetic purposes, convert ASCII numbers to binary. When converting from ASCII to binary format, check that the ASCII characters are valid: 30 though 39, decimal point, and possibly a minus sign.

QUESTIONS

13-1. Assume that the AX contains ASCII 9 and the BX contains ASCII 7. Explain the exact results of the following unrelated operations:

```
(a) ADD  AX,33H      (b) ADD  AX,BX
    AAA                  AAA
(c) SUB  AX,BX       (d) SUB  AX,0DH
    AAS                  AAS
```

13-2. An unpacked decimal field named UNPAK contains hex 01040705. Code a loop that causes its contents to be proper ASCII 31343735.

13-3. A field named ASCA contains the ASCII value 313733 and another field named ASCB contains 35. Code the instructions to multiply the ASCII numbers and to store the product in ASCPRO.

13-4. Use the same field as Question 13-3 to divide ASCA by ASCB and store the quotient in ASCQUO.

13-5. Provide the manual calculations for the following: (a) Convert ASCII 46328 to binary and show in hex; (b) Convert the hex value back to ASCII.

13-6. Code and run a program that determines the computer's memory size (INT 12H—see Chapter 2), converts the size to ASCII format, and displays it on the screen as follows:

Memory size is nnn bytes

CHAPTER 14

Table Processing

Objective: To cover the requirements for defining tables, for performing table searches, and for sorting table entries.

INTRODUCTION

Many program applications require *tables* of such data as names, descriptions, quantities, and prices. The definition and use of tables involves only one new assembler instruction, XLAT. Otherwise, it is simply a matter of technique and of applying what you have already learned.

This chapter begins by defining some conventional tables. Techniques for table searching are subject to the way in which tables are defined, and many variations of table definitions and search are possible.

DEFINING TABLES

To facilitate table searching, most tables are defined methodically, with each entry the same format (character or numeric), the same length, and in either ascending or descending order.

A table that you have been using throughout this book is the definition of the stack, which in the following is a table of 64 uninitialized words:

```
STACK   DW    64 DUP(?)
```

The following two tables initialize character and numeric values, respectively:

```
MONTAB  DB  'JAN', 'FEB', 'MAR', ..., 'DEC'
COSTAB  DB  205, 208, 209, 212, 215, 224, ...
```

MONTAB defines an alphabetic abbreviation of the months, and COSTAB defines a table of employee numbers. A table may also contain a mixture of numeric and character values, provided that the numeric values are consistent and the character values are consistent. In the following table of stock items, each numeric entry (stock number) is two digits (one byte) and each character entry (stock description) is nine bytes. The dots following the description "Paper" are to show that a space should be present and are not to be keyed into a program.

```
STOKTBL  DB  12, 'Computers',14,'Paper....',17,'Diskettes'
```

For added clarity, you may code table entries vertically:

```
STOKTBL  DB  12, 'Computers'
         DB  14, 'Paper....'
         DB  17, 'Diskettes'
```

Now let's examine different ways to use tables in a program.

DIRECT TABLE ACCESSING

Suppose that a terminal user enters a numeric month such as 03 and a program is to convert it to alphabetic, March. The routine to perform this conversion involves defining a table of alphabetic months, all of equal length. Since the longest name is September, the length is 9, as in the following definition:

```
MONTBL  DB  'January..'
        DB  'February.'
        DB  'March....'
         .
         .
         .
```

The entry 'January' is at MONTBL+0, 'February' is at MONTBL+9, and 'March' is at MONTBL+18. To locate month 03, the program has to perform the following steps:

1. Convert the entered month from ASCII 33 to binary 03.
2. Deduct 1 from the month: 03 – 1 = 02.
3. Multiply the month by 9: 02 × 9 = 18.
4. Add this product to the address of MONTBL; the result is the address of the required description: MONTBL+18.

Figure 14-1 provides an example of a direct access of a table of the months' names, although for brevity the descriptions are three rather

```
        page    60,132
TITLE   DIRECT (COM)  Direct table access
CODESG  SEGMENT PARA 'Code'
        ASSUME  CS:CODESG,DS:CODESG,SS:CODESG,ES:CODESG
        ORG     100H
BEGIN:  JMP     SHORT MAIN
; ---------------------------------------------------
THREE   DB      3
MONIN   DB      '11'
ALFMON  DB      '???','$'
MONTAB  DB      'JAN','FEB','MAR','APR','MAY','JUN'
        DB      'JUL','AUG','SEP','OCT','NOV','DEC'
; ---------------------------------------------------
MAIN    PROC    NEAR              ;Main procedure
        CALL    C10CONV           ;Convert to binary
        CALL    D10LOC            ;Locate month
        CALL    F10DISP           ;Display alpha month
        RET
MAIN    ENDP
;               Convert ASCII to binary:
;               -----------------------
C10CONV PROC
        MOV     AH,MONIN          ;Set up month
        MOV     AL,MONIN+1
        XOR     AX,3030H          ;Clear ASCII 3's
        CMP     AH,00             ;Month 01-09?
        JZ      C20               ;  Yes - bypass
        SUB     AH,AH             ;  No  - clear AH,
        ADD     AL,10             ;  correct for binary
C20:    RET
C10CONV ENDP
;               Locate month in table:
;               ---------------------
D10LOC  PROC
        LEA     SI,MONTAB
        DEC     AL                ;Correct for table
        MUL     THREE             ;Mult AL by 3
        ADD     SI,AX
        MOV     CX,03             ;Init'ze 3-char move
        CLD
        LEA     DI,ALFMON
        REP MOVSB                 ;Move 3 chars
        RET
D10LOC  ENDP
;               Display alpha month:
;               -------------------
F10DISP PROC
        LEA     DX,ALFMON
        MOV     AH,09
        INT     21H
        RET
F10DISP ENDP

CODESG  ENDS
        END     BEGIN
```

Figure 14-1 Direct Table Addressing.

than nine characters long. The entered month is defined as **MONIN**; assume that a routine has requested a user to enter an ASCII month number into this location.

The technique is *direct table accessing*. Since the algorithm directly calculates the required table address, the program does not have to search through the table.

Although direct table addressing is very efficient, it works only when entries have consecutive organization. That is, you could design such a table if entries are in order of 1, 2, 3, . . ., or 106, 107, 108, . . ., or even 5, 10, 15, ... You don't usually have such a neat arrangement of table entries. The next section examines tables with entries that are not consecutive.

TABLE SEARCHING

Some tables consist of numbers with no apparent pattern. A typical example is a table of stock items with consecutive numbers such as 134, 138, 141, 239, and 245. Another type of table contains ranges of values such as an income tax table. The following sections examine these types—tables with unique entries and with ranges—and the requirements for table searching.

Tables with Unique Entries

The stock item numbers for most firms are often not in consecutive order. Numbers tend to be grouped by category, with a leading number to indicate furniture or appliance, or to indicate department number. Also, over time, numbers are deleted and others are added. As a result, you have to attach a stock number to its particular description (and unit price, if required). Stock items and descriptions could be defined in separate tables, such as

```
STOKNOS  DB   '101','107','109,'...
STOKDCR  DB   'Excavators','Processors','Assemblers', ...
```

or in the same table, such as

```
STOKTAB  DB  '101','Excavators'
         DB  '107','Processors'
         DB  '109','Assemblers'
         ...
```

The program in Figure 14-2 defines the stock table and performs a table search. The table contains six pairs of item numbers and descrip-

```
         page     60,132
TITLE    TABSRCH (COM)  Table search
CODESG   SEGMENT PARA 'Code'
         ASSUME  CS:CODESG,DS:CODESG,SS:CODESG,ES:CODESG
         ORG     100H
BEGIN:   JMP     SHORT MAIN
; ---------------------------------------------------
STOKNIN DW      '23'
STOKTAB DB      '05','Excavators'
         DB      '08','Lifters   '
         DB      '09','Presses   '
         DB      '12','Valves    '
         DB      '23','Processors'
         DB      '27','Pumps     '
DESCRN   DB      10 DUP(?)
; ---------------------------------------------------
MAIN     PROC    NEAR
         MOV     AX,STOKNIN          ;Get stock#
         XCHG    AL,AH
         MOV     CX,06               ;No. of entries
         LEA     SI,STOKTAB          ;Init'ze table address
A20:
         CMP     AX,[SI]             ;Stock# : table
         JE      A30                 ;Equal - exit
         ADD     SI,12               ;Not equal - increment
         LOOP    A20
         CALL    R10ERR              ;Not in table
         RET
A30:
         MOV     CX,05               ;Length of descr'n
         LEA     DI,DESCRN           ;Addr of descr'n
         INC     SI
         INC     SI                  ;Extract description
         REP MOVSW                   ;  from table
         RET
MAIN     ENDP
;
R10ERR   PROC
;                <Display error message>
         RET
R10ERR   ENDP

CODESG   ENDS
         END     BEGIN
```

Figure 14-2 Table Searching.

tions. The search loop begins comparing the input stock number, STOKNIN, to the first stock number in the table. If the comparison is unequal, the routine adds to the table address in order to compare to the next table stock number. If the comparison is equal, the routine at A30 extracts the description from the table and stores it in DESCRN.

The search loop performs a maximum of six compares. If the required item number is not in the table, the program calls an error routine that displays an error message.

Note that table initialization contains an instruction that moves STOKNIN to the AX. Although STOKNIN is defined as 3233, the MOV instruction loads the AX with 3332. Since the table entries are not reversed, following the MOV is an XCHG instruction that "unreverses" the two bytes as 3233. However, since CMP expects bytes to be in reverse sequence, it compares first the rightmost bytes and then the leftmost bytes. Consequently, a test for equal is valid, but a high or low test would give invalid results. To compare for high or low, omit the XCHG instruction, MOV the table entry to, say, the BX, and then compare the AX to the BX as follows:

```
          MOV    AX,STOKNIN
          LEA    SI,STOKTAB
    C20:
          MOV    BX,[SI]
          CMP    AX,BX
          JA or JB ...
```

In a program of this nature, another table could define unit prices. The program could locate the item in the table, calculate selling price, (quantity times unit price), and display the description and selling price.

In Figure 14-2, the item number is two characters and the description is ten characters. Programming detail would vary for different number of entries and different lengths of entries. For example, if you compare three-byte fields, you could use REPE CMPSB, although the instruction also involves use of the CX register.

Tables with Ranges

Income tax provides a typical example of a table with ranges of values. Assume the following imaginary table of taxable income, rates, and correction factors:

Taxable Income	*Rate*	*Correction Factor*
0-1000.00	.10	0.00
1000.01-2500.00	.15	050.00
2501.01-4250.00	.18	125.00
4250.01-6000.00	.20	260.00
6000.01 and over	.23	390.00

In the tax table, rates increase as taxable income increases. Entries in the taxable income table contain the high amount for each step:

```
TAXTBL DD  100000,  250000,  425000,  600000,  999999
```

To perform a search of the table, the program compares the taxpayer's taxable income to the table's taxable income:

Low or equal: Use the associated rate and correction factor.

High: Increment for the next entry in the table.

The tax deduction is calculated as (taxable income × table rate) − correction factor.

Table Searching Using String Compares

If item numbers exceed two bytes, use REPE CMPS for the compare operation. Assume that the stock item table from Figure 14-2 is revised for a three-byte item number. If STOKNIN is the first field in the data area and STOKTAB is next, they could appear in memory as follows:

```
Data:     |123|035Excavators|038Lifters   |049Presses    | . . .
           |   |  |          |  |          |  |
Address:  00   03 06         16 19         29 32
```

The program in Figure 14-3 defines STOKTAB, including a last entry with '999' to force termination of the search. The search routine compares the contents of each table entry to STOKNIN as follows:

Table Entry	*STOKNIN*	*Result of Compare*
035	123	Low: check next entry
038	123	Low: check next entry
049	123	Low: check next entry
102	123	Low: check next entry
123	123	Equal: entry found

Note that the CMPSB operation in Figure 14-3 compares byte for byte as long as the bytes are equal and automatically increments the SI and DI registers.

The CX is initialized to 03, and the initial offset addresses in the SI and DI registers are 03 and 00, respectively. A comparison of the first table entry (035:123) causes termination after one byte; the SI contains 04, the DI contains 01, and the CX contains 02. For the next compare, the SI should contain 16 and the DI should contain 00. Correcting the DI address simply involves reloading the address of STOKNIN. For the address of the table entry that should be in the SI, however, the increment depends on whether the comparison ends after one, two, or three

```
        page    60,132
TITLE   STRSRCH (COM)  Table search using CMPSB
CODESG  SEGMENT PARA 'Code'
        ASSUME  CS:CODESG,DS:CODESG,SS:CODESG,ES:CODESG
        ORG     100H
BEGIN:  JMP     SHORT MAIN
; -----------------------------------------------------
STOKNIN DB      '123'
STOKTAB DB      '035','Excavators'      ;Start of table
        DB      '038','Lifters   '
        DB      '049','Presses   '
        DB      '102','Valves    '
        DB      '123','Processors'
        DB      '127','Pumps     '
        DB      '999', 10 DUP(' ')      ;End of table
DESCRN  DB      10 DUP(?)
; -----------------------------------------------------
MAIN    PROC    NEAR
        CLD
        LEA     SI,STOKTAB         ;Init'ze table address
A20:
        MOV     CX,03              ;Set to compare 3 bytes
        LEA     DI,STOKNIN         ;Init'ze stock# address
        REPE CMPSB                 ;Table : stock#
        JE      A30                ;Equal - exit
        JA      A40                ;High  - not in table
        ADD     SI,CX              ;Add CX value to offset
        ADD     SI,10              ;Next table item
        JMP     A20
A30:
        MOV     CX,05              ;Set to move 5 words
        LEA     DI,DESCRN          ;Init'ze addr of descr'n
        REP MOVSW                  ;Move descr'n from table
        RET
A40:
        CALL    R10ERR             ;Not in table
        RET
MAIN    ENDP

R10ERR  PROC
;               <Display error message>
        RET
R10ERR  ENDP

CODESG  ENDS
        END     BEGIN
```

Figure 14-3 Table Search Using CMPSB.

bytes. The CX contains the number of the remaining uncompared bytes, in this case, 02. Adding the CX value plus the length of the stock description gives the offset of the next table item as follows:

Address in SI after CMPSB	04
Add CX	02
Add length of description	10
Next table offset address	16

Since the CX contains the number of the remaining uncompared bytes (if any), the arithmetic works for all cases: termination after 1, 2, or 3 compares. On an equal compare, the CX contains 00 and the SI is already incremented to the address of the required description.

Tables With Variable-Length Entries

It is possible to define a table with variable-length entries. A special "delimiter" character such as hex 00 could follow each entry, and hex FF could distinguish the end of the table. However, be sure that no byte within an entry contains the bit configuration of a delimiter. For example, an arithmetic binary amount can contain any possible bit configuration. Use the SCAS instruction for the search.

THE TRANSLATE (XLAT) INSTRUCTION

The XLAT instruction translates the contents of a byte into another predefined value. You could use XLAT to validate the contents of data items, or, if you transfer data between a PC and an IBM mainframe computer, use XLAT to translate data between ASCII and EBCDIC formats.

The following example converts ASCII numbers 0 through 9 into EBCDIC. Since representation of ASCII is 30-39 and EBCDIC is F0-F9, you could make the change with an OR operation. However, let's also convert all other characters to EBCDIC blank, hex 40. For XLAT, you define a translate table that accounts for all 256 possible characters, with EBCDIC codes inserted in the ASCII positions:

```
XLTBL   DB   47 DUP(40H)                         ;EBCDIC blanks
        DB   0F0H,0F1H,0F2H,0F3H,   ...,0F9H ;EBCDIC 0-9
        DB   199 DUP(40H)                        ;EBCDIC blanks
```

XLAT expects the address of the table in the BX register and the byte to be translated (let's name it ASCNO) in the AL register. The following performs the initialization and translation:

```
LEA  BX,XLTBL
MOV  AL,ASCNO
XLAT
```

XLAT uses the AL value as an offset address, in effect, the address in the BX plus the offset in the AL. If ASCNO contains 00, for example, the

```
        page    60,132
TITLE   XLATE (COM)  Translate ASCII to EDCDIC
CODESG  SEGMENT PARA 'Code'
        ASSUME  CS:CODESG,DS:CODESG,SS:CODESG,ES:CODESG
        ORG     100H
BEGIN:  JMP     MAIN
;-------------------------------------------------------------
ASCNO   DB      '-31.5 '
EBCNO   DB      6 DUP(' ')
XLTAB   DB      45 DUP(40H)
        DB      60H, 2DH
        DB      5CH
        DB      0F0H,0F1H,0F2H,0F3H,0F4H,0F5H,0F6H,0F7H,0F8H,0F9H
        DB      199 DUP(40H)
;-------------------------------------------------------------
MAIN    PROC    NEAR                ;Main procedure
        LEA     SI,ASCNO            ;Address of ASCNO
        LEA     DI,EBCNO            ;Address of EBCNO
        MOV     CX,06               ;Length
        LEA     BX,XLTAB            ;Address of table
A20:
        MOV     AL,[SI]             ;Get ASCII character
        XLAT                        ;Translate
        MOV     [DI],AL             ;Store in EBCNO
        INC     SI
        INC     DI
        LOOP    A20                 ;Repeat 6 times
        RET
MAIN    ENDP
CODESG  ENDS
        END     BEGIN
```

Figure 14-4 Conversion of ASCII to EBCDIC.

table address would be XLTBL+0, and XLAT would replace the 00 in the AL with hex 40 from the table. If ASCN0 contains hex 32, the table address is XLTBL+50. This position contains hex F2 (EBCDIC 2), which XLAT inserts in the AL register.

The program in Figure 14-4 expands this example to convert ASCII decimal point (2E) and minus sign (2D) to EBCDIC (4B and 60, respectively) and to loop through a six-byte field. Initially, ASCNO contains –31.5 followed by a blank, or hex 2D33312E3520. At the end of the loop, EBCNO should contain hex 60F3F14BF540.

PROGRAM: DISPLAYING HEX AND ASCII

The program in Figure 14-5 displays almost all of the ASCII symbols as well as their hex values. For example, the ASCII symbol for hex 53 is the letter S, which the program displays as 53 S. The full display appears on the screen as a 16 by 16 matrix:

```
        page 60,132
TITLE   ASCHEX (COM)  Conversion of ASCII characters to hex
CODESG  SEGMENT PARA 'Code'
        ASSUME  CS:CODESG,DS:CODESG,SS:CODESG,ES:CODESG
        ORG     100H
BEGIN:  JMP     SHORT MAIN
; -------------------------------------------------------
DISPROW DB      16 DUP('     '), 13
HEXCTR  DB      00
XLATAB  DB      30H,31H,32H,33H,34H,35H,36H,37H,38H,39H
        DB      41H,42H,43H,44H,45H,46H
; -------------------------------------------------------
MAIN    PROC    NEAR                ;Main procedure
        CALL    Q10CLR              ;Clear screen
        LEA     SI,DISPROW
A20LOOP:
        CALL    C10HEX              ;Translate
        CALL    D10DISP             ;  & display
        CMP     HEXCTR,0FFH         ;Last hex value (FF)?
        JE      A50                 ;  yes - terminate
        INC     HEXCTR              ;  no  - incr next hex
        JMP     A20LOOP
A50:    RET
MAIN    ENDP

C10HEX  PROC    NEAR                ;Convert to hex
        MOV     AH,00
        MOV     AL,HEXCTR           ;Get hex pair
        SHR     AX,CL               ;Shift off right hex digit
        LEA     BX,XLATAB           ;Set table address
        MOV     CL,04               ;Set shift value
        XLAT                        ;Translate hex
        MOV     [SI],AL             ;Store left char

        MOV     AL,HEXCTR
        SHL     AX,CL               ;Shift off left digit
        SHR     AL,CL
        XLAT                        ;Translate hex
        MOV     [SI]+1,AL           ;Store right char
        RET
C10HEX  ENDP

D10DISP PROC    NEAR                ;Display
        MOV     AL,HEXCTR
        MOV     [SI]+3,AL
        CMP     AL,1AH              ;EOF char?
        JE      D20                 ;  yes - bypass
        CMP     AL,07H              ;Lower/equal 08?
        JB      D30                 ;  yes - ok
        CMP     AL,10H              ;Higher/equal 0F?
        JAE     D30                 ;  yes - ok
D20:
        MOV     BYTE PTR [SI]+3,20H
D30:
        ADD     SI,05               ;Inc next loc'n in row
        LEA     DI,DISPROW+80
        CMP     DI,SI
        JNE     D40
```

Figure 14-5 Displaying Hex and ASCII.

```
         MOV     AH,40H          ;Request display
         MOV     BX,01           ;Handle
         MOV     CX,81           ;Entire row
         LEA     DX,DISPROW
         INT     21H
         LEA     SI,DISPROW      ;Reset display row
D40:     RET
D10DISP  ENDP

Q10CLR   PROC    NEAR            ;Clear screen
         MOV     AX,0600H
         MOV     BH,03           ;Color (07 for BW)
         MOV     CX,0000
         MOV     DX,184FH
         INT     10H
         RET
Q10CLR   ENDP

CODESG   ENDS
         END     BEGIN
```

Figure 14-5 (Continued)

```
00 01 02 03 04 05 06 07 08 09 0A 0B 0C 0D 0E 0F
.  .  .  .  .  .  .  .  .  .  .  .  .  .  .  .
.  .  .  .  .  .  .  .  .  .  .  .  .  .  .  .
.  .  .  .  .  .  .  .  .  .  .  .  .  .  .  .
F0 F1 F2 F3 F4 F5 F6 F7 F8 F9 FA FB FC FD FE FF
```

As seen in Figure 8-1, displaying ASCII symbols is no problem. However, displaying a hex value as ASCII is more involved. For example, to display as ASCII, you have to convert hex 00 to hex 3030, hex 01 to hex 3031, and so forth.

The program initializes HEXCTR to 00 and subsequently increments it. The procedure C10HEX splits HEXCTR into its two hex digits. For example, assume that HEXCTR contains hex 4F. The routine extracts the hex 4 and uses its value for a translate operation against XLATAB. The value returned to the AL is hex 34. The routine then extracts the hex F and translates it to hex 46. The result, hex 3446, displays as 4F.

Since DOS function call hex 40 for displaying treats hex 1A as an end-of-file character, the program changes it to a blank. A program using DOS function call hex 09 would have to change the '$' terminator to a blank.

There are many other ways of converting hex digits to ASCII characters, and you could experiment with shifting and comparing.

PROGRAM: SORTING TABLE ENTRIES

Often an application requires sorting data in a table into ascending or descending sequence. For example, a user may want a list of stock descriptions in ascending sequence, or a list of salesmen's total sales in descending sequence. Typically, the data in the table is not defined as in previous examples, but is loaded from a terminal or disk. Let's make a clear distinction: this chapter covers sorting of table entries; a different application that involves sorting of disk records can be much more complex.

There are a number of table sort routines varying from not efficient but clear to efficient but obscure. The sort routine in this section is fairly efficient and could serve for most table sorting. Now you may not do a lot of table sorting, and even the least efficient routine may seem to execute at the speed of light. Also, the objective of this book is to explain assembler, not sort, techniques.

A general approach is to compare a table entry to the entry immediately following. If the comparison is high, exchange the entries. Continue in this fashion comparing entry 1 to entry 2, entry 2 to entry 3, to the end of the table, exchanging where necessary. If you made any exchanges, repeat the entire process from the start of the table, comparing entry 1 to entry 2. If you didn't make any exchanges, the table is in sequence and you can terminate the sort.

In the following pseudocode, assume that SWAP is an item that indicates whether an exchange was made (YES) or not made (NO).

```
G10:  Initialize address of last entry in table
G20:  Set SWAP to NO
      Initialize address of start of table
G30:  Table entry > next entry?
          Yes:  Exchange entries
                Set SWAP to YES
      Increment for next entry in table
      At end of table?
          No:   Jump to G30
          Yes:  Does SWAP = YES?
                Yes:  Jump to G20 (repeat sort)
                No:   End of sort
```

The program in Figure 14-6 allows a user to enter up to 30 names on a terminal. When all the names are entered, the program sorts the names into ascending sequence and displays the sorted names on the screen.

```
        page    60,132
TITLE   NMSORT (EXE)  Sort names entered from terminal
; ---------------------------------------------------
STACK   SEGMENT PARA STACK 'Stack'
        DW      32 DUP(?)
STACK   ENDS
; ---------------------------------------------------
DATASG  SEGMENT PARA 'Data'
NAMEPAR LABEL   BYTE               ;Name parameter list:
MAXNLEN DB      21                 ;  max. length
NAMELEN DB      ?                  ;  no. chars entered
NAMEFLD DB      21 DUP(' ')        ;  name

CRLF    DB      13, 10, '$'
ENDADDR DW      ?
MESSG1  DB      'Name? ', '$'
NAMECTR DB      00
NAMETAB DB      30 DUP(20 DUP(' ')) ;Name table
NAMESAV DB      20 DUP(?), 13, 10, '$'
SWAPPED DB      00
DATASG  ENDS
; ------------------------------------------------
CODESG  SEGMENT PARA 'Code'
BEGIN   PROC    FAR
        ASSUME CS:CODESG,DS:DATASG,SS:STACK,ES:DATASG
        PUSH    DS
        SUB     AX,AX
        PUSH    AX
        MOV     AX,DATASG
        MOV     DS,AX
        MOV     ES,AX
        CLD
        LEA     DI,NAMETAB
        CALL    Q10CLR             ;Clear screen
        CALL    Q20CURS            ;Set cursor
A20LOOP:
        CALL    B10READ            ;Accept name
        CMP     NAMELEN,00         ;Any more names?
        JZ      A30                ;  no  - go to sort
        CMP     NAMECTR,30         ;30 names entered?
        JE      A30                ;  yes - go to sort
        CALL    D10STOR            ;Store entered name in table
        JMP     A20LOOP
A30:                               ;End of input
        CALL    Q10CLR             ;Clear screen
        CALL    Q20CURS            ;  & set cursor
        CMP     NAMECTR,01         ;One or no name entered?
        JBE     A40                ;  yes - exit
        CALL    G10SORT            ;Sort stored names
        CALL    K10DISP            ;Display sorted names
A40:    RET                        ;Terminate
BEGIN   ENDP
;               Accept name as input:
;               --------------------
B10READ PROC
        MOV     AH,09
        LEA     DX,MESSG1          ;Display prompt
        INT     21H
```

Figure 14-6 Sorting a Table of Names.

```
         MOV     AH,0AH
         LEA     DX,NAMEPAR        ;Accept name
         INT     21H
         MOV     AH,09
         LEA     DX,CRLF           ;Return/line feed
         INT     21H

         MOV     BH,00             ;Clear characters after name
         MOV     BL,NAMELEN        ;Get count of chars
         MOV     CX,21
         SUB     CX,BX             ;Calc remaining length
B20:
         MOV     NAMEFLD[BX],20H ;Set to blank
         INC     BX
         LOOP    B20
         RET
B10READ ENDP
;                Store name in table:
;                -------------------
D10STOR PROC
         INC     NAMECTR           ;Add to number of names
         CLD
         LEA     SI,NAMEFLD
         MOV     CX,10
         REP MOVSW                 ;Move name to table
         RET
D10STOR ENDP
;                Sort names in table:
;                -------------------
G10SORT PROC
         SUB     DI,40             ;Set up stop address
         MOV     ENDADDR,DI
G20:
         MOV     SWAPPED,00        ;Set up start
         LEA     SI,NAMETAB        ; of table
G30:
         MOV     CX,20             ;Length of compare
         MOV     DI,SI
         ADD     DI,20             ;Next name for compare
         MOV     AX,DI
         MOV     BX,SI
         REPE CMPSB                ;Compare name to next
         JBE     G40               ;  no exchange
         CALL    H10XCHG           ;  exchange
G40:
         MOV     SI,AX
         CMP     SI,ENDADDR        ;End of table?
         JBE     G30               ;  no  - continue
         CMP     SWAPPED,00        ;Any swaps?
         JNZ     G20               ;  yes - continue
         RET                       ;  no  - end of sort
G10SORT ENDP
;                Exchange table entries:
;                ----------------------
H10XCHG PROC
         MOV     CX,10
         LEA     DI,NAMESAV
         MOV     SI,BX
```

Figure 14-6 (Continued)

```
          REP MOVSW                    ;Move lower item to save

          MOV     CX,10
          MOV     DI,BX
          REP MOVSW                    ;Move higher item to lower

          MOV     CX,10
          LEA     SI,NAMESAV
          REP MOVSW                    ;Move save to higher item
          MOV     SWAPPED,01           ;Signal that exchange made
          RET
H10XCHG   ENDP
;                 Display sorted names:
;                 --------------------
K10DISP   PROC
          LEA     SI,NAMETAB
K20:
          LEA     DI,NAMESAV           ;Init'ze start of table
          MOV     CX,10
          REP MOVSW
          MOV     AH,09
          LEA     DX,NAMESAV
          INT     21H                  ;Display
          DEC     NAMECTR              ;Is this last one?
          JNZ     K20                  ;  no  - loop
          RET                          ;  yes - exit
K10DISP   ENDP
;                 Clear screen:
;                 ------------
Q10CLR    PROC
          MOV     AX,0600H
          MOV     BH,61H               ;Color (07 for BW)
          SUB     CX,CX
          MOV     DX,184FH
          INT     10H
          RET
Q10CLR    ENDP
;                 Set cursor:
;                 ----------
Q20CURS   PROC
          MOV     AH,02
          SUB     BH,BH
          SUB     DX,DX                ;Set cursor to 00,00
          INT     10H
          RET
Q20CURS   ENDP

CODESG    ENDS
          END     BEGIN
```

Figure 14-6 (Continued)

TYPE, LENGTH, AND SIZE OPERATORS

The assembler supplies a number of special operators that you may find useful. For example, the length of a table may change from time to time and you may have to modify the program for the new definition and for routines that check for the table end. But the use of the TYPE, LENGTH, and SIZE operators can enable you to reduce the number of instructions that have to be changed.

Assume the following definition of a table of ten words:

```
TABLEX  DW    10 DUP(?)         ;Table with 10 words
```

The program can use the TYPE operator to determine the definition (DW in this case), the LENGTH operator to determine the DUP factor (10), and the SIZE operator to determine the number of bytes (10 × 2, or 20). The following examples illustrate the three operators:

```
MOV   AX,TYPE TABLEX               ;AX = 0002
MOV   BX,LENGTH TABLEX             ;BX = 000A (10)
MOV   CX,SIZE TABLEX               ;CX = 0014 (20)
```

You may use the values that LENGTH and SIZE return in order to terminate a table search or a sort. For example, if the SI register contains the incremented address of a table search, test it using

```
CMP   SI,SIZE TABLEX
```

Chapter 23, "Assembler PSEUDO-op Reference," describes TYPE, LENGTH, and SIZE in detail.

KEY POINTS TO REMEMBER

- For most purposes, define tables with related entries that are the same length and data format.
- Design tables based on their data format. For example, entries may be character or numeric and one, two, or more bytes each. It may be more practical to define two tables: one, for example, for item numbers that are three bytes long, and another for unit prices that are one word. The search could increment the address of the item number table by 3 and the address of the price table by 2. Or, keep a count of the number of loops; on finding an equal item multiply the count by 2 (SHL one bit), and use this value as an offset to the address of the price table. (Actually, initialize the count to –1.)
- Remember that DB permits numeric values with a maximum of 256 and that a numeric DW reverses the bytes. Also, CMP and CMPSW assume that words are reversed.

- If a table is subject to frequent changes or if several programs reference it, store it on disk. An updating program can handle changes to the table. Any program can load the table from disk and the programs need not be changed.
- Be especially careful when coding a sort routine. Use a trace to test the sort because a minor coding error can cause unpredictable results.

QUESTIONS

14-1. Define a table that contains the names of the days of the week, beginning with Sunday.

14-2. Given that Sunday equals 1, code the instructions that directly access the name from the table defined in Question 14-1. Use any suitable names.

14-3. Define three separate related tables that contain the following data: (a) Item numbers 06, 10, 14, 21, 24; (b) Item descriptions Videotape, Receivers, Modems, Keyboards, Diskettes; (c) Item prices 93.95, 82.25, 90.67, 85.80, 13.85

14-4. Code a program that allows a user to enter item number (ITEMIN) and quantity (QTYIN) from the keyboard. Using the tables defined in Question 14-3, include a table search routine using ITEMIN to locate an item number in the table. Extract description and price from the tables. Calculate value (quantity times price), and display description and value back on the screen.

14-5. Using the description table defined in Question 14-3, code the following: (a) A routine that moves the contents of the table to another (empty) table; (b) A routine that sorts the contents of this new table into ascending sequence.

CHAPTER 15

Disk Storage I: Organization

Objective: To examine the basic formats for hard disk and diskette storage, the directory, and the file allocation table.

INTRODUCTION

Disk is a popular storage medium for data that is to be kept (more or less) permanently. Processing for hard disk is similar to that for diskette, except that you may need to supply a path name to access files in subdirectories. In order to process files, it is useful to be familiar with disk organization. Each side of a conventional 5 1/4" diskette contains 40 concentric tracks, numbered 00 through 39. Each track is formatted into eight or nine sectors of 512 bytes each.

Data on disk is stored in the form of a file just as you have stored assembler programs. Although there is no restriction on the kind of data that you may keep in a file, a typical user file would consist of records for customers, for inventory supplies, or for name and address lists. Each record contains information about a particular customer or inventory item. Within a file, all records are the same length and format. A record contains one or more fields. A customer file, for example, could consist of records that contain such fields as customer number, customer name, and balance owing. These records could be in ascending sequence by customer number as follows:

```
 -----------    -----------    -----------          -----------
| #1|name|amt|  |#2|name|amt|  |#3|name|amt|  . . .  |#n|name|amt|
 -----------    -----------    -----------          -----------
```

For programming disk files, you need be generally familiar only with the concepts and terminology. In the absence of a specified disk size, this chapter refers to the 5 1/4" format.

DISK CAPACITY

Common diskette storage capacities are the following:

Version	*Tracks /side*	*Sectors /track*	*Bytes /sector*	*Total two sides*
Prior to DOS 2.0	40	8	512	327,680
DOS 2.0 and on	40	9	512	368,640
High density	80	15	512	1,228,800
3 1/2"	80	9	512	737,280

Common hard disk storage capacities are the following:

Version	*Tracks /side*	*Sectors /track*	*Bytes /sector*	*Total four sides*
10 megabytes	306	17	512	10,653,696
20 megabytes	614	17	512	21,377,024

A reference to disk sides (heads), tracks, and sectors is by number. Side and track numbers begin with 0, whereas sector numbers begin with 1.

THE DIRECTORY

In order to account for the information stored on disk, DOS reserves certain sectors for its own purposes. The organization of diskette and hard disk vary according to their capacity. A formatted two-sided diskette with nine sectors per track contains the following:

Side 0, track 0, sector 1	Boot record
Side 0, track 0, sectors 2-3	File Allocation Table (FAT)
Side 0, track 0, sectors 4-7	Directory
Side 1, track 0, sectors 1-3	Directory
Side 1, track 0, sectors 4 and on	Data files

Data records begin on side 1, track 0, sector 3 through sector 9. The system stores records next on side 0, track 1, then side 1, track 1, then side 0, track 2, and so forth. This feature of filling data on opposite tracks before proceeding to the next track reduces disk head motion and is also the method used on hard disk.

If you use FORMAT /S to format a diskette, the DOS modules IBMBIO.COM and IBMDOS.COM occupy the first sectors of the data area.

All files even if less than 512 bytes (or multiples of 512) begin on a sector boundary. DOS constructs a directory for each file in track 0 of the disk. Each directory entry describes the name, date, size, and location of a file on the disk. Directory entries have the following format:

Byte	*Purpose*
0-7	Filename as designated in the program that created the file. The first byte can also indicate file status: hex 00 means that the file has never been used, hex E5 means that the file has been deleted, and hex 2E means the entry is for a subdirectory.
8-10	Filename extension.
11	File attribute defining the type of file: Hex 00 normal file Hex 01 file that can only be read Hex 02 "hidden" file Hex 04 DOS system file Hex 08 volume label Hex 10 subdirectory Hex 20 archive file, relevant to hard disk.
12-21	Reserved for DOS.
22-23	Time of day when the file was created or last updated, stored in binary as |hhhhhmmmmmmsssss|
24-25	Date when the file was created or last updated, compressed into two bytes in binary format as |yyyyyyym|mmmddddd| where year begins at 1980 and can be 0-119, month can be 1-12, and day can be 1-31.
26-27	Starting cluster of the file. The number is relative to the last two sectors of the directory. The first data file (with no DOS COM modules) begins at relative cluster 002. The actual side, track, and cluster depend on disk capacity.
28-31	File size in bytes. When you create a file, DOS calculates and stores its size in this field.

For fields in the directory that exceed one byte, the bytes are stored in reverse sequence.

FILE ALLOCATION TABLE (FAT)

The purpose of the file allocation table (FAT) is to allocate disk space for files. If you create a new file or revise an existing file, DOS revises FAT entries according to the location of the file on disk. The boot record is at sector 1 and FAT begins at sector 2. FAT contains an entry for each cluster on the disk and varies in length depending on the disk storage device. A cluster on one-sided diskettes is one sector and on two-sided diskettes is an adjacent pair of sectors, so that a two-sided diskette can reference twice the data with the same number of FAT entries.

The first byte of FAT indicates the type of device:

FE	One-sided, 8 sectors
FC	One-sided, 9 sectors
FF	Two-sided, 8 sectors
FD	Two-sided, 9 sectors
F9	High capacity 1.2 meg
F8	Hard disk

The second and third bytes contain FFFF at the time of this writing. The following lists the organization for several types of devices, showing the starting and ending sector numbers. The column headed "Cluster" means the number of sectors per cluster:

Device	*Boot*	*FAT*	*Directory*	*Cluster*
One-sided, 8 sectors	1	2-3	4-7	1
One-sided, 9 sectors	1	2-5	6-9	1
Two-sided, 8 sectors	1	2-3	4-10	2
Two-sided, 9 sectors	1	2-5	6-12	2
High capacity 1.2 meg	1	2-15	16-29	1
XT hard disk	1	2-17	18-49	8
AT hard disk	1	2-83	84-115	4

From the fourth byte on, FAT entries reference sectors, and are each 12 bits in length. (From DOS 3 and on, FAT entries for hard disk may be 16 bits.) The first two FAT entries, known as relative sectors 000 and 001, respectively, reference the last two sectors of the directory to indicate its size and format. The first data file begins at relative sector 002. Each FAT entry consists of three hex digits (12 bits) to indicate the use of a particular sector in the following format:

000	The referenced cluster is currently unused.
nnn	The relative cluster number of the next cluster for a file.
FF7	Unusable cluster (bad track).
FFF	The last cluster of a file.

For example, assume that a diskette contains only one file named PAYROLL.ASM on relative sectors 002, 003, and 004. The directory entry for this file contains the filename PAYROLL, extension ASM, hex 00 to indicate a normal file, the creation date, 002 for the first relative sector of the file, and an entry for file size in bytes. The FAT could appear as follows, except that pairs of bytes would be reversed:

```
FAT entry:          |FDF|FFF|003|004|FFF|000|000|. . .|000|
Relative sector:      0   1   2   3   4   5   6  . . . end
```

The first two FAT entries reference the directory on relative sectors 000 and 001. In order to enter this file into memory, the system takes the following steps:

1. DOS accesses the diskette and searches the directory for the filename PAYROLL and extension ASM.
2. DOS then extracts from the directory the location of the first relative sector (002) of the file and delivers the contents of this sector to its buffer area in main memory.
3. For the second sector, DOS accesses the FAT entry that represents relative sector 002. From the diagram, this entry contains 003, meaning that the file continues on relative sector 003. DOS delivers the contents of this sector to the buffer in main memory.
4. For the third sector, DOS accesses the FAT entry that represents relative sector 003. This entry contains 004, meaning that the file continues on relative sector 004. DOS delivers the contents of this sector to the buffer in main memory.
5. The FAT entry for relative sector 004 contains hex FFF to indicate that there is no more data for this file.

The directory contains the starting cluster number for each file, and FAT contains a three-digit hex entry that indicates the location of each additional cluster, if any. At the least, FAT contains hex FFF for a file to indicate no more records past the first cluster.

As a simple example, a directory indicates a file stored beginning a relative cluster 15. To locate the first FAT entry:

- Multiply 15 by 1.5 to get 22.5.

- Access offset bytes 22 and 23 in FAT. Assume that they contain Fx FF.
- Reverse the bytes: FF Fx.
- Because the location, 15, was an odd number, use the first three digits, FFF, which tell you that there are no more clusters for this file.

Now consider a file that uses four clusters, beginning at location 15. FAT entries for bytes 22 and on, this time shown in proper reversed byte sequence, contain the following:

6x 01 17 80 01 FF xF

To find the first FAT entry, multiply 15 by 1.5 to get 22.5, and access bytes 22 and 23, as before. This time, the bytes contain 6x 01, which reverse as 01 6x. Since 15 was an odd number, use the first three digits, 016. The second cluster for the file, therefore, begins at cluster 016.

To find the third cluster, multiply 16 by 1.5 to get 24. Access bytes 24 and 25 of FAT. These contain 17 80, which reverse as 80 17. Since 16 was an even number, use the last three digits, 017. The third cluster for the file, therefore, begins at cluster 017.

To find the fourth cluster, multiply 17 by 1.5 to get 25.5. Access bytes 25 and 26 of FAT. These contain 80 01, which reverse as 01 80. Since 17 was an even number, use the first three digits, 018. The fourth cluster for the file, therefore, begins at cluster 018.

You can use the same procedure to locate the contents of the next FAT entry in offset locations 27 and 28, FF xF, which reverse as xF FF. Since 18 was an even number, use the last three digits, FFF, which mean that this is the last entry.

From the foregoing, you can see that all files begin on a cluster boundary. Also, what may not be so immediately clear is that a file need not be contained on adjacent clusters, but could be scattered on a disk in various sectors.

If your program has to determine the type of installed disk, it could check the FAT directly, or preferably could use DOS function call 1BH or 1CH.

KEY POINTS TO REMEMBER

- Regardless of size, all files begin on a cluster boundary.
- The directory contains an entry for each file on a disk and indicates the filename, extension, file attribute, time, date, starting sector, and file size.

- The file allocation table (FAT) contains one entry for each cluster for each file.

QUESTIONS

15-1. What is the length in bytes of a standard sector?

15-2. Where is the boot record located?

15-3. What is the indication in the directory for a deleted file?

15-4. What is the additional effect on a diskette when you use FORMAT /S to format?

15-5. Where and how does the FAT indicate that the device for this table is on hard disk?

15-6. Consider a file with a size of 2890 (decimal) bytes: (a) Where does the system store the size? (b) What is the size in hexadecimal format? Show the value as the system stores it.

CHAPTER 16

Disk Storage II: Original DOS Functions

Objective: To examine the basic programming requirments of the original DOS functions for processing disk files.

INTRODUCTION

This chapter first covers the original DOS functions that define a file control block (FCB) and then examines the requirements for creating and processing disk files defined as sequential and as random. All of these operations were introduced by the first versions of DOS and are available under all versions.

Disk processing under original DOS involves definition of a file control block (FCB) that defines the file and records. You provide its address to DOS for all disk input/output operations. No new assembler instructions are required.

A number of special interrupt calls handle input and output. Writing a file requires that it first be "created" so that DOS can generate an entry in the directory. When all records have been written, the program must "close" the file so that DOS can complete the directory. Reading a file requires that it first be "opened" to ensure that the file exists. Because records are fixed length and because of the directory's design, you may process records in a disk file either sequentially or randomly.

The method of disk accessing that supports use of a directory and "blocking" and "unblocking" of records is by means of DOS interrupt 21H. The next lower level, also via DOS, is by means of interrupts 25H and 26H but involves absolute addressing of disk sectors. The lowest level is via BIOS interrupt 13H, which requires direct addressing of track and sector numbers. The DOS methods perform some preliminary processing before linking to BIOS. Chapter 17 explains the use of the preferred extended DOS functions using file handles introduced by DOS 2, and Chapter 18 covers the basic BIOS disk operations. Reminder: The term *cluster* denotes one or more sectors of data, depending on the device.

FILE CONTROL BLOCK: FCB

For disk I/O under original DOS, you define an FCB in the data area. Since the FCB does not support path names, you use it primarily for processing files in the current directory. The FCB contains descriptive information about the file and its records, described in the following. You initialize bytes 0-15 and 32-36; DOS sets bytes 16-31.

Byte	*Purpose*
0	Disk drive. Code 01 for drive A, 02 for drive B, and so forth.
1-8	Filename. The name of the file, left-adjusted with trailing blanks, if any. The entry may be a reserved filename such as LPT1 for line printer, without a colon.
9-11	Filename extension. A subdivision of filename for further identification of the file, such as DTA or ASM. If less than three characters, left-adjust. DOS stores the filename and extension in the directory.
12-13	Current block number. A block consists of 128 records. Read and write operations use the current block number and current record number (byte 32) to locate a particular record. The number is relative to the beginning of the file, where the first block is 0, the second is 1, and so forth. An open operation sets this entry to zero.
14-15	Logical record size. An open operation initializes the record size to 128 (hex 80). After the open and before any read or write, you may set this entry to your own required record size.
16-19	File size. When a program creates a file, DOS calculates and stores its size (number of records times record size) in the directory. An open operation subsequently extracts the file size from the directory and stores it in this field. Your program may read this field but should not change it.
20-21	Date. DOS records the date in the directory when the file was created or last updated. An open operation extracts the date from the directory and stores it in this field.
22-31	Reserved by DOS.
32	Current record number. This entry contains the current record number (0-127) within the current block (see bytes 12-13). The system uses the current block/record to locate records in the disk file. Although the usual initial record number is 0, you may set this field to begin sequential processing at any number between 0 and 127.
33-36	Relative record number. For random read/write, this entry must contain a relative record number. For example, to randomly read record 25 (hex 19), set this entry to hex 19000000. To access a record randomly, the system automatically converts the relative record number to current block/record. Because there is a limit to the maximum size of a file (1,073,741,824 bytes), a file with a short record size can contain more

records and may have a higher maximum relative record number. If record size is greater than 64, byte 36 always contains 00.

Remember that numeric values in words and doublewords are stored in reversed byte sequence.

Preceding the FCB is an optional seven-byte extension, which you may use for processing files with special attributes. To use the extension, code the first byte with hex FF, the second with the file attribute, and the remaining five bytes with hex zeros.

USING AN FCB TO CREATE A DISK FILE

For each disk file referenced, a program contains a properly defined file control block. Disk I/O operations require the address of the FCB in the DX register and use this address to access fields within the FCB by means of DS:DX registers. On initialization, the program uses function call hex 16 and DOS interrupt 21H to create a new file as follows:

```
MOV  AH,16H       ;Create
LEA  DX,FCBname   ;  disk file
INT  21H          ;Call DOS
```

DOS searches the directory for a filename that matches the entry in the FCB. If found, DOS reuses the space in the directory, and if not found, DOS searches for a vacant entry. The operation then initializes the file size to 0 and "opens" the file. The open step checks for available disk space and sets the AL register as follows:

00 Space is available.
FF No space is available.

Open also initializes the FCB current block number to 0 and sets a default value in the FCB record size of 128 (hex 80) bytes. Before writing a record, you may override this default with your own record size.

The disk transfer area (DTA) is the start of the definition of your output record. Since the FCB contains the record size, the DTA does not require a delimiter to indicate the end of the record. Prior to a write operation, use function call hex 1A to supply DOS with the address of the DTA. There may be only one DTA active at any time. The following initializes the address of the DTA:

```
MOV  AH,1AH       ;Set address
LEA  DX,DTAname   ;  of DTA
INT  21H          ;Call DOS
```

If a program processes only one disk file, it needs to initialize the DTA only once for the entire execution. If a program processes more than one file, it must initialize the appropriate DTA immediately before each read or write.

To write a sequential disk record, use function call hex 15:

```
MOV   AH,15H       ;Write record
LEA   DX,FCBname   ;  sequentially
INT   21H          ;Call DOS
```

The write operation uses the information in the FCB and the address of the current DTA. If the record is the size of a sector, the operation writes the record. Otherwise, the operation fills records into a buffer area that is the length of a sector and writes the buffer when full. For example, if each record is 128 bytes long, the operation fills the buffer with four records (4 × 128 = 512) and writes the buffer into an entire disk sector.

On a successful write, DOS increments the FCB file size field (by adding the record size to it) and increments the current record number by 1. When the current record number exceeds 128, the operation sets it to 0 and increments the FCB current block number. The operation then returns a code to the AL register:

00 The write was successful.
01 The disk is full.
02 There is no space in the disk transfer area for one record.

When you have finished writing records, you may write an end-of-file marker (hex 1A), although it's not always necessary, and then use function call hex 10 to close the file:

```
MOV   AH,10H       ;Close the
LEA   DX,FCBname   ; file
INT   21H          ;Call DOS
```

The operation writes on disk any partial data still in the DOS disk buffer and updates the directory with the date and the file size. The following codes are returned to the AL register:

00 The write was successful.
FF The file was not in the correct position in the directory, perhaps caused by a user changing a diskette.

PROGRAM: USING AN FCB TO CREATE A DISK FILE

The program in Figure 16-1 creates a disk file of names that a user enters through the keyboard. The FCB, named FCBREC in the example, contains the following entries:

FCBDRIV	The program is to create a file on a disk in drive 4 (or D).
FCBNAME	Name of the file is NAMEFILE.
FCBEXT	File extension is DAT.
FCBBLK	Current block number is initialized to 0.
FCBRCSZ	Record size is undefined because the open operation sets this entry to 128.
FCBSQRC	Current record number is initialized to 0.

The program is organized with the following procedures:

BEGIN	Initializes segment registers, calls C10OPEN to create the file and to set the DTA address for DOS, and calls D10PROC to accept input. If no more input, the routine calls G10CLSE and terminates.
C10OPEN	Creates an entry for the file in the directory, sets the size of the record to 32 (hex 20), and initializes the address of the DTA.
D10PROC	Prompts and accepts input of names from the terminal and calls F10WRIT to write the entered name on disk.
E10DISP	Handles scrolling and setting of the cursor.
F10WRIT	Writes names onto the disk file.
G10CLSE	Writes an end-of-file marker and closes the file.
X10ERR	Displays an error message in the event of an invalid create or write operation.

Each write operation automatically adds 1 to FCBSQRC (the current record number) and hex 20 (the record size) to FCBFLSZ (the file size). Since each record is 32 bytes long, the operation fills the buffer with 16 records and then writes the entire buffer onto a disk sector. The following shows the DTA and the buffer:

```
                DTA:  |curr rec|
     Buffer:    |rec 00|rec 01|rec 02| ... |rec 15|
```

If a user enters 25 names, the record count increments from 1 to 25 (hex 19). The file size is, therefore,

25 × 32 bytes = 800 bytes, or hex 320

```
        page    60,132
TITLE   FCBCREAT (EXE)  Use FCB to create file of names
; ------------------------------------------------------
STACKSG SEGMENT PARA STACK 'Stack'
        DW      80 DUP(?)
STACKSG ENDS
; ------------------------------------------------------
DATASG  SEGMENT PARA 'Data'
RECLEN  EQU     32
NAMEPAR LABEL   BYTE              ;Name parameter list:
MAXNLEN DB      RECLEN            ;  max. length of name
NAMELEN DB      ?                 ;  no. chars entered, incl. CR
NAMEDTA DB      RECLEN DUP(' ')   ;  disk transfer area (DTA)

FCBREC  LABEL   BYTE              ;FCB for disk file:
FCBDRIV DB      04                ;  drive D
FCBNAME DB      'NAMEFILE'        ;  file name
FCBEXT  DB      'DAT'             ;  extension
FCBBLK  DW      0000              ;  current block#
FCBRCSZ DW      ?                 ;  logical record size
FCBFLSZ DD      ?                 ;  DOS file size
        DW      ?                 ;  DOS date
        DT      ?                 ;  DOS reserved
FCBSQRC DB      00                ;  current record #
        DD      ?                 ;  relative record #

CRLF    DB      13, 10, '$'
ERRCDE  DB      00
PROMPT  DB      'Name? ','$'
ROW     DB      01
OPNMSG  DB      '*** Open error ***',  '$'
WRTMSG  DB      '*** Write error ***', '$'
DATASG  ENDS
; ------------------------------------------------------
CODESG  SEGMENT PARA 'Code'
BEGIN   PROC    FAR
        ASSUME  CS:CODESG,DS:DATASG,SS:STACKSG,ES:DATASG
        PUSH    DS
        SUB     AX,AX
        PUSH    AX
        MOV     AX,DATASG
        MOV     DS,AX
        MOV     ES,AX
        MOV     AX,0600H
        CALL    Q10SCR            ;Clear screen
        CALL    Q20CURS           ;Set cursor
        CALL    C10OPEN           ;Open file, set DTA
        CMP     ERRCDE,00         ;Available space?
        JZ      A20LOOP           ;  yes - continue
        RET                       ;  no  - return to DOS
A20LOOP:
        CALL    D10PROC
        CMP     NAMELEN,00        ;End of input?
        JNE     A20LOOP           ;  no  - continue
        CALL    G10CLSE           ;  yes - close,
        RET                       ;  return to DOS
BEGIN   ENDP
;               Open disk file:
```

Figure 16-1 Creation of a Disk File.

```
;                  --------------
C10OPEN PROC       NEAR
        MOV        AH,16H            ;Request create
        LEA        DX,FCBREC
        INT        21H
        CMP        AL,00             ;Available space?
        JNZ        C20               ;  no - error

        MOV        FCBRCSZ,RECLEN    ;Record size (EQU)
        LEA        DX,NAMEDTA        ;Set address of DTA
        MOV        AH,1AH
        INT        21H
        RET
C20:
        LEA        DX,OPNMSG         ;Error message
        CALL       X10ERR
        RET
C10OPEN ENDP
;                  Accept input:
;                  ------------
D10PROC PROC       NEAR
        MOV        AH,09             ;Request display
        LEA        DX,PROMPT         ;Display prompt
        INT        21H

        MOV        AH,0AH            ;Request input
        LEA        DX,NAMEPAR        ;Accept name
        INT        21H
        CALL       E10DISP           ;Handle scrolling

        CMP        NAMELEN,00        ;Was a name entered?
        JNE        D20               ;  yes - process
        RET                          ;  no  - exit
D20:
        MOV        BH,00             ;Replace return char
        MOV        BL,NAMELEN
        MOV        NAMEDTA[BX],' '   ;Store blank
        CALL       F10WRIT           ;Call write routine

        CLD
        LEA        DI,NAMEDTA        ;Clear
        MOV        CX,RECLEN / 2     ;  name
        MOV        AX,2020H          ;  field
        REP STOSW
        RET                          ;Exit
D10PROC ENDP
;                  Scroll & set cursor:
;                  -------------------
E10DISP PROC       NEAR
        MOV        AH,09             ;Request display
        LEA        DX,CRLF           ;Carriage ret/line feed
        INT        21H               ;Call DOS
        CMP        ROW,18            ;Bottom of screen?
        JAE        E20               ;  yes - bypass
        INC        ROW               ;  no  - add to row
        RET
E20:
        MOV        AX,0601H          ;Scroll one row
        CALL       Q10SCR
```

Figure 16-1 (Continued)

```
        CALL    Q20CURS         ;Reset cursor
        RET
E10DISP ENDP
;               Write disk record:
;               -----------------
F10WRIT PROC    NEAR
        MOV     AH,15H          ;Request write
        LEA     DX,FCBREC
        INT     21H
        CMP     AL,00           ;Valid write?
        JZ      F20             ;  yes
        LEA     DX,WRTMSG       ;  no --
        CALL    X10ERR          ;  call error routine
        MOV     NAMELEN,00
F20:    RET
F10WRIT ENDP
;               Close disk file:
;               ---------------
G10CLSE PROC    NEAR
        MOV     NAMEDTA,1AH     ;Set EOF mark
        CALL    F10WRIT
        MOV     AH,10H          ;Request close
        LEA     DX,FCBREC
        INT     21H
        RET
G10CLSE ENDP
;               Scroll screen:
;               ------------
Q10SCR  PROC    NEAR            ;AX set on entry
        MOV     BH,1EH          ;Set yellow on blue
        MOV     CX,0000
        MOV     DX,184FH
        INT     10H             ;Scroll
        RET
Q10SCR  ENDP
;               Set cursor:
;               ----------
Q20CURS PROC    NEAR
        MOV     AH,02
        MOV     BH,00
        MOV     DL,00
        MOV     DH,ROW          ;Set cursor
        INT     10H
        RET
Q20CURS ENDP
;               Disk error routine:
;               ------------------
X10ERR  PROC    NEAR
        MOV     AH,09           ;DX contains
        INT     21H             ;  address of message
        MOV     ERRCDE,01       ;Set error code
        RET
X10ERR  ENDP

CODESG  ENDS
        END     BEGIN
```

Figure 16-1 (Continued)

The close operation writes the remaining nine records in the buffer onto a second sector and updates the directory for date and file size. The size is stored with reversed bytes as 20030000. The following shows the last buffer:

```
Buffer:   |rec 16|rec 17| ... |rec 24|hex 1A| ... | ... | ...
```

For simplicity, the program creates records that contain only one field. Most records, however, contain various alphabetic and binary fields and just require defining the record in the DTA. But if records contain binary numbers, do not use an EOF marker because a binary number could validly contain hex 1A.

To make the program more flexible, consider allowing a user to specify which drive contains the file. At the start, the program could display a message for the user to enter the disk drive number and could then change the first byte of the FCB.

SEQUENTIAL READING OF A DISK FILE

Under original DOS, a program that reads a disk file contains a file control block that defines the file exactly how it was created. At its start, the program uses the function call hex 0F to *open* the file:

```
MOV   AH,0FH       ;Open the
LEA   DX,FCBname   ;     file
INT   21H          ;Call DOS
```

The open operation checks that the directory contains an entry with the filename and extension defined in the FCB. If the entry is not in the directory, the operation sets the AL to hex FF. If the entry is present, the operation sets the AL to 00, the actual file size in the FCB, the FCB current block number to 0, and the FCB record size to hex 80. After the open, you may override this default with your own record size.

The DTA is the start of the definition of the input record, according to the format that was used to create the file. Use the function call hex 1A (not to be confused with the EOF marker 1A) to set the address of the DTA, just as for creating a disk file:

```
MOV   AH,1AH       ;Set address
LEA   DX,DTAname   ;  of DTA
INT   21H          ;Call DOS
```

To read a disk record sequentially, use function call hex 14:

```
MOV   AH,14H       ;Read record
LEA   DX,FCBname   ;  sequentially
INT   21H          ;Call DOS
```

The read operation uses the information in the FCB to deliver the disk record beginning at the address of the DTA. The operation then sets the AL register as follows:

00 A successful read.
01 End-of-file, no data in record.
02 Not enough space in the DTA to read one record.
03 End-of-file, has read a partial record filled out with zeros.

The first read operation reads an entire sector into the DOS buffer. The operation determines the record size from the FCB and delivers to the DTA the first record from the buffer. Subsequent reads cause remaining records (if any) to be delivered until the buffer contains no more records. At this point, the operation determines the address of the next sector and reads its contents into the buffer.

On a successful read, the operation automatically increments the current record number in the FCB. On completion of sequential reading, the program recognizes the end-of-file for which you should test. Because the directory would be unchanged, it is usually not necessary to close an input file. An exception: a program that successively opens and reads a number of files should close them because DOS limits the number of files that can be open at one time.

PROGRAM: USING AN FCB TO READ A DISK FILE

The program in Figure 16-2 reads the file that the previous program created and displays the input names on the screen. Both programs contain an identical FCB; although the names of the entries need not be the same, the operands for filename and extension must be identical.

The program is organized as follows:

BEGIN Initializes segment registers, calls E10OPEN to open the file and set the DTA, and calls F10READ to read a disk record. If end-of-file, the program terminates; if not end, the program calls G10DISP.

E10OPEN Opens the file, sets the record size to the correct length of 32 (hex 20), and initializes the address of the DTA.

```
TITLE   FCBREAD (EXE)  Read records created by CREATDSK
; ------------------------------------------------------
STACKSG SEGMENT PARA STACK 'Stack'
        DW      80 DUP(?)
STACKSG ENDS
; ------------------------------------------------------
DATASG  SEGMENT PARA 'Data'
FCBREC  LABEL   BYTE              ;FCB for disk file:
FCBDRIV DB      04                ;  drive D
FCBNAME DB      'NAMEFILE'        ;  file name
FCBEXT  DB      'DAT'             ;  extension
FCBBLK  DW      0000              ;  current block#
FCBRCSZ DW      0000              ;  logical record size
        DD      ?                 ;  DOS file size
        DW      ?                 ;  DOS date
        DT      ?                 ;  DOS reserved
FCBSQRC DB      00                ;  current record#
        DD      ?                 ;  relative record#

RECLEN  EQU     32                ;Record length
NAMEFLD DB      RECLEN DUP(' '), 13, 10, '$'

ENDCDE  DB      00
OPENMSG DB      '*** Open error ***', '$'
READMSG DB      '*** Read error ***', '$'
ROW     DB      00
DATASG  ENDS
;------------------------------------------------------
CODESG  SEGMENT PARA 'Code'
BEGIN   PROC    FAR
        ASSUME  CS:CODESG,DS:DATASG,SS:STACKSG,ES:DATASG
        PUSH    DS
        SUB     AX,AX
        PUSH    AX
        MOV     AX,DATASG
        MOV     DS,AX
        MOV     ES,AX
        MOV     AX,0600H
        CALL    Q10SCR            ;Clear screen
        CALL    Q20CURS           ;Set cursor
        CALL    E10OPEN           ;Open file, set DTA
        CMP     ENDCDE,00         ;Valid open?
        JNZ     A90               ;  no - terminate
A20LOOP:
        CALL    F10READ           ;Read disk record
        CMP     ENDCDE,00         ;Normal read?
        JNZ     A90               ;  no  - exit
        CALL    G10DISP           ;Display name
        JMP     A20LOOP           ;Continue
A90:    RET                       ;Terminate
BEGIN  ENDP

;               Open disk file:
;               --------------
E10OPEN PROC    NEAR
        LEA     DX,FCBREC
        MOV     AH,0FH            ;Request open
        INT     21H
```

Figure 16-2 Reading a Disk File.

```
        CMP     AL,00           ;File found?
        JNZ     E20             ;  no - error

        MOV     FCBRCSZ,RECLEN  ;Set record length (EQU)
        MOV     AH,1AH
        LEA     DX,NAMEFLD      ;Set address of DTA
        INT     21H
        RET
E20:
        MOV     ENDCDE,01       ;Error message
        LEA     DX,OPENMSG
        CALL    X10ERR
        RET
E10OPEN ENDP
;               Read disk record:
;               ----------------
F10READ PROC    NEAR
        MOV     AH,14H          ;Request read
        LEA     DX,FCBREC
        INT     21H
        CMP     NAMEFLD,1AH     ;EOF marker?
        JNE     F20             ;  no
        MOV     ENDCDE,01       ;  yes
        JMP     F90
F20:
        CMP     AL,00           ;Normal read?
        JZ      F90             ;  yes - exit
        MOV     ENDCDE,01       ;No:
        CMP     AL,01           ;End-of-file?
        JZ      F90             ;  yes - exit
        LEA     DX,READMSG      ;  no  - must be
        CALL    X10ERR          ;  invalid read
F90:
        RET
F10READ ENDP
;               Display record:
;               --------------
G10DISP PROC    NEAR
        MOV     AH,09           ;Request display
        LEA     DX,NAMEFLD
        INT     21H
        CMP     ROW,20          ;Bottom of screen?
        JAE     G30             ;  no  -
        INC     ROW             ;  yes - incr row
        JMP     G90
G30:
        MOV     AX,0601H
        CALL    Q10SCR          ;  scroll
        CALL    Q20CURS         ;  set cursor
G90:    RET
G10DISP ENDP
;               Scroll screen:
;               ------------
Q10SCR  PROC    NEAR            ;AX set on entry
        MOV     BH,1EH          ;Set color
        MOV     CX,0000
        MOV     DX,184FH        ;Request scroll
        INT     10H
        RET
```

Figure 16-2 (Continued)

```
Q10SCR   ENDP
;                Set cursor:
;                ----------
Q20CURS PROC     NEAR
         MOV     AH,02
         MOV     BH,00
         MOV     DH,ROW
         MOV     DL,00
         INT     10H
         RET
Q20CURS ENDP
;                Disk error routine:
;                ------------------
X10ERR   PROC    NEAR
         MOV     AH,09              ;DX contains address
         INT     21H                ;  of message
         RET
X10ERR   ENDP

CODESG   ENDS
         END     BEGIN
```

Figure 16-2 (Continued)

F10READ	Reads disk records sequentially. The read operation automatically increments the FCB current record number.
G10DISP	Displays the input record.
X10ERR	In the event of an invalid open or read operation, displays an error message.

The open operation checks that filename and extension exist in the directory. If so, it automatically sets the FCB entries for file size, date, and record size. The first read, which references current record number 00, accesses disk and reads a full sector (16 records) into the buffer. It then delivers the first record to the DTA and increments the current record number in the FCB from 00 to 01:

```
Buffer:   |rec 00|rec 01|rec 02| . . . |rec 15|
                 DTA:    |rec 00|
```

The second read executed does not have to access disk. Since the required record is already in the buffer, the operation simply transfers current record 01 from the buffer to the DTA and increments the current record number to 02. Each read operation continues in this manner until all 16 records in the buffer have been processed.

An attempt to read current record 16 causes the operation to physically read the entire next sector into the buffer. Subsequent reads then transfer each record successively from the buffer to the DTA. An attempt to read past the last record causes the operation to signal an end-of-file condition that sets the AL to hex 01.

RANDOM PROCESSING

Up to now, this chapter has discussed processing disk files sequentially, which is adequate for creating a file, for printing its contents, and for making changes to small files. To update a file with new data, a program restricted only to sequential processing has to read each record, change the specified ones, and write the records into another file (it could use the same DTA but would require a different FCB). A common practice is to read the input file from disk A and to write the updated file onto disk B. The advantage of this method is that it provides an automatic backup file.

Some applications involve accessing a particular record on a file for information on a few employees or stock part numbers. For example, to access the 300th record in a file, sequential processing could involve reading through the preceding 299 records before delivering the 300th (although the system could begin at a specific current block/record number).

Although you may create a file sequentially, you may access records sequentially or randomly. The requirements for random processing using a DOS call simply involve inserting the required record number in the FCB relative record field and issuing a random read or write command.

Random processing uses the relative record number (bytes 33-36) in the FCB. The value is a doubleword, stored in reverse byte sequence. To locate a random record, the system automatically converts relative record number to current block (bytes 12-13) and current record (byte 32).

Random Reading

The open operation and setting of the DTA is the same for both random and sequential processing. Consider a program that is to directly access relative record number 05. Insert the number 05 into the FCB field for relative record number and issue the instructions for random read. If successful, the operation returns the contents of the record to the DTA.

To read a record randomly, store the required relative record number in the FCB and use function call hex 21:

```
MOV AH,21H        ;Request random
LEA DX,FCBname    ;   read
INT 21H           ;Call DOS
```

The read operation converts relative record number to current block/record. It uses this value to locate the required disk record, delivers the record to the DTA, and sets the AL register as follows:

00 The read was successful.
01 No more data is available.
02 Terminated transfer because of insufficient room in the DTA.
03 Has read a partial record filled with zeros.

As you can see, there is no end-of-file test as such. The only valid response for a record that is supposed to exist is 00. You can cause invalid responses by such means as setting an invalid relative record number and failing to initialize a correct address in the DTA or FCB. Since these errors are easy to make, it is wise to test the AL for a nonzero code.

When a program first requests a random record, the operation uses the directory to locate the sector where the record resides, reads the entire sector from disk into the buffer, and delivers the record to the DTA. For example, assume that records are 128 bytes long and four to a sector. A request for random record number 23 causes the following four records to be read into the DTA:

| rel rec #20 | rel rec #21 | rel rec #22 | rel rec #23 |

When the program requests the next random record—for example, number 23—the operation first checks the buffer. Since the record is already there, it is transferred directly to the DTA. If the program requests a record such as number 35 that is not in the buffer, the operation uses the directory to locate the record, reads the entire sector into the buffer, and delivers the record to the DTA. Accordingly, it is more efficient to request random record numbers that are close together.

Random Writing

The create operation and setting of the DTA is the same for both random and sequential processing. For processing an inventory file, a program could randomly read an item, change the quantity on hand, and write the record back into the same disk location. With the relative record number initialized in the FCB, a *random write* uses the function call hex 22 as follows:

```
MOV AH,22H          ;Request random
LEA DX,FCBname      ;  write
INT 21H             ;Call DOS
```

The write operation sets the AL as follows:

- 00 The write was successful.
- 01 The disk is full.
- 02 Transfer ended because of insufficient space to write the record in the DTA.

You could get a nonzero return code when randomly creating a new file. But if you have read a record randomly and are now rewriting an updated record in the same disk location, you would expect the return code to be only 00.

The random relative record number in the FCB is a doubleword, four bytes, stored in reversed sequence. For a small file, you may have to initialize only the leftmost byte or two. But for large files, setting a record number for three or four bytes requires some care.

PROGRAM: READING A DISK FILE RANDOMLY

The program in Figure 16-3 reads the same file created in Figure 16-1. By keying in a relative record number that is within the bounds of the file, a user can request any record to display on the screen. If the file contains 25 records, then valid record numbers are 00 through 24. A number entered from the keyboard is in ASCII format, and in this case should be only one or two digits.

The program is organized as follows:

- C10OPEN Opens the file, sets the record size to 32, and sets the address of the DTA.
- D10RECN Accepts a record number from the keyboard and converts it to binary format in the FCB relative record field. An improvement would be to check that the number is valid, between 00 and 24.
- F10READ Uses the relative record number in the FCB to deliver a record to the DTA.
- G10DISP Displays the record.

The procedure D10RECN accepts a record number from the keyboard and checks its length in the parameter list. There are three possible lengths:

- 00 End of processing requested.
- 01 A one-digit request, stored in the AL.
- 02 A two-digit request, stored in the AX.

```
        page    60,132
TITLE   RANREAD (COM)  Random read records created by FCBCREAT
CODESG  SEGMENT PARA 'Code'
        ASSUME  CS:CODESG,DS:CODESG,SS:CODESG,ES:CODESG
        ORG     100H
BEGIN:  JMP     MAIN
; -------------------------------------------------------
FCBREC  LABEL   BYTE               ;FCB for disk file:
FCBDRIV DB      04                 ;  drive D
FCBNAME DB      'NAMEFILE'         ;  file name
FCBEXT  DB      'DAT'              ;  extension
FCBBLK  DW      0000               ;  current block#
FCBRCSZ DW      0000               ;  logical record size
        DD      ?                  ;  DOS file size
        DW      ?                  ;  DOS date
        DT      ?                  ;  DOS reserved
        DB      00                 ;  current record#
FCBRNRC DD      00000000           ;  relative record#

RECLEN  EQU     32                 ;Record length
RECDPAR LABEL   BYTE               ;Parameter list:
MAXLEN  DB      3                  ;
ACTLEN  DB      ?                  ;
RECDNO  DB      3 DUP(' ')         ;

NAMEFLD DB      RECLEN DUP(' '),13,10,'$' ;DTA

OPENMSG DB      '*** Open error ***',13,10,'$'
READMSG DB      '*** Read error ***',13,10,'$'
COL     DB      00
PROMPT  DB      'Record number? $'
ROW     DB      00
ENDCDE  DB      00
; -------------------------------------------------------
MAIN    PROC    NEAR
        CALL    Q10CLR             ;Clear screen
        CALL    Q20CURS            ;Set cursor
        CALL    C10OPEN            ;Open file, set DTA
        CMP     ENDCDE,00          ;Valid open?
        JZ      A20LOOP            ;  yes - continue
        RET                        ;  no  - terminate
A20LOOP:
        CALL    D10RECN            ;Request record #
        CMP     ACTLEN,00          ;Any more requests?
        JE      A40                ;  no  - exit
        CALL    F10READ            ;Random read
        CMP     ENDCDE,00          ;Normal read?
        JNZ     A30                ;  no  - bypass
        CALL    G10DISP            ;Call display routine
A30:
        JMP     A20LOOP
A40:    RET                        ;Terminate
MAIN    ENDP
;               Open disk routine:
;               -----------------
C10OPEN PROC    NEAR
        MOV     AH,0FH             ;Request open
        LEA     DX,FCBREC
```

Figure 16-3 Random Reading of Disk Records.

```
         INT     21H
         CMP     AL,00              ;Valid open?
         JNZ     C20                ;  no - error
         MOV     FCBRCSZ,RECLEN     ;Record size (EQU)
         MOV     AH,1AH
         LEA     DX,NAMEFLD         ;Set address of DTA
         INT     21H
         RET
C20:
         LEA     DX,OPENMSG
         CALL    X10ERR
         RET
C10OPEN  ENDP
;                Get record number:
;                -----------------
D10RECN  PROC    NEAR
         MOV     AH,09H             ;Request display
         LEA     DX,PROMPT
         INT     21H
         MOV     AH,0AH             ;Request input
         LEA     DX,RECDPAR
         INT     21H
         CMP     ACTLEN,01          ;Check length 0, 1, 2
         JB      D40                ;Length 0, terminate
         JA      D20
         SUB     AH,AH              ;Length 1
         MOV     AL,RECDNO
         JMP     D30
D20:
         MOV     AH,RECDNO          ;Length 2
         MOV     AL,RECDNO+1
D30:
         AND     AX,0F0FH           ;Clear ASCII 3's
         AAD                        ;Convert to binary
         MOV     WORD PTR FCBRNRC,AX
D40:
         MOV     COL,20
         CALL    Q20CURS            ;Set cursor
         RET
D10RECN  ENDP
;                Read disk record:
;                ----------------
F10READ  PROC    NEAR
         MOV     ENDCDE,00          ;Clear indicator
         MOV     AH,21H             ;Random read
         LEA     DX,FCBREC
         INT     21H
         CMP     AL,00              ;Normal read?
         JZ      F20                ;  yes - exit
         LEA     DX,READMSG         ;  no  - invalid,
         CALL    X10ERR             ;  call error routine
F20:     RET
F10READ  ENDP
;                Display name:
;                ------------
G10DISP  PROC    NEAR
         MOV     AH,09              ;Request display
         LEA     DX,NAMEFLD
```

Figure 16-3 (Continued)

```
         INT     21H
         INC     ROW
         MOV     COL,00
         RET
G10DISP  ENDP
;                Clear screen:
;                ------------
Q10CLR   PROC    NEAR
         MOV     AX,0600H          ;Request scroll
         MOV     BH,41H            ;Color (07 for BW)
         MOV     CX,0000
         MOV     DX,184FH
         INT     10H
         RET
Q10CLR   ENDP
;                Set cursor:
;                ----------
Q20CURS  PROC    NEAR
         MOV     AH,02             ;Request set
         MOV     BH,00             ;  cursor
         MOV     DH,ROW
         MOV     DL,COL
         INT     10H
         RET
Q20CURS  ENDP
;                Disk error routine:
;                ------------------
X10ERR   PROC    NEAR
         MOV     AH,09             ;DX contains address
         INT     21H               ;  of message
         INC     ROW
         MOV     ENDCDE,01
         RET
X10ERR   ENDP

CODESG   ENDS
         END     BEGIN
```

Figure 16-3 (Continued)

The procedure has to convert the ASCII number to binary. Since the value is in the AX, the AAD instruction works nicely for this purpose. The contents of the AX, now in binary, are moved to the leftmost two bytes of the FCB relative record field. As an example, if the entered number is ASCII 12, then the AX would contain 3132. AND converts this to 0102 and AAD further converts it to 000C. The result in the FCB random record field is C0000000.

RANDOM BLOCK PROCESSING

If there is sufficient space in a program, one random block operation can write an entire file from the DTA onto disk and can read the entire file from disk into the DTA. This feature is especially useful for storing tables on disk, which other programs can read into memory for processing.

You may begin with any valid relative record number and any number of records, although the block must be within the file's range of records. You still must first open the file and initialize the DTA.

For a *random block write,* initialize the required number of records in the CX register, set the starting relative record number in the FCB, and use function call hex 28:

```
MOV AH,28H          ;Request random block write
MOV CX,records      ;Set no. of records
LEA DX,FCBname      ;
INT 21H             ;Call DOS
```

The operation converts the FCB relative record number to current block/record. It uses this value to determine the starting disk location and sets a code in the AL register:

00 Successful write of all records.
01 No records written because of insufficient disk space.

The operation sets the FCB relative record field and the current block/record fields to the next record number. That is, if it wrote records 00-24, the next record is 25 (hex 19).

For *random block read,* initialize the required number of records in the CX and use function call hex 27:

```
MOV AH,27H          ;Request random block read
MOV CX,records      ;Initialize no. of records
LEA DX,FCBname      ;
INT 21H             ;Call DOS
```

The read operation returns a code in the AL register:

00 Successful read of all records.
01 Has read to end of file and last record is complete.
02 Read as many records as possible in the DTA.
03 Has read to end of file and last record is partial.

The operation stores in the CX the actual number of records read and sets the FCB relative record field and current block/record fields to the next record.

You may want to read an entire file but are uncertain of the number of records. Since the open operation initializes the FCB file size field, simply divide this value by the record length. For example, if the file size is hex 320 (800) and record length is hex 20 (32), then the number of records would be hex 19 (25).

PROGRAM: READING A RANDOM BLOCK

The program in Figure 16-4 performs a block read of the file created in Figure 16-1. The program initializes the starting relative record number to 00 and the CX to 25 records and displays the entire DTA on the screen (just to show that it really works!). Other variations could involve initializing at a record other than 00 and reading fewer than 25 records.

The program is organized as follows:

E10OPEN	Opens the file, sets the FCB record size to 32, and sets the address of the DTA.
F10READ	Initializes the number of records to 25 and performs the block read.
G10DISP	Displays the block on the screen.

The read operation converts the FCB relative record number 00 to current block 00 and current record hex 00. At the end of the read operation, the FCB current record number contains hex 19 and the relative record number contains hex 19000000.

ABSOLUTE DISK I/O

You can use DOS INT 25H and 26H for absolute reads and writes to process a disk directly. In this case, you lose the advantages of directory handling and blocking/deblocking of records that DOS INT 21H provides.

Since these operations treat all records as the size of a sector, they directly access a whole sector or block of sectors. Disk addressing is in terms of "logical record number" (absolute sector). To determine a logical record number on two-sided diskettes with nine sectors per track, count each sector from track 0, sector 1, as follows:

Track	*Sector*	*Logical Record Number*
0	1	0
0	2	1
1	1	9
1	9	17
2	9	26

```
TITLE   RANBLOK (COM) Random block read of name file
CODESG  SEGMENT PARA 'Code'
        ASSUME  CS:CODESG,DS:CODESG,SS:CODESG,ES:CODESG
        ORG     100H
BEGIN:  JMP     MAIN
; ---------------------------------------------------------
FCBREC  LABEL   BYTE              ;FCB for disk file:
FCBDRIV DB      04                ;  drive D
FCBNAME DB      'NAMEFILE'        ;  file name
FCBEXT  DB      'DAT'             ;  extension
FCBBLK  DW      0000              ;  current block #
FCBRCSZ DW      0000              ;  logical record size
FCBFLZ  DD      ?                 ;  DOS file size
        DW      ?                 ;  DOS date
        DT      ?                 ;  DOS reserved
        DB      00                ;  current record #
FCBRNRC DD      00000000          ;  relative record #

DSKRECS DB      1024 DUP(?),'$'  ;DTA for block of records

ENDCODE DB      00
NORECS  DW      25                ;Number of records
OPENMSG DB      '*** Open error ***',13,10,'$'
READMSG DB      '*** Read error ***',13,10,'$'
ROWCTR  DB      00
; ---------------------------------------------------------
MAIN    PROC    NEAR
        CALL    Q10CLR            ;Clear screen
        CALL    Q20CURS           ;Set cursor
        CALL    E10OPEN           ;Open file, set DTA
        CMP     ENDCODE,00        ;Valid open?
        JNZ     A30               ;  no - exit
        CALL    F10READ           ;Read records
        CALL    G10DISP           ;Call display
A30:    RET                       ;Terminate
MAIN    ENDP
;               Open disk file:
;               --------------
E10OPEN PROC    NEAR
        MOV     AH,0FH            ;Request open
        LEA     DX,FCBREC
        INT     21H
        CMP     AL,00             ;Valid open?
        JNZ     E20               ;  no - error

        MOV     FCBRCSZ,0020H     ;Record size
        MOV     AH,1AH
        LEA     DX,DSKRECS        ;Set address of DTA
        INT     21H
        RET
E20:
        LEA     DX,OPENMSG        ;Open error
        CALL    X10ERR
        RET
E10OPEN ENDP
;               Read disk block:
;               ---------------
F10READ PROC    NEAR
```

Figure 16-4 Reading a Random Block.

```
         MOV     AH,27H          ;Random block read
         MOV     CX,NORECS       ;No. of records
         LEA     DX,FCBREC
         INT     21H
         MOV     ENDCODE,AL      ;Save return condition
         RET
F10READ  ENDP
;                Display disk block:
;                -----------------
G10DISP  PROC    NEAR
         MOV     AH,09           ;Request display
         LEA     DX,DSKRECS
         INT     21H
         RET
G10DISP  ENDP
;                Clear screen routine:
;                --------------------
Q10CLR   PROC    NEAR
         MOV     AX,0600H        ;Request scroll
         MOV     BH,41H          ;Color (07 for BW)
         MOV     CX,0000
         MOV     DX,184FH
         INT     10H
         RET
Q10CLR   ENDP
;                Set cursor routine:
;                -----------------
Q20CURS  PROC    NEAR
         MOV     AH,02           ;Request set cursor
         MOV     BH,00
         MOV     DH,ROWCTR
         MOV     DL,00
         INT     10H
         INC     ROWCTR
         RET
Q20CURS  ENDP
;                Disk error routine:
;                -----------------
X10ERR   PROC    NEAR
         MOV     AH,09           ;DX contains address
         INT     21H             ;  of message
         MOV     ENDCODE,01
         RET
X10ERR   ENDP

CODESG   ENDS
         END     BEGIN
```

Figure 16-4 (Continued)

A convenient formula for two-sided diskettes is

Logical record number = (track x 9) + (sector – 1)

For example, the logical record number for track 2, sector 9, is

$$(2 \times 9) + (9 - 1) = 18 + 8 = 26$$

The required coding is the following:

```
MOV  AL,drive#      ;0 for A, 1 for B, etc.
MOV  BX,addr        ;Transfer address
MOV  CX,sectors     ;No. of sectors to read/write
MOV  DX,record#     ;Beginning logical record no.
INT  25H or 26H     ;DOS absolute read or write
```

Absolute disk read/write operations destroy all registers except the segment registers and set the CF flag to indicate if the operation was successful (0) or unsuccessful (1). If unsuccessful, the AL describes the error:

AL	*Reason*
10000000	Attachment failed to respond
01000000	Seek operation failed
00100000	Controller failure
00010000	Bad CRC on diskette read
00001000	DMA overrun on diskette read
00000100	Requested sector not found
00000011	Attempt to write on write-protected diskette
00000010	Address mark not found

The INT operation pushes the flags onto the stack. On return, since the original flags are still on the stack, pop them after checking the CF flag.

MISCELLANEOUS FEATURES

Among the original DOS functions are several useful disk operations.

Disk Reset: Hex D

Normally, closing a file properly writes all remaining records and updates the directory. Under special circumstances, such as between program steps or a disaster, a program may need to reset a disk. The DOS function call hex D flushes all file buffers but does not automatically update the directory; if necessary, first close all files.

```
MOV AH,0DH   ;Request reset disk
INT 21H      ;Call DOS
```

Select Default Disk Drive: Hex E

The main purpose of DOS function call hex E is to select a drive as the current default. Set the drive number in the DL, where 0 = A, 1 = B, and so forth:

```
MOV AH,0EH   ;Request set default
MOV DL,02    ;  drive C
INT 21H      ;Call DOS
```

The operation returns the number of drives (all types) in the AL. Because of a DOS requirement of at least two logical drives A and B, DOS returns the value 02 for a one-drive system. (Use INT 11H for determining the actual number of drives.)

Search for Directory Entries: Hex 11 and 12

A utility program may have to search a directory in order to access a file name, for example, to delete or rename. To access the first or only directory entry requires the address of an unopened FCB in the DX and function call 11H. If an extended FCB is used, you can also provide an attribute code—see the DOS Technical Reference manual.

```
MOV AH,11H        ;Request first directory entry
LEA DX,FCBname    ;Unopened FCB
INT 21H           ;Call DOS
```

The reference to FCBname could be location 5CH, the default DTA in the program segment prefix immediately preceding the program in memory (see Chapter 22).

The operation returns hex FF to the AL if it finds no match, and 00 if a match. The operation sets the contents of the DTA with drive number (1 = A, 2 = B, etc.), followed by file name and extension.

If a match to a multiple request, such as *.ASM, is found, use function call 12H for locating subsequent entries in the directory:

```
MOV AH,12H        ;Request next directory entry
LEA DX,FCBname    ;Unopened FCB
INT 21H           ;Call DOS
```

The operation returns the same values as function call 11H.

Delete a File: Hex 13

For deleting a file from within a program, use DOS function call 13H. The operation sets a delete byte in the first position of the file name in the directory.

```
MOV AH,13H        ;Request delete file
LEA DX,FCBname    ;Unopened FCB
INT 21H           ;Call DOS
```

If the operation finds and deletes an entry, it returns 00 to the AL, otherwise it returns hex FF.

Rename File: Hex 17

Use DOS function call hex 17 to rename files from within a program. Set the old file name (change from) in the FCB in the usual location. Set the new file name (change to) at FCB offset 16.

```
MOV AH,17H        ;Request rename file
LEA DX,FCBname    ;Address of FCB
INT 21H           ;Call DOS
```

Global characters ? and * in the new name cause the operation to duplicate corresponding positions from the old name. A successful operation returns 00 to the AL, and an unsuccessful operation (no match or new file name already exists) returns FF.

Get Default Drive: Hex 19

Use DOS function call hex 19 to determine the default disk drive:

```
MOV AH,19H  ;Get default drive
INT 21H     ;Call DOS
```

The operation returns a hex number in the AL register, where 0 = A, 1 = B, and so forth. You could next move this number directly into the FCB for accessing a file from the default drive.

Other function calls include get FAT information (1B and 1C), set random record field (24), set interrupt vector (25), create new program segment (26), and parse file name (29), explained in the DOS Technical Reference manual.

PROGRAM: SELECTIVELY DELETING FILES

The COM program named SDEL in Figure 16-5 illustrates DOS function calls 11H, 12H, and 13H to delete selected files. To request deletes, a user enters such commands as

```
SDEL *.*      (examine all file names)
SDEL *.BAK    (examine all BAK file names)
SDEL TEST.*   (examine all files named TEST)
```

The program, via DOS, locates each name in the directory that matches the request. On finding a match, DOS delivers the full program name to the PSP at hex 81 (the default DTA). The program displays the name and a prompt. You reply Y (if yes) to delete, N (if no) to keep, or press Return to terminate.

Be sure to create this as a COM program, because an EXE program requires different addressing for the use of locations hex 5C and 81 in the PSP. As a caution, use copied temporary files for testing.

```
TITLE   SELDEL (COM)    Delete selected files
;               Assumes default drive; enter as *.*, *.BAK, etc.
CODESG  SEGMENT PARA 'Code'
        ASSUME  CS:CODESG,DS:CODESG,SS:CODESG
        ORG     100H
BEGIN:  JMP     MAIN
; -------------------------------------------------------------
TAB     EQU     09
LF      EQU     10
CR      EQU     13
CRLF    DB      CR, LF, '$'
DELMSG  DB      TAB, 'Erase ','$'
ENDMSG  DB      CR, LF, 'No more directory entries', CR, LF, '$'
ERRMSG  DB      'Write-protected disk','$'
PROMPT  DB      'Y = Erase, N = Keep, Ret = Exit', CR, LF, '$'
; -------------------------------------------------------------
MAIN    PROC    NEAR                ;Main procedure
        MOV     AH,11H              ;Locate 1st entry
        CALL    D10DISK
        CMP     AL,0FFH             ;If no entries,
        JE      A90                 ;  exit
        LEA     DX,PROMPT           ;Initial prompt
        CALL    B10DISP
A20:
        LEA     DX,DELMSG           ;Display delete message
        CALL    B10DISP
        MOV     CX,11               ;11 chars
        MOV     SI,81H              ;Start of filename
A30:
        MOV     DL,[SI]             ;Get char for display
```

Figure 16-5 Selectively Deleting Files.

```
        CALL    C10CHAR
        INC     SI              ;Next char
        LOOP    A30
        MOV     DL,'?'
        CALL    C10CHAR

        MOV     AH,01           ;Accept 1-char
        INT     21H             ;  reply
        CMP     AL,0DH          ;Return char?
        JE      A90             ;  yes - exit
        OR      AL,00100000B    ;Force lowercase
        CMP     AL,'y'          ;Delete requested?
        JNE     A50             ;  no  - bypass
        MOV     AH,13H          ;  yes - delete entry
        MOV     DX,80H
        INT     21H
        CMP     AL,0            ;Was delete valid?
        JZ      A50             ;  yes - bypass
        LEA     DX,ERRMSG       ;  no -- warn
        CALL    B10DISP
        JMP     A90
A50:
        LEA     DX,CRLF         ;Return/line feed
        CALL    B10DISP
        MOV     AH,12H
        CALL    D10DISK         ;Get next dir entry
        CMP     AL,0FFH         ;Any more?
        JNE     A20             ;  yes - loop
A90:
        RET                     ;Exit to DOS
MAIN    ENDP
;               Display line:
;               ------------
B10DISP PROC    NEAR            ;DX set on entry
        MOV     AH,09
        INT     21H
        RET
B10DISP ENDP
;               Display character:
;               ----------------
C10CHAR PROC    NEAR            ;DL set on entry
        MOV     AH,02
        INT     21H
        RET
C10CHAR ENDP
;               Read directory entry:
;               --------------------
D10DISK PROC    NEAR
        MOV     DX,5CH          ;Set FCB
        INT     21H
        CMP     AL,0FFH         ;More entries?
        JNE     D90
        PUSH    AX              ;Save AL
        LEA     DX,ENDMSG
        CALL    B10DISP
        POP     AX              ;Restore AL
D90:    RET
D10DISK ENDP

CODESG  ENDS
        END     BEGIN
```

Figure 16-5 (Continued)

KEY POINTS TO REMEMBER

- A program using original DOS INT 21H function calls for disk I/O defines a file control block (FCB) for each file that it accesses.
- A block consists of 128 records. In the FCB, the current block number combined with the current record number indicates the disk record that is to be processed.
- The entries in the FCB for current block, record size, file size, and relative record number are stored in reversed byte sequence.
- All programs that reference a file define a similar FCB.
- The disk transfer area (DTA) is the location of the record that is to be written or read. You have to initialize each DTA in a program prior to a write or read operation.
- An open operation sets FCB entries for filename, extension, record size (hex 80), file size, and date. A program should change record size to the correct value.
- A program using DOS INT 21H for writing a file must close it at the end in order to write the records (if any) in the buffer and to complete the directory entries.
- On reads and writes under DOS INT 21H, the system automatically updates the current record number in the FCB.
- A DOS INT 21H read operation first checks the buffer for the required record and, if not present, performs a disk access.
- Random processing requires a record number in the relative record number entry in the FCB. Prior to performing a read or write, the system converts the number to current block/record.
- The eight bytes (doubleword) of the relative record number are stored in reversed sequence.
- If a required random record is already in the buffer, the system transfers it directly to the DTA. Otherwise, the operation accesses disk and reads into the buffer the entire sector containing the record.
- Where there is sufficient space, a random block read or write is more efficient. This feature is especially useful for loading tables.
- DOS INT 25H and 26H provide absolute disk read and write, but do not supply automatic directory handling, end-of-file operations, and record blocking and deblocking.

QUESTIONS

16-1. Provide the original DOS function calls for the following operations: (a) create, (b) set the DTA, (c) sequential write, (d) open, (e) sequential read.

16-2. A program uses the record size to which the open operation defaults: (a) How many records would a sector contain? (b) How many records would a diskette contain, assuming three tracks with nine sectors per track. (c) If the file in (b) is being read sequentially, how many physical disk accesses will occur?

16-3. Write a program that creates a disk file containing part number (five characters), part description (12 characters), and unit price (one word). Allow a user to enter these values on the terminal. Remember to convert the quantity from ASCII to binary.

16-4. Write a program that displays the contents of the file created in Question 16-3.

16-5. Determine the current block/record for the following random record numbers: (a) 45, (b) 73, (c) 150, (d) 260.

16-6. How does random record number (decimal) 2652 appear in the FCB relative record field?

16-7. Provide the hexadecimal function calls for the following operations: (a) random write, (b) random read, (c) random block write, (d) random block read.

16-8. Write the instructions to determine the number of records in a file. Assume that the open operation has already occurred. The name of the file size is FCBFLSZ and record size is FCBRCSZ.

16-9. Use the program from Question 16-4 to create part number, price, and description using the given data. Write a program that performs one block read for this file and displays each record down the screen.

```
Part# Price Description
 |023|00315|Assemblers  |
 |024|00430|Linkages    |
 |027|00525|Compilers   |
 |049|00920|Compressors |
 |114|11250|Extractors  |
 |117|00630|Haulers     |
 |122|10520|Lifters     |
 |124|21335|Processors  |
 |127|00960|Labelers    |
 |232|05635|Bailers     |
 |999|00000|            |
```

16-10. Revise the program in Question 16-9 so that price is stored in the disk record as a binary value.

16-11. Modify the program in Question 16-9 so that (a) it performs a random read, (b) a user can enter part number and quantity, and (c) it calculates and displays value (quantity times price).

CHAPTER 17

Disk Storage III: Extended DOS Functions

Objective: To cover the extended DOS function calls available since DOS 2.0 for handling disk files.

INTRODUCTION

Chapter 16 covered the original DOS function calls for file processing that are still available on all DOS versions. This chapter covers a number of extended functions introduced by DOS 2.0 and 3.0 that do not work on earlier versions. Make sure you have the correct DOS version before attempting to execute the operations covered in this chapter.

Many of these function calls are simpler than their direct counterparts in the original DOS functions. The DOS manual recommends using the new operations, which lead more naturally into UNIX-type systems. Some operations involve the use of an ASCIIZ string to initially identify a drive, path, and filename; a file handle for subsequent accessing of the file; and special error return codes.

THE ASCIIZ STRING

When using many of the extended functions for disk processing, you first tell DOS the address of an *ASCIIZ string* containing the location of the file, as disk drive, directory path, and filename (all optional), followed by a byte of hex zeros. Some examples:

```
PATHNM1    DB    'B:\TEST.ASM',0
PATHNM2    DB    'C:\UTILITY\NU.EXE',0
```

The back slash, which may also be a forward slash, acts as a path separator. A byte of zeros terminates the string, thus the name ASCIIZ string. For interrupts that require an ASCIIZ string, load its address in the DX register, for example as LEA DX,PATHNM1.

FILE HANDLES AND ERROR RETURN CODES

You access files by means of a handle, a one-word number that the open and create functions deliver in the AX. As discussed in Chapter 8, certain standard devices need not be opened, and you may use them directly: 0 = input, 1 = output, 2 = error output, 3 = auxiliary device, and 4 = printer.

For disk accessing, first either create or open a file using an ASCIIZ string and DOS function call hex 3C or 3D. If successful, the operation sets the CF flag to 0 and delivers the handle in the AX. Save the handle in a DW data item and use it for all subsequent disk accesses of the file. If not successful, the operation sets the CF flag to 1 and sets the AX to an error code, depending on the operation, as shown in Figure 17-1.

CREATING A DISK FILE

The following sections cover the requirements for creating, writing, and closing disk files for extended DOS.

Create File: Hex 3C

For creating a new file or overwriting an old file, first use function call hex 3C. Load the address of the ASCIIZ string in the DX and the required

01	Invalid function number	10	Invalid environment
02	File not found	11	Invalid format
03	Path not found	12	Invalid access code
04	Too many files open	13	Invalid data
05	Access denied	15	Invalid drive specified
06	Invalid handle	16	Attempt to remove directory
07	Memory control block destroyed	17	Not same device
08	Insufficient memory	18	No more files
09	Invalid memory block address		

Figure 17-1 Error Return Codes.

attribute in the CX. Chapter 15 covers the attribute byte; the code for a normal file is 0. An example that creates a normal file follows:

```
MOV AH,3CH          ;Request create
MOV CX,00           ;  normal file
LEA DX,PATHNM1      ;ASCIIZ string
INT 21H             ;Call DOS
JC  error           ;Exit if error
MOV HANDLE1,AX      ;Save handle in DW
```

For a valid open, the operation creates a directory entry with the given attribute, clears the CF flag, and sets the handle for the file in the AX. Use the handle for all subsequent operations. If a file by the given name already exists, the operation sets it to zero length for overwriting.

For error conditions, the operation sets the CF flag and returns an error code in the AX: 03, 04, or 05 (see Figure 17-1). Code 05 means that either the directory is full or the referenced filename has the read-only attribute. Be sure to check the CF flag first. For example, creating a file probably delivers handle 0005 to the AX, which could easily be confused with error code 05, access denied.

Write File: Hex 40

For writing records, use DOS function call hex 40. Set the file handle in the BX, the number of bytes to write in the CX, and the address of the output area in the DX. The following writes a 256-byte record from OUTREC:

```
HANDLE1 DW   ?
OUTREC  DB   256 DUP (' ')
        MOV AH,40H          ;Request write
        MOV BX,HANDLE1      ;Handle
        MOV CX,256          ;Record length
        LEA DX,OUTREC       ;Address of output area
        INT 21H             ;Call DOS
        JC  error2          ;Test for error
        CMP AX,256          ;All bytes written?
        JNE error3
```

A valid operation writes the record from memory, clears the CF flag, and sets the AX to the number of bytes actually written. A full disk may cause the number written to differ from the number requested. An invalid operation sets the CF flag and returns to the AX error code 05 (access denied) or 06 (invalid handle).

Close File: Hex 3E

When you have finished writing a file, set the file handle in the BX and use DOS function call hex 3E to close it. The operation writes any remaining records still in the memory buffer and updates the directory and FAT.

```
MOV AH,3EH        ;Request close
MOV BX,HANDLE1    ;File handle
INT 21H           ;Call DOS
```

The only possible error return in the AX is 06 (invalid handle).

PROGRAM: USING A HANDLE TO CREATE A FILE

The program in Figure 17-2 creates a file from names that a user enters from a keyboard. Major procedures are the following:

C10CREA	Uses function call hex 3C to create the file and saves the handle in a data item named HANDLE.
D10PROC	Accepts input from the keyboard and clears positions from the end of the name to the end of the input area to blank.
F10WRIT	Uses function call hex 40 to write records.
G10CLSE	At the end of processing, uses function call hex 3E to close the file in order to create a proper directory entry.

The input area is 30 bytes, followed by two bytes for a carriage return (hex 0DH) and line feed (hex 0AH), for 32 bytes in all. The program writes the 32 bytes as a fixed-length record. You could omit the return/line feed characters, but include them if you want to sort the file. The DOS SORT program requires these characters to indicate end of a record. For this example, the SORT command could be:

```
SORT B:<NAMEFILE.DAT >NAMEFILE.SRT
```

which sorts the records from NAMEFILE.DAT into ascending sequence in NAMEFILE.SRT. The program in Figure 17-3 later reads and displays the contents of NAMEFILE.SRT. Note two points: (1) The return/line feed

```
        page    60,132
TITLE   HANCREAT (EXE)  Create disk file of names
; ----------------------------------------------------
STACKSG SEGMENT PARA STACK 'Stack'
        DW      80 DUP(?)
STACKSG ENDS
; ----------------------------------------------------
DATASG  SEGMENT PARA 'Data'
NAMEPAR LABEL   BYTE                    ;Name parameter list:
MAXLEN  DB      30                      ;
NAMELEN DB      ?                       ;
NAMEREC DB      30 DUP(' '), 0DH, 0AH   ;  entered name,
                                        ;  CR/LF for writing
ERRCDE  DB      00
HANDLE  DW      ?
PATHNAM DB      'D:\NAMEFILE.DAT', 0
PROMPT  DB      'Name? '
ROW     DB      01
OPNMSG  DB      '*** Open error  ***', 0DH, 0AH
WRTMSG  DB      '*** Write error ***', 0DH, 0AH
DATASG  ENDS
; ----------------------------------------------------
CODESG  SEGMENT PARA 'Code'
BEGIN   PROC    FAR
        ASSUME  CS:CODESG,DS:DATASG,SS:STACKSG,ES:DATASG
        PUSH    DS
        SUB     AX,AX
        PUSH    AX
        MOV     AX,DATASG
        MOV     DS,AX
        MOV     ES,AX
        MOV     AX,0600H
        CALL    Q10SCR          ;Clear screen
        CALL    Q20CURS         ;Set cursor
        CALL    C10CREA         ;Create file, set DTA
        CMP     ERRCDE,00       ;Create error?
        JZ      A20LOOP         ;  yes - continue
        RET                     ;  no  - return to DOS
A20LOOP:
        CALL    D10PROC
        CMP     NAMELEN,00      ;End of input?
        JNE     A20LOOP         ;  no  - continue
        CALL    G10CLSE         ;  yes - close,
        RET                     ;  return to DOS
BEGIN   ENDP
;               Create disk file:
;               ----------------
C10CREA PROC    NEAR
        MOV     AH,3CH          ;Request create
        MOV     CX,00           ;Normal
        LEA     DX,PATHNAM
        INT     21H
        JC      C20             ;Error?
        MOV     HANDLE,AX       ;  no - save handle
        RET
C20:                            ;  yes --
        LEA     DX,OPNMSG       ;  error message
        CALL    X10ERR
```

Figure 17-2 Using a Handle to Create a File.

```
         RET
C10CREA  ENDP
;                 Accept input:
;                 ------------
D10PROC  PROC     NEAR
         MOV      AH,40H             ;Request display
         MOV      BX,01              ;Handle
         MOV      CX,06              ;Length of prompt
         LEA      DX,PROMPT          ;Display prompt
         INT      21H

         MOV      AH,0AH             ;Request input
         LEA      DX,NAMEPAR         ;Accept name
         INT      21H
         CMP      NAMELEN,00         ;Is there a name?
         JNE      D20                ;  yes --
         RET                         ;  no  - exit
D20:
         MOV      AL,20H             ;Blank for storing
         SUB      CH,CH
         MOV      CL,NAMELEN         ;Length
         LEA      DI,NAMEREC
         ADD      DI,CX              ;Address + length
         NEG      CX                 ;Calculate remaining
         ADD      CX,30              ;  length
         REP      STOSB              ;Set to blank
D90:
         CALL     F10WRIT            ;Write disk record
         CALL     E10SCRL            ;Check for scroll
         RET
D10PROC  ENDP
;                 Check for scroll:
;                 ----------------
E10SCRL  PROC     NEAR
         CMP      ROW,18             ;Bottom of screen?
         JAE      E10                ;  yes - bypass
         INC      ROW                ;  no  - add to row
         JMP      E90
E10:
         MOV      AX,0601H           ;Scroll one row
         CALL     Q10SCR
E90:     CALL     Q20CURS            ;Reset cursor
         RET
E10SCRL  ENDP
;                 Write disk record:
;                 -----------------
F10WRIT  PROC     NEAR
         MOV      AH,40H             ;Request write
         MOV      BX,HANDLE
         MOV      CX,32              ;30 for name + 2 for CR/LF
         LEA      DX,NAMEREC
         INT      21H
         JNC      F20                ;Valid write?
         LEA      DX,WRTMSG          ;  no --
         CALL     X10ERR             ;  call error routine
         MOV      NAMELEN,00
F20:
         RET
```

Figure 17-2 (Continued)

```
F10WRIT ENDP
;               Close disk file:
;               ---------------
G10CLSE PROC    NEAR
        MOV     NAMEREC,1AH      ;Set EOF mark
        CALL    F10WRIT
        MOV     AH,3EH           ;Request close
        MOV     BX,HANDLE
        INT     21H
        RET
G10CLSE ENDP
;               Scroll screen:
;               -------------
Q10SCR  PROC    NEAR             ;AX set on entry
        MOV     BH,1EH           ;Set yellow on blue
        MOV     CX,0000
        MOV     DX,184FH
        INT     10H              ;Scroll
        RET
Q10SCR  ENDP
;               Set cursor:
;               ----------
Q20CURS PROC    NEAR
        MOV     AH,02
        MOV     BH,00
        MOV     DH,ROW           ;Set cursor
        MOV     DL,00
        INT     10H
        RET
Q20CURS ENDP
;               Disk error routine:
;               ------------------
X10ERR  PROC    NEAR             ;DX contains
        MOV     AH,40H           ;  address of message
        MOV     BX,01
        MOV     CX,21            ;Length
        INT     21H
        MOV     ERRCDE,01        ;Set error code
        RET
X10ERR  ENDP

CODESG  ENDS
        END     BEGIN
```

Figure 17-2 (Continued)

characters are included following each record only to facilitate the sort, and could otherwise be omitted. (2) The records could be variable length, only up to the end of the names; this would involve some extra programming, as you'll see in Figure 17-4.

READING A DISK FILE

The following sections cover the requirements for opening and reading disk files for extended DOS.

Open File: Hex 3D

If your program is to read a file, first use function call hex 3D to open it. This operation checks that the name is valid and the file is available. Load the address of the required ASCIIZ string in the DX and set an access code in the AL:

0 Open the file only for input
1 Open the file only for output
2 Open the file for input and output

Other bits in the AL are used for file sharing under DOS 3.0 and on—see the DOS Technical Reference manual. Watch out—for writing a file, use the create function, hex 3C, not the open function. Following is an example that opens a file for reading:

```
MOV AH,3DH       ;Request open
MOV AL,00        ;Read only
LEA DX,PATHNM1   ;ASCIIZ string
INT 21H          ;Call DOS
JC  error4       ;Exit if error
MOV HANDLE2,AX   ;Save handle in DW
```

If a file by the given name exists, the operation sets the record length to 1, assumes its present attribute, clears the CF flag, and sets a handle for the file in the AX. Use the handle for all subsequent operations.

If the file does not exist, the operation sets the CF flag and returns an error code in the AX: 02, 04, 05, or 12 (see Figure 17-1). Be sure to check the CF flag first. For example, creating a file probably delivers handle 0005 to the AX, which could easily be confused with error code 05, access denied.

Read File: Hex 3F

For reading records, use DOS function call hex 3F. Set the file handle in the BX, the number of bytes to read in the CX, and the address of the input area in the DX. The following reads a 512-byte record:

```
HANDLE2 DW   ?
INPREC  DB   512 DUP(' ')
        MOV AH,3FH        ;Request read
        MOV BX,HANDLE2    ;Handle
        MOV CX,512        ;Record length
        LEA DX,INPREC     ;Address of input area
```

```
INT 21H            ;Call DOS
JC  error5         ;Test for error
CMP AX,00          ;Zero bytes read?
JE  endfile
```

A valid operation reads the record into memory, clears the CF flag, and sets the AX to the number of bytes actually read. Zero in the AX means an attempt to read from end of file. An invalid read sets the CF flag and returns to the AX error code 05 (access denied) or 06 (invalid handle).

Since DOS limits the number of files open at one time, a program that successively reads a number of files should close them.

PROGRAM: USING A HANDLE TO READ A FILE

The program in Figure 17-3 reads the file created in Figure 17-2 and sorted by the DOS SORT command. It uses function call hex 3D to open the file and saves the handle in a data item named HANDLE, which function call hex 3F subsequently uses to read the file.

Since a return/line feed pair already follows each record, this program does not have to advance the cursor on displaying records.

ASCII FILES

The preceding examples created files and read them, but you may also want to process ASCII files that DOS or an editor have created. All you need to know are the organization of the directory and the FAT and the way in which the system stores data in a sector. DOS stores your data in an ASM file, for example, exactly the way that you key it, including the characters for tab (hex 09), return (hex 0D), and line feed (hex 0A). To conserve disk space, DOS does not store blanks that appear on the screen immediately preceding a tab character nor blanks on a line to the right of a return character. The following illustrates an assembler instruction as it appears on the screen:

<tab>MOV<tab> AH,09<return>

```
        page    60,132
TITLE   HANREAD (EXE)  Read disk records created by HANCREAT
; -----------------------------------------------------------
STACKSG SEGMENT PARA STACK 'Stack'
        DW      80 DUP(?)
STACKSG ENDS
; -----------------------------------------------------------
```

Figure 17-3 Using a Handle to Read a File.

```
DATASG  SEGMENT PARA 'Data'
ENDCDE  DB      00
HANDLE  DW      ?
IOAREA  DB      32 DUP(' ')
PATHNAM DB      'D:\NAMEFILE.SRT',0
OPENMSG DB      '*** Open error ***', 0DH, 0AH
READMSG DB      '*** Read error ***', 0DH, 0AH
ROW     DB      00
DATASG  ENDS
;-----------------------------------------------------
CODESG  SEGMENT PARA 'Code'
BEGIN   PROC    FAR
        ASSUME  CS:CODESG,DS:DATASG,SS:STACKSG,ES:DATASG
        PUSH    DS
        SUB     AX,AX
        PUSH    AX
        MOV     AX,DATASG
        MOV     DS,AX
        MOV     ES,AX
        MOV     AX,0600H
        CALL    Q10SCR              ;Clear screen
        CALL    Q20CURS             ;Set cursor
        CALL    E10OPEN             ;Open file, set DTA
        CMP     ENDCDE,00           ;Valid open?
        JNZ     A90                 ;  no - terminate
A20LOOP:
        CALL    F10READ             ;Read disk record
        CMP     ENDCDE,00           ;Normal read?
        JNZ     A90                 ;  no  - exit
        CALL    G10DISP             ;  yes - display name,
        JMP     A20LOOP             ;  continue
A90:    RET                         ;Terminate
BEGIN  ENDP
;               Open file:
;               ---------
E10OPEN PROC    NEAR
        MOV     AH,3DH              ;Request open
        MOV     AL,00               ;Normal file
        LEA     DX,PATHNAM
        INT     21H
        JC      E20                 ;Error?
        MOV     HANDLE,AX           ;  no - save handle
        RET
E20:
        MOV     ENDCDE,01           ;  yes --
        LEA     DX,OPENMSG          ;  error message
        CALL    X10ERR
        RET
E10OPEN ENDP
;               Read disk record:
;               ----------------
F10READ PROC    NEAR
        MOV     AH,3FH              ;Request read
        MOV     BX,HANDLE
        MOV     CX,32               ;30 for name, 2 for CR/LF
        LEA     DX,IOAREA
        INT     21H
        JC      F20                 ;Error on read?
        CMP     AX,00               ;End of file?
```

Figure 17-3 (Continued)

```
        JE      F30
        CMP     IOAREA,1AH          ;EOF marker?
        JE      F30                 ;  yes - exit
        RET
F20:                                ;  no --
        LEA     DX,READMSG          ;  invalid read
        CALL    X10ERR
F30:
        MOV     ENDCDE,01           ;Force end
F90:    RET
F10READ ENDP
;               Display name:
;               ------------
G10DISP PROC    NEAR
        MOV     AH,40H              ;Request display
        MOV     BX,01               ;Set handle
        MOV     CX,32               ;  & length
        LEA     DX,IOAREA
        INT     21H
        CMP     ROW,20              ;Bottom of screen?
        JAE     G90                 ;   yes - bypass
        INC     ROW
        RET
G90:
        MOV     AX,0601H
        CALL    Q10SCR              ;Scroll
        CALL    Q20CURS             ;Set cursor
        RET
G10DISP ENDP
;               Scroll screen:
;               -------------
Q10SCR  PROC    NEAR                ;AX set on entry
        MOV     BH,1EH              ;Set color
        MOV     CX,0000
        MOV     DX,184FH            ;Request scroll
        INT     10H
        RET
Q10SCR  ENDP
;               Set cursor:
;               ----------
Q20CURS PROC    NEAR
        MOV     AH,02               ;Request set
        MOV     BH,00               ;  cursor
        MOV     DH,ROW              ;  row
        MOV     DL,00               ;  column
        INT     10H
        RET
Q20CURS ENDP
;               Disk error routine:
;               ------------------
X10ERR  PROC    NEAR
        MOV     AH,40H              ;DX contains address
        MOV     BX,01               ;Handle
        MOV     CX,20               ;Length
        INT     21H                 ;  of message
        RET
X10ERR  ENDP

CODESG  ENDS
        END     BEGIN
```

Figure 17-3 (Continued)

For the above, the contents of the ASCII file would be

094D4F560941482C30390D0A

When TYPE or an editor reads the file, the tab, return, and line feed characters automatically adjust the data on a screen.

Let's now examine the program in Figure 17-4 that reads and displays the file, HANREAD.ASM (the example from Figure 17-3), one

```
         page     60,132
TITLE    ASCREAD  (COM)  Read an ASCII file
CODESG   SEGMENT PARA 'Code'
         ASSUME   CS:CODESG,DS:CODESG,SS:CODESG,ES:CODESG
         ORG      100H
BEGIN:   JMP      MAIN
; ------------------------------------------------------
SECTOR   DB       512 DUP(' ')     ;Input area
DISAREA  DB       120 DUP(' ')     ;Display area
ENDCDE   DW       00
HANDLE   DW       0
OPENMSG  DB       '*** Open error ***'
PATHNAM  DB       'D:\HANREAD.ASM', 0
ROW      DB       00
; ------------------------------------------------------
MAIN     PROC     NEAR             ;Main procedure
         MOV      AX,0600H
         CALL     Q10SCR           ;Clear screen
         CALL     Q20CURS          ;Set cursor
         CALL     E10OPEN          ;Open file, set DTA
         CMP      ENDCDE,00        ;Valid open?
         JNE      A90              ;  no -- exit
A20LOOP:                           ;  yes - continue
         CALL     R10READ          ;Read 1st disk sector
         CMP      ENDCDE,00        ;End-file, no data?
         JE       A90              ;  yes - exit
         CALL     G10XFER          ;Display/read
A90:     RET                       ;Terminate
MAIN     ENDP
;                 Open disk file:
;                 --------------
E10OPEN  PROC     NEAR
         MOV      AH,3DH           ;Request open
         MOV      AL,00            ;Read only
         LEA      DX,PATHNAM
         INT      21H
         JNC      E20              ;Test CF flag,
         CALL     X10ERR           ;  error if set
         RET
E20:
         MOV      HANDLE,AX        ;Save handle
         RET
E10OPEN  ENDP
;                 Transfer data to display line:
;                 -----------------------------
G10XFER  PROC     NEAR
```

Figure 17-4 Reading an ASCII File.

```
        CLD                     ;Set left-to-right
        LEA     SI,SECTOR
G20:
        LEA     DI,DISAREA
G30:
        LEA     DX,SECTOR+512
        CMP     SI,DX           ;End of sector?
        JNE     G40             ;  no  - bypass
        CALL    R10READ         ;  yes - read next
        CMP     ENDCDE,00       ;End of file?
        JE      G80             ;  yes - exit
        LEA     SI,SECTOR
G40:
        LEA     DX,DISAREA+80
        CMP     DI,DX           ;End of DISAREA?
        JB      G50             ;  no  - bypass
        MOV     [DI],0D0AH      ;  yes - set CR/LF,
        CALL    H10DISP         ;  & display
        LEA     DI,DISAREA
G50:
        LODSB                   ;[SI] to AL, INC SI
        STOSB                   ;AL to [DI], INC DI
        CMP     AL,1AH          ;End-of-file?
        JE      G80             ;  yes - exit
        CMP     AL,0AH          ;Line feed?
        JNE     G30             ;  no  - loop
        CALL    H10DISP         ;  yes - display
        JMP     G20
G80:
        CALL    H10DISP         ;Display last line
G90:    RET
G10XFER ENDP
;               Display line:
;               ------------
H10DISP PROC    NEAR
        MOV     AH,40H          ;Request display
        MOV     BX,01           ;Handle
        LEA     CX,DISAREA      ;Calculate
        NEG     CX              ;  length of
        ADD     CX,DI           ;  line
        LEA     DX,DISAREA
        INT     21H
        CMP     ROW,22          ;Bottom of screen?
        JAE     H20             ;  no - exit
        INC     ROW
        JMP     H90
H20:
        MOV     AX,0601H        ;Scroll
        CALL    Q10SCR
        CALL    Q20CURS
H90:    RET
H10DISP ENDP
;               Read disk sector:
;               ----------------
R10READ PROC    NEAR
        MOV     AH,3FH          ;Request read
        MOV     BX,HANDLE       ;Device
        MOV     CX,512          ;Length
        LEA     DX,SECTOR       ;Buffer
        INT     21H
```

Figure 17-4 (Continued)

```
         MOV     ENDCDE,AX
         RET
R10READ  ENDP
;                Scroll screen:
;                -------------
Q10SCR   PROC    NEAR             ;AX set on entry
         MOV     BH,1EH           ;Set color
         MOV     CX,0000          ;Scroll
         MOV     DX,184FH
         INT     10H
         RET
Q10SCR   ENDP
;                Set cursor:
;                ----------
Q20CURS  PROC    NEAR
         MOV     AH,02            ;Request set
         MOV     BH,00            ;  cursor
         MOV     DH,ROW
         MOV     DL,00
         INT     10H
         RET
Q20CURS  ENDP
;                Disk error routine:
;                ------------------
X10ERR   PROC    NEAR
         MOV     AH,40H           ;Request display
         MOV     BX,01            ;Handle
         MOV     CX,18            ;Length
         LEA     DX,OPENMSG
         INT     21H
         MOV     ENDCDE,01        ;Error indicator
         RET
X10ERR   ENDP

CODESG   ENDS
         END     BEGIN
```

Figure 17-4 (Continued)

sector at a time. If you have already keyed and tested HANREAD, you can easily copy it to a new name.

The program performs much the same functions as DOS TYPE, where each line displays up to the return/line feed characters. Scrolling is a problem. If you perform no special tests for bottom of screen, the operation automatically displays new lines over old, and if the old line is longer, old characters still appear to the right. For proper scrolling, you have to count rows and test for the bottom of the screen. Since lines in an ASCII file are variable lengths, you have to scan for the end of each line before displaying it.

The program reads a full sector of data into SECTOR. The procedure G10XFER transfers one byte at a time from SECTOR to

DISAREA, where the characters are to be displayed. When a line feed is encountered, the routine displays the contents of DISAREA up to and including the line feed. (The display screen accepts tab characters (hex 09) and automatically sets the cursor on the next location evenly divisible by 8.)

The program has to check for end of sector (read another sector) and end of display area. For conventional ASCII files such as ASM files, each line is relatively short and is sure to terminate with a CR/LF pair. Non-ASCII files such as EXE and OBJ do not have "lines," and our program has to check for end of DISAREA to avoid crashing. The program is intended to display only ASCII files, but the test is insurance against unexpected files.

The steps in G10XFER are the following:

1. Initialize the address of SECTOR.
2. Initialize the address of DISAREA.
3. If at end of SECTOR, read the next sector. If at end-of-file, exit, otherwise initialize the address of SECTOR.
4. If at end of DISAREA, force CR/LF, display the line, and initialize DISAREA.
5. Get a character from SECTOR and store it in DISAREA.
6. If the character is end-of-file (hex 1A), exit.
7. If the character is line feed (hex 0A), display the line and go to step 2, otherwise go to step 3.

Try running this program under DEBUG. After each disk input, display the contents of the input area and see how DOS has formatted your records. To enhance this program, prompt a user to enter the filename and extension.

OTHER EXTENDED FUNCTION CALLS

Get Free Disk Space: Hex 36

This function delivers information about the space on a disk device. Set the drive number (0 = default, 1 = A, 2 = B, etc.) in the DL and request function hex 36:

```
MOV AH,36H   ;Request default
MOV DL,0     ;   drive
INT 21H      ;Call DOS
```

For an invalid device number, the operation sets the AX to hex FFFF; otherwise, it returns:

AX Number of sectors per cluster
BX Number of available clusters
CX Number of bytes per sector
DX Total number of clusters on device

DOS versions prior to 2.0 could use call hex 1B (get FAT information) for similar data.

Delete File: Hex 41

Use function call hex 41 to delete a file (but not "read-only") from within a program. Load the address of an ASCIIZ string containing device path and filename.

```
MOV AH,41H        ;Request delete
LEA DX,PATHNAM    ;  ASCIIZ string
INT 21H           ;Call DOS
```

Error returns in the AX are 02 (file not found) or 05 (access denied).

Move File Pointer: Hex 42

DOS maintains a file pointer that it initializes to 0 and increments for each record sequentially read or written. You can use the move file pointer function, hex 42, for reading records or writing records anywhere within a file, in effect, for random retrieval or updating.

Set the file handle in the BX and the required offset as bytes in the CX:DX. For a move up to 65,535, set 0 in the CX and the number in the DX. Also, set a method code in the AL that tells the operation the point from which to take the offset:

0 Take the offset from the start of the file.

1 Take the offset from the current location of the file pointer, which could be anywhere within the file, including the start.

2 Take the offset from the end-of-file. You can determine the size of a file (and its consequent end-of-file) by setting the CX:DX to zero and using method code 2.

The following example moves the pointer 1024 bytes from the start of a file:

```
MOV AH,42H          ;Request move pointer
MOV AL,00           ;  to start of file
LEA BX,HANDLE1      ;Set handle
MOV CX,00
MOV DX,1024         ;1024-byte offset
INT 21H             ;Call DOS
JC  error
```

A valid operation clears the CF flag and delivers the new pointer location in the DX:AX. An invalid operation sets the CF flag and returns in the AX code 01 (invalid method code) or 06 (invalid handle).

Check or Change Attribute: Hex 43

You may use function call hex 43H to check or change a file attribute in the directory. Set the address of an ASCIIZ string in the DX. To check attribute, set 00 in the AL. To change attribute, set 01 in the AL and the new attribute in the CX. The following sets normal attribute:

```
MOV AH,43H          ;Request set
MOV AL,01           ;  normal
MOV CX,00           ;  attribute
LEA DX,PATHNM2      ;ASCIIZ string
INT 21H             ;Call DOS
```

A check of attribute returns the current attribute to the CX; a change of attribute sets the directory entry to the attribute in the CX. An invalid operation returns to the AX error code 02, 03, or 05.

Get Current Directory: Hex 47

Use DOS function call hex 47 to determine the current directory for any drive. Define a space large enough to contain the longest possible pathname, and load its name in the DX. Identify the drive in the DL by 0 = default, 1 = A, 2 = B, and so forth. The operation delivers the current directory (but not the drive) to the named address, such as

```
ASSEMBLE\EXAMPLES0
```

A byte of hex zeros identifies the end of the pathname. If the requested directory is the root, the value returned is only a byte of hex 00. In this way, you can get the current pathname in order to access any file in a subdirectory. See the example in Figure 17-5.

Find Matching File: Hex 4E and 4F

These operations are similar to function call hex 11 and 12 of original DOS. Use call 4E to begin a search in a directory and call 4F to continue it. For begin search, set the DX with the address of an ASCIIZ string containing pathname; the string may contain global characters ? and *. Set the CX with the file attribute, any combination of normal, directory, hidden, or system bits.

```
MOV AH,4EH        ;Request first match
MOV CX,00H        ;Normal attribute
LEA DX,PATHNM1    ;ASCIIZ string
INT 21H           ;Call DOS
```

An operation that locates a match fills the current DTA in the FCB with the following:

00 Reserved by DOS for subsequent search
21 File attribute
22 File time
24 File date
26 File size: low word then high word
30 Name and extension as a 13-byte ASCIIZ string followed by hex 00

Error returns in the AX are 02 (not found) and 18 (no more files). If you used call hex 4E to begin a search for global names, then use call

```
TITLE   GETPATH (COM)  Get current directory
CODESG  SEGMENT PARA 'Code'
        ASSUME  CS:CODESG,DS:CODESG,ES:CODESG
        ORG     100H
BEGIN:  JMP     SHORT MAIN
; ------------------------------------------------
PATHNAM DB      65 DUP(' ')      ;Current pathname
; ------------------------------------------------
MAIN    PROC    NEAR
        MOV     AH,19H           ;Get default drive
        INT     21H
        ADD     AL,41H           ;Change hex no. to letter
        MOV     DL,AL            ;  0=A, 1=B, etc.
        CALL    B10DISP          ;Display drive no.,
        MOV     DL,':'
        CALL    B10DISP          ;  colon,
        MOV     DL,'\'
        CALL    B10DISP          ;  backslash

        MOV     AH,47H
        MOV     DL,00            ;Get pathname
        LEA     SI,PATHNAM
        INT     21H
A10LOOP:
        CMP     BYTE PTR [SI],0 ;End of pathname?
        JE      A20              ;  yes - exit
        MOV     AL,[SI]          ;Display pathname
        MOV     DL,AL            ;  one byte at
        CALL    B10DISP          ;  a time
        INC     SI
        JMP     A10LOOP
A20:    RET                      ;Exit to DOS
MAIN    ENDP

B10DISP PROC    NEAR             ;DL set on entry
        MOV     AH,02            ;Request display
        INT     21H
        RET
B10DISP ENDP

CODESG  ENDS
        END     BEGIN
```

Figure 17-5 Get Current Directory.

hex 4F to find subsequent entries. Between use of these operations, leave the current DTA intact.

```
MOV AH,4FH      ;Request next match
INT 21H         ;Call DOS
```

The only return code in the AX is 18 (no more files). Neither function call clears or sets the CF flag.

Rename a File: Hex 56

Use function call 56 to rename a file from within a program. Set the DX with the address of an ASCIIZ string containing the old drive, path, and name of the file to be renamed. Set the DI (actually ES:DI) with the address of an ASCIIZ string containing the new drive, path, and name. Drive numbers, if used, must be the same in both strings. Since paths need not be the same, the operation can both rename a file and move it to another directory.

```
MOV AH,56H          ;Request rename file
LEA DX,oldstring    ;DS:DX
LEA DI,newstring    ;ES:DI
INT 21H             ;Call DOS
```

Error returns in the AX are codes 03 (path not found), 05 (access denied), and 17 (not same device).

Other DOS function calls concerned with files include create directory (hex 39), remove directory entry (hex 3A), change current directory (hex 3B), I/O control for devices (hex 44), duplicate file handle (hex 45), force duplicate handle (hex 46), and get verify state (hex 54).

KEY POINTS TO REMEMBER

- Many of the extended DOS functions reference an ASCIIZ string that consists of a directory path followed by a byte of hex zeros.
- The create and open functions return a file handle that you use for subsequent file accessing.
- On errors, many of the functions set the CF flag and insert an error code in the AX.
- As a rule, use the create function when writing a file and the open function when reading a file.
- Close a file that has been written in order to update the directory.

QUESTIONS

17-1. What are the error return codes for "file not found" and for "invalid handle"?

17-2. Define an ASCIIZ string named PATH1 for a file named CUST.LST on drive C.

17-3. For the file in Question 17-2, provide the instructions to (a) define an item named CUSTHAN for the file handle, (b) create the file, (c) write a record from CUSTOUT (128 bytes), and (d) close the file. Test for errors.

17-4. For the file in Question 17-3, code the instructions to (a) open the file and (b) read records into CUSTIN. Test for errors.

17-5. Under what circumstances should you close a file that is used only for input?

17-6. Revise the program in Figure 17-4 so that a user at a keyboard can enter a filename for displaying. Provide for any number of requests and for pressing only the Return key to cause termination.

CHAPTER 18

Disk Storage IV: BIOS Disk I/O

Objective: To examine the basic programming requirements for using the BIOS functions to create and read disk files.

INTRODUCTION

You can code directly at the BIOS level for disk processing, although BIOS supplies no automatic use of the directory or blocking and deblocking of records. BIOS disk operation INT 13H treats all "records" as the size of a sector, and disk addressing is in terms of actual track number and sector number.

For disk read, write, and verify, initialize the following registers:

AH	The operation to perform: read, write, verify, or format.
AL	The number of sectors.
CH	Track number.
CL	Starting sector number.
DH	Head (side) number: 0 or 1 for diskette.
DL	Drive number: 0 = drive A, 1 = drive B, and so forth.
ES:BX	The address of the I/O buffer in the data area (except for verify operations).

BIOS DISK OPERATIONS

BIOS INT 13H requires a code in the AH register to identify the operation.

AH = 00: Reset Diskette System

This operation performs a hard reset to the diskette controller and requires only hex 00 in the AH for INT 13H to execute. Use this after another disk operation returns a serious error.

AH = 01: Read Diskette Status

This operation returns to the AL the status from the last diskette I/O operation (see Status Byte in the following section). Execution requires only hex 01 in the AH register.

AH = 02: Read Sectors

The operation reads a specified number of sectors on the same track into memory. The number is usually 1, 8, or 9. Load the BX with the memory address for the input area, but note that BX in this case is subject to ES, thus the form ES:BX. The following example reads one sector into an area named INSECT, which should be large enough to contain all the data:

```
MOV   AH,02          ;Request read
MOV   AL,01          ;One sector
LEA   BX,INSECT      ;Input buffer at ES:BX
MOV   CH,05          ;Track 05
MOV   CL,03          ;Sector 03
MOV   DH,00          ;Head 00
MOV   DL,01          ;Drive 01 (B)
INT   13H            ;Call BIOS
```

On return, the AL contains the number of sectors that the operation actually reads. The DS, BX, CX, and DX registers are preserved.

For most situations, a program would specify only one sector or all sectors for a track. It would initialize the CH and CL and would increment them to read sectors sequentially. Note that when the sector number exceeds the maximum for a track, you have to either reset it to 01 and increment the track number or change from side 0 to side 1 for two-sided diskettes.

AH = 03: Write Sectors

This operation writes a specified area from memory (presumably 512 bytes or a multiple of 512) onto a designated sector or sectors. Load registers and handle processing just as for reading disk (code 02). On return, the AL contains the number of sectors that the operation actually wrote. The DS, BX, CX, and DX registers are preserved.

AH = 04: Verify Sector

This operation simply checks that the specified sectors can be found and performs a type of parity check. You could use it after a write (code 03) to ensure more reliable output at a cost of more I/O time. Set the registers just as for code 03, but since the operation does not perform true verification, there is no need to set an address in the ES:BX. On return, the AL contains the number of sectors actually verified. The DS, BX, CX, and DX registers are preserved.

AH = 05: Format Tracks

Use this operation to format a designated number of tracks according to one of four different sizes (the standard for the PC system is 512). Read/write operations require the format information to locate a requested sector. For this operation, the ES:BX registers must contain an address that points to a group of address fields for the track. For each sector on a track, there must be one four-byte entry of the form T/H/S/B, where

T = track number
H = head number
S = sector number
B = bytes per sector (00 = 128, 01 = 256, 02 = 512, 03 = 1024)

For example, if you format track 03, head 00, and 512 bytes per sector, then the first entry for the track is hex 03000102, followed by one entry for each remaining track. The AT Technical Reference manual contains a number of additional BIOS operations.

STATUS BYTE

For all AH codes 02, 03, 04, and 05, if the operation is successful, the CF flag and the AH are set to 0. If the operation fails, the CF flag is set to 1 and the AH contains a status code identifying the cause. This is the same status that AH call 01 returns to the AL.

AH	*Reason*
00000001	Bad command was passed for diskette I/O.
00000010	Could not find address mark on disk.
00000011	Attempted to write on protected disk.
00000100	Could not find required sector.
00001000	Operation overran DMA (direct memory access).
00001001	Attempted to DMA across a 64K boundary.
00010000	Encountered a bad CRC on a read.
00100000	Failure by diskette controller.
01000000	Seek operation failed.
10000000	Attachment failed to respond.

If the interrupt operation returns an error, the usual action is to reset the disk (AH code 00) and to retry the operation three times. If there is still an error, display a message and give the user a chance to change the diskette.

PROGRAM: USING BIOS TO READ SECTORS

Now let's examine the program in Figure 18-1 that uses BIOS instruction INT 13H to read sectors from disk. The program is based on the example in Figure 16-3 with the following changes:

1. There is now no FCB definition or open routine.
2. The program has to calculate each disk address. After each read, it increments the sector number. In C10ADDR, when the sector reaches 10, the routine resets the sector to 01. If the side is 1, the program increments track number; side number is then changed, if 0 to 1 and if 1 to 0.
3. CURADR contains the beginning track/sector (which the program increments) and ENDADR contains the ending track/sector. One way to enhance the program is to prompt a user for starting and ending track/sector.

Suggestion: Run this program under DEBUG. Trace through the instructions that initialize the segment registers and then adjust the start and end sectors to the location of the FAT (its location varies by operating

```
TITLE   BIOREAD (COM)  Read disk sectors via BIOS
CODESG  SEGMENT PARA 'Code'
        ASSUME  CS:CODESG,DS:CODESG,SS:CODESG,ES:CODESG
        ORG     100H
BEGIN:  JMP     MAIN
; ------------------------------------------------------
RECDIN  DB      512 DUP(' ')       ;Input area
ENDCDE  DB      00
CURADR  DW      0304H              ;Beginning tr/sector
ENDADR  DW      0501H              ;Ending track/sector
READMSG DB      '*** Read error ***$'
SIDE    DB      00
; ------------------------------------------------------
MAIN    PROC    NEAR
        MOV     AX,0600H           ;Request scroll
A20LOOP:
        CALL    Q10SCR             ;Clear screen
        CALL    Q20CURS            ;Set cursor
        CALL    C10ADDR            ;Calculate disk address
        MOV     CX,CURADR
        MOV     DX,ENDADR
        CMP     CX,DX              ;At ending sector?
        JE      A90                ; yes - exit
        CALL    F10READ            ;Read disk record
        CMP     ENDCDE,00          ;Normal read?
        JNZ     A90                ; no  - exit
        CALL    G10DISP            ;Display sector
        JMP     A20LOOP            ;Repeat
A90:    RET                        ;Terminate
MAIN    ENDP
;               Calculate next disk address:
;               ----------------------------
C10ADDR PROC    NEAR
        MOV     CX,CURADR          ;Get track/sector
        CMP     CL,10              ;Past last sector?
        JNE     C90                ; no - exit
        CMP     SIDE,00            ;Bypass if side 0
        JE      C20
        INC     CH                 ;Increment track
C20:
        XOR     SIDE,01            ;Change side
        MOV     CL,01              ;Set sector to 1
        MOV     CURADR,CX
C90:    RET
C10ADDR ENDP
;               Read disk sector:
;               ----------------
F10READ PROC    NEAR
        MOV     AL,01              ;No. of sectors
        MOV     AH,02              ;Request read
        LEA     BX,RECDIN          ;Address of buffer
        MOV     CX,CURADR          ;Track/sector
        MOV     DH,SIDE            ;Side
        MOV     DL,01              ;Drive B
        INT     13H                ;Request input
        CMP     AH,00              ;Normal read?
        JZ      F90                ; yes - exit
        MOV     ENDCDE,01          ; no:
        CALL    X10ERR             ; invalid read
```

Figure 18-1 Using BIOS to Read a Disk File.

```
F90:
        INC     CURADR          ;Increment sector
        RET
F10READ ENDP
;               Display sector:
;               --------------
G10DISP PROC    NEAR
        MOV     AH,40H          ;Request display
        MOV     BX,01           ;Handle
        MOV     CX,512          ;Length
        LEA     DX,RECDIN
        INT     21H
        RET
G10DISP ENDP
;               Clear screen:
;               ------------
Q10SCR  PROC    NEAR
        MOV     AX,0600H        ;Full screen
        MOV     BH,1EH          ;Set color
        MOV     CX,0000         ;Request scroll
        MOV     DX,184FH
        INT     10H
        RET
Q10SCR  ENDP
;               Set cursor:
;               ----------
Q20CURS PROC    NEAR
        MOV     AH,02           ;Request set
        MOV     BH,00           ;  cursor
        MOV     DX,0000
        INT     10H
        RET
Q20CURS ENDP
;               Disk error routine:
;               ------------------
X10ERR  PROC    NEAR
        MOV     AH,40H          ;Request display
        MOV     BX,01           ;Handle
        MOV     CX,18           ;Length of message
        LEA     DX,READMSG
        INT     21H
        RET
X10ERR  ENDP

CODESG  ENDS
        END     BEGIN
```

Figure 18-1 (Continued)

system version). Use G (go) to execute and examine the input area for the FAT and directory entries.

As an alternative to DEBUG, you could convert the ASCII characters in the input area to their hex equivalents and display the hex values just as DEBUG does (see the program back in Figure 14-5). In this way, you could examine the contents of any sector, even "hidden" ones and could allow a user to enter changes and write the changed sector back onto disk.

Note that when DOS creates a file, it may insert records in available sectors, which may not be contiguous on disk. Thus, you can't expect BIOS INT 13H to read a file sequentially.

KEY POINTS TO REMEMBER

- BIOS INT 13H provides direct access to track and sector.
- BIOS INT 13H does not supply automatic directory handling, end-of-file operations, and blocking and deblocking of records.
- The verify sector operation performs an elementary check of data written at some cost of processing time.
- Check the status byte after each BIOS disk operation.

QUESTIONS

18-1. Code the instructions to reset the diskette controller.

18-2. Code the instructions to read the diskette status.

18-3. Code the instructions for BIOS INT 13H to read one sector using memory address INDSK, drive A, head 0, track 6, and sector 3.

18-4. Code the instructions for BIOS INT 13H to write three sectors using memory address OUTDSK, drive B, head 0, track 8, and sector 1.

18-5. After the write in Question 18-4, how would you check for an attempt to write on a protected disk?

18-6. Based on Question 18-4, code the instructions to verify the write operation.

CHAPTER 19

Printing

Objective: To describe the requirements for printing in assembler language.

INTRODUCTION

Compared to screen and disk handling, printing appears to be a simple process. There are only a few operations involved, all done either through DOS INT 21H or through BIOS INT 17H. The commands to the printer include form feed, line feed, and carriage return.

One classification of printers is according to print quality. A dot matrix printer produces symbols as patterns of tiny dots in a defined box, or matrix, and can provide normal, compressed, or expanded characters. More advanced matrix printers produce dot graphics, slanted printing, and emphasized and double-strike symbols, and are able to print such characters as happy faces, hearts, and clubs. A letter-quality printer is restricted to the characters on a replaceable daisy-wheel or thimble but provides excellent quality of type and variety of font styles. Many letter-quality printers can print 10, 12, or 15 characters per inch and provide proportional spacing, underlining, shadowing, and bold printing. A laser printer provides the advantages of both dot matrix for graphics and letter quality for text.

Another classification is according to printer interface. The IBM PC is designed for parallel printers, which accept eight bits at a time from the processor. A serial printer accepts data from the processor one bit at a time.

Many printers have a memory buffer that can hold several thousand bytes. Printers also may accept either even parity, odd parity, or no parity bit at all. A printer must understand a signal from the processor, for example, to eject to a new page, to feed one line down a page, or to tab across a page. The processor also must understand a signal from a printer that indicates it is busy or out of paper.

Unfortunately, many types of printers respond differently to signals from a processor, and one of the more difficult tasks for software specialists is to interface their programs to printers.

COMMON PRINT CONTROL CHARACTERS

The standard characters that control printing include the following:

Decimal	*Hex*	*Function*
08	08	Backspace
09	09	Horizontal tab
10	0A	Line feed (advance one line)
11	0B	Vertical tab
12	0C	Form feed (advance to next page)
13	0D	Carriage return (return to left margin)

Horizontal Tab. Horizontal tab (hex 09) works only on printers that have the feature and the printer tabs are set up. Otherwise, the printer ignores the command. Print blank spaces to get around an inability to tab.

Line Feed. Use a line feed (hex 0A) to advance a single line and use two successive line feeds to double-space.

Form Feed. Initializing the paper when you power up a printer determines the starting position for the top of a page. The default length for a page is 11 inches. Neither the processor nor the printer automatically checks for the bottom of a page. If your program continues printing down a page, it eventually prints over the page perforation and onto the top of the next page. To control paging, count the lines as they print, and on reaching the maximum for a page (such as 55 lines), execute a form feed (hex 0C), then reset the line count to 0 or 1.

At the end of printing, deliver a command such as line feed or form feed to force printing the last line still in the printer's buffer. The use of form feed at the end of execution also facilitates tearing off the last page.

PRINTING USING EXTENDED DOS

DOS 2.0 introduced file handles, which we have used in the chapters on screen handling and disk processing. To print, use DOS function call hex 40 and the standard file handle 04. The following prints 25 characters from a data item named HEADG:

```
HEADG DB   'Industrial Bicycle Mfrs', ODH, OAH
      ...
      MOV AH,40H          ;Request output
      MOV BX,04           ;Handle for printer
      MOV CX,25           ;25 characters
      LEA DX,HEADG        ;Print area
      INT 21H             ;Call DOS
```

An unsuccessful operation sets the CF flag and returns a code in the AX.

PROGRAM: PRINTING WITH PAGE OVERFLOW AND HEADINGS

The program in Figure 19-1 is similar to the one in Figure 9-1 that accepts names from the keyboard and displays them down the screen. This program, however, directs the names to the printer. Each printed page contains a heading followed by a double space and the entered names in the following format:

```
List of Employee Names  Page 01

Clancy Alderson
Janet Brown
David Christie
...
```

The program counts each line printed and, on reaching the "bottom" of a page, ejects the forms to the top of the next page. Major procedures are the following:

- D10INPT Prompts for and accepts a name from the keyboard.
- E10PRNT If at the end of a page, calls M10PAGE; prints the name (its length is based on the actual length in the input parameter list).
- M10PAGE Advances to a new page; prints the heading; resets line count and adds to page count.
- P10OUT Common routine, handles actual request to print.

At the beginning of execution, it is necessary to print a heading, but not to eject to a new page. M10PAGE therefore bypasses the form feed if PAGECTR contains 01, its initial value. PAGECTR is defined as

```
PAGECTR  DB   '01'
```

which generates an ASCII number, hex 3031. The routine in M10PAGE increments PAGECTR by 1 so that it becomes progressively 3032, 3033,

```
TITLE    PRTNAME (COM)  Accept & print input names
CODESG   SEGMENT PARA PUBLIC 'Code'
         ASSUME  CS:CODESG,DS:CODESG,SS:CODESG,ES:CODESG
         ORG     100H
BEGIN:   JMP     SHORT MAIN
; -----------------------------------------------------
NAMEPAR LABEL   BYTE            ;Parameter list:
MAXNLEN DB      20              ;  maximum length of name
NAMELEN DB      ?               ;  actual length entered
NAMEFLD DB      20 DUP(' ')     ;  name entered
                                ;Heading line:
HEADG   DB      'List of Employee Names    Page  '
PAGECTR DB      '01', 0AH, 0AH

FFEED   DB      0CH             ;Form feed
LFEED   DB      0AH             ;Line feed
LINECTR DB      01
PROMPT  DB      'Name? '
; -----------------------------------------------------
MAIN    PROC    NEAR
        CALL    Q10CLR          ;Clear screen
        CALL    M10PAGE         ;Page heading
A20LOOP:
        MOV     DX,0000         ;Set cursor to 00,00
        CALL    Q20CURS
        CALL    D10INPT         ;Provide for input of name
        CALL    Q10CLR
        CMP     NAMELEN,00      ;Name entered? (indicates end)
        JE      A30             ;  if not, exit
        CALL    E10PRNT         ;  if so, prepare printing
        JMP     A20LOOP
A30:
        MOV     CX,01           ;End --
        LEA     DX,FFEED        ;  one character
        CALL    P10OUT          ;  for form feed,
        RET                     ;  return to DOS
MAIN    ENDP
;               Accept input of name:
;               --------------------
D10INPT PROC    NEAR
        MOV     AH,40H          ;Request
        MOV     BX,01           ;  display
        MOV     CX,05           ;  5 characters
        LEA     DX,PROMPT
        INT     21H             ;Call DOS
        MOV     AH,0AH          ;Request input
        LEA     DX,NAMEPAR
        INT     21H             ;Call DOS
        RET
D10INPT ENDP
;               Prepare for printing:
;               --------------------
E10PRNT PROC    NEAR
        CMP     LINECTR,60      ;End of page?
        JB      E20             ;  no  - bypass
        CALL    M10PAGE         ;  yes - print heading
E20:    MOV     CH,00
        MOV     CL,NAMELEN      ;Set no. chars
```

Figure 19-1 Printing with Page Overflow and Headings.

```
        LEA     DX,NAMEFLD          ;Init'ze addr of name
        CALL    P10OUT              ;Print name
        MOV     CX,01               ;One
        LEA     DX,LFEED            ;  line feed
        CALL    P10OUT
        INC     LINECTR             ;Add to line count
        RET
E10PRNT ENDP
;               Page heading routine:
;               --------------------
M10PAGE PROC    NEAR
        CMP     WORD PTR PAGECTR,3130H  ;First page?
        JE      M30                 ;  yes - bypass
        MOV     CX,01               ;
        LEA     DX,FFEED            ;  no --
        CALL    P10OUT              ;  form feed,
        MOV     LINECTR,03          ;  reset line count
M30:
        MOV     CX,36               ;Length of heading
        LEA     DX,HEADG            ;Address of heading
M40:
        CALL    P10OUT
        INC     PAGECTR+1           ;Add to page count
        CMP     PAGECTR+1,3AH       ;Page no. = hex 3A?
        JNE     M50                 ;  no  - bypass
        MOV     PAGECTR+1,30H       ;  yes - set to ASCII
        INC     PAGECTR             ;
M50:    RET
M10PAGE ENDP
;               Print routine:
;               -------------
P10OUT  PROC    NEAR                ;CX & DX set on entry
        MOV     AH,40H              ;Request print
        MOV     BX,04               ;Handle
        INT     21H                 ;Call DOS
        RET
P10OUT  ENDP
;               Clear screen:
;               ------------
Q10CLR  PROC    NEAR
        MOV     AX,0600H            ;Request scroll
        MOV     BH,60H              ;Color (07 for BW)
        MOV     CX,0000             ;From 00,00
        MOV     DX,184FH            ;  to 24,79
        INT     10H                 ;Call BIOS
        RET
Q10CLR  ENDP
;               Set cursor row/col:
;               -------------------
Q20CURS PROC    NEAR                ;DX set on entry
        MOV     AH,02               ;Request set cursor
        MOV     BH,00               ;Page #0
        INT     10H                 ;Call BIOS
        RET
Q20CURS ENDP
CODESG  ENDS
        END     BEGIN
```

Figure 19-1 (Continued)

and so forth. The value is valid up to 3039 and then becomes 303A, which would print as a colon (:). If the rightmost byte of PAGECTR contains hex 3A, the routine changes it to hex 30 and adds 1 to the leftmost byte. Hex 303A would become 3130, or 10.

Placing a test for end of page *before* (rather than after) printing a name ensures that the last page has at least one name under the title.

PRINTING ASCII FILES AND HANDLING TABS

A common procedure, performed for example by the video adapter, is to expand a tab character (09) with blanks to the next location evenly divisible by 8. Thus, tab stops, if requested, are at locations 8, 16, 24, and so forth. Many printers, however, ignore tab characters. A program such as DOS PRINT that prints ASCII files (such as assembler source programs) has to check each character that it sends to the printer. If a tab, the program expands blanks to the next 8-byte location.

The program in Figure 19-2 requests a user to enter the name of a file and prints its contents. The program is similar to that in Figure 17-3 that displays files, but this one has to expand tab stops for the printer. In effect, all locations between 0 and 7 become 8, those between 8 and 15 become 16, and so forth. You'll find the logic in G10XFER, following label G60. Three examples of tab stops follow:

```
Present print location:      1          9          21
Binary value:             00000001   00001001   00010101
Clear rightmost 3 bits:   00000000   00001000   00010000
Add 8:                    00001000   00010000   00011000
New tabbed location:         8         16          24
```

The program is organized as follows:

- C10PRMP Requests the user to enter a file name. Pressing only the return key causes the program to assume the user is finished.
- E10OPEN Opens the requested disk file.
- G10XFER Checks for end of sector, end of file, end of display area, line feed, and tab character. Basically, sends regular characters to the display area.
- P10PRNT Prints the display line and clears it.
- R10READ Reads a sector from the file.

Carriage returns, line feeds, and form feeds should work on all printers. You could modify this program to count the lines printed and force a form feed (hex 0C) when near the bottom of a page, at line 62

```
TITLE    PRINASC (COM)  Read & print disk records
CODESG   SEGMENT PARA 'Code'
         ASSUME  CS:CODESG,DS:CODESG,SS:CODESG,ES:CODESG
         ORG     100H
BEGIN:   JMP     MAIN
; ----------------------------------------------------
PATHPAR LABEL    BYTE              ;Parameter list for
MAXLEN   DB      32                ;  input of
NAMELEN DB       ?                 ;  filename
FILENAM DB       32 DUP(' ')

SECTOR   DB      512 DUP(' ')      ;Input area for file
DISAREA DB       120 DUP(' ')      ;Display area
COUNT    DW      00
ENDCDE   DW      00
FFEED    DB      0CH
HANDLE   DW      0
OPENMSG DB       '*** Open error ***'
PROMPT   DB      'Name of file? '
; ------------------------------------------------------
MAIN     PROC    NEAR              ;Main procedure
         CALL    Q10SCR            ;Clear screen
         CALL    Q20CURS           ;Set cursor
A10LOOP:
         MOV     ENDCDE,00         ;Initialize
         CALL    C10PRMP           ;Request filename
         CMP     NAMELEN,00        ;Any request?
         JE      A90               ;  No -- exit
         CALL    E10OPEN           ;Open file, set DTA
         CMP     ENDCDE,00         ;Valid open?
         JNE     A80               ;  no -- request again
         CALL    R10READ           ;Read 1st disk sector
         CMP     ENDCDE,00         ;End-file, no data?
         JE      A80               ;  yes -- request next
         CALL    G10XFER           ;Print/read
A80:
         JMP     A10LOOP
A90:     RET                       ;Terminate
MAIN     ENDP
;                Request file name:
;                -----------------
C10PRMP PROC     NEAR
         MOV     AH,40H            ;Prompt for filename
         MOV     BX,01
         MOV     CX,13
         LEA     DX,PROMPT
         INT     21H
         MOV     AH,0AH            ;Accept filename
         LEA     DX,PATHPAR
         INT     21H
         MOV     BL,NAMELEN        ;Insert
         MOV     BH,00             ;  zero at end
         MOV     FILENAM[BX],0     ;  filename
C90:     RET
C10PRMP ENDP
;                Open disk file:
;                --------------
E10OPEN PROC     NEAR
```

Figure 19-2 Printing an ASCII file.

```
         MOV     AH,3DH            ;Request open
         MOV     AL,00             ;Read only
         LEA     DX,FILENAM
         INT     21H
         JNC     E20               ;Test CF flag,
         CALL    X10ERR            ;  error if set
         RET
E20:
         MOV     HANDLE,AX         ;Save handle
         MOV     AX,2020H
         MOV     CX,256            ;Clear sector
         LEA     DI,SECTOR         ;  area to blank
         REP STOSW
         RET
E10OPEN  ENDP
;                Transfer data to print line:
;                ----------------------------
G10XFER  PROC    NEAR
         CLD                       ;Set left-to-right
         LEA     SI,SECTOR         ;Initialize
G20:
         LEA     DI,DISAREA
         MOV     COUNT,00
G30:
         LEA     DX,SECTOR+512
         CMP     SI,DX             ;End of sector?
         JNE     G40
         CALL    R10READ           ;  yes -- read next
         CMP     ENDCDE,00         ;End of file?
         JE      G80               ;  yes -- exit
         LEA     SI,SECTOR
G40:
         MOV     BX,COUNT
         CMP     BX,80             ;At end of display area?
         JB      G50               ;  no -- bypass
         MOV     [DI+BX],0D0AH     ;  yes - set CR/LF
         CALL    P10PRNT
         LEA     DI,DISAREA        ;Reinitialize
         MOV     COUNT,00
G50:
         LODSB                     ;[SI] to AL, INC SI
         MOV     BX,COUNT
         MOV     [DI+BX],AL        ;Char to print line
         INC     BX
         CMP     AL,1AH            ;End-of-file?
         JE      G80               ;  yes -- exit
         CMP     AL,0AH            ;Line feed?
         JNE     G60
         CALL    P10PRNT           ;  & print
         JMP     G20
G60:
         CMP     AL,09H            ;Tab char?
         JNE     G70
         DEC     BX                ;  yes -- reset BX
         MOV     BYTE PTR [DI+BX],20H ;Clear tab to blank
         AND     BX,0FFF8H         ;Clear rightmost 3 bits
         ADD     BX,08             ;  & add 8 -> tab stop
G70:
```

Figure 19-2 (Continued)

```
         MOV     COUNT,BX
         JMP     G30
G80:     MOV     BX,COUNT           ;End of file
         MOV     BYTE PTR [DI+BX],0CH     ;Form feed
         CALL    P10PRNT            ;Print last line
G90:     RET
G10XFER ENDP
;                Print routine:
;                -------------
P10PRNT PROC     NEAR
         MOV     AH,40H             ;Request print
         MOV     BX,04
         MOV     CX,COUNT           ;Length
         INC     CX
         LEA     DX,DISAREA
         INT     21H
         MOV     AX,2020H           ;Clear display line
         MOV     CX,60
         LEA     DI,DISAREA
         REP STOSW
         RET
P10PRNT ENDP
;                Read disk sector:
;                ----------------
R10READ PROC     NEAR
         MOV     AH,3FH             ;Request read
         MOV     BX,HANDLE          ;Device
         MOV     CX,512             ;Length
         LEA     DX,SECTOR          ;Buffer
         INT     21H
         MOV     ENDCDE,AX
         RET
R10READ ENDP
;                Scroll screen:
;                ------------
Q10SCR   PROC    NEAR
         MOV     AX,0600H
         MOV     BH,1EH             ;Set color
         MOV     CX,0000            ;Scroll
         MOV     DX,184FH
         INT     10H
         RET
Q10SCR   ENDP
;                Set cursor:
;                ----------
Q20CURS PROC     NEAR
         MOV     AH,02              ;Request set
         MOV     BH,00              ;  cursor
         MOV     DX,00
         INT     10H
         RET
Q20CURS ENDP
;                Disk error routine:
;                ------------------
X10ERR   PROC    NEAR
         MOV     AH,40H             ;Request display
         MOV     BX,01              ;Handle
         MOV     CX,18              ;Length
```

Figure 19-2 (Continued)

```
              LEA     DX,OPENMSG        ;Error message
              INT     21H
              MOV     ENDCDE,01         ;Error indicator
              RET
      X10ERR  ENDP
      CODESG  ENDS
              END     BEGIN
```

Figure 19-2 (Continued)

or so. Some users prefer to use an editor program to embed form feed characters directly in their ASCII files, at the exact location where they want a page break, such as at the end of an assembler procedure. You could also revise this program for original DOS function call 05 to send each character directly to the printer, thereby eliminating the definition and use of a display area.

PRINTING USING ORIGINAL DOS

To print using original DOS, insert function call 05 in the AH register, the character that you want to print in the DL, and issue an INT 21H command as follows:

```
MOV  AH,05       ;Request print function
MOV  DL,char     ;Character to print
INT  21H         ;Call DOS
```

These instructions are adequate for sending print control characters. However, printing typically involves a full or partial line of text and requires stepping through a line formatted in the data area.

The following illustrates printing a full line. It first initializes the address of HEADG in the SI register and sets the CX to the length of HEADG. The loop at P20 extracts each character successively from HEADG and sends it to the printer. Since the first character in HEADG is a form feed and the last two characters are line feeds, the heading prints at the top of a new page and is followed by a double space.

```
HEADG DB     0CH,'Industrial Bicycle Mfrs',0DH,0AH,0AH

      LEA    SI,HEADG       ;Init'ze address &
      MOV    CX,27          ; length of heading
```

```
P20:
        MOV     AH,05           ;Request to print
        MOV     DL,[SI]         ;Char from heading
        INT     21H             ;Call DOS
        INC     SI              ;Next char in heading
        LOOP    P20
```

If the printer power is not on, DOS returns a message "Out of paper" repetitively. If you turn on the power, the program begins printing correctly. You can also press Ctrl/Break to cancel the program.

SPECIAL PRINTER COMMANDS

We have already examined use of a number of commands that are basic to most printers. Other commands include

Decimal	*Hex*	
15	0F	Turn on condensed mode
14	0E	Turn on expanded mode
18	12	Turn off condensed mode
20	14	Turn off expanded mode

Some commands require a preceding Esc (escape) character (hex 1B). Some of these, depending on the printer, include:

1B 30	Set line spacing to 8 lines per inch
1B 32	Set line spacing to 6 lines per inch
1B 45	Set on emphasized printing mode
1B 46	Set off emphasized printing mode

You can send command codes to a printer in two different ways:

1. Define commands in the data area. The following sets condensed mode, 8 lines per inch, prints a title, and then causes a carriage return and a line feed:

```
HEADG DB 0FH, 1BH, 30H, 'Title ... ', 0DH, 0AH
```

2. Use immediate instructions:

```
MOV AH,05        ;Request print
MOV DL,0FH       ;Set condensed mode
INT 21H
```

All following characters print in condensed mode until the program sends a command that resets the mode.

These commands don't necessarily work for all printer models. Check your printer manual for its specific commands.

PRINTING USING BIOS INT 17H

BIOS interrupt 17H provides three different operations specified in the AH register:

AH = 0: This operation causes printing of one character and allows for three printers, numbered 0, 1, and 2 (0 is the standard default).

```
MOV   AH,00       ;Request print
MOV   AL,char     ;Character to be printed
MOV   DX,00       ;Select printer #0
INT   17H         ;Call BIOS
```

If the operation cannot print the character, it sets the AH register to 01.

AH = 1: Initialize the printer port as follows:

```
MOV   AH,01   ;Request initialize port
MOV   DX,00   ;Select printer port #0
INT   17H     ;Call BIOS
```

Since the operation sends a form feed character, use it to set the printer to the top-of-page position, although most printers do this automatically when turned on.

AH = 2: Read the printer port status as follows:

```
MOV    AH,02          ;Request read port
MOV    DX,00          ;Select printer port #0
INT    17H            ;Call BIOS
TEST   AH,00101001B   ;Ready?
JNZ    errormsg       ;No -- display message
```

The purpose of AH=1 and AH=2 is to determine the status of the printer. The operations set the AH bits to 1 as follows:

Bit	*Cause*
7	Not busy
6	Acknowledged from printer
5	Out of paper
4	Selected
3	Input/output error
0	Time out

If the printer is already switched on, the operation returns hex 90, or binary 10010000—the printer is not "busy" and it is "selected," a valid condition. Printer "errors" are bit 5 (out of paper) and bit 3 (output error). If the printer is not switched on, the operation returns hex B0, or binary 10110000, indicating "Out of paper."

When the program runs, if the printer is not initially turned on, BIOS is unable to return a message automatically—your program is supposed to test and act upon the printer status. If your program does not check the status, your only indication is the cursor blinking. If you turn on the printer at this point, some of the output data is lost. Consequently, before print operations using BIOS, check the port status; if there is an error, display a message. (The DOS operation performs this checking automatically, although its message "Out of paper" applies to various conditions.) When the printer is switched on, the message no longer displays and printing begins normally with no loss of data.

At any time, a printer may run out of forms or may be inadvertently switched off. Consequently, if you are writing a program that others are to use, include a status test before every attempt to print.

KEY POINTS TO REMEMBER

- Before attempting to print, turn on the power and have the printer loaded with an adequate supply of paper.
- After printing is completed, use a line feed or form feed to clear the printer buffer.
- DOS provides a message if there is a printer error, but BIOS returns only a status code. When using BIOS INT 17H, check the printer status before printing.

QUESTIONS

19-1. Code a program using extended DOS for the following requirements: (a) Eject the forms to the next page; (b) Print your name;

(c) Perform a line feed and print your address; (d) Perform a line feed and print your city/state; (e) Eject the forms.

19-2. Revise Question 19-1 for using original DOS.

19-3. Code a heading line that provides for carriage return, form feed, set condensed mode, a title (any name), and turn off condensed mode.

19-4. Revise Question 19-1 for using BIOS INT 17H. Include a test for printer status.

19-5. Revise Question 19-1 so that the program performs (b), (c), and (d) five times.

19-6. Revise Figure 19-1 to run under original DOS.

19-7. Revise Figure 19-2 so that it also displays printed lines.

CHAPTER 20

Macro Writing

Objective: To explain the definition and use of assembler macro instructions.

INTRODUCTION

For each coded instruction, the assembler generates one machine language instruction. But for each coded statement, a compiler language such as Pascal or C generates one or more (often many) machine language instructions. In this regard, you can think of a compiler language as consisting of *macro* statements.

The large (MASM) assembler also has macro facilities, but you—as programmer—define the macros. You define a specific name for a macro, the MACRO pseudo-op, the various assembler instructions that the macro is to generate, and terminate the macro definition with the MEND pseudo-op. Then, whenever you need to execute the instructions, simply code the name of the macro. The assembler generates the defined instructions.

Macros are useful for the following purposes:

- To simplify and to reduce the amount of coding.
- To streamline an assembler program to make it more readable.
- To reduce errors caused by repetitive coding.

Examples of macros could be input/output operations that initialize registers and perform interrupts, conversion of ASCII and binary data, multiple-word arithmetic operations, string handling routines such as MOVS, and divide by subtraction.

This chapter covers most of the features in the macro facility, including explanations of features that the assembler manual does not make clear. However, you should still refer to the assembler manual for some of the less-used operations.

A SIMPLE MACRO DEFINITION

A macro definition must appear before any defined segment. Let's examine a simple *macro definition* named INIT1, that initializes the segment registers for an EXE program:

```
INIT1 MACRO                                        ;Define macro
      ASSUME  CS:CSEG,DS:DSEG,SS:STACK,ES:DSEG     ; }
      PUSH    DS                                   ; } Body
      SUB     AX,AX                                ; }  of
      PUSH    AX                                   ; }  the
      MOV     AX,DSEG                              ; }  macro
      MOV     DS,AX                                ; }  defin'n
      MOV     ES,AX                                ; }
      ENDM                                         ;End macro
```

The MACRO pseudo-op tells the assembler that the following instructions up to ENDM are to be part of a macro definition. The name of the macro is INIT1, although any other unique valid assembler name is acceptable. The ENDM pseudo-op terminates the macro definition. The seven instructions between MACRO and ENDM comprise the *body* of the macro definition.

The names referenced in the macro definition, CSEG, DSEG, and STACK, must be defined elsewhere in the program. You use the *macro instruction* INIT1 in the code segment where you want to initialize the registers. When the assembler encounters the instruction INIT1, it scans a table of symbolic instructions, and failing to find an entry, checks for macro instructions. Since the program contains a definition of the macro INIT1, the assembler substitutes the body of the definition, generating the instructions—the *macro expansion.* A program would use this macro instruction only once, although other macros are designed to be used any number of times, and each time the assembler generates the same macro expansion.

Figure 20-1 provides the assembled program. The listing of the macro expansion shows a plus (+) sign to the left of each instruction to indicate that a macro instruction generated it. Also, the macro expansion does not list the ASSUME pseudo-op because it generates no object code.

A later section, "Includes From a Macro Library," discusses how to catalog macros in a library and how to include them automatically into any program.

USE OF PARAMETERS IN MACROS

The previous macro definition requires fixed names for the segments: CSEG, DSEG, and STACK. To make a macro more flexible so that it can

```
                                 TITLE  MACRO1  (EXE) Simple macro to initialize
                                 ; ---------------------------------------------
                                 INIT1  MACRO  ;Define a macro
                                        ASSUME  CS:CSEG,DS:DSEG,SS:STACK,ES:DSEG
                                        PUSH    DS
                                        SUB     AX,AX
                                        PUSH    AX
                                        MOV     AX,DSEG
                                        MOV     DS,AX
                                        MOV     ES,AX
                                        ENDM                     ;End of macro
                                 ; ----------------------------------------------
0000                             STACK  SEGMENT PARA STACK 'Stack'
0000      20 [ ???? ]                   DW      32 DUP(?)
0040                             STACK  ENDS
                                 ; ----------------------------------------------
0000                             DSEG   SEGMENT PARA 'Data'
0000  54 65 73 74 20 6F          MESSGE DB 'Test of macro-instruction', 13
      66 20 6D 61 63 72
      6F 2D 69 6E 73 74
      72 75 63 74 69 6F
      6E 0D
001A                             DSEG   ENDS
                                 ; ----------------------------------------------
0000                             CSEG   SEGMENT PARA 'Code'
0000                             BEGIN  PROC    FAR
                                        INIT1                    ;Macro-instruction
0000  1E                       +        PUSH    DS
0001  2B C0                    +        SUB     AX,AX
0003  50                       +        PUSH    AX
0004  B8 ---- R                +        MOV     AX,DSEG
0007  8E D8                    +        MOV     DS,AX
0009  8E C0                    +        MOV     ES,AX
000B  B4 40                             MOV     AH,40H           ;Request display

000D  BB 0001                           MOV     BX,01            ;Handle
0010  B9 001A                           MOV     CX,26            ;Length
0013  8D 16 0000 R                      LEA     DX,MESSGE        ;Message
0017  CD 21                             INT     21H
0019  CB                                RET
001A                             BEGIN  ENDP
001A                             CSEG   ENDS
                                        END   BEGIN

Macros:
                 N a m e          Length
INIT1. . . . . . . . . . . . .    0004

Segments and Groups:
                 N a m e          Size    Align   Combine Class
CSEG . . . . . . . . . . . . .    001A    PARA    NONE    'CODE'
DSEG . . . . . . . . . . . . .    001A    PARA    NONE    'DATA'
STACK. . . . . . . . . . . . .    0040    PARA    STACK   'STACK'

Symbols:
                 N a m e          Type    Value   Attr
BEGIN. . . . . . . . . . . . .    F PROC  0000    CSEG    Length =001A
MESSGE . . . . . . . . . . . .    L BYTE  0000    DSEG
```

Figure 20-1 Simple Assembled Macro Instruction.

accept any segment name, define the names in the macro as *dummy arguments*:

```
INIT2   MACRO   CSNAME,DSNAME,SSNAME ;Dummy arguments
        ASSUME  CS:CSNAME,DS:DSNAME,SS:SSNAME,ES:DSNAME
        PUSH    DS
        SUB     AX.AX
        PUSH    AX
        MOV     AX,DSNAME
        MOV     DS,AX
        MOV     ES,AX
        ENDM
                                     ;End macro
```

The dummies in the macro definition tell the assembler to match these names with any occurrence of the same names in the macro body. The three dummy arguments CSNAME, DSNAME, and SSNAME all occur in the ASSUME statement, and DSNAME occurs in a later MOV instruction. A dummy argument may have any valid assembler name and need not be the same as that of the data segment.

Now when using the macro instruction INIT2, supply as parameters the actual names of the three segments in the specified sequence. For example, the following macro instruction contains three parameters that match the dummy arguments in the original macro definition:

```
Macro definition: INIT2  MACRO  CSNAME,DSNAME,SSNAME (arguments)
                                    |      |      |
Macro instruction:       INIT2   CSEG,DSEG,STACK     (parameters)
```

The assembler has already matched arguments in the original macro definition with statements in the body. It now substitutes the parameters of the macro instruction entry for entry with the dummy arguments in the macro definition:

- Parameter 1 for argument 1: CSEG matches with CSNAME in the macro definition. The assembler substitutes CSEG for the occurrence of CSNAME in the ASSUME.
- Parameter 2 for argument 2: DSEG matches with DSNAME in the macro definition. The assembler substitutes DSEG for the two occurrences of DSNAME in the ASSUME and for one in a MOV.
- Parameter 3 for argument 3: STACK matches with SSNAME in the macro definition. The assembler substitutes STACK for the occurrence of SSNAME in the ASSUME.

The macro definition and the macro expansion are shown in Figure 20-2.

```
                          TITLE  MACRO2  (EXE) Use of Parameters
                          ; ----------------------------------------
                          INIT2  MACRO   CSNAME,DSNAME,SSNAME
                                 ASSUME  CS:CSNAME,DS:DSNAME,SS:SSNAME,ES:DSNAME
                                 PUSH    DS
                                 SUB     AX,AX
                                 PUSH    AX
                                 MOV     AX,DSNAME
                                 MOV     DS,AX
                                 MOV     ES,AX
                                 ENDM                    ;End of macro
                          ; ----------------------------------------
0000                      STACK  SEGMENT PARA STACK 'Stack'
0000     20 [ ???? ]             DW      32 DUP(?)
0040                      STACK  ENDS
                          ; ----------------------------------------
0000                      DSEG   SEGMENT PARA 'Data'
0000 54 65 73 74 20 6F    MESSGE DB      'Test of macro', '$'
     66 20 6D 61 63 72
     6F 24
000E                      DSEG   ENDS
                          ; ----------------------------------------
0000                      CSEG   SEGMENT PARA 'Code'
0000                      BEGIN  PROC    FAR
                                 INIT2   CSEG,DSEG,STACK
0000 1E                 +        PUSH    DS
0001 2B C0              +        SUB     AX,AX
0003 50                 +        PUSH    AX
0004 B8 ---- R          +        MOV     AX,DSEG
0007 8E D8              +        MOV     DS,AX
0009 8E C0              +        MOV     ES,AX
000B B4 09                       MOV     AH,09           ;Request display
000D 8D 16 0000 R                LEA     DX,MESSGE       ;Message
0011 CD 21                       INT     21H
0013 CB                          RET
0014                      BEGIN  ENDP
0014                      CSEG   ENDS
                                 END     BEGIN
```

Figure 20-2 Use of Macro Parameters.

A dummy argument may have any legal assembler name, including a register name such as CX, which the assembler replaces with a parameter. As a consequence, the macro definition does not recognize register names and names defined in the data area as such. You may define a macro with any number of dummy arguments, separated by commas, up to column 120 of a line.

COMMENTS

Comments may appear in a macro definition in order to clarify its purpose. A COMMENT pseudo-op or a semicolon indicates a comment line, as in the following macro named PROMPT:

```
PROMPT  MACRO   MESSGE
;       This macro permits display of messages
        MOV     AH,09H
        LEA     DX,MESSGE
        INT     21H
        ENDM
```

Because the default is to list only instructions that generate object code, the assembler does not automatically display a comment when the macro definition just mentioned is expanded. If you want a comment to appear with an expansion, use the listing pseudo-op .LALL ("list all," including the leading period) prior to requesting the macro instruction:

```
.LALL
PROMPT  MESSAG1
```

A macro definition could contain a number of comments, some of which you may want to list and some to suppress. Still use .LALL, but code the double semicolons (;;) before comments that are always to be suppressed. The assembler default is .XALL, which causes a listing only of instructions that generate object code. Finally, you may not want any of the assembler code of a macro expansion to list, especially if the macro instruction is used several times in a program. Code the listing pseudo-op .SALL ("suppress all"), which reduces the size of the printed program, although it has no effect on the size of the object module.

A listing pseudo-op holds effect throughout a program until another listing pseudo-op is encountered. You can place them in a program to cause some macros to display comments, some to display the macro expansion, and some to suppress these.

The program in Figure 20-3 demonstrates the preceding features. The program defines the two macros, INIT2 and PROMPT, described earlier. The code segment contains the listing pseudo-op .SALL to suppress the expansion of INIT2 and the first expansion of PROMPT. For the second use of PROMPT, the listing pseudo-op .LALL causes the assembler to print the comment and the expansion of the macro. Note however in the macro definition for PROMPT that the comment containing a double semicolon (;;) still does not print in this macro expansion.

USE OF A MACRO WITHIN A MACRO DEFINITION

A macro definition may contain a reference to another defined macro. Consider a simple macro named DOS21 that inserts a DOS function into the AH register and calls INT 21H:

```
DOS21 MACRO DOSFUNC
      MOV   AH,DOSFUNC
      INT   21H
      ENDM
```

```
                              TITLE  MACRO3  (EXE)  Use of .LALL & .SALL
                              ; -----------------------------------------------
                              INIT2  MACRO    CSNAME,DSNAME,SSNAME
                                     ASSUME   CS:CSNAME,DS:DSNAME,SS:SSNAME,ES:DSNAME
                                     PUSH     DS
                                     SUB      AX,AX
                                     PUSH     AX
                                     MOV      AX,DSNAME
                                     MOV      DS,AX
                                     MOV      ES,AX
                                     ENDM
                              ; -----------------------------------------------
                              PROMPT MACRO    MESSGE
                              ;      This macro displays any message
                              ;;     Generates code that links to DOS
                                     MOV      AH,09            ;Request display
                                     LEA      DX,MESSGE
                                     INT      21H
                                     ENDM
                              ; -----------------------------------------------
0000                          STACK  SEGMENT PARA STACK 'Stack'
0000     20 [ ???? ]                 DW       32 DUP(?)
0040                          STACK  ENDS
                              ; -----------------------------------------------
0000                          DATA   SEGMENT PARA 'Data'
0000 43 75 73 74 6F 6D        MESSG1 DB       'Customer name?', '$'
     65 72 20 6E 61 6D
     65 3F 24
000F 43 75 73 74 6F 6D        MESSG2 DB       'Customer address?', '$'
     65 72 20 61 64 64
     72 65 73 73 3F 24
0021                          DATA   ENDS
                              ; -----------------------------------------------
0000                          CSEG   SEGMENT PARA 'Code'
0000                          BEGIN  PROC     FAR
                                     .SALL
                                     INIT2    CSEG,DATA,STACK
                                     PROMPT   MESSG1
                                     .LALL
                                     PROMPT   MESSG2
                            + ;      This macro displays any message
0013 B4 09                  +        MOV      AH,09            ;Request display
0015 8D 16 000F R           +        LEA      DX,MESSG2
0019 CD 21                  +        INT      21H
001B CB                              RET
001C                          BEGIN  ENDP
001C                          CSEG   ENDS
                                     END      BEGIN
```

Figure 20-3 Listing and Suppression of Macro Expansions.

To use the macro to accept input from the keyboard, code

```
LEA    DX,NAMEPAR
DOS21 0AH
```

Suppose you have another macro that uses 02 in the AH register to display a character:

```
DISP  MACRO  CHAR
      MOV    AH,02
      MOV    DL,CHAR
      INT    21H
      ENDM
```

To display an asterisk, for example, code the macro as DISP '*'. You could change DISP to take advantage of the DOS21H macro, as

```
DISP  MACRO  CHAR
      MOV    DL,CHAR
      DOS21  02
      ENDM
```

Now if you code the DISP macro as DISP '*', the assembler generates

```
MOV   DL,'*'
MOV   AH,02
INT   21H
```

THE LOCAL PSEUDO-OP

Some macros require definition of a data item or of an instruction label. If you use the macro more than once in the same program, the assembler defines the data field or label for each occurrence, and generates an error message because of duplicate names. Use the LOCAL pseudo-op to ensure that each generated name is unique, and code it immediately after the MACRO statement, even before comments. Its general format is:

```
LOCAL  dummy-1, dummy-2, ... ;One or more dummy arguments
```

Figure 20-4 illustrates the use of LOCAL. The purpose of the program is to perform division by successive subtraction. The routine subtracts the divisor from the dividend and adds 1 to the quotient until

```
                       TITLE  MACRO4  (COM)  Use of LOCAL
                       ; -----------------------------------------------
                       DIVIDE MACRO   DIVIDEND,DIVISOR,QUOTIENT
                              LOCAL   COMP
                              LOCAL   OUT
                       ;      AX = div'd, BX = divisor, CX = quotient
                              MOV     AX,DIVIDEND       ;Set dividend
                              MOV     BX,DIVISOR        ;Set divisor
                              SUB     CX,CX             ;Clear quotient
                       COMP:
                              CMP     AX,BX             ;Div'd < div'r?
                              JB      OUT               ; yes -- exit
                              SUB     AX,BX             ;Div'd -- divisor
                              INC     CX                ;Add to quotient
                              JMP     COMP
                       OUT:
                              MOV     QUOTIENT,CX       ;Store quotient
                              ENDM
                       ; -----------------------------------------------
0000                   CSEG   SEGMENT PARA 'Code'
                              ASSUME  CS:CSEG,DS:CSEG,SS:CSEG,ES:CSEG
0100                          ORG     100H
0100  EB 06            BEGIN: JMP     SHORT MAIN
                       ; -----------------------------------------------
0102  0096             DIVDND DW      150               ;Dividend
0104  001B             DIVSOR DW      27                ;Divisor
0106  ????             QUOTNT DW      ?                 ;Quotient
                       ; -----------------------------------------------
0108                   MAIN   PROC    NEAR
                              .LALL
                              DIVIDE  DIVDND,DIVSOR,QUOTNT
                     + ;      AX = div'd, BX = divisor, CX = quotient
0108  A1 0102 R      +        MOV     AX,DIVDND         ;Set dividend
010B  8B 1E 0104 R   +        MOV     BX,DIVSOR         ;Set divisor
010F  2B C9          +        SUB     CX,CX             ;Clear quotient
0111                 + ??0000:
0111  3B C3          +        CMP     AX,BX             ;Div'd < div'r?
0113  72 05          +        JB      ??0001            ; yes -- exit
0115  2B C3          +        SUB     AX,BX             ;Div'd -- divisor
0117  41             +        INC     CX                ;Add to quotient
0118  EB F7          +        JMP     ??0000
011A                 + ??0001:
011A  89 0E 0106 R   +        MOV     QUOTNT,CX         ;Store quotient
011E  C3                      RET
011F                   MAIN   ENDP
011F                   CSEG   ENDS
                              END     BEGIN
```

Figure 20-4 Use of LOCAL.

the dividend is less than the divisor. For this purpose, two labels are required: COMP, for the loop address, and OUT, for exiting on completion. Both COMP and OUT are defined as LOCAL and may have any legal assembler names.

In the macro expansion, the generated symbolic label for COMP is ??0000 and for OUT is ??0001. If the DIVIDE macro instruction were used again in the same program, the symbolic labels for the next macro expansion would become ??0002 and ??0003, respectively. In this way, the feature ensures that generated labels are unique.

INCLUDES FROM A MACRO LIBRARY

Defining a macro such as INIT1 or INIT2 and using it just once in a program may seem pointless. A better approach is to catalog all your macros in a disk library under any descriptive name, such as MACRO.LIB:

```
INIT     MACRO    CSNAME,DSNAME,SSNAME
         .
         .
         ENDM
PROMPT   MACRO    MESSGE
         .
         .
         ENDM
```

Now in order to use any of the cataloged macros, instead of a MACRO definition at the start of the program, use an INCLUDE pseudo-op:

```
INCLUDE C:MACRO.LIB
   .
   .
INIT     CSEG,DATA,STACK
```

The assembler accesses the file named MACRO.LIB (in this case) on drive C, and includes both macro definitions INIT and PROMPT into the program. In this example, only INIT is actually required. As coded, the assembled listing will contain a copy of the macro definition indicated by the letter C in column 30 of the LST file. Following the macro instruction is the expansion of the macro along with its generated object code indicated by + in column 31.

Since the assembly is a two-pass operation, you can use the following statements to cause INCLUDE to occur only on pass 1 (instead of both passes):

```
IF1
         INCLUDE C:MACRO.LIB
ENDIF
```

IF1 and ENDIF are conditional pseudo-ops. IF1 tells the assembler to access the named library only on pass 1 of the assembly. ENDIF terminates the IF logic. Now the copy of the macro definition does not appear on the listing—a saving of both time and space.

The program in Figure 20-5 contains the previously described IF1, INCLUDE, and ENDIF statements, although on the LST file the assembler lists only the ENDIF. The two macro instructions used in the code segment, INIT and PROMPT, are both cataloged in MACRO.LIB. They were simply recorded together as a disk file under that name by means of an editor program.

The placement of INCLUDE is not critical, but must appear before a macro instruction that references the library entry.

The Purge Pseudo-Op

An INCLUDE statement causes the assembler to include all the macro definitions that are in the specified library. For example, a library contains the macros INIT, PROMPT, and DIVIDE, but a program requires

```
                                TITLE  MACRO5  (EXE) Test of INCLUDE
                                ENDIF
                                ; ----------------------------------------
0000                            STACK  SEGMENT PARA STACK 'Stack'
0000     20 [????]                     DW      32 DUP(?)
0040                            STACK  ENDS
                                ; ----------------------------------------
0000                            DATA   SEGMENT PARA 'Data'
0000 54 65 73 74 20 6F          MESSGE DB      'Test of macro','$'
     66 20 6D 61 63 72
     6F 24
000E                            DATA   ENDS
                                ; ----------------------------------------
0000                            CSEG   SEGMENT PARA 'Code'
0000                            BEGIN  PROC    FAR
                                       INIT    CSEG,DATA,STACK
0000 1E                    +           PUSH    DS
0001 2B C0                 +           SUB     AX,AX
0003 50                    +           PUSH    AX
0004 B8 ---- R             +           MOV     AX,DATA
0007 8E D8                 +           MOV     DS,AX
0009 8E C0                 +           MOV     ES,AX
                                       PROMPT  MESSGE
000B B4 09                 +           MOV     AH,09           ;Request display
000D 8D 16 0000 R          +           LEA     DX,MESSGE
0011 CD 21                 +           INT     21H
0013 CB                                RET
0014                            BEGIN  ENDP
0014                            CSEG   ENDS
                                       END     BEGIN
```

Figure 20-5 Use of Library Include.

only INIT. The PURGE pseudo-op enables you to "delete" unwanted macros PROMPT and DIVIDE from the current assembly:

```
IF1
        INCLUDE MACRO.LIB ;Include full library
ENDIF
PURGE   PROMPT,DIVIDE      ;Delete unneeded macros
   ...
INIT    CSEG,DATA,STACK    ;Use remaining macro
```

A PURGE operation facilitates only the assembly and has no effect on macros still stored in the macro library.

CONCATENATION (&)

The ampersand (&) character tells the assembler to join (concatenate) text or symbols. The following MOVE macro provides for either MOVSB or MOVSW:

```
MOVE    MACRO    TAG
        REP MOVS&TAG
        ENDM
```

A user could code the macro instruction either as MOVE B or as MOVE W. The assembler concatenates the parameter with the MOVS instruction, as REP MOVSB or REP MOVSW. This example is somewhat trivial and is for illustrative purposes.

REPETITION: REPT, IRP, AND IRPC

The repetition pseudo-ops cause the assembler to repeat a block of statements, terminated by ENDM. These pseudo-ops do not have to be contained in a MACRO definition, but if they are, one ENDM is required to terminate the repetition and a second ENDM to terminate the MACRO definition.

REPT: Repetition

The REPT operation causes repetition of a block of statements up to ENDM according to the number of times in the expression entry:

```
REPT expression
```

The following initializes the value N to 0, and then repeats generation of DB N five times:

```
N =     0
REPT    5
N =     N + 1
DB      N
ENDM
```

The result is five generated DB statements, DB 1 through DB 5. A use for REPT could be to define a table or part of a table. As another example, the following code generates five MOVSB instructions and is equivalent to REP MOVSB where the CX contains 05:

```
REPT 5
MOVSB
ENDM
```

IRP: Indefinite Repeat

The IRP operation causes a repeat of a block of instructions up to the ENDM. The following is the general format:

```
IRP   dummy,<arguments>
```

The arguments, contained in angle brackets, are any number of legal symbols, string, numeric, or arithmetic constants. The assembler generates a block of code for each argument. In the following example the assembler generates DB 3, DB 9, DB 17, DB 25, and DB 28:

```
IRP  N,<3,9,17,25,28>
DB   N
```

IRPC: Indefinite Repeat Character

The IRPC operation causes a repeat of the block of statements up to the ENDM. The following is the general format:

```
IRPC dummy,string
```

The assembler generates a block of code for each character in the "string." In the following example, the assembler generates DW 3 through DW 8:

```
IRPC   N,345678
DW     N
ENDM
```

CONDITIONAL PSEUDO-OPERATIONS

The assembler supports a number of conditional pseudo-ops. We used IF1 earlier to include a library entry only during pass 1 of the assembly. Conditional pseudo-ops are most useful within a macro definition but are not limited to that purpose. Every IF pseudo-op must have a matching ENDIF to terminate the tested condition. One optional ELSE may provide an alternative action:

```
IFxx     (condition)
  .                              }
  .                              }  conditional
ELSE     (optional)              }
  .                              }    block
  .                              }
ENDIF    (end of IF)
```

Omission of ENDIF causes an error message: "Undeterminated conditional." If a condition being examined is true, the assembler executes the conditional block up to the ELSE, or if no ELSE up to the ENDIF. If the condition is false, the assembler executes the conditional block following the ELSE, or if no ELSE it does not generate any of the conditional block.

The following explains the various conditional pseudo-ops:

IF expression	If the assembler evaluates the expression to nonzero, it assembles the statements within the conditional block.
IFE expression	If the assembler evaluates the expression to zero, it assembles the statements within the conditional block.
IF1 (no expression)	If the assembler is processing pass 1, it acts on the statements in the conditional block.
IF2 (no expression)	If the assembler is processing pass 2, it acts on the statements in the conditional block.
IFDEF symbol	If the symbol is defined in the program or is declared as EXTRN, the assembler processes the statements in the conditional block.
IFNDEF symbol	If the symbol is not defined or is not declared as EXTRN, the assembler processes the statements in the conditional block.

IFB <argument> — If the argument is blank, the assembler processes the statements in the conditional block. The argument requires angle brackets.

IFNB <argument> — If the argument is not blank, the assembler processes the statements in the conditional block. The argument requires angle brackets.

IFIDN <arg-1>,<arg-2> — If the argument-1 string is identical to the argument-2 string, the assembler processes the statements in the conditional block. The arguments require angle brackets.

IFDIF <arg-1>,<arg-2> — If the argument-1 string is different from the argument-2 string, the assembler processes the statements in the conditional block. The arguments require angle brackets.

Here's a simple example of IFNB (if not blank). For DOS INT 21H, all requests require a function in the AH register, whereas only some requests also require a value in the DX. The following macro handles this situation:

```
DOS21   MACRO   DOSFUNC,DXADDRES
        MOV     AH,DOSFUNC
        IFNB    <DXADDRES>
        MOV     DX,OFFSET DXADDRES
        ENDIF
        INT     21H
        ENDM
```

Using DOS21 for simple keyboard input requires 01 in the AH, as:

```
DOS21   01
```

The assembler generates MOV AH,01 and INT 21H. Input of a character string requires 0AH in the AH and the input address in the DX, as:

```
DOS21   0AH,IPFIELD
```

The assembler generates both MOV instructions and INT 21H.

THE EXITM PSEUDO-OP

A macro definition may contain a conditional pseudo-op that tests for a serious condition. If the condition is true, the assembler is to exit from any further macro expansion. The EXITM pseudo-op serves this purpose:

```
IFxx  [condition]
  .
  .     (invalid condition)
  .
EXITM
  .
  .
ENDIF
```

If the assembler encounters EXITM in its expansion, it discontinues the macro expansion and resumes after the ENDM pseudo-op. You can also use EXITM to terminate REPT, IRP, and IRPC even if they are contained within a macro definition.

MACRO USING IF AND IFNDEF CONDITIONS

The skeleton program in Figure 20-6 contains a macro definition named DIVIDE that generates a routine to perform division by successive subtraction. A user has to code the macro instruction with parameters for

```
TITLE  MACRO6 (COM)  Test of IF and IFNDEF
; ---------------------------------------------
DIVIDE MACRO    DIVIDEND,DIVISOR,QUOTIENT
       LOCAL    COMP
       LOCAL    OUT
       CNTR     = 0
;      AX = div'nd, BX = div'r, CX = quot't
       IFNDEF   DIVIDEND
;               Dividend not defined
       CNTR     = CNTR +1
       ENDIF
       IFNDEF   DIVISOR
;               Divisor not defined
       CNTR     = CNTR +1
       ENDIF
       IFNDEF   QUOTIENT
;               Quotient not defined
       CNTR = CNTR + 1
       ENDIF
       IF       CNTR
;               Macro expansion terminated
       EXITM
       ENDIF
       MOV      AX,DIVIDEND       ;Set dividend
       MOV      BX,DIVISOR        ;Set divisor
       SUB      CX,CX             ;Clear quot
```

Figure 20-6 Use of IF and IFNDEF.

```
                    COMP:
                          CMP     AX,BX            ;Div'd < div'r?
                          JB      OUT              ;  yes - exit
                          SUB     AX,BX            ;Div'd - div'r
                          INC     CX               ;Add to quot
                          JMP     COMP
                    OUT:
                          MOV     QUOTIENT,CX      ;Store quot
                          ENDM
                    ; ------------------------------------------
0000                CSEG  SEGMENT PARA 'Code'
                          ASSUME  CS:CSEG,DS:CSEG,SS:CSEG,ES:CSEG
0100                      ORG     100H
0100  EB 06         BEGIN: JMP    SHORT MAIN
                    ; ------------------------------------------
0102  0096          DIVDND DW     150              ;Dividend
0104  001B          DIVSOR DW     27               ;Divisor
0106  ????          QUOTNT DW     ?                ;Quotient
                    ; ------------------------------------------
0108                MAIN  PROC    NEAR
                          .LALL
                          DIVIDE  DIVDND,DIVSOR,QUOTNT
= 0000              +             CNTR    = 0
                    + ;   AX = div'nd, BX = div'r, CX = quot't
                    +     ENDIF
                    +     ENDIF
                    +     ENDIF
                    +     ENDIF
0108  A1 0102 R     +     MOV     AX,DIVDND        ;Set dividend
010B  8B 1E 0104 R  +     MOV     BX,DIVSOR        ;Set divisor
010F  2B C9         +     SUB     CX,CX            ;Clear quot
0111                + ??0000:
0111  3B C3         +     CMP     AX,BX            ;Div'd < div'r?
0113  72 05         +     JB      ??0001           ;  yes - exit
0115  2B C3         +     SUB     AX,BX            ;Div'd - div'r
0117  41            +     INC     CX               ;Add to quot
0118  EB F7         +     JMP     ??0000
011A                + ??0001:
011A  89 0E 0106 R  +     MOV     QUOTNT,CX        ;Store quot
                          DIVIDE  DIDND,DIVSOR,QUOT
= 0000              +     CNTR    = 0
                    + ;   AX = div'nd, BX = div'r, CX = quot't
                    +     IFNDEF  DIDND
                    + ;           Dividend not defined
= 0001              +     CNTR    = CNTR +1
                    +     ENDIF
                    +     ENDIF
                    +     IFNDEF  QUOT
                    + ;           Quotient not defined
= 0002              +     CNTR = CNTR + 1
                    +     ENDIF
                    +     IF      CNTR
                    + ;           Macro expansion terminated
                    +     EXITM
011E  C3                  RET
011F                MAIN  ENDP
011F                CSEG  ENDS
                          END     BEGIN
```

Figure 20-6 (Continued)

dividend, divisor, and quotient, in that order. The macro uses IFNDEF to check if the program actually contains their definitions. For any entry not defined, the macro increments a field named CNTR. Technically, CNTR could have any legal name and is for temporary use in a macro definition. After checking all three parameters, the macro checks CNTR for nonzero:

```
          IF    CNTR
;           Macro expansion terminated
          EXITM
```

If CNTR has been set to a nonzero value, the assembler generates the comment and exits (EXITM) from any further macro expansion. Note that an initial instruction clears CNTR to 0, and also that the IFNDEF blocks need only to set CNTR to 1 rather than increment it.

If the assembler passes all the tests safely, it generates the macro expansion. In the code segment, the first DIVIDE macro instruction contains an invalid dividend and quotient and generates only comments. One way to improve the macro would be to test that the divisor is nonzero and that the dividend and divisor have the same sign; for this purpose, use assembler code rather than conditional pseudo-ops.

MACRO USING IFIDN CONDITION

The skeleton program in Figure 20-7 contains a macro definition named MOVIF that generates a MOVSB or MOVSW depending on a supplied parameter. A user has to code the macro instruction with a parameter B (for byte) or W (for word) to indicate if the MOVS is to be MOVSB or MOVSW.

Note the first two statements of the macro definition:

```
MOVIF    MACRO    TAG
         IFIDN    <&TAG>,<B>
```

The IFIDN conditional compares the supplied parameter (supposedly B or W) to the string B. If the two are identical, the assembler generates REP MOVSB. The normal use of the ampersand (&) operator is for concatenation. However, the operand <TAG> without the ampersand does not work.

If a user supplies neither B nor W, the assembler generates a comment and a default to MOVSB.

The examples in the code segment test MOVIF three times: for a B, for a W, and for invalid. Don't attempt to execute this program as it stands, since the CX and DX registers need to contain proper values.

```
                          TITLE  MACRO7 (COM)  Tests of IFIDN
                          ; -------------------------------------
                          MOVIF  MACRO   TAG
                                 IFIDN   <&TAG>,<B>
                                 REP MOVSB
                                 EXITM
                                 ENDIF
                                 IFIDN   <&TAG>,<W>
                                 REP MOVSW
                                 ELSE
                          ;      No B or W tag -- default to B
                                 REP MOVSB
                                 ENDIF
                                 ENDM
                          ; -------------------------------------
0000                      CSEG   SEGMENT PARA 'Code'
                                 ASSUME  CS:CSEG,DS:CSEG,SS:CSEG,ES:CSEG
0100                             ORG     100H
0100  EB 00               BEGIN: JMP     SHORT MAIN
                          ;      ...
0102                      MAIN   PROC    NEAR
                                 .LALL
                                 MOVIF   B
                         +       IFIDN   <B>,<B>
0102  F3/ A4             +       REP MOVSB
                         +       EXITM
                                 MOVIF   W
                         +       ENDIF
                         +       IFIDN   <W>,<W>
0104  F3/ A5             +       REP MOVSW
                         +       ENDIF
                                 MOVIF
                         +       ENDIF
                         +       ELSE
                         + ;     No B or W tag -- default to B
0106  F3/ A4             +       REP MOVSB
                         +       ENDIF
0108  C3                         RET
0109                      MAIN   ENDP
0109                      CSEG   ENDS
                                 END     BEGIN
```

Figure 20-7 Use of IFIDN.

Admittedly, this macro is not very useful; its purpose is to illustrate the use of conditional pseudo-ops in a simple manner. By this point, however, you should have sufficient direction to be able to code some large useful macros.

KEY POINTS TO REMEMBER

- Macro facilities are available only under the large (MASM) assembler.

- The use of macros in assembler programs can result in more readable and more productive code.
- A macro definition requires a MACRO pseudo-op, a block of one or more statements known as the body that the macro definition is to generate, and an ENDM pseudo-op to terminate the definition.
- A macro instruction is the use of the macro in a program. The code that a macro instruction generates is the macro expansion.
- The use of .SALL, .LALL, and .XALL controls the listing of comments and the generated object code in a macro expansion.
- The LOCAL pseudo-op facilitates using names within a macro definition, and must appear immediately after the macro statement.
- The use of dummy arguments in a macro definition allows a user to code parameters for more flexibility.
- A macro library makes macros available to all your other assembler programs.
- Conditional pseudo-ops enable you to validate macro parameters.

QUESTIONS

20-1. Specify the required instructions: (a) to suppress all instructions that a macro generates and (b) to list only instructions that generate object code.

20-2. Code two macro definitions that perform multiplication: (a) MULTBY is to generate code that multiplies byte times byte; (b) MULTWD is to generate code that multiplies word times word.

Include the multiplicands and multipliers as dummy arguments in the macro definition. Test execution of the macros with a small program that also defines the required data fields.

20-3. Store the macros defined in Question 20-2 in a "macro library." Revise the program to INCLUDE the library entries during pass 1 of the assembly.

20-4. Write a macro named BIPRINT that uses BIOS INT 17H to print. The macro should include a test for status and should provide for any defined print line with any length.

20-5. Revise the macro in Figure 20-6 to test if the divisor is zero (bypass the divide).

CHAPTER 21

Linking to Subprograms

Objective: To cover the programming techniques involved in linking and executing assembled programs.

INTRODUCTION

Up to this point, program examples have consisted of one assembly step. It is possible, however, to execute a program module that consists of more than one assembled program. In such a case, you could look at the program as consisting of a main program and one or more subprograms. Reasons for organizing a program into subprograms include the following:

- It may be desirable to link between languages—for example, to combine the computing power of a high-level language with the efficiency of assembler.
- A program written as one module could be too large for the assembler to process.
- Parts of a program may be written by different teams who assemble their modules separately.
- Because of the large size of an executable module, it may be necessary to overlay parts of it during execution.

Each program is assembled separately and generates its own unique object (OBJ) module. The LINK program then links the object modules into one combined executable (EXE) module. Typically, the main program is the one that begins execution, and it calls one or more subprograms. Subprograms in turn may call other subprograms.

Figure 21-1 shows two examples of a hierarchy of a main program and three subprograms. In Figure 21-1(a), the main program calls subprograms 1, 2, and 3. In Figure 21-1(b), the main program calls subprograms 1 and 2, and only subprogram 1 calls subprogram 3.

There are numerous variations of subprogram organization, but the organization has to make sense to the assembler, to the linker, and to

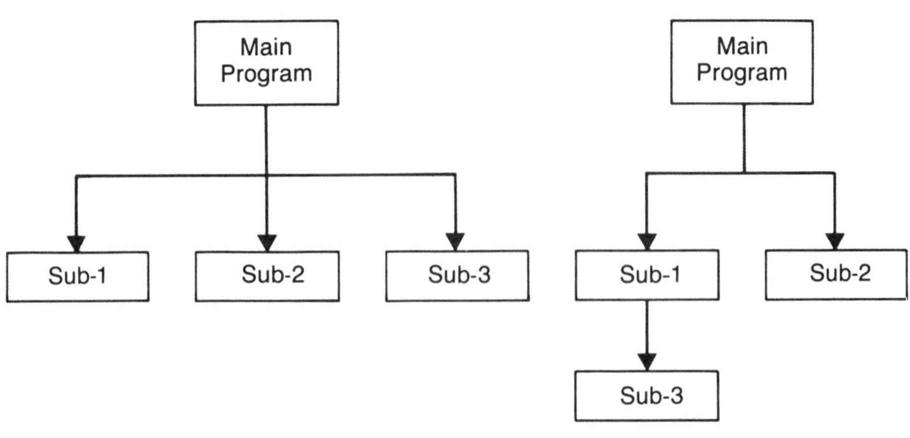

Figure 21-1 Program Hierarchy.

execution. You also have to watch out for situations in which, for example, subprogram 1 calls subprogram 2, which calls subprogram 3, which in turn calls subprogram 1. This process, known as recursion, can be made to work, but if not handled carefully, can cause interesting execution bugs.

INTERSEGMENT CALLS

CALL instructions used to this point have been *intra*segment (near) calls—that is, within the same code segment. An intrasegment CALL may be near (if within +127 or −128 bytes) or far (if exceeding these values). The operation pushes the IP register onto the stack and replaces the IP with the offset of the destination address.

For example, an intrasegment CALL could consist of the following object code: E8 2000. Hex E8 is the operation code for a conventional intrasegment CALL. The operation stores the 2000 as offset 0020 in the IP. The processor then combines the current address in the CS with the offset in the IP for the next instruction to execute. On exit from the called procedure, the RET instruction pops the stored IP off the stack and into the IP and returns to the instruction following the CALL.

A CALL outside of the code segment is an *inter*segment (far) CALL. This operation first pushes the contents of the CS register onto the stack and inserts an intersegment address into the CS. It then pushes the IP onto the stack and inserts an offset address in the IP. In this way, both the address in the code segment and the offset are saved for the return from the called subprogram.

For example, an intersegment CALL could consist of the following object code:

```
9A 0002 AF04
```

Hex 9A is the operation code for an intersegment CALL. The operation stores the 0002 as 0200 in the IP and stores the AF04 as 04AF in the CS. These combine to establish the address of the first instruction to execute in the called subprogram:

```
Code segment          04AF0
Offset in IP           0200
                      -----
Effective address     04CF0
```

On exit from the called procedure, an intersegment RET pops both the original CS and IP addresses back into their respective registers and returns to the instruction following the CALL.

THE EXTRN AND PUBLIC ATTRIBUTES

Let's consider a main program (MAINPROG) that calls one subprogram (SUBPROG). An intersegment CALL is required as shown in Figure 21-2.

The CALL in MAINPROG has to know that SUBPROG exists outside this segment (or else the assembler generates an error message that SUBPROG is an undefined symbol). An EXTRN pseudo-op performs this function—it notifies the assembler that any reference to SUBPROG is to a FAR label that is defined in another assembly. Because the assembler has no way of knowing if this is true, it generates "empty" object code operands for the linker to fill:

```
9A 0000 ---- E
```

SUBPROG contains a PUBLIC pseudo-op that tells the assembler and linker that another module has to know the address of SUBPROG. In a later step, when both MAINPROG and SUBPROG are successfully assembled into object modules, they may be linked as follows:

LINK Prompt	*Reply:*
`Object Modules [.OBJ]:`	`B:MAINPROG+B:SUBPROG`
`Run File [filespec.EXE]:`	`B:COMBPROG  (or any legal name)`
`List File [NUL.MAP]:`	`CON`
`Libraries [.LIB]:`	`[return]`

```
          EXTRN   SUBPROG:FAR
MAINPROG:   .
            .
          CALL    SUBPROG
            .
            .
---------------------------------
          PUBLIC  SUBPROG
SUBPROG:    .
            .
            .
          RET
```

Figure 21-2 Intersegment CALL.

The linker matches EXTRNs in one object module with PUBLICs in the other and inserts any required offset addresses. It then combines the two object modules into one executable module. If unable to match references, the linker supplies error messages—watch for these before attempting to execute.

The EXTRN Pseudo-op

The EXTRN pseudo-op has the following format:

```
EXTRN name:type [, ... ]
```

You can define more than one name up to the end of a line or code additional EXTRN statements. Another assembly module must define the name and identify it as PUBLIC. The type entry may be ABS, BYTE, DWORD, FAR, NEAR, WORD, or a name defined by an EQU and must be valid in terms of the actual definition of name.

THE PUBLIC Pseudo-op

The PUBLIC pseudo-op tells the assembler and linker that the address of a specified symbol is to be available to other programs. The general format is

```
PUBLIC symbol [, ... ]
```

You can define more than one symbol up to the end of a line or code additional PUBLIC statements. The symbol entry can be a label (including PROC labels), a variable, or a number. Invalid entries include register names and EQU symbols that define values greater than two bytes.

Let's now examine three different ways of linking programs.

PROGRAM: USE OF EXTRN AND PUBLIC FOR A LABEL

The program in Figure 21-3 consists of a main program, CALLMUL1, and a subprogram, SUBMUL1. The main program defines segments for the stack, data, and code. The data segment defines QTY and PRICE. The code segment loads the AX with PRICE and the BX with QTY and then calls the subprogram. An EXTRN in the main program defines the entry point to the subprogram as SUBMUL.

The subprogram contains a PUBLIC statement (after the ASSUME) that makes SUBMUL known to the linker as the entry point for execution. This subprogram simply multiplies the contents of the AX (price) by the BX (quantity). The product is developed in the DX:AX pair as hex 002E 4000.

Since the subprogram does not define any data, it does not need a data segment; it could, but only this subprogram would recognize such data.

As well, the subprogram does not define a stack segment because it references the same stack addresses as the main program. As a consequence, the stack defined in the main program is available to the subprogram. The linker requires definition of at least one stack, and the definition in the main program serves this purpose.

Now let's examine the symbol tables following each assembly. Notice that the symbol table for the main program shows SUBMUL as FAR and External. The symbol table for the subprogram shows SUBMUL as F (for FAR) and Global. This latter term implies that the name is known "globally" outside of this subprogram.

The link map listed at the end of the subprogram depicts the organization of the program in memory. Note that there are two code segments, one for each assembly, but at different starting addresses. These appear in the sequence that you enter when linking, and the main program is normally first. In this case, the main program starts at offset hex 00000, and the subprogram at hex 00020.

A trace of program execution disclosed that CALL SUBMUL generated

```
9A 0000 D413
```

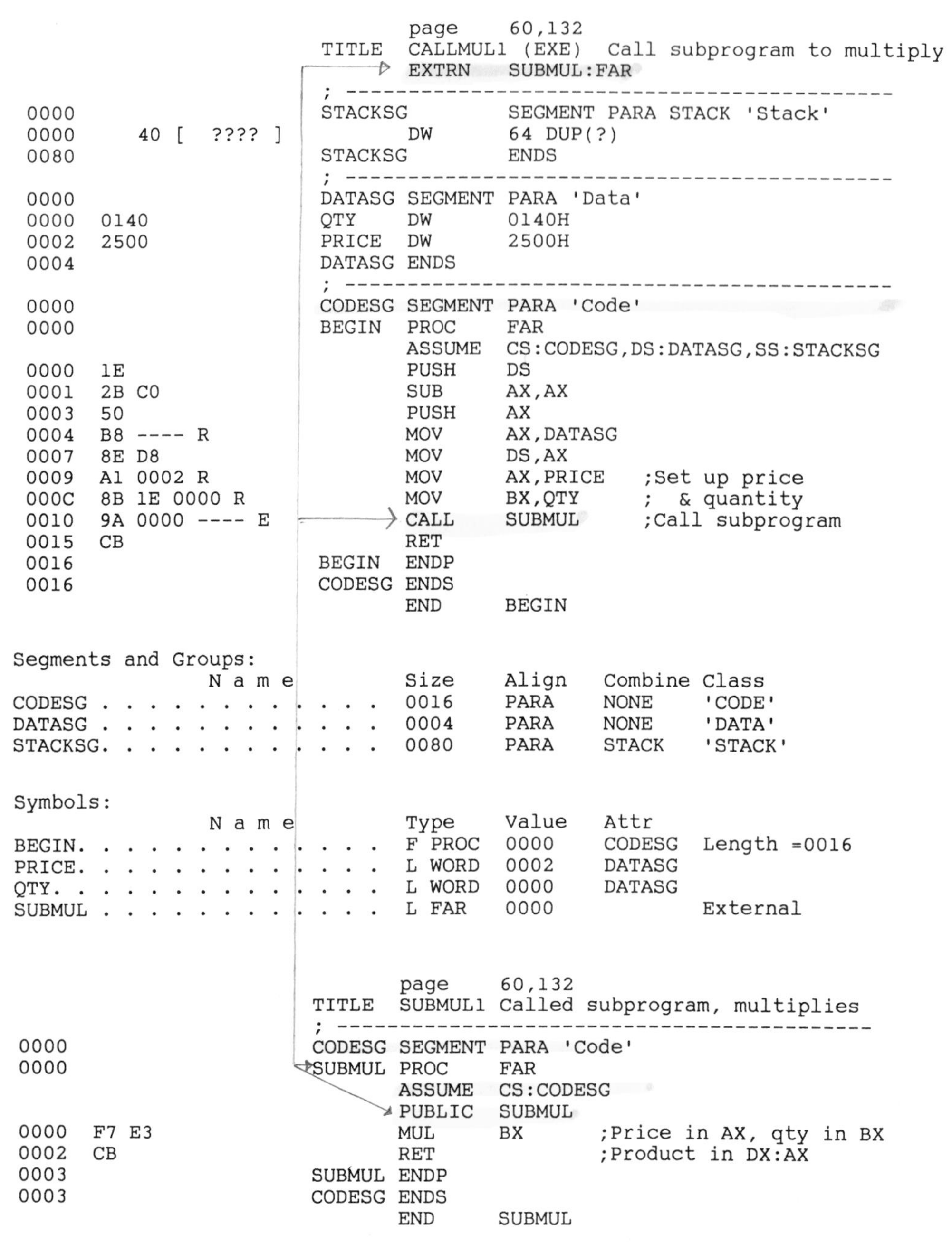

```
                                     page     60,132
                               TITLE CALLMUL1 (EXE)  Call subprogram to multiply
                                     EXTRN    SUBMUL:FAR
                               ; --------------------------------------------
 0000                          STACKSG        SEGMENT PARA STACK 'Stack'
 0000      40 [  ???? ]              DW       64 DUP(?)
 0080                          STACKSG        ENDS
                               ; --------------------------------------------
 0000                          DATASG SEGMENT PARA 'Data'
 0000  0140                    QTY    DW      0140H
 0002  2500                    PRICE  DW      2500H
 0004                          DATASG ENDS
                               ; --------------------------------------------
 0000                          CODESG SEGMENT PARA 'Code'
 0000                          BEGIN  PROC    FAR
                                      ASSUME  CS:CODESG,DS:DATASG,SS:STACKSG
 0000  1E                             PUSH    DS
 0001  2B C0                          SUB     AX,AX
 0003  50                             PUSH    AX
 0004  B8 ---- R                      MOV     AX,DATASG
 0007  8E D8                          MOV     DS,AX
 0009  A1 0002 R                      MOV     AX,PRICE     ;Set up price
 000C  8B 1E 0000 R                   MOV     BX,QTY       ;  & quantity
 0010  9A 0000 ---- E                 CALL    SUBMUL       ;Call subprogram
 0015  CB                             RET
 0016                          BEGIN  ENDP
 0016                          CODESG ENDS
                                      END     BEGIN

Segments and Groups:
                    N a m e           Size    Align   Combine Class
CODESG . . . . . . . . . . . . . .    0016    PARA    NONE    'CODE'
DATASG . . . . . . . . . . . . . .    0004    PARA    NONE    'DATA'
STACKSG. . . . . . . . . . . . . .    0080    PARA    STACK   'STACK'

Symbols:
                    N a m e           Type    Value   Attr
BEGIN. . . . . . . . . . . . . . .    F PROC  0000    CODESG  Length =0016
PRICE. . . . . . . . . . . . . . .    L WORD  0002    DATASG
QTY. . . . . . . . . . . . . . . .    L WORD  0000    DATASG
SUBMUL . . . . . . . . . . . . . .    L FAR   0000            External


                                     page     60,132
                               TITLE SUBMUL1  Called subprogram, multiplies
                               ; --------------------------------------------
 0000                          CODESG SEGMENT PARA 'Code'
 0000                          SUBMUL PROC    FAR
                                      ASSUME  CS:CODESG
                                      PUBLIC  SUBMUL
 0000  F7 E3                          MUL     BX        ;Price in AX, qty in BX
 0002  CB                             RET               ;Product in DX:AX
 0003                          SUBMUL ENDP
 0003                          CODESG ENDS
                                      END     SUBMUL
```

Figure 21-3 Use of EXTRN and PUBLIC.

```
Segments and Groups:
                N a m e           Size    Align   Combine Class
CODESG . . . . . . . . . . . .    0003    PARA    NONE    'CODE'

Symbols:
                N a m e           Type    Value   Attr
SUBMUL . . . . . . . . . . . .    F PROC  0000    CODESG  Global  Length =0003
```

```
LINK
IBM Personal Computer Linker
Version 2.30 (C) Copyright IBM Corp 1981, 1985
Object Modules: B:CALLMUL1+B:SUBMUL1
Run File: [B:CALLMUL1.EXE]: <return>
List File: [NUL.MAP]: CON
Libraries [.LIB]: <return>

 Start   Stop   Length  Name               Class

 00000H 00015H 0016H   CODESG              CODE  <-- Note: 2 code
 00020H 00022H 0003H   CODESG              CODE  <--    segments
 00030H 00033H 0004H   DATASG              DATA
 00040H 000BFH 0080H   STACKSG             STACK

 Program entry point at 0000:0000
```

Figure 21-3 (Continued)

The machine code for an intersegment CALL is hex 9A. The operation pushed the IP register onto the stack and loaded the IP with 0000. It then pushed the CS register containing 13D2 onto the stack and loaded the CS with hex D413. The next instruction to execute was CS:IP, or hex 13D40 plus 0000. What is at 13D40? Well, the main program begins with the CS register containing hex 13D2, or technically 13D20. The map shows that the subprogram begins at offset hex 00020. Adding these two values supplies the effective address of the code segment for the subprogram:

```
CS address           13D20
IP offset            00020
Effective address    13D40
```

The linker determines this value just as we have and substitutes it in the CALL operand.

PROGRAM: USE OF PUBLIC IN THE CODE SEGMENT

Our next example in Figure 21-4 provides a variation on Figure 21-3. There is one change in the main program and one change in the sub-

```
                             page    60,132
                       TITLE  CALLMUL2 (EXE)  Call subprogram to multiply
                              EXTRN   SUBMUL:FAR
                       ; -------------------------------------------
0000                   STACKSG        SEGMENT PARA STACK 'Stack'
0000     40 [ ???? ]                  DW      64 DUP(?)
0080                   STACKSG        ENDS
                       ; -------------------------------------------
0000                   DATASG SEGMENT PARA 'Data'
0000  0140             QTY     DW     0140H
0002  2500             PRICE    DW    2500H
0004                   DATASG ENDS
                       ; -------------------------------------------
0000                   CODESG SEGMENT PARA PUBLIC 'Code'
0000                   BEGIN  PROC    FAR
                              ASSUME  CS:CODESG,DS:DATASG,SS:STACKSG
0000  1E                      PUSH    DS
0001  2B C0                   SUB     AX,AX
0003  50                      PUSH    AX
0004  B8 ---- R               MOV     AX,DATASG
0007  8E D8                   MOV     DS,AX
0009  A1 0002 R               MOV     AX,PRICE     ;Set up price
000C  8B 1E 0000 R            MOV     BX,QTY       ; & quantity
0010  9A 0000 ---- E          CALL    SUBMUL       ;Call subprogram
0015  CB                      RET
0016                   BEGIN  ENDP

0016                   CODESG ENDS
                              END     BEGIN
```

```
Segments and Groups:
                N a m e         Size    Align   Combine Class
CODESG . . . . . . . . . . . . . 0016    PARA    PUBLIC  'CODE'
DATASG . . . . . . . . . . . . . 0004    PARA    NONE    'DATA'
STACKSG. . . . . . . . . . . . . 0080    PARA    STACK   'STACK'

Symbols:
                N a m e          Type   Value   Attr
BEGIN. . . . . . . . . . . . . . F PROC  0000    CODESG  Length =0016
PRICE. . . . . . . . . . . . . . L WORD  0002    DATASG
QTY. . . . . . . . . . . . . . . L WORD  0000    DATASG
SUBMUL . . . . . . . . . . . . . L FAR   0000            External
```

```
                             page    60,132
                       TITLE  SUBMUL2 Called subprogram, multiplies
                       ; -------------------------------------------
0000                   CODESG SEGMENT PARA PUBLIC 'Code'
0000                   SUBMUL PROC    FAR
                              ASSUME  CS:CODESG
                              PUBLIC  SUBMUL
0000  F7 E3                   MUL     BX    ;Price in AX, qty in BX
0002  CB                      RET           ;Product in DX:AX
0003                   SUBMUL ENDP
0003                   CODESG ENDS
                              END     SUBMUL
```

Figure 21-4 Code Segment Defined as PUBLIC.

```
Segments and Groups:
                N a m e         Size    Align   Combine Class
CODESG . . . . . . . . . . . . 0003     PARA    PUBLIC  'CODE'

Symbols:
                N a m e         Type    Value   Attr
SUBMUL . . . . . . . . . . . . F PROC   0000    CODESG  Global  Length =0003


LINK
IBM Personal Computer Linker
Version 2.30 (C) Copyright IBM Corp 1981, 1985
Object Modules: B:CALLMUL2+B:SUBMUL2
Run File: [B:CALLMUL2.EXE]: <return>
List File: [NUL.MAP]: CON
Libraries [.LIB]: <return>

 Start   Stop   Length  Name                 Class

 00000H 00022H 0023H  CODESG                 CODE  <-- Note: 1 code segment
 00030H 00033H 0004H  DATASG                 DATA
 00040H 000BFH 0080H  STACKSG                STACK

Program entry point at 0000:0000
```

Figure 21-4 (Continued)

program, both involving the use of PUBLIC in the SEGMENT pseudo-op for both code segments:

```
CODESG  SEGMENT  PARA PUBLIC 'CODE'
```

There is an interesting result in the link map and in the CALL object code.

Note the symbol table following each assembly: The combine-type for CODESG is PUBLIC (in Figure 21-3 it is NONE). More interesting is the Link Map at the end that now shows only one code segment! The fact that both segments have the same name (DATASG), class ('CODE'), and PUBLIC attribute has caused the linker to combine the two logical code segments into one physical code segment. Further, a trace of machine execution shows that the CALL instruction in the subprogram is now the following:

```
9A 2000 D213
```

This instruction stores hex 2000 in the IP and hex D213 in the CS register. Because the subprogram shares a common code segment with the main program, the CS register is set to the same starting address, hex D213. But there is now an offset of 0020:

```
CS address            13D20
IP offset              0020
Effective address     13D40
```

The code segment of the subprogram therefore presumably begins at hex 13D40. Is this correct? The link map doesn't make this point entirely clear, but you can infer the address from the listing of the main program—its size ends at offset 0016. Since the code segment for the subprogram is defined as SEGMENT, it must begin on a paragraph boundary (evenly divisible by hex 10, so that the rightmost digit is 0). The linker sets the subprogram at the first paragraph boundary immediately following the main program—and this offset address is 00020. Therefore, the code segment of the subprogram begins at 13D20 plus 0020, or 13D40.

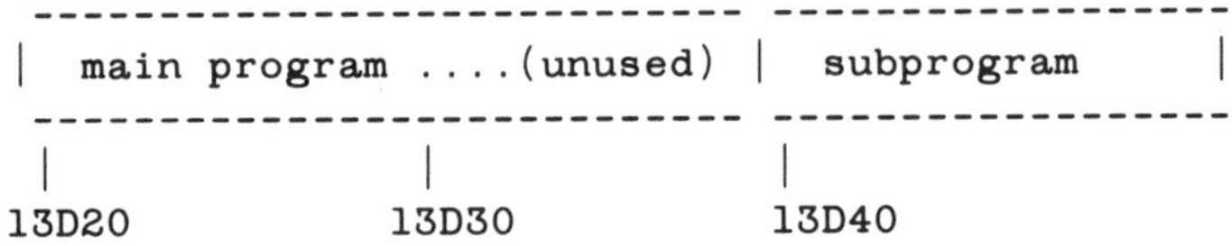

Let's see how the linker handles data defined in a main program and referenced in a subprogram.

PROGRAM: COMMON DATA IN SUBPROGRAMS

A common requirement is to process data in one assembly module that is defined in another assembly module. Let's modify the preceding examples so that although the main program still defines QTY and PRICE, the subprogram now inserts their values into the BX and AX. Figure 21-5 gives the revised coding. The new changes are the following:

- The main program defines QTY and PRICE as PUBLIC. The data segment is also defined with the PUBLIC attribute. Note in the symbol table the Global attribute for QTY and PRICE.
- The subprogram defines QTY and PRICE as EXTRN, and both as WORD. This definition informs the assembler as to the length of the two fields. The assembler can now generate the correct operation code for the MOV instructions, but the linker will have to complete the operands. Note in the symbol table that PRICE and QTY are External.

The assembler lists the MOV instructions in the subprogram as

```
A1 0000 E         MOV   AX,PRICE
8B 1E 0000 E      MOV   BX,QTY
```

```
                           page    60,132
                    TITLE  CALLMUL3 (EXE)  Call subprogram, multiplies
                           EXTRN   SUBMUL:FAR
                           PUBLIC  QTY,PRICE
                    ; ------------------------------------------
0000                STACKSG        SEGMENT PARA STACK 'Stack'
0000     40 [ ???? ]       DW      64 DUP(?)
0080                STACKSG        ENDS
                    ; ------------------------------------------
0000                DATASG SEGMENT PARA PUBLIC 'Data'
0000  0140          QTY    DW      0140H
0002  2500          PRICE   DW     2500H
0004                DATASG ENDS
                    ; ------------------------------------------
0000                CODESG SEGMENT PARA PUBLIC 'Code'
0000                BEGIN  PROC    FAR
                           ASSUME  CS:CODESG,DS:DATASG,SS:STACKSG
0000  1E                   PUSH    DS
0001  2B C0                SUB     AX,AX
0003  50                   PUSH    AX
0004  B8 ---- R            MOV     AX,DATASG
0007  8E D8                MOV     DS,AX
0009  9A 0000 ---- E       CALL    SUBMUL     ;Call subprogram
000E  CB                   RET
000F                BEGIN  ENDP

000F                CODESG ENDS
                           END     BEGIN
```

```
Segments and Groups:
                N a m e         Size    Align   Combine Class
CODESG . . . . . . . . . . . .  000F    PARA    PUBLIC  'CODE'
DATASG . . . . . . . . . . . .  0004    PARA    PUBLIC  'DATA'
STACKSG. . . . . . . . . . . .  0080    PARA    STACK   'STACK'

Symbols:
                N a m e         Type    Value   Attr
BEGIN. . . . . . . . . . . . .  F PROC  0000    CODESG  Length =000F
PRICE. . . . . . . . . . . . .  L WORD  0002    DATASG  Global
QTY. . . . . . . . . . . . . .  L WORD  0000    DATASG  Global
SUBMUL . . . . . . . . . . . .  L FAR   0000            External
```

```
                           page    60,132
                    TITLE  SUBMUL3 Called subprogram, multiplies
                           EXTRN   QTY:WORD,PRICE:WORD
                    ; ------------------------------------------
0000                CODESG SEGMENT PARA PUBLIC 'CODE'
0000                SUBMUL PROC    FAR
                           ASSUME  CS:CODESG
                           PUBLIC  SUBMUL
0000  A1 0000 E            MOV     AX,PRICE
0003  8B 1E 0000 E         MOV     BX,QTY
0007  F7 E3                MUL     BX        ;Product in DX:AX
0009  CB                   RET
000A                SUBMUL ENDP
000A                CODESG ENDS
                           END     SUBMUL
```

Figure 21-5 Common Data in Subprograms.

```
Segments and Groups:
                N a m e          Size    Align   Combine Class
CODESG . . . . . . . . . . . .   000A    PARA    PUBLIC  'CODE'

Symbols:
                N a m e          Type    Value   Attr
PRICE. . . . . . . . . . . . . V WORD    0000            External
QTY. . . . . . . . . . . . . . V WORD    0000            External
SUBMUL . . . . . . . . . . . . F PROC    0000    CODESG  Global  Length =000A
```

```
LINK
IBM Personal Computer Linker
Version 2.30 (C) Copyright IBM Corp 1981, 1985
Object Modules: B:CALLMUL3+B:SUBMUL3
Run File: [B:CALLMUL3.EXE]: <return>
List File: [NUL.MAP]: CON
Libraries [.LIB]: <return>

 Start   Stop   Length  Name                 Class

 00000H 00019H 001AH  CODESG                CODE
 00030H 00033H 0004H  DATASG                DATA
 00040H 000BFH 0080H  STACKSG               STACK

Program entry point at 0000:0000
```

Figure 21-5 (Continued)

Object code hex A1 means move a word from memory to the AX, whereas hex 8B means move a word from memory to the BX (AX operations often require fewer bytes). Tracing execution reveals that the linker has completed the object code operands as follows:

```
A1 0200
8B 1E 0000
```

The object code is now identical to that generated for the previous examples where the MOV instructions are in the calling program. This is a logical result because the operands in all three programs reference the same DS register and the same offset addresses.

The main program and the subprogram may define any other data items, but only those defined as PUBLIC and EXTRN are known in common.

If you follow the general rules discussed in this chapter, you should be able to link a program consisting of more than two assembly modules and to make data known in all the modules. But watch out for the size of the stack—for large programs, defining 64 words could be a wise precaution.

Chapter 23 provides additional features of segments, including defining more than one code or data segment in the same assembly module and the use of GROUP to combine these into a common segment.

PASSING PARAMETERS

Another way of making data known to a called subprogram is by *passing parameters,* in which a program passes data physically via the stack. In this case, ensure that each PUSH references a word, in either memory or a register.

The program in Figure 21-6 pushes both PRICE and QTY prior to calling SUBMUL. After the CALL, the stack appears as follows:

```
. . .   | 1600 | D213 | 4001 | 0025 | 0000 | C213 |
           6      5      4      3      2      1
```

1. The initializing instruction PUSH DS pushed the address onto the stack. This address may vary by DOS version.
2. PUSH AX loaded the zero address onto the stack.
3. A PUSH instruction loaded PRICE (2500) onto the stack.
4. A PUSH instruction loaded QTY (0140) onto the stack.
5. CALL pushed the contents of the CS register (D213).
6. Since this is an intersegment CALL, it also pushed the contents of the IP register, 1600.

The called program requires use of the BP to access the parameters in the stack. Its first action is to save the contents of the BP for the calling program by pushing it onto the stack. In this case, the BP happens to contain zero, and it is stored at the top of the stack, to the left.

The program then inserts the contents of the SP into the BP because the BP (but not the SP) is usable as an index register. The operation loads the BP with the value 0072. Initially, the SP contained the size of the stack—hex 80. Each word pushed onto the stack decrements the SP by 2:

```
      | 0000 | 1600 | D213 | 4001 | 0025 | 0000 | C213 |
        |      |      |      |      |      |      |
SP:     72     74     76     78     7A     7C     7E
```

Because the BP now also contains 0072, the price parameter is at BP + 8 and the quantity parameter is at BP + 6. The routine moves these values from the stack to the AX and BX, respectively, and performs the multiplication.

```
                                     page    60,132
                              TITLE  CALLMUL4 (EXE)  Pass parameters to subprogram
                                     EXTRN   SUBMUL:FAR
                              ; ---------------------------------------------
0000                          STACKSG        SEGMENT PARA STACK 'Stack'
0000      40 [???? ]                 DW      64 DUP(?)
0080                          STACKSG        ENDS
                              ; ---------------------------------------------
0000                          DATASG SEGMENT PARA 'Data'
0000  0140                    QTY    DW      0140H
0002  2500                    PRICE   DW     2500H
0004                          DATASG ENDS
                              ; ---------------------------------------------
0000                          CODESG SEGMENT PARA PUBLIC 'Code'
0000                          BEGIN  PROC    FAR
                                     ASSUME  CS:CODESG,DS:DATASG,SS:STACKSG
0000  1E                             PUSH    DS
0001  2B C0                          SUB     AX,AX
0003  50                             PUSH    AX
0004  B8 ---- R                      MOV     AX,DATASG
0007  8E D8                          MOV     DS,AX
0009  FF 36 0002 R                   PUSH    PRICE
000D  FF 36 0000 R                   PUSH    QTY
0011  9A 0000 ---- E                 CALL    SUBMUL     ;Call subprogram
0016  CB                             RET
0017                          BEGIN  ENDP
0017                          CODESG ENDS
                                     END     BEGIN
```

```
Segments and Groups:
                N a m e          Size     Align    Combine Class
CODESG . . . . . . . . . . . . . 0017     PARA     PUBLIC  'CODE'
DATASG . . . . . . . . . . . . . 0004     PARA     NONE    'DATA'
STACKSG. . . . . . . . . . . . . 0080     PARA     STACK   'STACK'

Symbols:
                N a m e          Type     Value    Attr
BEGIN. . . . . . . . . . . . . . F PROC   0000     CODESG  Length =0017
PRICE. . . . . . . . . . . . . . L WORD   0002     DATASG
QTY. . . . . . . . . . . . . . . L WORD   0000     DATASG
SUBMUL . . . . . . . . . . . . . L FAR    0000             External
```

```
                                   page    60,132
                            TITLE  SUBMUL4 Called subprogram, multiplies
0000                        CODESG SEGMENT PARA PUBLIC 'Code'
0000                        SUBMUL PROC    FAR
                                   ASSUME  CS:CODESG
                                   PUBLIC  SUBMUL
0000  55                           PUSH    BP
0001  8B EC                        MOV     BP,SP
0003  8B 46 08                     MOV     AX,[BP+8]  ;Price
0006  8B 5E 06                     MOV     BX,[BP+6]  ;Quantity
0009  F7 E3                        MUL     BX         ;Product in DX:AX
000B  5D                           POP     BP
000C  CA 0004                      RET     4
```

Figure 21-6 Passing Parameters.

```
000F                        SUBMUL ENDP
000F                        CODESG ENDS
                                   END
```

```
Segments and Groups:
                N a m e         Size    Align   Combine Class
CODESG . . . . . . . . . . . .  000F    PARA    PUBLIC  'CODE'

Symbols:
                N a m e         Type    Value   Attr
SUBMUL . . . . . . . . . . . .  F PROC  0000    CODESG  Global  Length =000F
```

```
LINK
IBM Personal Computer Linker
Version 2.30 (C) Copyright IBM Corp 1981, 1985
Object Modules: B:CALLMUL4+B:SUBMUL4
Run File: [B:CALLMUL4.EXE]: <return>
List File: [NUL.MAP]: CON
Libraries [.LIB]: <return>

 Start   Stop   Length  Name                 Class

 00000H 00019H 001AH   CODESG               CODE
 00030H 00033H 0004H   DATASG               DATA
 00040H 000BFH 0080H   STACKSG              STACK

Program entry point at 0000:0000
```

Figure 21-6 (Continued)

On returning to the calling program, the routine pops the BP (returning the zero address to the BP) and increments the SP by 2, from 72 to 74.

The last instruction, RET, is a "far" return to the calling program that performs the following:

- Pops the word now at the top of the stack (1600) to the IP.
- Increments the SP by 2, from 74 to 76.
- Pops the word now at the top (D213) onto the CS.
- Increments the SP by 2, from 76 to 78.

This operation returns correctly to the calling program—but there is one remaining explanation. The instruction is coded as

```
RET   4
```

The 4, known as a *pop-value,* contains the number of bytes in the passed parameters (two one-word parameters in this case). The RET operation also adds the pop-value to the SP, correcting it to 7C. In effect, because the parameters in the stack are no longer required, they are discarded. Be especially careful restoring the SP register—errors can create very interesting results.

LINKING BASIC INTERPRETER AND ASSEMBLER

The BASIC manual for the IBM PC provides methods of linking the BASIC interpreter with assembler routines. Two reasons for linking these languages are to make use of BIOS interrupt routines through assembler and to generate a more efficient program. The purpose of this section is to give a general overview of the linkage requirements; technical details in the BASIC manual need not be repeated here.

For linking to BASIC, code the assembler routine separately and assemble and link it. You have a choice of allocating space for the machine language subroutine either inside or outside the 64K memory area to which BASIC is restricted.

Two ways of loading a machine code subroutine into memory are to either use the BASIC POKE statement or combine an edited linked module with the BASIC program.

Use of the BASIC POKE Statement

Although the simplest method, BASIC POKE is suitable only for very short subroutines. First determine the object code of the assembler routine either through the LST file or through DEBUG. Code the hex values directly in the BASIC program as DATA statements. A BASIC READ statement reads each hex byte successively, and a BASIC POKE plugs each byte into memory for execution.

Linked Assembler Modules

A larger assembler subroutine is normally easier to handle if it is assembled and linked as an execute module. You then have to organize the BASIC program and the executable module into a working program. Use BSAVE (BASIC save) to store the program permanently, and use BLOAD to load it for execution.

Before coding the BASIC and assembler programs, decide which of two ways you want to interface them. The two BASIC methods are USR (user) function and the CALL statement. For both methods on entry, the DS, ES, and SS registers contain the address of BASIC's address space.

The CS contains the current value that the latest DEF SEG (if any) specified. The SP references a stack of only eight words, so you may need to set up a stack within the subroutine; if so, on entry save the location of the current stack, and on exit restore it. For both methods on exit, restore segment registers and the SP and return to BASIC with an intersegment RET.

Link your assembled object file so that it is at the high end of memory; use LINK's second prompt, as B:name/HIGH. Use DEBUG to load the EXE subroutine and use R to determine the values in the CS and IP registers: these supply the starting address of the subroutine. While still in DEBUG, name (N) BASIC and load (L) it.

The two ways of linking a BASIC program to an EXE subroutine are by using USRn or CALL. During the DEBUG session, you determined the starting address of the EXE subroutine; insert this address either in the BASIC USRn or in the BASIC CALL statement. The IBM BASIC manual provides details of the USRn function and the CALL statement, along with various examples.

Program: Linking BASIC and Assembler

Let's now study a simple example that links a BASIC interpreter program with an assembler subprogram. In this example, the BASIC program prompts for input of hours and rate and displays the product (wage). A FOR/NEXT loop provides for five entries of hours and rate and then terminates. We are just going to get the BASIC program to link to an assembler module that clears the screen.

Figure 21-7 shows the original BASIC program and assembler subprogram. Note the following features in the BASIC program: Statement 10 clears 32K bytes of memory; statements 20, 30, 40, and 50 temporarily contain comments.

Later, we will insert BASIC statements to facilitate linking to an assembler module. You could test this program right now. Enter the command BASIC and key in each numbered statement just as it appears on the example. Then press F2 to run the program. Remember to save it using

```
SAVE "B:BASTEST.BAS"
```

Note the following features in the assembler subprogram:

- There is no defined stack (BASIC supplies it); this subprogram is not intended to be run alone, nor can it.
- The subprogram saves the contents of the BP register on the stack and stores the SP register in the BP.

```
LOAD"D:BASTEST.BAS

LIST
010      CLEAR ,32768!
020      ' for BLOAD later
030      ' for DEFSEG
040      ' for entry-point for CALL
050      ' to CALL ASM module
060      FOR N = 1 TO 5
070      INPUT "Hours "; H
080      INPUT "Rate "; R
090      W = H * R
100      PRINT "Wage = " W
110      NEXT N
120      END
```

```
TITLE    LINKBAS Assembler subroutine linked from BASIC
CODESG   SEGMENT PARA 'CODE'
         ASSUME  CS:CODESG
CLRSCRN  PROC    FAR
         PUSH    BP                ;Save BP
         MOV     BP,SP             ;Set base param list
         MOV     AX,0600H          ;Request scroll
         MOV     BH,07             ;  of entire
         MOV     CX,0000           ;  screen
         MOV     DX,184FH
         INT     10H
         POP     BP
         RET                       ;Terminate
CLRSCRN  ENDP
CODESG   ENDS
         END
```

Figure 21-7 BASIC Main Program and Assembler Subprogram.

- The subprogram only clears the screen, although you could revise it to perform other features, such as scroll up or down or set the cursor.

All that's left is to link these programs together. The following assumes that your DOS diskette is in drive A and working programs are in drive B:

1. Key in the assembler subprogram, save it as B:LINKBAS.ASM, and assemble it.
2. Use LINK to generate an object module that will load in the high portion of memory:

   ```
   LINK B:LINKBAS,B:LINKBAS/HIGH,CON;
   ```

3. Use DEBUG to load the BASIC compiler: DEBUG BASIC.COM.

4. Use the DEBUG R command to display the registers. Record the contents of the SS, CS, and IP registers.
5. Now name and load the linked assembly module as follows:

```
N B:LINKBAS.EXE
L
```

6. Use the R command to display the registers and record the contents of the CX, CS, and IP.
7. Change the contents of the SS, CS, and IP registers to the values from step 4 (use R SS, R CS, and R IP for this purpose).
8. Enter the DEBUG G (go) command in order to transfer control to BASIC. At this point, the screen should show the BASIC prompt.
9. In order to save the assembler module, enter the following commands (with no statement numbers):

```
DEF SEG = &Hxxxx          (value in CS from step 6)
BSAVE "B:CLRSCRN.MOD",0,&Hxx  (value in CX from step 6)
```

   The first entry supplies the address in memory where the module is to load for execution. The second entry identifies the name of the module, the relative entry point, and the size of the module. At this point, the system should write the module onto drive B.

10. Now you have to modify the BASIC program for the linkage. You could load it right now while still in DEBUG, but instead, key in SYSTEM to exit from BASIC and key in Q to exit from DEBUG. The DOS prompt should now appear on the screen.
11. Enter the command BASIC, load the BASIC program, and display it:

```
BASIC
LOAD "B:BASTEST.BAS"
LIST
```

12. Change statements 20, 30, 40, and 50 as follows:

```
20 BLOAD "B:CLRSCRN.MOD"
30 DEF SEG = &Hxxxx   (value in CS from step 6)
40 CLRSCRN = 0        (entry point to subprogram)
50 CALL CLRSCRN       (invoke subprogram)
```

13. List, run, and save the revised BASIC program.

If you have entered the correct BASIC and assembler instructions and the correct hex values from registers, the linked program should immediately clear the screen and display prompts for hours and rate. Figure 21-8 provides a printout of the steps, but watch out—the values differ for versions of operating system and memory size.

The example is intentionally simple to illustrate linkage. You could perform more advanced techniques by passing parameters from the BASIC program to the assembler subprogram using

```
CALL subprogram (parameter-1, parameter-2, ... )
```

```
D>LINK

IBM Personal Computer Linker
Version 2.30 (C) Copyright IBM Corp. 1981, 1985

Object Modules [.OBJ]: LINKBAS
Run File [LINKBAS.EXE]: LINKBAS/HIGH
List File [NUL.MAP]: CON
Libraries [.LIB]:
Warning: no stack segment

 Start  Stop   Length Name                         Class
 00000H 00011H 00012H CODESG                       CODE

D>DEBUG BASIC.COM
-R
AX=0000  BX=0000  CX=4580  DX=0000  SP=FFFE  BP=0000  SI=0000  DI=0000
DS=1410  ES=1410  SS=1410  CS=1410  IP=0100   NV UP EI PL NZ NA PO NC
1410:0100 E9E03E        JMP     3FE3
-N D:LINKBAS.EXE
-L
-R
AX=FFA3  BX=0000  CX=0012  DX=0000  SP=0000  BP=0000  SI=0000  DI=0000
DS=1410  ES=1410  SS=9FE0  CS=9FE0  IP=0000   NV UP EI PL NZ NA PO NC
9FE0:0000 55            PUSH    BP
-R SS
SS 9FE0
:1410
-R CS
CS 9FE0
:1410
-R IP
IP 0000
:0100
-G
Ok
DEF SEG = &H9FE0
Ok
BSAVE "D:CLRSCRN.MOD",0,&H12
Ok
SYSTEM
```

Figure 21-8 Steps in Linking BASIC and Assembler.

```
Program terminated normally
-Q
D>BASIC
IBM Personal Computer Basic
Version D3.10 Copyright IBM Corp. 1981, 1985
61310 Bytes free
Ok
LOAD"D:BASTEST.BAS"
Ok
20       BLOAD "D:CLRSCRN.MOD"
30       DEF SEG = &H9FE0
40       CLRSCRN = 0
50       CALL CLRSCRN
LIST

10       CLEAR ,32768!
20       BLOAD "D:CLRSCRN.MOD"
30       DEF SEG = &H9FE0
40       CLRSCRN = 0
50       CALL CLRSCRN
60       FOR N = 1 TO 5
70       INPUT "Hours"; H
80       INPUT "Rate"; R
90       W = H * R
100      PRINT "Wage = " W
110      NEXT N
120      END
Ok
```

Figure 21-8 (Continued)

The assembler subprogram can access these parameters by using the BP register as [BP], just as Figure 21-3 did earlier. You also have to supply a pop-value in the RET operand to account for the parameter addresses on the stack. For example, if CALL delivers three parameters, code RET 6.

LINKING PASCAL AND ASSEMBLER

This section explains how to link IBM and MicroSoft Pascal to assembler. The program in Figure 21-9 shows a simple Pascal program that links to an assembler subprogram. The Pascal program is compiled to produce an OBJ module and the assembler program is assembled to produce an OBJ module. The LINK program then links together these two OBJ modules into one EXE executable module.

The Pascal program defines two items named temp_row and temp_col and accepts entries for row and column from the keyboard into these variables. It then sends the addresses of temp_row and temp_col as parameters to the assembler subprogram to set the cursor to this loca-

```
program pascall ( input, output );

    procedure move_cursor( const row: integer;
                           const col: integer ); extern;
    var
        temp_row:       integer;
        temp_col:       integer;

    begin
        write( 'Enter cursor row: ' );
        readln( temp_row );

        write( 'Enter cursor column: ' );
        readln( temp_col );

        move_cursor( temp_row, temp_col );
        write( 'New cursor location' );
    end.
```

```
TITLE   MOVCUR  Assembler subprogram called by Pascal
        PUBLIC  MOVE_CURSOR
;-------------------------------------------------------------
;    MOVE_CURSOR:  Set cursor on screen at passed location
;    Passed:     const row        Row and column where
;                const col        cursor is to be moved
;    Returned:   nothing
;-------------------------------------------------------------
CODESEG SEGMENT PARA PUBLIC 'CODE'

MOVE_CURSOR PROC FAR
        ASSUME  CS:CODESEG
ROWPAR  EQU     8                  ;Row parameter loc'n
COLPAR  EQU     6                  ;Col parameter loc'n

        PUSH    BP                 ;Save caller's BP register
        MOV     BP,SP              ;Point BP to parameters passed

        MOV     SI,[BP+ROWPAR]     ;SI points to row
        MOV     DH,[SI]            ;Move row to DH

        MOV     SI,[BP+COLPAR]     ;SI points to column
        MOV     DL,[SI]            ;Move column to DL

        MOV     AH,02              ;Move cursor
        SUB     BH,BH              ;Page #0
        INT     10H

        POP     BP                 ;Return to caller
        RET     4
MOVE_CURSOR     ENDP
CODESEG ENDS
        END
```

Figure 21-9 Linking Pascal to Assembler.

tion. The Pascal program defines the name of the assembler subprogram in a procedure as move_cursor and defines the two parameters as extern. The statement in the Pascal program that "calls" the name of the assembler subprogram and passes the parameters is

```
move_cursor( temp_row, temp_col );
```

Values pushed onto the stack are the calling program's frame pointer, return segment pointer, return offset, and the addresses of the two passed parameters. The following shows the offsets for each entry in the stack:

00 Caller's frame pointer
02 Caller's return segment pointer
04 Caller's return offset
06 Address of second parameter
08 Address of first parameter

Since the assembler subprogram is going to use the BP register, you have to PUSH it onto the stack in order to save its address for the return to the Pascal calling program. Note that the steps in the called subprogram are similar to the earlier example in Figure 21-6.

The SP register normally addresses entries in the stack. But since you cannot use the SP to act as an index register, the step after pushing the BP is to move the address in the SP to the BP. This step enables you to use the BP as an index register to access entries in the stack.

The next step is to access the addresses of the two parameters in the stack. The first passed parameter, the row, is at offset 08 in the stack and can be accessed by BP + 08. The second passed parameter, the column, is at offset 06 and can be accessed by BP + 06.

The two addresses in the stack have to be transferred to one of the available index registers: BX, DI, or SI. This example uses [BP+08] to move the address of the row to the SI and then uses [SI] to move the contents of the passed parameter to the DH register.

The column is transferred to the DL register in a similar way. Then the subprogram uses the row and column in the DX register to call BIOS to set the cursor. On exit, the subprogram pops the BP. The RET instruction requires an operand value that is two times the number of parameters—in this case, 2 × 2, or 4. Values are automatically popped off the stack and control transfers back to the calling program.

If you change a segment register, be sure to PUSH it on entry and POP it on exit. You can also use the stack to pass values from a subprogram to a calling program. Although this subprogram doesn't return values, Pascal would expect a subprogram to return a single word in the AX and a pair of words in the DX:AX.

Following the two programs is the map that the linker generated. The first entry is for the Pascal program named PASCALL; the second entry is for the assembler subprogram named CODESEG (the name of the code segment). A number of Pascal subroutines follow. This rather trivial program has resulted in hex 5720 bytes of memory—over 20K. A compiler language typically generates considerable overhead regardless of the size of the program.

LINKING C AND ASSEMBLER

The problem with describing linkage of C to assembler is that versions of C have different conventions, and for precise requirements, refer to your C manual. Some points of interest:

- Most versions of C pass parameters onto the stack in a sequence that is reverse to that of other languages. Typically, you access two passed parameters via the stack as follows:

```
PUSH    BP
MOV     BP,SP
MOV     DH,[BP+4]
MOV     DL,[BP+6]
...
POP     BP
RET
```

- Some versions are sensitive to uppercase and lowercase, so the name of the assembler module should be the same case as the C program's reference.
- Some C versions require that an assembler program that changes the DI and SI registers should push them on entry and pop them on exit.
- The assembler program should return values, if required, as one word in the AX or two words in the DX:AX pair.
- For some C versions, an assembler program that sets the DF flag should clear it (CLD) before returning.

KEY POINTS TO REMEMBER

- In a main program that calls a subprogram, define the entry point as EXTRN; in the subprogram define the entry point as PUBLIC.

- Handle recursion carefully—that is, subprogram 1 calls subprogram 2, which in turn calls subprogram 1.
- If two code segments are to be linked into one segment, define them with the same name, same class, and the PUBLIC combine-type.
- To simplify programming, begin execution with the main program.
- It is also generally easier (but not necessary) to define common data in the main program. The main program defines the common data as PUBLIC and the subprogram (or subprograms) defines the common data as EXTRN.

QUESTIONS

21-1. Assume that a program named MAINPRO is to call a subprogram named SUBPRO. (a) What instruction in MAINPRO tells the assembler that the name SUBPRO is defined outside of its own assembly? (b) What instruction in SUBPRO is required to make its name known to MAINPRO?

21-2. Assume that MAINPRO has defined variables named QTY as DB, VALUE as DW, and PRICE as DW. SUBPRO is to divide VALUE by QTY and is to store the quotient in PRICE. (a) How does MAINPRO tell the assembler that the three variables are to be known outside this assembly? (b) How does SUBPRO tell the assembler that the three variables are defined in another assembly?

21-3. Combine Questions 21-1 and 21-2 into a working program and test it.

21-4. Revise Question 21-3 so that MAINPRO passes all three variables as parameters. Note, however, that SUBPRO is to return the calculated price intact in its parameter.

21-5. Here's an exercise that should keep you occupied. Expand Question 21-4 so that MAINPRO permits a user to enter quantity and value on the keyboard; SUBCONV converts the ASCII amounts to binary; SUBCALC calculates the price; and SUBDISP converts the binary price to ASCII and displays the result.

CHAPTER 22

Program Loader

Objective: To describe the requirements for loading an executable module into memory for execution.

INTRODUCTION

This chapter describes the general DOS organization and the steps that DOS takes in loading an executable module into memory for execution. Each of the four major DOS programs provides a particular service:

1. The boot record is on track 0, sector 1, of the DOS diskette and on any disk that you use FORMAT /S to format. When you initiate the system (assuming that DOS is in drive A or C), the system automatically loads the boot record from disk into memory. This program then loads the three programs described next from disk into memory.
2. IBMBIO.COM is a low-level interface to the BIOS routines in ROM and loads in memory beginning at hex 00600. On initiation, IBMBIO.COM determines device and equipment status and then loads COMMAND.COM. IBMBIO.COM handles input/output between memory and external devices such as video monitor and disk.
3. IBMDOS.COM is a high-level interface to programs and loads into memory beginning at hex 00B00. IBMDOS.COM manages the directory and files on disk, handles blocking and deblocking of disk records, handles INT 21H functions, and contains a number of other service functions.
4. COMMAND.COM handles the various commands such as DIR and CHKDSK and runs requested COM, EXE, and BAT programs. It consists of three parts: a small resident portion, an initialization portion, and a transient portion. COMMAND.COM, covered in detail in the next section, is responsible for loading executable programs from disk into memory.

Figure 22-1 shows a map of memory. Details may vary by computer model.

Beginning Address	*Program*
00000	Interrupt vector table (details in Chapter 23)
00400	ROM communication area
00500	DOS communication area
00600	IBMBIO.COM
XXXX0	IBMDOS.COM: Directory buffer Disk buffer Drive parameter block/file allocation table (FAT, one for each disk drive)
XXXX0	Resident portion of COMMAND.COM
XXXX0	External command or utility (COM or EXE files)
XXXX0	User stack for COM files (256 bytes)
XXXX0	Transient portion of COMMAND.COM, stored in highest portion of memory.

Figure 22-1 Map of DOS in Memory.

COMMAND.COM

The system loads the three portions of COMMAND.COM into memory either permanently during a session or temporarily as required. The following describes the three parts of COMMAND.COM:

1. The *resident portion* immediately loads IBMDOS.COM (and its data areas) where it resides during processing. The resident portion handles all errors for disk I/O and the following interrupts:

INT 22H	Terminate address.
INT 23H	Ctrl/Break handler.
INT 24H	Error detection on disk read/write or a bad memory image of the file allocation table (FAT).
INT 27H	Terminate but stay resident.

2. The *initialization portion* immediately follows the resident portion and contains the setup for AUTOEXEC files. When the system starts up, this portion initially takes control, prompts for the date, and

determines the segment address where the system is to load programs for execution.

None of these initialization routines is required again during a session. Consequently, the first command that you enter which causes a program to load from disk overlays this section of memory.

3. The *transient portion* is loaded into the highest area of memory. "Transient" implies that DOS may overlay this area with other requested programs, if necessary.

This portion of COMMAND.COM displays the A> or C> prompt, and accepts and executes requests. It contains a relocation loader facility that loads COM and EXE files from disk into memory for execution. When you request a program be executed, the transient portion constructs a program segment prefix (PSP) immediately following the resident portion of COMMAND.COM. It then loads your requested executable program from disk into offset hex 100 of the program segment, sets exit addresses, and gives control to your loaded program. The following shows the sequence:

IBMBIO.COM
IBMDOS.COM
COMMAND.COM (resident)
Program segment prefix
Executable program
...
COMMAND.COM (transient, may be overlaid)

Execution of RET or INT 20H at the end causes a return to the resident portion of COMMAND.COM. If the transient portion was overlaid, the resident portion reloads it into memory.

PROGRAM SEGMENT PREFIX

A program segment prefix (PSP) of 256 (hex 100) bytes immediately precedes each COM and EXE program that is to execute. The PSP contains the following fields according to relative hex position:

00 An INT 20H instruction (hex CD20).

02 Total size of available memory, as xxxx0. For example, 512K is indicated as hex 8000 instead of hex 80000.

04 Reserved.

05 Long call to DOS function dispatcher.

0A Terminate address.

0E Ctrl/Break exit address.

12	Critical error exit address.
16	Reserved.
2C	Segment address of environment for storing ASCIIZ strings.
50	Call to DOS function (an INT 21H and RETF).
5C	Parameter area 1, formatted as standard unopened file control block (FCB #1).
6C	Parameter area 2, formatted as standard unopened file control block (FCB #2); overlaid if FCB at hex 5C is opened).
80-FF	Buffer for default disk transfer area (DTA).

Default DTA Buffer

The portion of the PSP beginning at hex 80 is a default buffer for the disk transfer area. It contains a number in the first byte indicating the number of keys (if any) pressed immediately following the entered program name, followed by the actual characters entered (if any). Following is any garbage already in memory from a previous program. An examination of the contents of the buffer should clarify its purpose.

Example 1: Command with No Operand. Suppose that you cause a program named CALCIT.EXE to execute by entering CALCIT [return]. When DOS constructs the PSP for this program, it inserts hex 000D in the buffer at hex 80. The first byte contains the number of bytes keyed in after the name CALCIT, not including the return character. Since no keys other than Return were pressed, the number of bytes is zero. The second byte contains the return character, hex 0D. Thus, hex 80 and 81 contain 000D.

Example 2: Command with Text Operand. Suppose you type text (not a filename) following a command, such as COLOR BY, meaning execute a program named COLOR, and you want to pass a parameter "BY" that tells the program to set color blue on yellow background. DOS sets the following at hex 80:

```
80: 03 20 42 59 0D
```

The bytes mean length of 3, a space, "BY," and the return character, respectively.

Example 3: Command with a Filename Operand. Programs like DEL allow users to enter a file name after the program name. If you key in DEL B:CALCIT.OBJ [return], the PSP contains the following at hex 5C and 80:

```
5C: 02 43 41 4C 43 49 54 20 20 4F 42 4A
       C  A  L  C  I  T        O  B  J
80: 0D 20 42 3A 43 41 4C 43 49 54 2E 4F 42 4A 0D
          B  :  C  A  L  C  I  T  .  O  B  J
```

Hex 5C begins an "unopened" FCB, not the name of the program that is executing, but the name of the file that it is to reference, CALCIT.OBJ. The first character indicates drive number (02 = B in this case). Following CALCIT are two blanks that complete the 8-character filename and then the extension, OBJ. If you enter two parameters, such as

```
progname A:FILEA,B:FILEB
```

DOS sets an FCB for FILEA at hex 5C and one for FILEB at hex 6C.

The bytes at hex 80 contain the number of characters entered (16), a space (hex 20), A:FILEA,B:FILEB, and the return character (0D).

Since the PSP immediately precedes your program, you can access its areas in order to process specified files or to take special action. To locate the DTA, a COM program can simply set hex 80 in the SI register and access the bytes, as follows:

```
MOV SI,80H              ;Address of DTA
CMP BYTE PTR[SI],0      ;Zero in buffer?
JE  EXIT
```

An EXE program can't always assume that its code segment immediately follows the PSP. However, on initialization, the DS and ES contain the address of the PSP, so you could save the ES after initializing the DS:

```
MOV   AX,DSEG
MOV   DS,AX
MOV   SAVEPSP,ES
```

Later, you could use the saved address for accessing the PSP buffer:

```
MOV   SI,SAVEPSP
CMP   BYTE PTR[SI+80H],0 ;Zero in buffer?
JE    EXIT
```

DOS versions 3.0 and on provide INT 62H that delivers the address of the current PSP in the BX register, which you may use to access data in the PSP.

EXECUTING A COM PROGRAM

Unlike an EXE file, a COM file does not contain a header record on disk. Since the organization of a COM file is much simpler, DOS needs to know only that the file extension is COM.

As described earlier, a program segment prefix precedes COM and EXE programs loaded in memory. The first two bytes contain the INT 20H instruction (return to DOS). On loading a COM program, DOS sets the four segment registers with the address of the first byte of the PSP. It then sets the stack pointer to the end of the 64K segment, hex FFFE, or to the end of memory if the segment is not large enough and pushes a zero word on the stack. DOS sets the instruction pointer to hex 100 (the size of the PSP) and allows control to proceed to the address generated by CS:IP, the first location immediately following the PSP. This is the first byte of your program, and should contain an executable instruction.

On exit from the program, RET pops the zero (that was pushed initially onto the stack) into the IP. CS:IP now generates an address that is the location of the first byte of the PSP, containing INT 20H. When that instruction executes, control returns to the resident portion of COMMAND.COM. (If a program terminates with INT 20H instead of RET, control passes directly to COMMAND.COM.)

EXECUTING AN EXE PROGRAM

The linker produces an EXE module that consists of the following two parts: (1) a header record containing control and relocation information and (2) the actual load module.

The header contains information about the size of the executable module, where it is to be loaded in memory, the address of the stack, and relocation offsets to be inserted into incomplete machine addresses, according to relative hex position:

00 Hex 4D5A. The linker inserts this code to identify the file as a valid EXE file.

02 Number of bytes in the last block of the EXE file.

04 Size of the file including the header, in 512-byte block increments.

08 Size of the header in 16-byte (paragraph) increments, to help locate the start of the executable module following this header.

0A Minimum count of paragraphs that must reside above the end of the program when loaded.

0C High/low loader switch. You decide when linking whether the program is to load for execution at a low (the usual) or a high memory address. Hex 0000 indicates high and hex FFFF indicates low. Otherwise, this location contains the maximum count of paragraphs that must reside above the end of the loaded program.

0E Offset location in the executable module of the stack segment.

10 Address that the loader is to insert in the SP register when transferring control to the executable module.

12 Checksum value—the sum of all the words in the file (ignoring overflows) used as a validation check for lost data.

14 Offset that the loader is to insert in the IP register when transferring control to the executable module.

16 Offset location in the executable module of the code segment, which the loader inserts in the CS register.

18 Offset of the first relocation item in this file.

1A Overlay number: zero means that the header references the resident portion of the EXE file.

1C Relocation table containing a variable number of relocation items, as identified at offset 06.

The header is a minimum of 512 bytes in size and may be longer if there are many relocatable items. Position 06 of the header indicates the number of items in the executable module that are to be relocated. Each relocation item, beginning at header position 1C, consists of a two-byte offset value and a two-byte segment value.

The system constructs the program segment prefix following the resident portion of COMMAND.COM, which performs the load operation. Following are the steps that COMMAND.COM performs:

- Reads the formatted part of the header into memory.
- Calculates the size of the executable module (total file size in position 04 minus header size in position 08) and reads the module into memory at the start segment.
- Reads the relocation table items into a work area and adds the value of each table item to the start segment value (position 0E).
- Sets SS and SP registers to the values in the header and adds the start segment value to the SS.
- Sets DS and ES registers to the segment address of the program segment prefix.
- Sets CS to the address of the PSP and adds the CS offset value in the header (position 16) to the CS. If your code segment immediately follows the PSP, the offset in the header is 256 (hex 100). The CS:IP pair provide the starting address of the code segment and, in effect, your program as well.

On initialization, the CS and SS registers are set correctly, but your program has to set the DS (and ES) for its own data segment:

```
1.  PUSH DS                ;Push address of PSP on stack.
2.  SUB AX,AX              ;Push zero value on stack
3.  PUSH AX                ;  to facilitate exiting program.
4.  MOV AX,datasegname     ;Set DS register to address
5.  MOV DS,AX              ;  of data segment.
```

When the program terminates, RET pops the zero (that was initially pushed onto the stack) into the IP. The CS:IP now generate an address that is the location of the first byte of the PSP, containing INT 20H. When that instruction executes, control returns to DOS.

EXAMPLE EXE PROGRAM

Assume the following MAP for a linked program:

```
Start     Stop      Length    Name    Class
00000H    0003AH    003BH     CSEG    CODE
00040H    0005AH    001BH     DSEG    DATA
00060H    0007FH    0020H     STACK   STACK
Program entry point at 0000:0000
```

The MAP provides the relative (not the actual) location of each of the three segments. The H following each value indicates hexadecimal format. Note that the linker may arrange these segments differently from the sequence in which you coded them.

According to the MAP, the code segment, named CSEG, is to start at 00000—its relative location is the beginning of the executable module, and its length is hex 003B bytes. The next segment, named DSEG, begins at hex 00040 and has a length of hex 001B. This is the first address following CSEG that aligns on a paragraph boundary (evenly divisible by hex 10). The last segment, STACK, begins at hex 00060, the first address following DSEG that aligns on a paragraph boundary.

DEBUG is no help in examining a header record because when loading a program for execution, DOS replaces the header with a PSP. However, there are various utility programs on the market (or you can write your own) that allow you to view the hex contents of any disk sector. The header for this example program contains the following relevant information, according to hex location. Byte contents are in reverse sequence:

00 Hex 4D5A

02 Number of bytes in last block: 5B00.

04 Size of file including header in 512-byte blocks: 0200. (Hex 0002 × 512 = 1024.)

06 Number of relocation table items following formatted portion of header: 0100, that is, 0001.

08 Size of header in 16-byte increments: 2000. (Hex 0020 = 32, and 32 × 16 = 512.)

0C Load in low memory: hex FFFF.

0E Offset location of stack segment: 6000, or hex 60.

10 Address to insert in SP: 2000, or hex 20.

14 Offset for IP: 0000.

16 Offset for CS: 0000.

18 Offset for first relocation item: 1E00, or hex 1E.

When the program was loaded under DEBUG, the registers contained the following:

```
SP = 0020   DS = 138F   ES = 138F
SS = 13A5   CS = 139F   IP = 0000
```

For EXE modules, the loader sets the DS and ES to the address of the program segment prefix, loaded at an available memory location, and sets the IP, SS, and SP to values from the header record.

SP Register

The loader uses hex 20 from the header to initialize the stack pointer to the length of the stack. In this example, the stack was defined as 16 DUP(?), that is, 16 two-byte fields = 32, or hex 20. The SP points to the current top of the stack.

CS Register

According to the DS register when the program loaded, the address of the PSP is at hex 138F(0). Since the PSP is hex 100 bytes long, the executable module follows immediately at hex 138F0 + 100 = 139F0 which the loader inserts in the CS register. The CS register indicates the starting address of the code portion (CSEG) of the program. You can use the DEBUG dump command, D CS:0000, to view the machine code in memory and note that it is identical to the hex portion of the assembler LST printout, other than operands tagged as R.

SS Register

The loader has also used the value in the header to set the SS register:

```
Start address of PSP (see DS)  138F0
Length of PSP                    100
Offset of stack (see the map)     60
Address of stack               13A50
```

DS Register

The loader uses the DS register to establish the starting point for the PSP. Because the header does not contain a starting address, you have to initialize the DS, as follows:

```
0004 B8 ---- R  MOV  AX,DSEG
0007 8E D8      MOV  DS,AX
```

The assembler has left unfilled the machine address of DSEG, which becomes an entry in the relocation table in the header, discussed earlier. DEBUG shows the completed instruction as

```
B8 A313
```

A313 loads into the DS as 13A3. We now have

Register	*Address*	*MAP Offset*
CS	139F0	00
DS	13A30	40
SS	13A50	60

As an exercise, trace any of your linked programs through DEBUG and note the changed values in the registers:

Instruction	*Registers Changed*
PUSH DS	IP and SP
SUB AX,AX	IP and AX (if already nonzero)
PUSH AX	IP and SP
MOV AX,DSEG	IP and AX
MOV DS,AX	IP and DS

The DS now contains the correct address of the data segment. You can use D DS:00 to view the contents of DSEG and use D SS:00 to view the contents of the stack.

LOAD OR EXECUTE A PROGRAM FUNCTION

Let's now examine how to load and execute a program from within another program. The hex 4B function call enables one program to load another program into memory for optional execution. Load the address of an ASCIIZ string in the DX and a parameter block in the BX (actually ES:BX). Set the AL with a function value 0 or 3:

AL = 0 Load and execute. The operation establishes a program segment prefix for the new program and sets the control-break and terminate addresses to the instruction following this function. Since all registers, including the stack, are changed, this operation is not for novices. The parameter block addressed by the ES:BX has the following format:

Offset	*Purpose*
0	Word segment address of environment string to be passed.
2	Doubleword pointer to command line at PSP+80H.
6	Doubleword pointer to default FCB at PSP+5CH.
10	Doubleword pointer to default FCB at PSP+6CH.

AL = 3 Load Overlay. The operation loads a program or block of code, but does not establish a PSP or begin execution. Thus, the requested code could be a program overlay. The parameter block addressed by the ES:BX has the following format:

Offset	*Purpose*
0	Word segment address where file is to be loaded.
2	Word relocation factor to apply to the image.

Possible error codes in the AX are 01, 02, 05, 08, 10, and 11. The program in Figure 22-2 requests DOS to perform the DIR command for drive D. Run this as an EXE program. (Thanks to *PC Magazine* for the idea.)

```
TITLE   EXDOS    (EXE) DOS call 4BH to execute DIR
CSEG    SEGMENT PARA 'Code'
        ASSUME  CS:CSEG,DS:CSEG,SS:CSEG,ES:CSEG
BEGIN:  JMP     SHORT MAIN
; ----------------------------------------------------
PARAREA DW      ?                ;Address of envir. string
        DW      OFFSET DIRCOM    ;Pointer to command line
        DW      CSEG
        DW      OFFSET FCB1      ;Pointer to default FCB1
        DW      CSEG
        DW      OFFSET FCB2      ;Pointer to default FCB2
        DW      CSEG

DIRCOM  DB      17,'/C DIR D:',13,0
FCB1    DB      16 DUP(0)
FCB2    DB      16 DUP(0)
PROGNAM DB      'D:COMMAND.COM',0
; ----------------------------------------------------
MAIN    PROC    FAR
        MOV     AH,4AH           ;Allocate 64K memory space
        MOV     BX,100H          ;  in paragraphs
        INT     21H
        JC      E10ERR           ;Not enough space?

        MOV     DI,2CH           ;Get segment address of
        MOV     AX,[DI]          ;  environment
        LEA     SI,PARAREA       ;  & store in
        MOV     [SI],AX          ;  1st word of para block
        MOV     AX,CS            ;Set DS & ES
        MOV     DS,AX            ;  with address
        MOV     ES,AX            ;  of CSEG

        MOV     AH,4BH           ;Request load
        MOV     AL,00            ;  & execute
        LEA     BX,PARAREA       ;  COMMAND.COM
        LEA     DX,PROGNAM
        INT     21H              ;Call DOS
        JC      E20ERR           ;Exec error?
        MOV     AL,00            ;No error code
        JMP     X10XIT
E10ERR:
        MOV     AL,01            ;Error code 1
        JMP     X10XIT
E20ERR:
        MOV     AL,02            ;Error code 2
        JMP     X10XIT
X10XIT:
        MOV     AH,4CH           ;Request terminate
        INT     21H              ;Call DOS
MAIN    ENDP
CSEG    ENDS
        END
```

Figure 22-2 Execution of DIR From Within a Program.

CHAPTER 23

BIOS and DOS Interrupts

Objective: To describe the BIOS and DOS interrupt functions.

INTRODUCTION

An interrupt is an operation that interrupts execution of a program so that the system can take special action. The two main reasons for an interrupt are an intentional request for such action as input from a device and output to a device and an unintentional serious error such as a divide overflow.

BIOS (basic input/output system), which is based in ROM, handles all interrupts for the system. We have already used a number of interrupts for video display, disk input/output, and printing. This chapter describes various BIOS and DOS interrupts, the implementing of resident programs, and the use of the IN and OUT instructions.

INTERRUPT SERVICES

On the PC, ROM resides beginning at location FFFF0H. When you turn on the power, the processor enters a reset state, performs a parity check, and sets the CS register to FFFFH and the IP register to zero. The first instruction to execute therefore is at FFFF:0, or FFFF0, the entry point to BIOS. BIOS checks the various computer ports to determine and initialize devices that are attached. BIOS then establishes beginning at location 0 of memory an interrupt service table that contains addresses for interrupts which occur. Two operations that BIOS performs are INT 11H (equipment determination) and INT 12H (memory size determination).

BIOS next determines if a disk(ette) is present containing DOS, and, if so, it executes INT 19H to access the first disk sector containing the bootstrap loader. This program reads DOS files IBMBIO.COM, IBMDOS.COM, and COMMAND.COM from disk into memory. At this point, RAM and ROM memory appear as follows:

Interrupt services table

BIOS data

IBMBIO.COM and IBMDOS.COM

Resident portion of COMMAND.COM

Available for use

Transient portion of COMMAND.COM

End of RAM

ROM BASIC

ROM BIOS

External devices signal for attention via an INTR pin on the processor. The processor responds to a request if the interrupt (IF) flag is enabled (equals 1) and, under most circumstances, ignores an interrupt if the IF flag is disabled (equals 0).

The operand of an interrupt instruction such as INT 12H contains an interrupt type that identifies the request. For each type, the system maintains an address in the interrupt services table beginning in location 0000. Since there are 256 entries each four bytes long, the table occupies the first 1024 bytes of memory, from hex 0 through hex 3FF. Each address relates to a routine that handles a specific interrupt type and consists of a code segment address and an offset, which the interrupt inserts into the CS and IP registers, respectively. See Figure 23-1 for a list of table entries.

An interrupt pushes on the stack the contents of the flags register, the CS, and the IP. For example, the table address of interrupt 12H (which returns the memory size in the AX register) is hex 0048 (hex 12 × 4 = hex 48). The operation extracts the four-byte address from location 0048 and stores two bytes in the IP and two in the CS. The address that results from the CS:IP registers is the start of a routine in the BIOS area, which now executes. The interrupt returns via an IRET (Interrupt Return) instruction that pops the flags, CS, and IP from the stack and returns to the instruction following the interrupt.

BIOS INTERRUPTS

This section covers the main BIOS interrupts.

INT 05H Print Screen. Causes the contents of the screen to print. Issuing INT 05H activates it internally, and pressing the Ctrl/PrtSc keys activates it externally. The operation enables interrupts and saves the cursor position.

Address (hex)	*Interrupt Function (hex)*	
0-3	0	Divide by zero
4-7	1	Single step (trace used by DEBUG)
8-B	2	Nonmaskable interrupt (NMI)
C-F	3	Break point instruction (used by DEBUG)
10-13	4	Overflow
14-17	5	Print Screen
18-1F	6, 7	Reserved
20-23	8	Timer
24-27	9	Keyboard interrupt
28-37	A, B, C, D	Used by AT
38-3B	E	Diskette interrupt
3C-3F	F	Printer
40-43	10	Video screen (Chapters 8, 9, 10)
44-47	11	Equipment check (Chapter 9)
48-4B	12	Memory size check (Chapter 2)
4C-4F	13	Disk I/O (Chapter 18)
50-53	14	Communications I/O
54-57	15	Cassette I/O and special AT functions
58-5B	16	Keyboard input (Chapter 9)
5C-5F	17	Printer output (Chapter 19)
60-63	18	ROM Basic entry code
64-67	19	Bootstrap loader
68-6B	1A	Read and set time
6C-6F	1B	Get control on keyboard break
70-73	1C	Get control on timer interrupt
74-77	1D	Pointer to video initialization table
78-7B	1E	Pointer to diskette parameter table
7C-7F	1F	Pointer to graphics table
80-83	20	DOS program terminate
84-87	21	DOS function call
88-8B	22	DOS terminate address
8C-8F	23	DOS ctrl/break exit address
90-93	24	DOS fatal error vector

Figure 23-1 Table of Interrupt Addresses.

94-97	25	DOS absolute disk read
98-9B	26	DOS absolute disk write
9C-9F	27	DOS terminate but stay resident
A0-FF	28-3F	DOS operations
100-1FF	40-7F	Reserved
200-217	80-85	Reserved by BASIC
218-3C3	86-F0	Used by BASIC interpreter
3C4-3FF	F1-FF	Reserved

Note: Interrupts 00-1F are BIOS and 20-FF are DOS and BASIC.

Figure 23-1 (Continued)

INT 10H Video Display I/O. Provides for screen and keyboard operations, described in detail in Chapter 9.

INT 11H Equipment Determination. Determines the optional devices on the system and returns a value to the AX. At power-up time, the system executes this operation and stores the AX in location hex 410:

Bit	*Device*
15,14	Number of printers attached.
13	Serial printer attached.
12	Game adapter attached.
11-9	Number of RS232 serial adapters.
7,6	Number of diskette devices, only if bit 0 = 1: 00 = 1, 01 = 2, 10 = 3, and 11 = 4.
5,4	Initial video mode: 00 = unused. 01 = 40 x 25 using a color card. 10 = 80 x 25 using a color card. 11 = 80 x 25 BW using a BW card.
1	A value of 1 means a math coprocessor is present.
0	A value of 1 indicates that the system contains one or more disk devices and is to load the operating system from disk

INT 12H Memory Size Determination. Returns in the AX the size of memory in terms of 1K bytes such that 512K memory is hex 200, as determined during power-on. This operation is useful for adjusting program size according to available memory.

INT 13H Disk Input/Output. Provides for diskette and hard disk I/O, covered in Chapter 16.

INT 14H Communications Input/Output. Provides byte stream I/O to the RS232 communication port. The DX should contain the number (0 or 1) of the RS232 adapter. Four calls established via the AH facilitate transmitting and receiving characters and return the status of the communications port.

INT 15H Cassette I/O and AT Advanced Features. Provides operations for cassette I/O and special AT operations.

INT 16H Keyboard Input. Provides three keyboard input commands, covered in detail in Chapter 9.

INT 17H Printer Output. Provides for printing, discussed in detail in Chapter 19.

INT 18H ROM Basic Entry. Calls BASIC from ROM.

INT 19H Bootstrap Loader. If a disk(ette) device is available, reads track 0, sector 1, into the boot location in memory, segment 0, offset 7C00 and transfers control to this location. If there is no disk drive, the operation transfers to the ROM BASIC entry point via INT 18H. It is possible to use this as a software interrupt; it does not clear the screen or initialize data in ROM BIOS.

INT 1AH Time of Day. Sets and reads the clock according to a value in the AH. To determine how long a routine executes, you could set the clock to zero, then read it at the end of processing. Counts occur at about 18.2 per second. Set a code in the AH according to the required operation:

AH = 00 Read Clock. Sets the CX to the high portion of the count and the DX to the low portion. If the time has passed 24 hours since the last read, the operation sets the AL to nonzero.

AH = 01 Set Clock. Sets the CX with the high portion of the count and the DX with the low portion.

Codes 02 and 06 handle time and date for the AT.

INT 1FH Pointer to Graphics Table. In graphics mode, enables access to characters 128-255 in a 1K table containing eight bytes per character. Graphics mode offers direct access only to the first ASCII characters 0-127.

DOS INTERRUPTS

The two DOS modules, IBMBIO.COM and IBMDOS.COM, facilitate using BIOS. Since the DOS modules provide much of the additional required testing, the DOS operations are generally easier to use than their BIOS counterparts and are generally more machine independent.

IBMBIO.COM provides a low-level interface to BIOS. This is an I/O handler program that facilitates reading data from external devices into memory and writing data from memory onto external devices.

IBMDOS.COM contains a file manager and a number of service functions such as blocking and deblocking disk records. When a user program requests INT 21H, the operation delivers to IBMDOS information via the contents of registers. To complete the request, IBMDOS.COM translates the information into one or more calls to IBMBIO.COM, which in turn calls BIOS. The following shows the relationship:

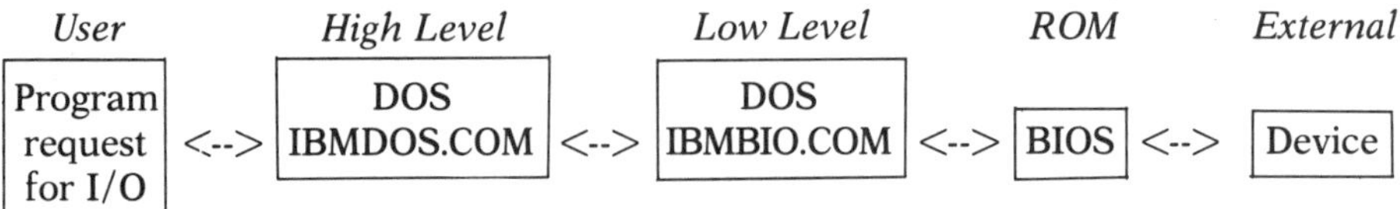

As discussed earlier, interrupts hex 20 through hex 62 are reserved for DOS operations. Following are the major operations:

INT 20H Program Terminate. Terminates execution and returns control to DOS. It should normally be placed in the main procedure.

INT 21H DOS Function Request. The main DOS operation, which requires a function code in the AH. The next section describes the functions.

INT 22H Terminate Address. See INT 24H.

INT 23H Ctrl/Break Address. See INT 24H.

INT 24H Critical Error Handler Vector. Along with the preceding two interrupts, is concerned with the addresses that DOS initializes in the program segment prefix and that you can revise for your own purposes. See the DOS Technical Reference manual for details.

INT 25H Absolute Disk Read. Chapter 17.

INT 26H Absolute Disk Write. Chapter 17.

INT 27H Terminate but Stay Resident. Causes a COM program to remain in memory. For details, see the later section, "Resident Programs."

DOS INT 21H FUNCTION CALLS

Following are the original function calls for DOS INT 21H. The function call is in the AH register:

00	Program terminate (same as INT 20H).
01	Keyboard input with echo.
02	Display output.
03	Auxiliary (asynchronous communications) input.
04	Auxiliary (asynchronous communications) output.
05	Printer output (Chapter 19).
06	Direct keyboard and display.
07	Direct keyboard input without echo.
08	Keyboard input without echo.
09	Display string (Chapter 8).
0A	Buffered keyboard input (Chapter 8).
0B	Check keyboard status.
0C	Clear keyboard buffer and invoke input.
0D	Reset disk (Chapter 16).
0E	Select current disk drive (Chapter 16).
0F	Open file (Chapter 16).
10	Close file (Chapter 16).
11	Search for first disk entry (Chapter 16).
12	Search for next disk entry (Chapter 16).
13	Delete file (Chapter 16).
14	Sequential read (Chapter 16).
15	Sequential write (Chapter 16).
16	Create file (Chapter 16).
17	Rename file (Chapter 16).
19	Determine default disk drive (Chapter 16).
1A	Set disk transfer area (Chapter 16).
1B	Get FAT information for current drive.
1C	Get FAT information for any drive.
21	Read random record (Chapter 16).
22	Write random record (Chapter 16).

23	Determine file size.
24	Set random record field.
25	Set interrupt vector.
26	Create program segment.
27	Read random disk block (Chapter 16).
28	Write random disk block (Chapter 16).
29	Parse filename.
2A	Get date (CX = year, DH = month, DL = day, in binary).
2B	Set date.
2C	Get time (CH = hours, CL = mins, DH = secs, DL = hundredths secs).
2D	Set time.
2E	Set/reset disk verification.

The following extended functions are available under DOS 2.0 and on:

2F	Get address of disk transfer area (returned via ES:BX).
30	Get version number of DOS (returned via AX).
31	Terminate but stay resident.
33	Ctrl/break check.
35	Get interrupt vector.
36	Get free disk space.
38	Return country-dependent information.
39	Create subdirectory (MKDIR).
3A	Remove subdirectory (RMDIR).
3B	Change current directory (CHDIR).
3C	Create file (Chapter 17).
3D	Open file (Chapter 17).
3E	Close file (Chapter 17).
3F	Read from file (Chapters 8, 17, 19).
40	Write to file (Chapters 8, 17, 19).
41	Delete file from directory (Chapter 17).
42	Move file pointer (Chapter 17).
43	Change file attribute (Chapter 17).
44	I/O control for devices.
45	Duplicate a file handle.
46	Force duplicate of handle.
47	Get current directory (Chapter 17).
48	Allocate memory.

49 Free allocated memory.
4A Modify allocated memory blocks.
4B Load/execute a program.
4C Terminate a process (return from a called program).
4D Retrieve return code of a subprocess.
4E Find first directory entry (Chapter 17).
4F Find next directory entry (Chapter 17).
54 Get verify state.
56 Rename a file (Chapter 17).
57 Get/set file date and time.

The following extended functions are available under DOS 3.0 and on:

59 Get extended error code.
5A Create temporary file.
5B Create new file.
5C Lock/unlock file access.
62 Get address of PSP.

The DOS Technical Reference manual provides a detailed description of each operation.

RESIDENT PROGRAMS

A number of popular commercial programs such as Prokey, Superkey, Homebase, and Sidekick are designed to reside in memory while other programs run, and you can activate their services through special keystrokes. These are known as resident programs that you load after DOS loads and before activating other normal processing programs.

The easy part of writing a resident COM program is getting it to reside. Instead of RET or INT 20H, you exit by means of INT 27H or DOS function call hex 31. For INT 27H, you deliver to DOS the size of the program in the DX register prior to the INT:

```
MOV   DX,prog-size
INT   27H
```

When you execute the initialization routine, DOS reserves the memory block where the program resides and loads subsequent programs in higher memory.

The not-so-easy part of writing a resident program involves activating it after it is resident. Although attached to DOS, it is not internal to DOS, as are DIR, COPY, and CLS. A common approach is to modify the interrupt services table so that the resident program interrupts all keystrokes, acts on a special keystroke or combination, and passes on all other keystrokes. The effect is that a resident program typically, but not necessarily, consists of the following:

1. A section that redefines locations in the interrupt services table.
2. A procedure that executes only the first time the program runs and that performs the following:
   - Replaces the address in the interrupt services table with its own address.
   - Establishes the size of the portion that is to remain resident.
   - Uses an interrupt that tells DOS to terminate this program and to attach the specified portion in memory.
3. A procedure that remains resident and that is activated, for example, by keyboard input or in some cases by the timer clock.

In effect, the initialization procedure sets up all the conditions to make the resident program work, and then—the supreme sacrifice—allows itself to be erased. The organization of memory now appears as follows:

Interrupt services table	
IBMBIO.COM & IBMDOS.COM	
COMMAND.COM	
Resident portion of program	} stays in memory
Initialization portion of program	} overlaid by next program
Rest of available memory	

The program in Figure 23-2 illustrates a resident program that sets the screen to color when you press the Alt and Left Shift keys together. The following points are of interest:

INTTAB defines the interrupt services table beginning at location 0, in particular the address of interrupt 9, keyboard input, called here KBADDR.

ROMAREA defines the segment beginning at hex 400, in particular the keyboard flags byte, called here KBFLAG, that reflects the status of the keyboard. The bit 3 flag on means that Alt is pressed and the bit 1 flag on means that Left Shift is pressed.

```
TITLE    RESIDENT (COM) Resident program to clear screen &
;                       set colors when Alt/Left Shift pressed
; --------------------------------------------------------------

INTTAB   SEGMENT AT 0H            ;Area for interrupt INTTAB:
         ORG     9H*4             ;  Int 9H address,
KBADDR   LABEL   DWORD            ;  doubleword
INTTAB   ENDS
; --------------------------------------------------------------

ROMAREA SEGMENT AT 40H            ;BIOS parameter area at 400H:
         ORG     17H              ;  location of keyboard flag,
KBFLAG   DB      ?                ;  status of Alt & Shift
ROMAREA ENDS
; --------------------------------------------------------------

CSEG     SEGMENT PARA             ;Code segment
         ASSUME  CS:CSEG
         ORG     100H
BEGIN:   JMP     INITZE           ;Do this first time thru only

KBSAVE   DD      ?                ;To save address of BIOS INT 9

;                Clear screen & set colors:
;                -------------------------
COLORS   PROC    NEAR             ;Procedure that executes when
         PUSH    AX               ;  user presses Alt/Left Shift
         PUSH    BX
         PUSH    CX               ;Save registers
         PUSH    DX
         PUSH    SI
         PUSH    DI
         PUSH    DS
         PUSH    ES
         PUSHF
         CALL    KBSAVE           ;Force interrupt
         ASSUME  DS:ROMAREA
         MOV     AX,ROMAREA       ;Set DS for
         MOV     DS,AX            ;  accessing Alt/Shift
         MOV     AL,KBFLAG        ;  status
         CMP     AL,00001010B     ;Alt/Left Shift keys pressed?
         JNE     EXIT             ;  no  - exit
         MOV     AX,0600H         ;Request scroll
         MOV     BH,61H           ;Set color
         MOV     CX,00
         MOV     DX,184FH
         INT     10H
EXIT:
         POP     ES               ;Restore registers
         POP     DS
         POP     DI
         POP     SI
         POP     DX
         POP     CX
         POP     BX
         POP     AX
         IRET                     ;Return
COLORS   ENDP
```

Figure 23-2 Resident Program.

```
;               Initialization routine:
;               ----------------------
INITZE  PROC    NEAR              ;Execute this only once
        ASSUME  DS:INTTAB
        PUSH    DS                ;Facilitate return to DOS
        MOV     AX,INTTAB         ;Init. data segment
        MOV     DS,AX
        CLI                       ;Prevent interrupts for following
                                  ;Exchange int addresses:
        MOV     AX,WORD PTR KBADDR      ;Insert BIOS address in
        MOV     WORD PTR KBSAVE,AX      ;  our location
        MOV     AX,WORD PTR KBADDR+2
        MOV     WORD PTR KBSAVE+2,AX
        MOV     WORD PTR KBADDR,OFFSET COLORS ;Change BIOS address
        MOV     WORD PTR KBADDR+2,CS          ;  to our address
        STI                       ;Allow interrupts
        MOV     DX,OFFSET INITZE ;Set size of res. program
        INT     27H               ;Terminate, stay resident
INITZE  ENDP

CSEG    ENDS
        END     BEGIN
```

Figure 23-2 (Continued)

CSEG begins the segment of a normal COM program. The first executable instruction, JMP INITZE, transfers past the resident portion to the INITZE procedure near the end. This routine establishes the address of INTTAB (the interrupt services table) in the DS register. It then transfers the table address for INT 9 (called KBADDR) into KBSAVE in the resident procedure. The next step sets up the address of the resident procedure, COLORS, in KBADDR in the table, followed by the contents of the CS register. Thus, KBADDR now contains two altered bytes: an offset and a CS value that together point to the address of COLORS in memory, and where keyboard entries are now directed. The routine establishes the size of COLORS in the DX (the address of INITZE is one byte greater than the end of COLORS) and uses INT 27H to exit.

COLORS is the name of the resident procedure that is activated when a user presses a key. Since this may happen, for example, while in DOS or in an editor or word processing program, this program has to save all registers that it uses (plus a few others as a wise precaution). An instruction calls KBSAVE, which contains the true address for interrupt, and then accesses the keyboard flag to determine if the Alt/Left Shift keys were pressed. If so, the program sets the required colors. Final instructions involve restoring the pushed registers—in reverse sequence—and executing IRET, interrupt return.

Since this program is intended to be illustrative, you can modify or expand it for your own purposes. A few commercial programs that also replace the table address of interrupt 9 don't allow concurrent use of a resident program like this one.

PORTS

A port is a device that connects a processor to the external world. Through a port a processor receives a signal from an input device and sends a signal to an output device. The processor can theoretically handle up to 65,536 ports, beginning with number 0. It is possible to use the IN and OUT instructions to handle I/O directly at the port level:

- IN transfers data from an input port to the AL if byte and AX if word. The general format is

```
IN   accum-reg,port
```

- OUT transfers data to an output port from the AL if a byte and from the AX if a word. The general format is

```
OUT port,accum-reg
```

You can specify a port number statically or dynamically:

1. *Statically.* Use an operand from 0 through 255 directly as

```
Input:     IN   AL,port#      ;Input one byte
Output     OUT  port#,AX      ;Output one word
```

2. *Dynamically.* Use the contents of the DX register, 0 through 65,535, indirectly. This method is suitable for incrementing the DX in order to process consecutive port numbers. The following example uses port 60H:

```
MOV   DX,60H          ;Port hex 60 (keyboard)
IN    AL,DX           ;Get byte
```

Following is a list of some port numbers, shown in hex:

21	Interrupt mask registers.
40-42	Timer/counter.
60	Input from the keyboard.
61	Speaker (bits 0 and 1).
201	Game control.

3B0-3BF Monochrome display and parallel printer adapter.
3D0-3DF Color/graphics adapter.
3F0-3F7 Disk controller.

For example, when a program requests input from the keyboard, it issues an interrupt instruction INT 16H. The system links to a routine in BIOS that issues an IN instruction to access a character from port hex 60.

The recommended practice is to use DOS and BIOS interrupts. You may safely bypass BIOS when you access ports 21, 40-42, 60, and 201. The BIOS listings in the IBM Technical Reference manual contain further examples of IN and OUT.

GENERATING SOUND

The PC generates sound by means of a built-in permanent magnet speaker. You can select one of two ways to drive the speaker or combine both ways: (1) Use bit 1 of port 61H to activate the Intel 8255A-5 Programmable Peripheral Interface (PPI) chip or (2) use the gating of the Intel 8353-5 Programmable Interval Timer (PIT). The clock generates a 1.19318 Mhz signal. The PPI controls gate 2 at bit 0 of port 61H.

The program in Figure 23-3 generates a series of notes in ascending frequency. DURTION provides the length of each note and TONE determines its frequency. The program initially accesses port 61H and saves the value that the operation delivers. A CLI instruction clears the interrupt flag to enable a constant tone. The interval timer generates a clock tick of 18.2 ticks per second that (unless you code CLI) interrupts execution of your program and causes the tone to wobble.

The contents of TONE determines its frequency; high values cause low frequencies and low values cause high frequencies. After the routine B10SPKR plays each note, it increases the frequency of TONE by means of a right shift of 1 bit (effectively halving its value). Since decreasing TONE in this example also reduces how long it plays, the routine also increases DURTION by means of a left shift of 1 bit (effectively doubling its value).

The program terminates when TONE is reduced to 0. The initial values in DURTION and TONE don't have any technical significance. You can experiment with other values and try execution without the CLI. You could also revise the program to generate notes that decrease in frequency; initialize TONE to 01 and DURTION to a high value. On each loop, increase the value in TONE, decrease the value in DURTION, and terminate when DURTION equals 0.

You could use any variation of the logic to play a sequence of notes, in order, for example, to draw a user's attention.

```
TITLE   SOUND   (COM)  Produce sound from speaker
SOUNSG SEGMENT PARA 'Code'
        ASSUME  CS:SOUNSG,DS:SOUNSG,SS:SOUNSG
        ORG     100H
BEGIN:  JMP     SHORT MAIN
; ---------------------------------------------
DURTION DW      1000               ;Length of tone
TONE    DW      256H               ;Frequency
; ---------------------------------------------
MAIN    PROC    NEAR
        IN      AL,61H             ;Get port data
        PUSH    AX                 ;  & save
        CLI                        ;Clear interrupts
        CALL    B10SPKR            ;Produce sound
        POP     AX                 ;Reset
        OUT     61H,AL             ;  port value
        STI                        ;Reset interrupts
        RET
MAIN    ENDP

B10SPKR PROC    NEAR
B20:    MOV     DX,DURTION         ;Set duration of sound
B30:
        AND     AL,11111100B       ;Clear bits 0 & 1
        OUT     61H,AL             ;Transmit to speaker
        MOV     CX,TONE            ;Set length
B40:
        LOOP    B40                ;Time delay
        OR      AL,00000010B       ;Set bit 1 on
        OUT     61H,AL             ;Transmit to speaker
        MOV     CX,TONE            ;Set length
B50:
        LOOP    B50                ;Time delay
        DEC     DX                 ;Reduce duration
        JNZ     B30                ;Continue?
        SHL     DURTION,1          ;  no - increase length
        SHR     TONE,1             ;Reduce frequency
        JNZ     B20                ;Now zero?
        RET                        ;  yes - exit
B10SPKR ENDP

SOUNSG ENDS
        END     BEGIN
```

Figure 23-3 Generating Sound.

CHAPTER 24

Assembler Pseudo-Op Reference

Objective: To describe in detail assembler operators and pseudo-operations.

INTRODUCTION

The various assembler features at first tend to be somewhat overwhelming. But once you have become familiar with the simpler and more common features described in earlier chapters, you should find the descriptions in this chapter more easily understood and a handy reference. This chapter describes indexed memory, the attribute operators, value-returning operators, and data pseudo-ops. The assembler manual contains a few other marginally useful features.

INDEXED MEMORY

For a *direct* memory reference, one operand of an instruction specifies the name of a defined variable, as shown by COUNTER in the following:

```
ADD   CX,COUNTER
```

During execution, the processor locates the specified variable in memory by combining the offset value of the variable with the address in the data segment.

For *indexed* memory, an operand references a base or index register, constants, offset variables, and variables. Square brackets indicate indexed memory operands and act like a plus (+) sign. You can use the following operations to reference indexed memory:

- Base register BX as [BX] in association with the DS segment register, and base register BP as [BP] in association with the SS segment register. For example, use the offset address in the BX (combined with the segment address in the DS register) and move the referenced item to the DX:

```
MOV  DX,[BX]        ;Base register
```

- Index register DI as [DI] and index register SI as [SI], both in association with the DS segment register. For example, combine the address in the DS with the offset address in the SI, and move the referenced item to the AX:

```
MOV  AX,[SI]        ;Index register
```

- [constant] containing an immediate number or name in square brackets. For example, combine the DS address, the BX offset, the SI offset, plus the constant 4, and move the the contents of the AX to the referenced address:

```
MOV  [BX+SI+4],AX    ;Base + index + constant
```

- A displacement (+ or -) used with an indexed operand. There is little difference between the use of a constant and a displacement. For example, combine the DS address, the displacement 8, the DI offset, plus the constant 4, and move the referenced item to the DX:

```
MOV  DX,8[DI][4]    ;Displacement + index + constant
```

You can combine these operands in any sequence, but don't combine two base registers [BX + BP] or two index registers [DI + SI]. A typical use of indexed addresses is to locate data items in tables.

ASSEMBLER OPERATORS

The three types of assembler operators are *attribute* operators, *value-returning* operators, and *record-specific* operators. This section covers the first two types; record-specific operators, MASK, shift count, and WIDTH are associated with the RECORD pseudo-op, covered in a later section.

LENGTH Operator

The LENGTH operator returns the number of entries defined by a DUP operand. The following MOV instruction returns the length 10 to the DX:

```
TABLEA DW   10 DUP(?)
```

```
        . . .
        MOV   DX,LENGTH TABLEA
```

If the operand does not contain a DUP entry, the operator returns the value 01. See also SIZE and TYPE in this section.

OFFSET Operator

The OFFSET operator returns the offset address of a variable or label (that is, the relative address within the data segment or code segment). The general format is

```
OFFSET variable or label
```

The following MOV returns the offset address of TABLEA. (Note that LEA would return the same value without using OFFSET.)

```
MOV   DX,OFFSET TABLEA
```

PTR Operator

The PTR operator uses BYTE, WORD, or DWORD to override the defined type (DB, DW, or DD) and uses NEAR and FAR to override implied distance. Its general format is

```
type PTR  expression
```

The type field is the new attribute such as BYTE. The expression refers to a variable or constant. Following are examples of the PTR operator:

```
FLDB  DB   22H
      DB   35H
FLDW  DW   2672H                 ;Stored as 7226
      . . .
      MOV  AH,BYTE PTR FLDW      ;Move first byte (72)
      ADD  BL,BYTE PTR FLDW+1    ;Add second byte (26)
      MOV  BYTE PTR FLDW,05      ;Move 05 to first byte
      MOV  AX,WORD PTR FLDB      ;Move two bytes (2235) to AX
      CALL FAR PTR[BX]           ;Call far procedure
```

A feature that performs a similar function to PTR is the LABEL pseudo-op, described in the next section.

SEG Operator

The SEG operator returns the address of the segment in which a specified variable or label is placed. Programs that combine separately assembled segments would most likely use this operator. The general format is

```
SEG variable or label
```

The following MOV instructions return the address of the segment in which they are defined:

```
MOV   DX,SEG FLDW   ;Address of data segment
MOV   DX,SEG A20    ;Address of code segment
```

SHORT Operator

The purpose of the SHORT operator is to modify the NEAR attribute of a JMP destination if it is within +127 and −128 bytes.

```
JMP SHORT label
```

The assembler reduces the machine code operand from two bytes to one. This feature is useful for near jumps that branch forward, since the assembler doesn't know the distance of the jump address.

SIZE Operator

The SIZE operator returns the product of LENGTH times TYPE and is useful only if the referenced variable contains the DUP entry. The general format is

```
SIZE variable
```

See TYPE Operator for an example.

TYPE Operator

The TYPE operator returns the number of bytes according to the definition of the referenced variable:

Definition	*Number of bytes*
DB	1
DW	2
DD	4
DQ	8
DT	10
STRUC	Number of bytes defined by STRUC
NEAR label	Hex FFFF
FAR label	Hex FFFE

The general format of TYPE is

```
TYPE variable or label
```

The following example illustrates TYPE, LENGTH, and SIZE:

```
FLDB    DB   ?
TABLEA  DW   20 DUP(?)          ;Define 20 words
        ...
        MOV  AX,TYPE FLDB       ;AX = 0001
        MOV  AX,TYPE TABLEA     ;AX = 0002
        MOV  CX,LENGTH TABLEA   ;CX = 000A (10)
        MOV  DX,SIZE TABLEA     ;DX = 0014 (20)
```

Since TABLEA is defined as DW, TYPE returns 0002, LENGTH returns hex 000A based on the DUP entry, and SIZE returns type times length, or hex 14 (20).

ASSEMBLER PSEUDO-OPERATIONS

This section describes most of the assembler pseudo-operations. Chapter 5 covers in detail the pseudo-ops for defining data (DB, DW, etc.).

ASSUME Pseudo-Operation

The purpose of ASSUME is to enable the assembler to associate segments with segment registers CS, DS, ES, and SS. The general format is

```
ASSUME  seg-reg:name [, ... ]
```

Valid names are segment registers, GROUPs, and a SEG expression. One ASSUME statement may assign up to four segment registers, in any sequence:

```
ASSUME  CS:CODESG,DS:DATASG,SS:STACK,ES:DATASG
```

Use of the keyword NOTHING cancels any previous ASSUME for a specified segment register as follows:

```
ASSUME  ES:NOTHING
```

Suppose that you do not assign the DS register or use NOTHING to cancel it. In order to reference a data item in the data segment, an instruction operand makes a specific reference to the DS register as follows:

```
MOV  AX,DS:[BX]    ;Use indexed address
MOV  AX,DS:FLDW    ;Move contents of FLDW
```

Of course, the DS register must contain a valid address.

EXTRN Pseudo-Operation

The purpose of the EXTRN pseudo-op is to inform the assembler of variables and labels that this assembly references but that another assembly defines. The general format is

```
EXTRN   name:type [, ... ]
```

Chapter 21 covers EXTRN in detail.

GROUP Pseudo-Operation

A program may contain several segments of the same type (code, data, stack). The purpose of the GROUP pseudo-op is to collect them under one name so that they reside within a 64K segment. The general format is

```
name GROUP   seg-name [, ... ]
```

The following GROUP combines SEG1 and SEG2 in the same assembly module:

```
GROUPX    GROUP      SEG1, SEG2
SEG1      SEGMENT    PARA 'CODE'
```

```
              ASSUME     CS:GROUPX
              ...
SEG1          ENDS
;
SEG2          SEGMENT    PARA 'CODE'
              ASSUME     CS:GROUPX
              ...
SEG2          ENDS
```

INCLUDE Pseudo-Operation

You may have sections of assembly code or macro instructions that various programs use. You can store these in separate disk files available for use by any program. Let's say that a routine which converts ASCII code to binary is stored on drive C in a file named CONVERT.LIB. To access the file, insert an INCLUDE statement such as

```
INCLUDE C:CONVERT.LIB
```

at the location in the source program where you would normally code the ASCII conversion routine. The assembler locates the file on disk and includes the statements in with your own program. (If the assembler cannot find the file, it issues an error message and ignores the INCLUDE.)

For each included line, the assembler prints a C in column 30 of the LST file (column 33 begins the source code).

Chapter 20 on macros gives a practical example of INCLUDE and explains how to include only for pass 1 of an assembly.

LABEL Pseudo-Operation

The LABEL pseudo-op enables you to redefine the attribute of a defined name. The general format is

```
name LABEL   type
```

You can use the type entry as BYTE, WORD, or DWORD to redefine data fields and the names of structures and records. You can also use LABEL to redefine executable code as NEAR or FAR. LABEL enables you, for example, to define a field as both DB and DW. The following illustrates the use of BYTE and WORD types:

```
REDEFB  LABEL  BYTE
FIELDW  DW     2532H
REDEFW  LABEL  WORD
```

```
FIELDB  DB    25H
        DB    32H
        . . .
        MOV   AL,REDEFB     ;Move 1st byte
        MOV   BX,REDEFW     ;Move 2 bytes
```

The first MOV instruction moves only the first byte of FIELDW. The second MOV moves the two bytes beginning at FIELDB. The PTR operator performs a similar function.

NAME Pseudo-Operation

The NAME pseudo-op provides another way to assign a name to a module, coded as

```
NAME name
```

The assembler selects the module name according to the following sequence:

1. If NAME is present, its operand becomes the name.
2. If NAME is not present, the assembler uses the first six characters from TITLE, if any.
3. If neither NAME nor TITLE is present, the name of the source file becomes the module name.

The assembler passes the selected name to the linker.

ORG Pseudo-Operation

The assembler uses a location counter to account for its relative position in a data or code segment. Assume a data segment with the following definitions:

Offset	*Name*	*Oper'n*	*Operand*	*Location Counter*
00	FLDA	DW	2542H	02
02	FLDB	DB	36H	03
03	FLDC	DW	212EH	05
05	FLDD	DD	00000705H	09

Initially, the location counter is set to 00. Since FLDA is two bytes, the location counter is incremented to 02 for the location of the next item. Since FLDB is one byte, the location counter is incremented to 03, and so forth. You can use the ORG pseudo-op to change the contents of the location counter and accordingly the location of the next defined items. The general format is

```
ORG   expression
```

The expression may be an absolute number, not a symbolic name, and must form a two-byte absolute number. Consider the following data items to be defined immediately after FLDD in the previous definition:

Offset	*Name*	*Oper'n Operand*	*Location Counter*
		ORG 0	00
00	FLDX	DB ?	01
01	FLDY	DW ?	02
03	FLDZ	DB ?	04
		ORG $+5	09

The first ORG sets the location counter back to 00. The variables that follow, FLDX, FLDY, and FLDZ, define the same memory locations as FLDA, FLDB, and FLDC:

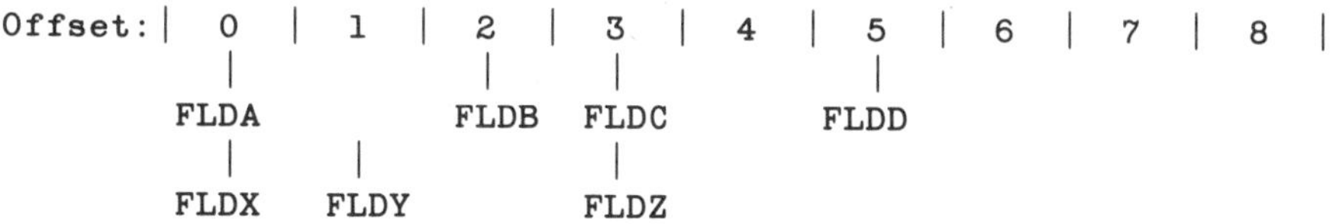

An operand containing the dollar symbol ($) as in the second ORG previously given refers to the current value in the location counter. The operand $+5 therefore sets the location counter to 04 + 5, or 09, which is the same setting after the definition of FLDD.

A reference to FLDC is to a one-word field at offset 03, and a reference to FLDZ is to a one-byte field at offset 03:

```
MOV   AX,FLDC     ;One word
MOV   AL,FLDZ     ;One byte
```

You can use this ORG feature to redefine memory locations. But be sure that ORG sets the location counter back to the correct value and that you account for all redefined memory locations. Also, the redefined variables should not contain defined constants—these would overlay constants on top of the original constants. You cannot use ORG within a STRUC definition.

PROC Pseudo-Operation

A procedure is a block of code that begins with the DOS PROC pseudo-op and terminates with ENDP. A typical use is for a subroutine within the code segment. Although technically you can enter a procedure in-line or by a JMP instruction, the normal practice is to use CALL to enter and RET to exit.

A procedure that is in the same segment as the calling procedure is a NEAR procedure:

```
proc-name    PROC [NEAR]
```

An omitted operand defaults to NEAR. If a procedure is external to the calling segment, you should use only CALL and the called procedure must be declared as PUBLIC. Further, if a called procedure is under a different ASSUME CS value, it must have the FAR attribute:

```
          PUBLIC proc-name
proc-name PROC FAR
```

If you CALL a procedure, be sure to use RET to exit from it.

PUBLIC Pseudo-Operation

The purpose of the PUBLIC pseudo-op is to inform the assembler that the identified symbols in an assembly are to be referenced by other assembly modules. The general format is

```
PUBLIC  symbol [, ... ]
```

Chapter 20, "Subprograms," covers PUBLIC in detail.

RECORD Pseudo-Operation

The RECORD pseudo-op enables you to define patterns of bits. One purpose would be to define switch indicators either as one-bit or as multibit. The general format is:

```
record-name RECORD field-name:width[=exp] [, ... ]
```

Record name and field names may be any unique valid identifiers. Following each field name is a colon (:) and a "width"—the number of bits. The range of the width entry is 1 to 16 bits:

No. of defined bits	*Default size*
1 - 8	8
9 - 16	16

Any length up to 8 becomes 8 bits, and 9 to 16 becomes 16, right-adjusted if necessary. The following example defines RECORD:

```
BITREC  RECORD  BIT1:3,BIT2:7,BIT3:6
```

BIT1 defines the first 3 bits of BITREC, BIT2 defines the next 7, and BIT3 defines the last 6. The total is 16 bits, or one word. You can initialize values in RECORD as follows:

```
BITREC2 RECORD  BIT1:3=101B,BIT2:7=0110110B,BIT3:6=011010B
```

Let's say that the definition of a RECORD is in front of the data segment. Within the data segment there should be another statement that allocates storage for the record. Define a unique valid name, the record name, and an operand consisting of angle brackets (the less than, greater than symbols):

```
DEFBITS BITREC  <>
```

The above allocation generates object code hex AD9A (stored as 9AAD) in the data segment. The angle brackets may also contain entries that redefine BITREC.

The program in Figure 24-1 illustrates defining BITREC as RECORD, but without initial values in the record fields. In this case, an allocation statement in the data segment initializes each field as shown within angle brackets.

Record-specific operators are WIDTH, shift count, and MASK. The use of these operators permits you to change a RECORD definition without having to change the instructions that reference it.

WIDTH Operator. The WIDTH operator returns a width as the number of bits in a RECORD or in a RECORD field. For example, in Figure 24-1 following A10 are two examples of WIDTH. The first MOV returns the width of the entire RECORD BITREC (16 bits); the second MOV returns the width of the record field BIT2 (7 bits). In both cases, the assembler has generated an immediate operand for width.

Shift Count. A direct reference to a RECORD field such as

```
MOV   CL,BIT2
```

```
                       TITLE  TRECORD (COM)  Test of RECORD Pseudo-op
0000                   CODESG SEGMENT PARA 'Code'
                              ASSUME  CS:CODESG,DS:CODESG,SS:CODESG
0100                          ORG     100H
0100   EB 02           BEGIN:         JMP     SHORT MAIN
                       ; ----------------------------------------------------
                       BITREC RECORD  BIT1:3,BIT2:7,BIT3:6     ;Define record
0102   9A AD           DEFBITS BITREC <101B,0110110B,011010B> ;Init'ze record
                       ; ----------------------------------------------------
0104                   MAIN   PROC    NEAR
0104                   A10:                                ;Width:
0104   B7 10                  MOV     BH,WIDTH BITREC      ;  of record (16)
0106   B0 07                  MOV     AL,WIDTH BIT2        ;  of field (07)
0108                   B10:                                ;Shift count:
0108   B1 0D                  MOV     CL,BIT1              ;  hex 0D
010A   B1 06                  MOV     CL,BIT2              ;      06
010C   B1 00                  MOV     CL,BIT3              ;      00
010E                   C10:                                ;Mask:
010E   B8 E000                MOV     AX,MASK BIT1         ;  hex E000
0111   BB 1FC0                MOV     BX,MASK BIT2         ;      1FC0
0114   B9 003F                MOV     CX,MASK BIT3         ;      003F
0117                   D10:                                ;Isolate BIT 2:
0117   A1 0102 R              MOV     AX,DEFBITS           ;  get record
011A   25 1FC0                AND     AX,MASK BIT2         ;  clear BIT 1 & 3
011D   B1 06                  MOV     CL,BIT2              ;  get shift 06
011F   D3 E8                  SHR     AX,CL                ;  shift right
0121                   E10:                                ;Isolate BIT 1:
0121   A1 0102 R              MOV     AX,DEFBITS           ;  get record
0124   B1 0D                  MOV     CL,BIT1              ;  get shift 13
0126   D3 E8                  SHR     AX,CL                ;  shift right
0128   C3                     RET
0129                          MAIN    ENDP
0129                   CODESG ENDS
                              END     BEGIN
```

```
Structures and records:
                   N a m e        Width   # fields
                                          Shift    Width    Mask     Initial
  BITREC . . . . . . . . . . . . . 0010   0003
  BIT1 . . . . . . . . . . . . . . 000D   0003     E000     0000
  BIT2 . . . . . . . . . . . . . . .      0006     0007     1FC0     0000
  BIT3 . . . . . . . . . . . . . . 0000   0006     003F     0000

Segments and Groups:
                   N a m e        Size    Align    Combine Class
CODESG . . . . . . . . . . . .    0129    PARA     NONE    'CODE'

Symbols:
                   N a m e       Type     Value    Attr
A10. . . . . . . . . . . . . . . L NEAR   0104     CODESG
B10. . . . . . . . . . . . . . . L NEAR   0108     CODESG
BEGIN. . . . . . . . . . . . . . L NEAR   0100     CODESG
C10. . . . . . . . . . . . . . . L NEAR   010E     CODESG
D10. . . . . . . . . . . . . . . L NEAR   0117     CODESG
DEFBITS. . . . . . . . . . . . . L WORD   0102     CODESG
E10. . . . . . . . . . . . . . . L NEAR   0121     CODESG
MAIN . . . . . . . . . . . . . . N PROC   0104     CODESG  Length =0025
```

Figure 24-1 Use of RECORD Pseudo-op.

does not refer to the contents of BIT2 (indeed, that would be rather difficult). Instead, the assembler generates an immediate operand that contains a "shift count" to help you isolate the field. The immediate value represents the number of bits that you would have to shift BIT2 to right-adjust it. In Figure 24-1, the three examples following B10 return the shift count for BIT1, BIT2, and BIT3.

MASK Operator. The MASK operator returns a "mask" of 1-bits representing the specified field, and in effect defines the bit positions that the field occupies. For example, the MASK for each of the fields defined in BITREC are:

Field	*Binary*	*Hex*
BIT1	1110000000000000	E000
BIT2	0001111111000000	1FC0
BIT3	0000000000111111	003F

In Figure 24-1, the three instructions following C10 return the MASK values for BIT1, BIT2, and BIT3. The instructions following D10 and E10, respectively, illustrate isolating BIT2 and BIT1 from BITREC. D10 gets the record into the AX register and then ANDs it using a MASK of BIT2:

Record	101 0110110 011010
AND MASK BIT2:	000 1111111 000000
Result:	000 0110110 000000

The effect is to clear all bits except those of BIT2. The next two instructions cause the AX to shift six bits so that BIT2 is right-adjusted:

```
0000000000110110          (hex 0036)
```

The example following E10 gets the record into the AX, and because BIT1 is the leftmost field, the routine simply uses its shift factor to shift right 13 bits:

```
0000000000000101          (hex 0005)
```

SEGMENT Pseudo-Operation

An assembly module consists of one or more segments, part of a segment, or even parts of several segments. The general format is

```
seg-name  SEGMENT [align] [combine] [class]
```

```
                .
                .
                .
seg-name   ENDS
```

All operands are optional. The following describes the entries for align, combine, and class:

Align. The align operand indicates the starting boundary for the segment, where x represents a hex digit:

PAGE = xxx00
PARA = xxxx0 (default boundary)
WORD = xxxxe (even)
BYTE = xxxxx

Combine. The combine operand indicates the way LINK is to handle the segment:

NONE (default): The segment is to be logically separate from other segments, although it may end up to be physically adjacent. The segment is presumed to have its own base address.

PUBLIC: LINK loads PUBLIC segments of the same name and class adjacent to one another. One base address is presumed for all such PUBLIC segments.

STACK: LINK treats STACK the same as PUBLIC. There must be at least one STACK defined in a linked program. If there is more than one, the stack pointer (SP) is set to the start of the first stack.

COMMON: If COMMON segments have the same name and class, the linker gives them the same base address. For execution, the second segment overlays the first one. The largest segment determines the length of the common area.

AT paragraph-address: The paragraph must be previously defined. The entry facilitates defining labels and variables at fixed offsets within fixed areas of memory, such as ROM or the interrupt table in low memory. For example, the code in ROM defines the location of the video display buffer as:

```
VIDEO_RAM   SEGMENT   AT 0B800H
```

'class': The class entry may contain any legal name, contained in single quotes. LINK uses it to relate segments that have the same name and class. Typical examples are 'STACK' and 'CODE'.

LINK combines the following two segments into one physical segment under the same segment register:

```
          ------------------------------------
Assembly  SEG1    SEGMENT PARA PUBLIC 'CODE'
module 1          ASSUME  CS:SEG1
                  ...
          SEG1    ENDS
          ------------------------------------
Assembly  SEG2    SEGMENT PARA PUBLIC  'CODE'
module 2          ASSUME  CS:SEG1
                  ...
          SEG2    ENDS
          ------------------------------------
```

You may nest segments provided that a nested segment is completely contained within the other:

```
SEG1    SEGMENT
        ...             SEG1 begins
SEG2    SEGMENT
        ...             SEG2 area
SEG2    ENDS
        ...             SEG1 resumes
SEG1    ENDS
```

For combining segments into groups, see the GROUP pseudo-op.

STRUC Pseudo-Operation

The STRUC pseudo-op (not supported by the small assembler) facilitates defining related fields within a structure. Its general format is

```
struc-name  STRUC
            ...
          [ defined fields ]
            ...
struc-name  ENDS
```

A structure begins with its name and the pseudo-op STRUC and terminates with the structure name and the pseudo-op ENDS. The assembler stores the contained defined fields one after the other from the start of the structure. Valid entries are DB, DW, DD, DQ, and DT definitions with optional field names.

In Figure 24-2, STRUC defines a parameter list named PARLIST for input of a name from the keyboard. A subsequent statement allocates storage for the structure:

```
PARAMS  PARLIST   <>
```

```
                          TITLE  DSTRUC  (COM)  Definition of a structure
0000                      CODESG SEGMENT PARA 'Code'
                                 ASSUME  CS:CODESG,DS:CODESG,SS:CODESG
0100                             ORG     100H
0100 EB 29                BEGIN: JMP     SHORT MAIN
                          ; ---------------------------------------------
                          PARLIST        STRUC            ;Parameter list
0000 19                   MAXLEN DB      25               ;
0001 ??                   ACTLEN DB      ?                ;
0002    19 [ 20 ]         NAMEIN DB      25 DUP(' ')      ;
001B                      PARLIST        ENDS
                                                          ;
0102 19                   PARAMS PARLIST <>               ;Allocate structure
0103 ??
0104    19 [ 20 ]
011D 57 68 61 74 20 69    PROMPT DB      'What is name?', '$'
     73 20 6E 61 6D 65
     3F 24
                          ; ---------------------------------------------
012B                      MAIN   PROC    NEAR
012B B4 09                       MOV     AH,09            ;Display prompt
012D 8D 16 011D R                LEA     DX,PROMPT
0131 CD 21                       INT     21H
0133 B4 0A                       MOV     AH,0AH           ;Accept input
0135 8D 16 0102 R                LEA     DX,PARAMS
0139 CD 21                       INT     21H
013B A0 0103 R                   MOV     AL,PARAMS.ACTLEN ;Length of input
                          ;      ...
013E C3                          RET
013F                      MAIN   ENDP
013F                      CODESG ENDS
                                 END     BEGIN
```

```
Structures and records:
                N a m e          Width  # fields
                                 Shift  Width   Mask    Initial
PARLIST. . . . . . . . . . . . . 001B   0003
  MAXLEN . . . . . . . . . . . . 0000
  ACTLEN . . . . . . . . . . . . 0001
  NAMEIN . . . . . . . . . . . . 0002

Segments and Groups:
                N a m e          Size   Align   Combine Class
CODESG . . . . . . . . . . .     013F   PARA    NONE    'CODE'

Symbols:
                N a m e          Type   Value   Attr
BEGIN. . . . . . . . . . . . . L NEAR   0100    CODESG
MAIN . . . . . . . . . . . . . N PROC   012B    CODESG  Length =0014
PARAMS . . . . . . . . . . . . L 001B   0102    CODESG
PROMPT . . . . . . . . . . . . L BYTE   011D    CODESG
```

Figure 24-2 Example Structure.

The allocate statement makes the structure addressable within the program. The angle brackets (less than, greater than symbols) in the operand are empty in this example, but you may use them to redefine ("override") data within a structure.

Instructions may reference a structure name directly. To reference fields within a structure, instructions must qualify them by using the allocate name of the structure (**PARAMS** in the example) followed by a period that connects it with the field name, as:

```
MOV   AL,PARAMS.ACTLEN
```

You can use the allocate statement to redefine the contents of fields within a structure. For the rules of this practice, see your assembler manual.

CHAPTER 25

Instruction Reference

Objective: To explain machine code and to provide a description of the instruction set.

INTRODUCTION

This chapter explains machine code and provides an alphabetic listing of symbolic instructions with an explanation of their purpose.

Many instructions have a specific purpose so that a one-byte instruction code is adequate. The following are examples:

```
Obj. code: Symbolic instruction:
    40        INC   AX             ;Increment AX
    50        PUSH  AX             ;Push AX
    C3        RET (short)          ;Short return from procedure
    CB        RET (far)            ;Far return from procedure
    FD        STD                  ;Set direction flag
```

None of the instructions just given makes a direct reference to memory. Other instructions that specify an immediate operand, an 8-bit register, two registers, or a reference to memory require more complex machine code.

REGISTER NOTATION

Instructions that reference a register may contain three bits that indicate the particular register and a "w" bit that signifies if the "width" is byte or word. Also, only certain instructions may access segment registers. Figure 25-1 shows the complete register notations.

Here's a MOV instruction with a one-byte immediate operand:

```
MOV   AH,00      10110 100 00000000
                     |   |
                     w reg = AH
```

```
General, Base, and Index Registers:
    Bits         w = 0        w = 1
    000           AL           AX
    001           CL           CX
    010           DL           DX
    011           BL           BX
    100           AH           SP
    101           CH           BP
    110           DH           SI
    111           BH           DI
      Bits: Segment register:
             00       ES
             01       CS
             10       SS
             11       DS
```

Figure 25-1 Register Notation.

In this case, the first byte of machine code indicates a width of one byte (w = 0) and refers to the AH register (100). Here's a MOV instruction that contains a one-word immediate operand:

```
MOV   AX,00      10111 000 00000000 00000000
                     |   |
                     w reg = AX
```

The first byte of machine code indicates a width of one word (w = 1) and refers to the AX register (000). Don't generalize too much from these examples—for other instructions, w and reg may occupy different positions.

ADDRESSING MODE BYTE

The mode byte, where it exists, occupies the second byte of machine code and consists of the following three elements:

1. *mod* A two-bit mode, where 11 refers to a register and 00, 01, and 10 reference a memory location.
2. *reg* A three-bit reference to a register.
3. *r/m* A three-bit reference to register or memory, where r signifies which register and m indicates a memory address.

As well, the first byte of machine code may contain a "d" bit that indicates the direction of flow between operand 1 and operand 2.

Here's an example of adding the AX to the BX:

```
ADD   BX,AX      00000011  11 011 000
                         dw mod reg r/m
```

In this example, d = 1 means that mod (11) and reg (011) describe operand 1 and r/m (000) describes operand 2. Since w = 1, the width is a word. Therefore, the instruction is to add the AX (000) to the BX (011).

The second byte of the object instruction indicates most modes of addressing memory. The next section examines the addressing mode in more detail.

The MOD Bits

The two mod bits distinguish between addressing of registers and memory. The following explains their purpose:

00 The r/m bits supply the exact addressing option, and there is no offset byte.

01 The r/m bits supply the exact addressing option, and there is one offset byte.

10 The r/m bits supply the exact addressing option, and there are two offset bytes.

11 The r/m specifies a register. The "w" bit (in the operation code byte) determines if a reference is to an 8- or 16-bit register.

The REG Bits

The three reg bits, in association with the w bit, determine the actual register, either 8- or 16-bit.

The R/M Bits. The three r/m (register/memory) bits, in association with mod, determine the addressing mode, as shown in Figure 25-2.

TWO-BYTE INSTRUCTIONS

The first example adds the AX to the BX:

```
ADD  BX,AX  0000 0011   11 011 000
                   dw   mod reg r/m
```

r/m	mod=00	mod=01	mod=10	mod=1.1 w=0	mod=11 w=1
000	BX+SI	BX+SI+disp	BX+SI+disp	AL	AX
001	BX+DI	BX+DI+disp	BX+DI+disp	CL	CX
010	BP+SI	BP+SI+disp	BP+SI+disp	DL	DX
011	BP+DI	BP+DI+disp	BP+DI+disp	BL	BX
100	SI	SI+disp	SI+disp	AH	SP
101	DI	DI+disp	DI+disp	CH	BP
110	Direct	BP+disp	BP+disp	DH	SI
111	BX	BX+disp	BX+disp	BH	DI

Figure 25-2 The r/m Bits.

d 1 implies that reg plus w describe operand 1 (BX), and mod plus r/m plus w describe operand 2 (AX).

w 1 indicates that the width is word.

mod 11 means that operand 2 is a register.

reg 011 means that operand 1 is the BX register.

r/m 000 means that operand 2 is the AX register.

The second example multiplies the AL by the BL:

```
MUL   BL 11110110   11 100 011
                    w mod reg r/m
```

The MUL instruction assumes that the AL contains the multiplicand. The width (w=0) is byte, mod references a register, and the register is the BL (011). Reg = 100 is not meaningful here.

THREE-BYTE INSTRUCTIONS

The following MOV generates three bytes of machine code:

```
MOV   mem,AX 10100001 dddddddd dddddddd
```

A move from the accumulator (AX or AL) needs to know only if the operation is byte or word. In this example, w=1 means word, and the 16-bit AX is understood. Use of AL in operand-2 would cause the w bit to be 0. Byte-2 and byte-3 contain the offset to the memory location. Instructions using the accumulator often generate more efficient machine code.

FOUR-BYTE INSTRUCTIONS

The first example multiplies the AL by a memory location. The processor assumes that the multiplicand is in the AL if byte and in the AX if word.

```
MUL  mem_byte 11110110  00 100 110
                         w mod reg r/m
```

For this instruction, reg is always 100. Mod = 00 indicates a memory reference, and r/m = 110 means a direct reference to memory. The machine instruction also contains two following bytes that provide the offset to this memory location.

The second example illustrates the LEA instruction, which always specifies a word address:

```
LEA  DX,mem   10001101  00 010 110
                   LEA   mod reg r/m
```

Reg = 010 designates the DX register. Mod = 00 and r/m = 110 indicate a direct reference to a memory address. Two following bytes provide the offset to this location.

INSTRUCTIONS IN ALPHABETIC SEQUENCE

This section covers the instruction set in alphabetic sequence. Some instructions such as shift and rotate are grouped together for brevity. The 80186, 80286, and 80386 support a number of specialized instructions that are outside the scope of this book. In addition to the preceding discussion of the mode byte and the width bit, the following abbreviations are relevant:

addr	Address of a memory location.
addr-high	Rightmost byte of an address.
addr-low	Leftmost byte of an address.
data	Immediate operand (8-bit if w=0 and 16-bit if w=1).
data-high	Rightmost byte of an immediate operand.
data-low	Leftmost byte of an immediate operand.
disp	Displacement (offset value).
reg	Reference to a register.

AAA: ASCII Adjust for Addition

Operation: Corrects the sum of two ASCII bytes in the AL. If the rightmost four bits of AL have a value greater than 9 or if the AF flag is set to 1, AAA adds 1 to the AH and sets the AF and CF flags. The instruction always clears the leftmost four bits of the AL.

Flags: Affects AF and CF (OF, PF, SF, and ZF are undefined).

Object code: 00110111 (no operands)

AAD: ASCII Adjust for Division

Operation: Corrects for division of ASCII values. Use AAD before dividing into an unpacked decimal value in the AX (strip out ASCII 3s). AAD corrects the dividend to a binary value in the AL for a subsequent binary divide. It multiplies the AH by 10, adds the product to the AL, and clears the AH. AAD has no operands.

Flags: Affects PF, SF, ZF (AF, CF, and OF are undefined).

Object code: |11010101|00001010|

AAM: ASCII Adjust for Multiplication

Operation: Use AAM to correct the product generated by multiplying two unpacked decimal values. AAM divides the AL by 10 and stores the quotient in the AH and the remainder in the AL.

Flags: Affects PF, SF, and ZF (AF, CF, and OF are undefined).

Object code: |11010100|00001010| (no operands)

AAS: ASCII Adjust for Subtraction

Operation: Corrects subtraction of two ASCII bytes in the AL. If the rightmost four bits have a value greater than 9 or if the CF flag is 1, AAS subtracts 6 from the AL, subtracts 1 from the AH, and sets the AF and CF flags. The instruction always clears the leftmost four bits of the AL.

Flags: Affects AF and CF (OF, PF, SF, and ZF are undefined).

Object code: 00111111 (no operands)

ADC: Add with Carry

Operation: Typically used in multiword binary addition to carry an overflowed 1-bit into the next stage of arithmetic. If the CF flag is set, ADC first adds 1 to operand 1. The instruction always adds operand 2 to operand 1, just as ADD does.

Flags: Affects AF, CF, OF, PF, SF, and ZF.

Object code (three formats):

Reg/mem with reg: |000100dw|modregr/m|
Immed to accum'r: |0001010w| data |data if w=1|
Immed to reg/mem: |100000sw|mod010r/m|---data----|data if sw=01|

ADD: Add Binary Numbers

Operation: Adds byte or word values in memory, register, or immediate to a register, or adds byte or word values in a register or immediate to memory.

Flags: Affects AF, CF, OF, PF, SF, and ZF.

Object code (three formats):

Reg/mem with reg: |000000dw|modregr/m|
Immed to accum'r: |0000010w|-- data--|data if w=1|
Immed to reg/mem:
|100000sw|mod000r/m|---data ---|data if sw=01|

AND: Logical AND

Operation: Performs a logical AND operation on bits of two operands. The two operands are both bytes or both words in a register or memory; operand 2 may be immediate. AND matches the two operands bit for bit.

If both matched bits are 1, AND sets the operand 1 bit to 1; otherwise it is set to 0. See also OR, XOR, and TEST.

Flags: Affects CF, OF, PF, SF, and ZF (AF is undefined).

Object code (three formats):

```
Reg/mem with reg:   |001000dw|modregr/m|
Immed to accum'r:   |0010010w|---data----|data if w=1|
Immed to reg/mem:
    |1010000w|mod100r/m|---data----|data if w=1|
```

CALL: Call a Procedure

Operation: Calls a near or far procedure for subroutine linkage. Use RET to return from the procedure. CALL decrements the SP by 2 and pushes the address of the next instruction (in the IP) onto the stack. It then loads the IP with the destination offset address. A subsequent RET instruction undoes these steps on return. There are four types of CALL instructions for transferring within and between segments. An intersegment CALL first decrements the SP, pushes the CS onto the stack, and loads an intersegment pointer onto the stack.

Flags: None.

Object code (four formats):

```
Direct within segment: |11101000|disp-low  |disp-high|
Indir. within segment: |11111111|mod010r/m|
Indirect intersegment: |11111111|mod011r/m|
Direct intersegment:
    |10011010|offset-low|offset-high|seg-low|seg-high|
```

CBW: Convert Byte to Word

Operation: Extends a one-byte arithmetic value in the AL to a word. CBW duplicates the sign (bit 7) of the AL through the bits in the AH. See also CWD.

Flags: None.

Object code: 10011000 (no operands)

CLC: Clear Carry Flag

Operation: Clears the CF flag to 0 so that, for example, an ADC does not add a 1-bit. CLC has no operands. See also STD.

Flags: CF (becomes 0).

Object code: 11111000

CLD: Clear Direction Flag

Operation: Clears the DF flag to 0. The effect is to cause string operations such as CMPS and MOVS to process from left to right. See also STD.

Flags: DF (becomes 0).

Object code: 11111100 (no operands)

CLI: Clear Interrupt Flag

Operation: Disables maskable external interrupts that appear on the processor's INTR line, and thus clears the IF flag to 0. See also STI.

Flags: IF (becomes 0).

Object code: 11111010 (no operands)

CMC: Complement Carry Flag

Operation: Complements the CF flag: reverses the CF bit value -- 0 becomes 1 and 1 becomes 0.

Flags: CF (reversed).

Object code: 11110101 (no operands)

CMP: Compare

Operation: Compares the contents of two data fields. CMP internally subtracts operand 2 from operand 1, but does not change the values.

Operands should be either both byte or both word. CMP may compare register, memory, or immediate to a register or compare register or immediate to memory. See also CMPS.

Flags: Affects AF, CF, OF, PF, SF, and ZF.

Object code (three formats):

```
Reg/mem with reg:   |001110dw|modregr/m|
Immed to accum'r:   |0011110w|---data--|data if w=1|
Immed to reg/mem:
    |100000sw|mod111r/m|---data----|data if sw=0|
```

CMPS/CMPSB/CMPSW: Compare Byte or Word String

Operation: Compares strings of any length. A REPn prefix normally precedes these instructions, for example as REPE CMPSB. CMPSB compares bytes and CMPSW compares words in memory. The DS:SI registers address operand 1 and the ES:DI registers address operand 2. If the DF flag is 0, the operation compares from left to right and increments the SI and DI. If the DF is 1, it compares from right to left and decrements the SI and DI.

Flags: Affects AF, CF, OF, PF, SF, and ZF.

Object code: 1010011w

CWD: Convert Word to Doubleword

Operation: Extends a one-word arithmetic value in the AX to a doubleword by duplicating the sign (bit 15) of the AX through the DX, typically to generate a 16-bit dividend. See also CBW.

Flags: None.

Object code: 10011001 (no operands)

DAA: Decimal Adjust for Addition

Operation: Corrects the result of adding two BCD (packed decimal) items in the AL. If the rightmost four bits have a value greater than 9 or the

AF flag is 1, DAA adds 6 to the AL and sets the AF. If the AL contains a value greater than hex 9F or the CF flag is 1, DAA adds hex 60 to the AL and sets the CF flag. See also DAS.

Flags: Affects AF, CF, PF, SF, and ZF (OF undefined).

Object code: 00100111 (no operands)

DAS: Decimal Adjust for Subtraction

Operation: Corrects the result of subtracting two BCD (packed decimal) fields in the AL. If the rightmost four bits have a value greater than 9 or the AF is 1, DAS subtracts hex 60 from the AL and sets the CF flag. See also DAA.

Flags: Affects AF, CF, PF, SF, and ZF.

Object code: 00101111 (no operands)

DEC: Decrement by 1

Operation: Decrements 1 from a byte or word in a register or memory, used for example as DEC CX. See also INC.

Flags: Affects AF, OF, PF, SF, and ZF.

Object code (two formats):

```
Register:       |01001reg|
Reg/memory:     |1111111w|mod001r/m|
```

DIV: Divide

Operation: Divides an unsigned dividend (16 or 32-bit) by an unsigned divisor (8 or 16-bit). DIV treats a leftmost 1-bit as a data bit, not a minus sign. A 16-bit dividend is in the AX and its 8-bit divisor is in a register or memory, coded, for example, as DIV BH. The quotient is generated in the AL and the remainder in the AH. A 32-bit dividend is in the DX:AX and its 16-bit divisor is in a register or memory, coded, for example, as DIV CX. The quotient is generated in the AX and the remainder in the DX. See also IDIV.

Flags: Affects AF, CF, OF, PF, SF, and ZF (all undefined).

Object code: |1111011w|mod110r/m|

ESC: Escape

Operation: Facilitates use of coprocessors to perform special operations. Some operations require the use of a coprocessor such as the 8087 and 80287 for floating point. An ESC instruction provides the coprocessor with an instruction and operand for execution.

Flags: None.

Object code: |11011xxx|modxxxr/m| (x-bits are not important)

HLT: Enter Halt State

Operation: Causes the processor to enter its halt state while waiting for an interrupt. HLT terminates with the CS and IP registers pointing to the instruction following the HLT. When an interrupt occurs, the processor pushes the CS and IP on the stack and executes the interrupt routine. On return, an IRET instruction pops the stack and processing resumes following the original HLT.

Flags: None.

Object code: 11110100 (no operands)

IDIV: Integer (Signed) Division

Operation: Divides a signed dividend (16 or 32-bit) by a signed divisor (8 or 16-bit). IDIV treats a leftmost 1-bit as a negative sign. A 16-bit dividend is in the AX and its 8-bit divisor is in a register or memory, coded, for example, as IDIV DL. The quotient is generated in the AL and remainder in the AH. A 32-bit dividend is in the DX:AX and its 16-bit divisor is in a register or memory, coded, for example, as IDIV BX. The quotient is generated in the AX and the remainder in the DX. See CBW and CWD to extend the length of a signed dividend. See also DIV.

Flags: Affects AF, CF, OF, PF, SF, and ZF.

Object code: |1111011w|mod111r/m|

IMUL: Integer (Signed) Multiplication

Operation: Multiplies a signed multiplier (8 or 16-bit). IMUL treats a leftmost 1-bit as a negative sign. For 8-bit multiplication, the multiplicand is in the AL and the multiplier is in a register or memory, coded, for example, as IMUL BL. The product is developed in the AX. For 16-bit multiplication, the multiplicand is in the AX and the multiplier is in a register or memory, coded, for example, as IMUL BX. The product is developed in the DX:AX. See also MUL.

Flags: Affects CF and OF (AF, PF, SF, and ZF are undefined).

Object code: `|1111011w|mod101r/m|`

IN: Input Byte or Word

Operation: Transfers from an input port a byte to the AL or a word to the AX. Code the port as a fixed numeric operand (as IN AX,port#) or as a variable in the DX (as IN AX,DX). The 80186, 80286, and 80386 also support an INS (Input String) instruction. See also OUT.

Flags: None.

Object code (two formats):

Variable port: `|1110110w|`
Fixed port: `|1110010w|--port--|`

INC: Increment by 1

Operation: Increments by 1 a byte or word in a register or memory, coded, for example, as INC CX. See also DEC.

Flags: Affects AF, OF, PF, SF, and ZF.

Object code (two formats):

Register: `|01000reg|`
Reg/memory: `|1111111w|mod000r/m|`

INT: Interrupt

Operation: Interrupts processing of a program and transfers control to one of the 256 interrupt (vector) addresses. INT performs the following:

(1) Decrements the SP by 2, pushes the flags onto the stack, and resets the IF and TF flags; (2) decrements the SP by 2, pushes the CS onto the stack, and places the high-order word of the interrupt vector in the CS; and (3) decrements the CS by 2, pushes the IP onto the stack, and fills the IP with the low-order word of the interrupt vector.

Flags: Affects IF and TF.

Object code: |1100110v|--type--| (if v = 0 type is 3)

INTO: Interrupt on Overflow

Operation: Causes an interrupt if an overflow has occurred (the OF flag is set to 1) and performs an INT 4. The interrupt address is at location hex 10H. See also INT.

Flags: None.

Object code: 11001110 (no operands)

IRET: Interrupt Return

Operation: Provides a return from an interrupt routine. IRET performs the following: (1) Pops the word at the top of the stack into the IP, increments the SP by 2, and pops the top of the stack into the CS; (2) increments the SP by 2 and pops the top of the stack into the flags register. This procedure undoes the steps that the interrupt originally took and performs a return. See also RET.

Flags: Affects all.

Object code: 11001111 (no operands)

JA/JNBE: Jump Above or Jump if Not Below/Equal

Operation: Used after a test of unsigned data to transfer to another address. If the CF flag is 0 (no carry) and the ZF flag is 0 (nonzero), the instruction adds the operand offset to the IP and performs a jump.

Flags: None.

Object code: |01110111|--disp--|

JAE/JNB: Jump if Above/Equal or Jump if Not Below

Operation: Used after a test of unsigned data to transfer to another address. If the CF flag is 0 (no carry), the instruction adds the operand offset to the IP and performs a jump.

Flags: None.

Object code: `|01110011|--disp--|`

JB/JNAE: Jump if Below or Jump if Not Above/Equal

Operation: Used after a test of unsigned data to transfer to another address. If the CF flag is 1 (carry), the instruction adds the operand offset to the IP and performs a jump.

Flags: None.

Object code: `|01110010|--disp--|`

JBE/JNA: Jump if Below/Equal or Jump if Not Above

Operation: Used after a test of unsigned data to transfer to another address. If the CF flag is 1 (carry) or the AF flag is 1, the instruction adds the operand offset to the IP and performs a jump.

Flags: None.

Object code: `|01110110|--disp--|`

JC: Jump if Carry

Operation: See JB/JNAE (identical operations).

JCXZ: Jump if CX is Zero

Operation: Jumps to a specified address if the CX contains zero. JCXZ could be useful at the start of a loop.

Flags: None.

Object code: `|11100011|--disp--|`

JE/JZ: Jump if Equal or Jump if Zero

Operation: Used after a test of signed or unsigned data to transfer to another address. If the ZF flag is 1 (zero condition), the instruction adds the operand offset to the IP and performs a jump.

Flags: None.

Object code: `|01110100|--disp--|`

JG/JNLE: Jump if Greater or Jump if Not Less/Equal

Operation: Used after a test of signed data to transfer to another address. If the ZF flag is 0 (nonzero) and the SF flag equals the OF flag (both 0 or both 1), the instruction adds the operand offset to the IP and performs a jump.

Flags: None.

Object code: `|01111111|--disp--|`

JGE/JNL: Jump if Greater/Equal or Jump if Not Less

Operation: Used after a test of signed data to transfer to another address. If the SF flag equals the OF flag (both 0 or both 1), the instruction adds the operand offset to the IP and performs a jump.

Flags: None.

Object code: `|01111101|--disp--|`

JL/JNGE: Jump if Less or Jump if Greater/Equal

Operation: Used after a test of signed data to transfer to another address. If the SF flag is not equal to the OF flag, the instruction adds the operand offset to the IP and performs a jump.

Flags: None.

Object code: `|01111100|--disp--|`

JLE/JNG: Jump if Less/Equal or Jump if Not Greater

Operation: Used after a test of signed data to transfer to another address. If the ZF flag is 1 (zero condition) or if the SF flag is not equal to the OF flag, the instruction adds the operand offset to the IP and performs a jump.

Flags: None.

Object code: `|01111110|--disp--|`

JMP: Unconditional Jump

Operation: Jumps to a designated address under any condition. JMP replaces the IP with a destination offset address. There are five types of JMP operations for transferring control within segments and between segments. An intersegment jump also replaces the CS with a new segment address.

Flags: None.

Object code (five formats):

```
Direct within segment:      |11101001|disp-low |disp-high|
Direct within seg short:    |11101011|--disp---|
Indirect within segment:    |11111111|mod100r/m|
Indirect intersegment:      |11111111|mod101r/m|
Direct intersegment:
    |11101010|offset-low|offset-high|seg-low|seg-high|
```

JNC: Jump No Carry

Operation: See JAE/JNB (identical operations).

JNE/JNZ: Jump Not Equal or Jump Not Zero

Operation: Used after a test of signed data to transfer to another address. If the ZF flag is 0 (nonzero), the instruction adds the operand offset to the IP and performs a jump.

Flags: None.

Object code: `|01110101|--disp--|`

JNO: Jump No Overflow

Operation: Used to jump to a designated address on a test for no overflow. If the OF flag is 0 (no overflow), the instruction adds the operand offset to the IP and performs a jump. See also JO.

Flags: None.

Object code: `|01110001|--disp--|`

JNP/JPO: Jump No Parity or Jump Parity Odd

Operation: Causes a jump to a designated address if an operation caused no (or odd) parity. Odd parity here means that an operation has caused the low order eight bits to be an odd number of bits. If the PF flag is 0 (odd parity), the instruction adds the operand offset to the IP and performs a jump. See also JP/JPE.

Flags: None.

Object code: `|01111011|--disp--|`

JNS: Jump No Sign

Operation: Causes a jump to a designated address if an operation caused the sign to be set to positive. If the SF flag is 0 (positive), JNS adds the operand offset to the IP and performs a jump. See also JS.

Flags: None.

Object code: `|01111001|--disp--|`

JO: Jump if Overflow

Operation: Causes a jump to a designated address if an operation caused an overflow. If the OF flag is 1 (overflow set), JO adds the operand offset to the IP and performs a jump. See also JNO.

Flags: None.

Object code: |01110000|--disp--|

JP/JPE: Jump on Parity or Jump on Parity Even

Operation: Causes a jump to a designated address if an operation caused even parity. Even parity here means that an operation has caused the low order eight bits to be an even number of bits. If the PF flag is 1 (even parity), the instruction adds the operand offset to the IP and performs a jump. See also JNP/JPO.

Flags: None.

Object code: |01111010|--disp--|

JS: Jump on Sign

Operation: Jumps to a designated address if an operation caused the sign to be set to negative. If the SF flag is 1 (negative), JS adds the operand offset to the IP and performs a jump.

Flags: None.

Object code: |01111000|--disp--|

LAHF: Load AH from Flags

Operation: Loads the flags register into the AH. The instruction provides compatibility with the 8080 processor. See also SAHF. LAHF (coded with no operands) inserts the rightmost byte of the flags register into the AH as follows:

S Z * A * P * C (* denotes unused bit)

Flags: None.

Object code: 10011111

LDS: Load Data Segment Register

Operation: Initializes the start address for the data segment and offset address of a variable so that succeeding instructions can access the variable. LDS transfers four bytes in memory containing an offset address and a segment address to a pair of destination registers. The segment address loads in the DS and the offset address transfers to any of the general, index, or pointer registers. The following loads the offset address in the DI:

```
LDS  DI,memory-addr
```

Flags: None.

Object code: |11000101|mod reg r/m|

LES: Load Extra Segment Register

Operation: Initializes the start address for the extra segment and offset address of a variable so that succeeding instructions can access the variable. See also LDS.

Flags: None.

Object code: |11000100|mod reg /m|

LOCK: Lock Bus

Operation: Prevent other (co)processors from changing a data item at the same time. LOCK is a one-byte prefix that you may code immediately before any instruction, for use with an 8087 or other coprocessor. The operation sends a signal to the other processor to prevent it from using the data until the next instruction is completed.

Flags: None.

Object code: 11110000

LODS/LODSB/LODSW: Load Byte or Word String

Operation: Loads the AL with a byte or the AX with a word from memory. Although LODS is a string operation, there is no reason to use it with a REP prefix. The DS:SI registers address a byte (if LODSB) or a word (if LODSW) and load it from memory into the AL or AX. If the DF flag is 0, the operation adds 1 (if byte) or 2 (if word) to the SI; otherwise it subtracts 1 or 2.

Flags: None.

Object code: 1010110w (no operands)

LOOP: Loop until Complete

Operation: Controls executing a routine a specified number of times. The CX should contain a count before starting the loop. LOOP appears at the end of the loop and decrements the CX by 1. If the CX is nonzero, the instruction transfers to the operand address (adds the offset in the IP); otherwise it drops through to the next instruction.

Flags: None.

Object code: `|11100010|--disp--|`

LOOPE/LOOPZ: Loop if Equal or Loop if Zero

Operation: Controls executing a routine a specified number of times or until the ZF flag is set (to 1). LOOPE/LOOPZ is similar to LOOP except that this operation terminates if the CX is 0 or if the ZF flag is 0 (nonzero condition). See also LOOPNE/LOOPNZ.

Flags: None.

Object code: `|11100001|--disp--|`

LOOPNE/LOOPNZ: Loop if Not Equal or Loop if Not Zero

Operation: Controls executing a routine a specified number of times or until the ZF flag is set (to 1). LOOPNE/LOOPNZ is similar to LOOP except that this operation terminates if the CX is 0 or if the ZF flag is set to 1 (zero condition). See also LOOPE/LOOPZ.

Flags: None.

Object code: `|11100000|--disp--|`

MOV: Move Data

Operation: Transfers a byte or word of data between two registers or between a register and memory, and transfers immediate data to a register or memory. MOV cannot transfer between two memory locations -- see MOVS for that feature. There are seven types of MOV instructions.

Flags: None.

Object code (seven formats):

```
Reg/mem to/from reg:    |100010dw|modregr/m|
Immed to reg/mem:
    |1100011w|mod000r/m|---data---|data if w=1|
Immed to register:      |1011wreg|---data--|data if w=1|
Mem to accumulator:     |1010000w| addr-low| addr-high |
Accumulator to mem:     |1010001w| addr-low| addr-high |
Reg/mem to seg reg:     |10001110|mod0sgr/m| (sg = seg reg)
Seg reg to reg/mem:     |10001100|mod0sgr/m| (sg = seg reg)
```

MOVS/MOVSB/MOVSW: Move Byte or Word String

Operation: Moves data between memory locations. Normally used with the REP prefix, MOVSB moves any number of bytes and MOVSW moves any number of words. ES:DI addresses operand 1 and DS:SI addresses operand 2. If the DF flag is 0, the operation moves data from left to right and increments the DI and SI. If the DF flag is 1, the operation moves data from right to left and decrements the DI and SI.

Flags: None.

Object code: 1010010w (no operand).

MUL: Multiply Unsigned

Operation: Multiplies an unsigned multiplicand (8- or 16-bit) by an unsigned multiplier (8- or 16-bit). MUL treats a leftmost 1-bit as a data bit, not a negative sign. For 8-bit multiplication, the multiplicand is in the AL and the multiplier is in a register or memory, coded as MUL CL. The product is developed in the AX. For 16-bit multiplication, the multiplicand is in the AX and the multiplier is in a register or memory, coded as MUL BX. The product is developed in the DX:AX. See also IMUL.

Flags: Affects CF and OF (AF, PF, SF, and ZF are undefined).

Object code: |1111011w|mod100r/m|

NEG: Negate

Operation: Reverses a binary value from positive to negative and from negative to positive. NEG provides two's complement of the specified operand: subtracts the operand from zero and adds 1. Operands may be a byte or word in a register or memory. See also NOT.

Flags: Affects AF, CF, OF, PF, SF, and ZF.

Object code: |1111011w|mod011r/m|

NOP: No Operation

Operation: Used where you want to delete or insert machine code or to delay execution for purposes of timing. NOP simply performs XCHG AX,AX which changes nothing.

Flags: None.

Object code: 10010000 (no operands)

NOT: Logical NOT

Operation: Changes 0-bits to 1-bits and vice versa. The operand is a byte or word in a register or memory. See also NEG.

Flags: None.

Object code: |1111011w|mod 010 r/m|

OR: Logical OR

Operation: Performs logical OR on bits of two operands. The two operands are both bytes or both words in a register or memory; operand

2 may be immediate. OR matches the two operands bit for bit. If either matched bit is 1, the operand 1 bit becomes 1, and is otherwise unchanged. See also AND and XOR.

Flags: Affects CF, OF, PF, SF, and ZF (AF is undefined).

Object code (three formats):

```
Reg/mem with reg:  |000010dw|modregr/m|
Immed to accum'r:  |0000110w|---data--|data if w=1|
Immed to reg/mem:
    |1000000w|mod001r/m|---data----|data if w=1|
```

OUT: Output Byte or Word

Operation: Transfers to an output port a byte from the AL or a word from the AX. Code the port as a fixed numeric operand (as OUT port#,AX) or as a variable in the DX (as OUT DX,AX). The 80186, 80286, and 80386 also support an OUTS (Out String) instruction. See also IN.

Flags: None.

```
Object code: Variable port: |1110111w|
             Fixed port:    |1110011w|--port--|
```

POP: Pop Word off Stack

Operation: Transfers a word (previously pushed on the stack) to a specified destination. The SP register points to the current word at the top of the stack. POP transfers the word to the specified destination and increments the SP by 2. There are three types of POP instructions depending on whether the destination is a general register, segment register, or memory word. See also PUSH.

Flags: None.

Object code (three formats):

```
Register:      |01011reg|
Segment reg:   |000sg111|  (sg implies segment reg)
Reg/memory:    |10001111|mod 000 r/m|
```

POPA: Pop All General Registers (80188, 80186, 80286)

Operation: Pops the DI, SI, BP, SP, BX, DX, CX, AX in that order from the stack and increments the SP by 8. Normally a PUSHA has pushed the registers. The SP value is discarded rather than loaded.

Flags: Affects none.

Object code: 0110 0001 (no operands)

POPF: Pop Flags off Stack

Operation: Transfers bits (previously pushed on the stack) to the flags register. See also PUSHF and POP. The SP register points to the current word at the top of the stack. POPF (coded with no operand) transfers the bits from this word to the flags register and increments the SP by 2. Normally a PUSHF instruction has pushed the flags onto the stack, and POPF restores the bits to the originating flag positions.

Flags: Affects all.

Object code: 10011101 (no operands)

PUSH: Push Word onto Stack

Operation: Saves a word value (address or data item) on the stack for later use. The SP register points to the current word at the top of the stack. PUSH decrements the SP by 2 and transfers a word from the specified operand to the new top of the stack. There are three types of PUSH instructions depending on whether the source is a general register, segment register, or memory word. See also POP and PUSHF.

Flags: None.

Object code (three formats):

```
Register:      |01010reg|
Segment reg:   |000sg110|
Reg/memory:    |11111111|mod 110 r/m|
```

PUSHA: Push All General Registers (80188, 80186, 80286)

Operation: Pushes the AX, CX, DX, BX, SP, BP, SI, DI, in that order, on the stack and decrements the SP by 16. Normally a POPA later pops the registers.

Flags: Affects none.

Object code: 0110 0000 (no operands)

PUSHF: Push Flags onto Stack

Operation: Preserves the contents of the flags register on the stack for later use. The SP register points to the current word at the top of the stack. PUSHF decrements the SP by 2 and transfers the flags to the new top of the stack. See also POPF and PUSH.

Flags: Affects none.

Object code: 10011100 (no operands)

RCL AND RCR: Rotate Left Through Carry and Rotate Right Through Carry

Operation: Rotates bits left or right through the CF flag. The operation can act on a byte or word in a register or memory and can rotate bits left or right. Rotating one bit can specify an operand as 1; rotating more than one bit requires a reference to the CL containing a count. For RCL, the leftmost bit enters the CF flag and the CF bit enters bit-0 of the destination; all other bits shift left. For RCR, bit-0 enters the CF flag and the CF bit enters the leftmost bit of the destination; all other bits shift right. See also ROL and ROR.

Flags: Affects CF and OF.

Object code: RCL: |110100cw|mod010r/m| (if c=0 shift is 1;
RCR: |110100cw|mod011r/m| if c=1 shift is in CL)

REP/REPE/REPZ/REPNE/REPNZ: Repeat String

Operation: Repeats a string operation a specified number of times. These are optional repeat prefixes coded before string instructions CMPS,

MOVS, SCAS, and STOS. Load the CX with a count prior to execution. The operation decrements the CX by 1 for each execution of the string instruction. For REP, the operation repeats until CX is 0. For REPE/REPZ, the operation repeats until CX is nonzero or until ZF is 0 (nonzero condition). For REPNE/REPNZ, the operation repeats until CX is 0 or until ZF is 1 (zero condition).

Flags: See the associated string instruction.

Object code: REP/REPNE: 11110010
REPE: 11110011

RET: Return from a Procedure

Operation: Returns from a procedure previously entered by a CALL. CALL references either a near or far procedure. RET moves the word at the top of the stack to the IP and increments the SP by 2. For an intersegment return, RET also moves the word now at the top of the stack to the CS and again increments the SP by 2. Any numeric operand (a pop-value as RET 4) is added to the SP.

Flags: None.

Object code (four formats):

Within a segment: |11000011|
Within a segment with pop-value:
|11000010|data-low|data-high|
Intersegment |11001011|
Intersegment with pop-value:
|11001010|data-low|data-high|

ROL AND ROR: Rotate Left and Rotate Right

Operation: Rotates bits left or right. The operation can act on a byte or word in a register or memory and can rotate bits left or right. Rotating one bit can specify an operand as 1; rotating more than one bit requires a reference to the CL containing a count. For ROL, the leftmost bit enters bit-0 of the destination; all other bits shift left. For ROR, bit-0 enters the leftmost bit of the destination; all other bits shift right. See also RCL and RCR.

Flags: Affects CF and OF.

Object code: ROL: |110100cw|mod000r/m| (if c=0 count=1;
ROR: |110100cw|mod001r/m| if c=1 count is in CL)

SAHF: Store AH Contents in Flags

Operation: Provides compatibility with the 8080 processor for storing bits from the AH in the flags. See also LAHF. SAHF transfers specific bits from the AH to the flags register as follows:

S Z * A * P * C (* denotes unused bit)

Flags: Affects AF, CF, PF, SF, and ZF.

Object code: 10011110.

SAL, SAR, SHL, and SHR: Shift Left or Shift Right

Operation: Acts on a byte or word in a register or memory and shifts bits left or right. Shifting one bit can specify an operand as 1; shifting more than one bit requires a reference to the CL containing a count. SAR is an arithmetic shift that considers the sign of the referenced field. SHL and SHR are logical shifts that treat the sign bit as a data bit. SAL acts exactly like SHL.

SAL and SHL shift bits left a specified number and fill 0-bits in vacated positions to the right. SHR shifts bits to the right a specified number and fills 0-bits in vacated positions to the left. SAR shifts bits to the right a specified number and fills the sign bit (0 or 1) in vacated positions to the left. In all cases, bits shifted off are lost.

Flags: Affects CF, OF, PF, SF, and ZF (AF is undefined).

Object code: SAL/SHL: |110100cw|mod100r/m| (If c=0 count=1;
SAR: |110100cw|mod111r/m| if c=1 count in CL)
SHR: |110100cw|mod101r/m|

SBB: Subtract with Borrow

Operation: Typically used in multiword binary subtraction to carry an overflowed 1-bit into the next stage of arithmetic. If the CF flag is set

SBB first subtracts 1 from operand 1. SBB always subtracts operand 2 from operand 1, just as SUB does. See also ADC.

Flags: Affects AF, CF, OF, PF, SF, and ZF.

Object code (three formats):

```
Reg/mem with reg:        |000110dw|modregr/m|
Immed from accum'r:      |0001110w|---data--|data if w=1|
Immed from reg/mem:
    |100000sw|mod011r/m|---data----|data if sw=01|
```

SCAS/SCASB/SCASW: Scan Byte or Word String

Operation: Scans a string for a specified byte or word value. For SCASB load a value in the AL, and for SCASW load a value in the AX. ES:DI reference the string in memory that is to be scanned. The operations are normally used with a REPE/REPNE prefix. If the DF flag is 0, the operation scans memory from left to right and increments the DI. If the DF flag is 1, the operation scans memory from right to left and decrements the DI.

Flags: Affects AF, CF, OF, PF, SF, and ZF.

Object code: 1010111w (no operands)

STC: Set Carry Flag

Operation: Sets the CF flag to 1. See also CLC.

Flags: CF (becomes 1).

Object code: 11111001 (no operands)

STD: Set Direction Flag

Operation: Sets the direction flag to 1, which causes string operations such as MOVS and CMPS to process from right to left. See also CLD.

Flags: DF (becomes 1).

Object code: 11111101 (no operands)

STI: Set Interrupt Flag

Operation: Enables maskable external interrupts after execution of the next instruction and sets the IF flag to 1. See also CLI.

Flags: IF (becomes 1).

Object code: 11111011 (no operands)

STOS/STOSB/STOSW: Store Byte or Word String

Operation: Stores a byte or word in memory. When used with a REP prefix, the operation duplicates a string value a specified number of times, suitable for such actions as clearing an area of memory. For STOSB load a byte in the AL, and for STOSW load a word in the AX. ES:DI reference a location in memory where the byte or word is to be stored. If the DF flag is 0, the operation stores in memory from left to right and increments the DI. If the DF flag is 1, the operation stores from right to left and decrements the DI.

Flags: None.

Object code: 1010101w (no operands)

SUB: Subtract Binary Numbers

Operation: Subtracts byte or word binary values in a register, memory, or immediate from a register or subtracts byte or word values in a register or immediate from memory. See also SBB.

Flags: Affects AF, CF, OF, PF, SF, and ZF.

Object code (three formats):

```
Reg/mem with reg:        |001010dw|modregr/m|
Immed from accum'r:      |0010110w|---data--|data if w=1|
Immed from reg/mem:
    |100000sw|mod101r/m|---data----|data if sw=01|
```

TEST: Test Bits

Operation: Tests a byte or word for a specific bit configuration. TEST acts like AND but does not change the destination operand. The two operands are both bytes or both words in a register or memory; operand-2 may be immediate. The instruction sets flags according to AND logic.

Flags: Affects CF, OF, PF, SF, and ZF (AF is undefined).

Object code (three formats):

```
Reg/mem with reg:     |1000010w|modregr/m|
Immed to accum'r:     |1010100w|---data--|data if w=1|
Immed to reg/mem:
    |1111011w|mod000r/m|---data----|data if w=1|
```

WAIT: Put Processor in Wait State

Operation: Allows the processor to remain in a wait state until an external interrupt occurs in order to synchronize it with external devices or with a coprocessor. The processor waits until the external device (or coprocessor) finishes executing and resumes processing on receiving a signal in the TEST pin.

Flags: None.

Object code: 10011011

XCHG: Exchange

Operation: Exchanges two bytes or two words between two registers (as XCHG AH,BL) or between a register and memory (as XCHG CX,word).

Flags: None.

Object code (two formats):

```
Reg with accumulator: |10010reg|
Reg/mem with reg:     |1000011w|mod reg r/m|
```

XLAT: Translate

Operation: Translates bytes into a different format, such as lowercase to uppercase or ASCII to EBCDIC. You have to define a table and load its address in the BX. Load the AL with a byte that XLAT is to translate.

The operation uses the AL value as an offset into the table, selects the byte from the table, and stores it in the AL.

Flags: none.

Object code: 11010111 (no operands)

XOR: Exclusive OR

Operation: Performs logical exclusive OR on bits of two operands, both bytes or both words in a register or memory; operand 2 may be immediate. XOR matches the two operands bit for bit. If the matched bits are the same, XOR sets the operand 1 bit to 0, and if different to 1. See also AND and OR.

Flags: Affects CF, OF, PF, SF, and ZF (AF is undefined).

Object code: (three formats):

Reg/mem with reg: `|001100dw|mod reg r/m|`

Immed to reg/mem:
`|1000000w|mod 110 r/m|---data----|data if w=1|`

Immed to accum'r:
`|0011010w|---data----|data if w=1|`

APPENDIX A

ASCII Character Codes

Following is the representation for the first 128 ASCII character codes. The BASIC manual provides the remaining 128 characters. Note that hex 20 is the standard space or blank.

Table A-1 ASCII Character Set.

Dec	Hex	Char	Dec	Hex	Char	Dec	Hex	Char	Dec	Hex	Char
000	00H	Null	032	20H	sp	064	40H	@	096	60H	`
001	01H	Start heading	033	21H	!	065	41H	A	097	61H	a
002	02H	Start text	034	22H	"	066	42H	B	098	62H	b
003	03H	End text	035	23H	#	067	43H	C	099	63H	c
004	04H	End transmit	036	24H	$	068	44H	D	100	64H	d
005	05H	Enquiry	037	25H	%	069	45H	E	101	65H	e
006	06H	Acknowledge	038	26H	&	070	46H	F	102	66H	f
007	07H	Bell	039	27H	'	071	47H	G	103	67H	g
008	08H	Back space	040	28H	(	072	48H	H	104	68H	h
009	09H	Horiz. tab	041	29H	)	073	49H	I	105	69H	i
010	0AH	Line feed	042	2AH	*	074	4AH	J	106	6AH	j
011	0BH	Vertical tab	043	2BH	+	075	4BH	K	107	6BH	k
012	0CH	Form feed	044	2CH	,	076	4CH	L	108	6CH	l
013	0DH	Carriage ret	045	2DH	–	077	4DH	M	109	6DH	m
014	0EH	Shift out	046	2EH	.	078	4EH	N	110	6EH	n
015	0FH	Shift in	047	2FH	/	079	4FH	O	111	6FH	o
016	10H	Data line esc	048	30H	0	080	50H	P	112	70H	p
017	11H	Dev ctl 1	049	31H	1	081	51H	Q	113	71H	q
018	12H	Dev ctl 2	050	32H	2	082	52H	R	114	72H	r
019	13H	Dev ctl 3	051	33H	3	083	53H	S	115	73H	s
020	14H	Dev ctl 4	052	34H	4	084	54H	T	116	74H	t
021	15H	Neg acknowledg	053	35H	5	085	55H	U	117	75H	u
022	16H	Synch idle	054	36H	6	086	56H	V	118	76H	v
023	17H	End tran block	055	37H	7	087	57H	W	119	77H	w
024	18H	Cancel	056	38H	8	088	58H	X	120	78H	x
025	19H	End of medium	057	39H	9	089	59H	Y	121	79H	y
026	1AH	Substitute	058	3AH	:	090	5AH	Z	122	7AH	z
027	1BH	Escape	059	3BH	;	091	5BH	[	123	7BH	{
028	1CH	File separator	060	3CH	<	092	5CH	\	124	7CH	¦
029	1DH	Group separ.	061	3DH	=	093	5DH		125	7DH	}
030	1EH	Record separ.	062	3EH	>	094	5EH	^	126	7EH	~
031	1FH	Unit separ.	063	3FH	?	095	5FH	_	127	7FH	DEL

APPENDIX B

Hexadecimal/Decimal Conversion

This appendix provides the steps in converting between hexadecimal and decimal formats. The first section shows how to convert hex A7B8 to decimal 42,936 and the second section shows how to convert 42,936 back to hex A7B8.

CONVERTING HEXADECIMAL TO DECIMAL

To convert hex number A7B8 to a decimal number, start with the leftmost hex digit (A), continuously multiply each hex digit by 16, and accumulate the results. Since multiplication is in decimal, convert hex digits A through F to decimal 10 through 15.

First digit: A (10)	10
Multiply by 16	×16
	160
Add next digit, 7	7
	167
Multiply by 16	×16
	2672
Add next digit, B (11)	11
	2683
Multiply by 16	×16
	42,928
Add next digit, 8	8
Decimal value	42,936

You can also use a conversion table. For hex number A7B8, think of the rightmost digit (8) as position 1, the next digit to the left (B) as position 2, the next digit (7) as position 3, and the leftmost digit (A) as position 4. Refer to Table B-1 and locate the value for each hex digit:

Table B-1 Hexadecimal/Decimal Conversion Table.

	HEX	DEC	HEX	DEC	HEX		HEX	DEC	HEX	DEC	HEX	DEC	HEX	DEC	HEX	DEC
	0	0	0	0	0	0	0	0	0	0	0	0	0	0	0	0
	1	268,435,456	1	16,777,216	1	1,048,576	1	65,536	1	4,096	1	256	1	16	1	1
	2	536,870,912	2	33,554,432	2	2,097,152	2	131,072	2	8,192	2	512	2	32	2	2
	3	805,306,368	3	50,331,648	3	3,145,728	3	196,608	3	12,288	3	768	3	48	3	3
	4	1,073,741,824	4	67,108,864	4	4,194,304	4	262,144	4	16,384	4	1,024	4	64	4	4
	5	1,342,177,280	5	83,886,080	5	5,242,880	5	327,680	5	20,480	5	1,280	5	80	5	5
	6	1,610,612,736	6	100,663,296	6	6,291,456	6	393,216	6	24,576	6	1,536	6	96	6	6
	7	1,879,048,192	7	117,440,512	7	7,340,032	7	458,752	7	28,672	7	1,792	7	112	7	7
	8	2,147,483,648	8	134,217,728	8	8,388,608	8	524,288	8	32,768	8	2,048	8	128	8	8
	9	2,415,919,104	9	150,994,944	9	9,437,184	9	589,824	9	36,864	9	2,304	9	144	9	9
	A	2,684,354,560	A	167,772,160	A	10,485,760	A	655,360	A	40,960	A	2,560	A	160	A	10
	B	2,952,790,016	B	184,549,376	B	11,534,336	B	720,896	B	45,056	B	2,816	B	176	B	11
	C	3,221,225,472	C	201,326,592	C	12,582,912	C	786,432	C	49,152	C	3,072	C	192	C	12
	D	3,489,660,928	D	218,103,808	D	13,631,488	D	851,968	D	53,248	D	3,328	D	208	D	13
	E	3,758,096,384	E	234,881,024	E	14,680,064	E	917,504	E	57,344	E	3,584	E	224	E	14
	F	4,026,531,840	F	251,658,240	F	15,728,640	F	983,040	F	61,440	F	3,840	F	240	F	15
Hexadecimal Positions	8		7		6		5		4		3		2		1	

For position 1 (8), column 1 equals	8
For position 2 (B), column 2 equals	176
For position 3 (7), column 3 equals	1,792
For position 4 (A), column 4 equals	40,960
Decimal value	42,936

CONVERTING DECIMAL TO HEXADECIMAL

To convert decimal number 42,936 to hexadecimal, first divide the original number 42,936 by 16; the remainder becomes the rightmost hex digit, 6. Next divide the new quotient 2683 by 16; the remainder, 11 or B, becomes the next hex digit to the left. Develop the hex number from the remainders of each step of the division. Continue in this manner until the quotient is zero.

	Quotient	*Remainder*	*Hex*	
42,936 / 16	2683	8	8	(rightmost)
2,683 / 16	167	11	B	
167 / 16	10	7	7	
10 / 16	0	10	A	(leftmost)

You can also use Table B-1 to convert decimal to hexadecimal. For decimal number 42,936, locate the number that is equal to or next smaller.

Note the equivalent hex number and its position in the table. Subtract the decimal value of that hex digit from 42,936, and locate the difference in the table. The procedure works as follows:

	Decimal	*Hex*
Starting decimal value	42,936	
Subtract next smaller number	40,960	A000
Difference	1,976	
Subtract next smaller number	1,792	700
Difference	184	
Subtract next smaller number	176	B0
Difference	8	8
Final hex number		A7B8

APPENDIX C

Reserved Words

Many of the following reserved words if used to define a data item may confuse the assembler or may cause an assembler error, in some cases a serious one:

Register Names

AH	BH	CH	DH	CS	SS	BP
AL	BL	CL	DL	DS	SI	SP
AX	BX	CX	DX	ES	DI	

Symbolic Instructions

AAA	DIV	JLE	JS	OR	SBB
AAD	ESC	JMP	JZ	OUT	SCAS
AAM	HLT	JNA	LAHF	POP	SHL
AAS	IDIV	JNAE	LDS	POPF	SHR
ADC	IMUL	JNB	LEA	PUSH	STC
ADD	IN	JNBE	LES	PUSHF	STD
AND	INC	JNE	LOCK	RCL	STI
CALL	INT	JNG	LODS	RCR	STOS
CBW	INTO	JNGE	LOOP	REP	SUB
CLC	IRET	JNL	LOOPE	REPE	TEST
CLD	JA	JNLE	LOOPNE	REPNE	WAIT
CLI	JAE	JNO	LOOPNZ	REPNZ	XCHG
CMC	JB	JNP	LOOPZ	REPZ	XLAT
CMP	JBE	JNS	MOV	RET	XOR
CMPS	JCXZ	JNZ	MOVS	ROL	
CWD	JE	JO	MUL	ROR	
DAA	JG	JP	NEG	SAHF	
DAS	JGE	JPE	NOP	SAL	
DEC	JL	JPO	NOT	SAR	

Assembler Pseudo-Operations

ASSUME	END	EXTRN	IFNB	LOCAL	PURGE
COMMENT	ENDIF	GROUP	IFNDEF	MACRO	RECORD
DB	ENDM	IF	IF1	NAME	REPT
DD	ENDP	IFB	IF2	ORG	SEGMENT
DQ	ENDS	IFDEF	INCLUDE	OUT	STRUC
DT	EQU	IFDIF	IRP	PAGE	SUBTTL
DW	EVEN	IFE	IRPC	PROC	TITLE
ELSE	EXITM	IFIDN	LABEL	PUBLIC	

Miscellaneous Items

BYTE	FAR	LENGTH	MOD	PRT	THIS
COMMENT	GE	LINE	NE	SEG	TYPE
CON	GT	LT	NEAR	SHORT	WIDTH
DUP	HIGH	LOW	NOTHING	SIZE	WORD
EQ	LE	MASK	OFFSET	STACK	

APPENDIX D

Assembler and Link Options

ASSEMBLING A PROGRAM

The assembler package contains two versions. ASM.EXE is a smaller version with some features omitted; MASM.EXE has all the features and is the preferred version. Insert the assembler diskette in drive A and your program diskette in drive B. Users of hard disk or RAM disk can substitute the appropriate drive in these examples. Key in the command MASM (or ASM), which causes the assembler program to load from disk into memory. The screen displays:

```
source filename [.ASM]:
object filename [filename.OBJ]:
source listing [NUL.LST]:
cross reference [NUL.CRF]:
```

The cursor is placed at the first line, waiting for you to enter the name of the file. Type the drive (if it's not the default) and the file name. Do not type the extension ASM—the assembler assumes it. The second prompt assumes the same file name, which you may change. If necessary, enter the drive number. The third prompt assumes that you do not want a listing of the assembled program. The last prompt assumes that you do not want a cross-reference listing. To get one on drive B, type B:.

For the last three prompts, press Return if you want to accept the default. Here's an example of prompts and replies in which the assembler is to produce OBJ, LST, and CRF files on drive B:

```
source filename [.ASM]:B:ASMPROG [Return]
object filename [filename.OBJ]:B: [Return]
source listing [NUL.LST]:B: [Return]
cross reference [NUL.CRF]:B: [Return]
```

An alternative to cause assembly is the following:

```
MASM B:name.ASM,B:name.OBJ,B:name.LST,B:name.CRF
```

The following short-cut command allows for defaults:

```
MASM B:filename,B:,B:,B:;
```

- B: filename identifies the source program that is to be assembled.
- The second B: tells the assembler to write the machine language object module onto drive B under filename.OBJ.
- The third B: tells the assembler to write an assembled listing onto drive B under filename.LST.
- The fourth B: generates a cross-reference file under filename.CRF.
- The semicolon at the end of the command tells the assembler to ignore any further options. Although there are none, it is a good habit to code the semicolon for other versions of the command.

For errors, the ASM version lists only a code that is explained in the assembler manual, whereas the MASM version lists a code and explanation. There are in total about 100 error messages.

Assembler options include the following:

MASM /A	Arrange source segments in alphabetic sequence (the default).
MASM /D	Produce an LST file on both pass 1 and 2.
MASM /E	Accept 8087 instructions and generate linkage to FORTRAN and Pascal Emulation Package.
MASM /N	Suppress generation of symbol table.
MASM /R	Accept 8087 instructions (same as /E).
MASM /S	Leave source segments in original sequence.

CROSS-REFERENCE FILE

Use the CRF file to produce a cross-reference listing of labels, symbols, and variables. To request the file, reply to the fourth assembler prompt, assuming that it is to be on drive B:

```
cross-reference [NUL.CRF]:B: [Return]
```

To convert the resulting CRF file to a proper sorted cross-reference, use the assembler CREF program. Enter the command CREF; the screen displays two prompts:

```
Cref filename [.CRF]:
List filename [cross-ref.REF]:
```

For the first prompt, enter the name of the CRF file, such as B:ASMPROG. For the second prompt, you can enter the drive number only and accept the default file name. This choice causes CRF to write a cross reference file named filename.REF on drive B. You can also code the entire command in one line:

```
CREF B:filename.CRF,CON or CREF B:filename.CRF,B:
```

The first example displays the cross-reference on the "console" (screen). The second example writes a file onto disk under the name B:progname.REF.

LINK OPTIONS

To link an EXE module, insert the DOS diskette in drive A and your program diskette in drive B. Users of hard disk or RAM disk can substitute the appropriate drive in these examples. The simplest approach, keying in the command LINK, causes the linker to load from disk into memory. The screen displays:

```
Object Modules [.OBJ]:
Run File [d:filename.EXE]:
List File [NUL.MAP]:
Libraries [.LIB]:
```

The cursor is placed at the first line, waiting for you to enter a file name. Type the drive (if it's not the default) and the file name. Accept the extension OBJ, which the linker assumes. The second prompt assumes the same file name, which you may change. If necessary, enter the drive number. The third prompt assumes that you do not want a listing of the link map. The last prompt is a reference to the DOS library option.

For the last three prompts, just press Return if you want to accept the default. Here's an example of prompts and replies in which the linker is to produce EXE and CON files:

```
Object Modules [.OBJ]:B:ASMPROG [return]
Run File [ASMPROG.EXE]:B: [return]
List File [NUL.MAP]:CON [return]
Libraries [.LIB]: [return]
```

The entry CON causes a display of the link map, which you can check for error messages. You can also enter drive numbers and file names in the LINK command, as

```
LINK B:ASMPROG,B:,CON
```

See the DOS manual for other LINK options.

EXE2BIN OPTIONS

Use the DOS EXE2BIN program to convert EXE modules to COM modules, provided they have been coded according to correct COM requirements. Insert the DOS diskette in drive A and the diskette containing the EXE file in drive B. Hard disk users assume drive C. Enter the following command:

```
EXE2BIN B:filename,B:filename.COM
```

The first operand is the name of the EXE file, which you enter without an extension. The second operand is the name of the COM file; you may change the name, but be sure to code a COM extension. Delete the OBJ and EXE files.

Answers to Selected Questions

1-1. (a) 01001101; (c) 00111111.

1-2. (a) 0101; (c) 10101.

1-3. (a) 00100010; (c) 00100000.

1-4. (a) 11101101; (c) 11000110.

1-5. (a) 00111000; (c) 10000000.

1-6. (a) 51; (c) 5D.

1-7. (a) 23C8; (c) 8000.

1-8. (a) 13; (c) 59; (e) FFF.

1-9. (a) Stack, data, and code; (c) paragraph.

1-10. (a) AX, BX, CX, DX, DI, SI; (c) AX and DX; (e) flags.

1-11. (a) ROM (read-only memory) is permanent and performs startup procedures and handles input/output. (b) RAM (random/access memory) is temporary and is the area where programs and data reside when executing.

2-1. (a) B82946.

2-2. E CS:101 54.

2-3. (a)
```
MOV AX,3004
ADD AX,3000
RET
```
(c) R and IP to set the IP to 0.

2-4. The product is hex 0612.

2-6. Use the N command to name the program (as COM), set the length in the CX, and use the W command to write it.

3-1. TITLE and PAGE.

3-2. (a), (b), and (c) are valid; (d) is invalid because it starts with a number; (e) is valid only if it refers to the AX register.

3-4. (a) END; (c) ENDS.

3-6. RET is an instruction that causes control to return to the operating system; END is a pseudo-op that tells the assembler that there are no more instructions to assemble.

3-7. `ASSUME CS:CDSEG,DS:DATSEG,SS:STKSEG.`

3-8.
```
PUSH DS
SUB AX,AX
PUSH AX
```

4-1. (a) Code the MASM command and reply to the prompts as B:TEMPY, B:, B:, and B:.

4-2. (a) DEBUG B:TEMPY.EXE; (b) B:TEMPY

4-3. (a) Backup of the source file; (c) assembled listing file with source and object code; (e) assembled object file; (g) link map.

4-4.
```
        MOV     AX,DATSEG
        MOV     DS,AX
```

4-5.
```
        MOV     AL,30H
        SHL     AL,1
        MOV     BL,18H
        MUL     BL
```

4-6. The data segment should appear as follows:
```
FLDA    DB      28H
FLDB    DB      14H
FLDC    DW      ?
```

5-1. (a) 2; (c) 10; (e) 8.

5-2. `CONAME DB 'RGB Electronics'`

5-3.
(a) `FLDA DD 73H`
(c) `FLDC DW ?`
(e) `FLDE DW 16, 19, 20, 27, 30`

5-4. (a) ASCII 3236; (b) hex 1A.

5-5. (a) 26; (c) 3A732500.

5-6.
(a) `MOV AX,320`
(c) `ADD BX,40H`
(e) `SHL FLDB,1 (or SAL)`

6-1. 64K.

6-3. It uses the high area of the COM program, or if insufficient space, uses the end of memory.

6-4. `EXE2BIN SAMPLE,SAMPLE.COM.`

7-1. +127 and −128. The operand is a one-byte value allowing for hex 00 through 7F (0 through +128) and hex 80 through FF (−128 through −1).

7-2. (a) 62B; (c) 5EA (convert C6 to two's complement).

7-3. Following is one of many possible solutions:

```
        MOV     AX,00
        MOV     BX,01
        MOV     CX,12
        MOV     DX,00
B20:
        ADD     AX,BX           ;No. is in AX
        MOV     BX,DX
        MOV     DX,AX
        LOOP    B20
```

7-4. (a) `CMP DX,CX` `JA address` (c) `JCXZ address` or `CMP CX,0` `JZ address` (e) `CMP BX,AX` `JLE or JNG`

7-5. (a) OF (1); (c) ZF (1); (e) DF (1).

7-7. The first (main) PROC must be FAR because the operating system links to its address for execution. A NEAR attribute means that the address is within this particular program (i.e., within the assembly).

7-9. Three (one for each CALL).

7-10. (a) 1001 1010; (c) 1111 1011; (e) 0001 1100.

7-12. (a) 01011100 11011100; (c) 11001101 11001000.

8-1. Row = hex 18 and column = hex 27.

8-3.

```
        MOV     AX,0600H        ;Request
        MOV     BH,07           ; clear
        MOV     CX,0C00H        ; screen
        MOV     DX,164FH
        INT     10H
```

8-4. (a) Original DOS function call:

```
MSSGE   DB      'What is the date (mm/dd/yy)?',07H,'$'
        MOV     AH,09           ;Request display
        LEA     DX,MSSGE        ; of date
        INT     21H
```

8-5. (a) Original DOS function call:

```
DATEPAR LABEL   BYTE
MAXLEN  DB      9       ;Space for slashes and return
ACTLEN  DB      ?
DATEFLD DB      9 DUP(' ')
        DB      '$'
        MOV     AH,0AH          ;Request input
        LEA     DX,DATEPAR      ; of date
        INT     21H
```

9-1. (a) 1000 0001; (c) 0111 1000.

9-2. (a)
```
        MOV     AH,00           ;Request set mode
        MOV     AL,02           ; 80-column BW
        INT     10H
```
(c)
```
        MOV     AH,060AH        ;Request scroll 10 lines
        MOV     BH,07           ;Normal video
        MOV     CX,0000         ;Entire screen
        MOV     DX,184FH
        INT     10H
```

9-3. (a) 48; (c) 47.

9-5. Use INT 10H for input and test for the scan code.

10-1. Eight colors for background and 16 for foreground.

10-2. (a) 1011 0101; (c) 1000 1100.

10-3. Low resolution: four bits per pixel gives 16 colors. Medium resolution: two bits per pixel gives 4 colors. High resolution: one bit per pixel gives 2 "colors" (BW).

10-4.
```
        MOV AH,09           ;Display
        MOV AL,04           ;Diamond
        MOV BH,00           ;Page #0
        MOV BL,01011010B    ;Light green on magenta
        MOV CX,05           ;Five times
        INT 10H
```

10-6. First set graphics mode, then use INT 10H (AH=OBH) to set background color.

10-7. First set graphics mode.
```
        MOV AH,0DH          ;Read dot
        MOV CX,13           ;Column
        MOV DX,12           ;Row
        INT 10H
```

11-1. (a)
```
        JCXZ    label2
label1: MOV     AX,[SI]
        MOV     [DI],AX
        INC     DI
        INC     DI
        INC     SI
        INC     SI
        LOOP    label1
label2: ...
```

11-2. Set the DF for right-to-left move. For MOVSB, initialize at NAME1+9 and NAME2+9. For MOVSW, initialize at NAME1+8 and NAME2+8.

The routine at H10SCAS can use

```
MOV AX,'mb'
```

and use SCASW for the scan.

11-3. (a)

```
        CLD                             ;Left to right
        LEA        SI,CONAME            ;Initialize
        LEA        DI,PRLINE            ; to move
        MOV        CX,20                ; 20 bytes
        REP MOVSB
```

(c)

```
        CLD
        LEA        SI,CONAME+2          ;Start at 3rd byte
        LODSW                           ;Load 2 bytes
```

(e)

```
        CLD                             ;Left to right
        MOV        CX,20                ;20 bytes
        LEA        SI,CONAME            ;Initialize
        LEA        DI,PRLINE            ; address
        REPE CMPSB                      ;Compare
```

11-4. One solution is the following:

```
H10SCAS PROC NEAR
        CLD                             ;Left to right
        MOV        CX,10                ;10 bytes
        LEA        DI.NAME1             ;Initialize address
        MOV        AL,'e'               ; & scan character
H20:
        REPNE SCASB                     ;Scan
        JNE        H30                  ;Found?
        CMP        BYTE PTR[DI],'r';Yes — next byte
        JNE        H20                  ; equals r ?
        MOV        AH,03
H30:    RET
H10SCAS ENDP
```

11-5.

```
PATTERN DB 03H,04H,05H,0B4H
DISPLAY DB 80 DUP(' '),'$'
        CLD                             ;Left to right
        LEA        SI,PATTERN           ;Initialize
        LEA        DI,DISPLAY           ; address
        MOV        CX,20                ;20 bytes
        REP MOVSW                       ;Move pattern
```

Then use INT 21H to display the variable DISPLAY.

12-1. (a)

```
        MOV        AX,DATAY
        ADD        AX,DATAX
        MOV        DATAY,AX
```

(b) See Figure 12-2 for multiword addition.

12-2. STC sets the CF flag. The sum is hex 0148 plus hex 0237 plus 1.

12-3. (a)

```
MOV     AX,DATAX
MUL     DATAY
```

(b) See Figure 12-4 for multiplying doubleword by word.

12-5. (a)

```
MOV     AX,DATAX
MOV     BL,25
DIV     BL
```

13-1. (a) ADD generates hex 6C, and AAA generates hex 0102.
(c) SUB generates hex 02, and AAS has no effect.

13-2.

```
        LEA     SI,UNPAK        ;Initialize address
        MOV     CX,04           ; & 4 loops
B20:
        OR      [SI],30H        ;Insert ASCII 3
        INC     SI              ;Increment for next byte
        LOOP    B20             ;Loop 4 times
```

13-3. Use Figure 13-2 as a guide, but initialize CX to 03.

13-4. Use Figure 13-3 as a guide, but initialize CX to 03.

13-5. (a) Convert ASCII to binary:

	Decimal	*Hex*
$8 \times 1 =$	8	8
$2 \times 10 =$	20	14
$3 \times 100 =$	300	12C
$6 \times 1000 =$	6000	1770
$4 \times 10000 =$	40000	9C40
		B4F8

14-1.

```
WKDAYS  DB      'Sunday...'
        DB      'Monday...'
        DB      'Tuesday..'
                ....
```

14-2.

```
DAYNO   DB      ?
DAYNAM  DB      9 DUP(?)
NINE    DB      9
        LEA     SI,WKDAYS   ;Address of table
        SUB     AH,AH       ;Clear AH
        MOV     AL,DAYNO    ;Day of week
        DEC     AL          ;Decrement day,
        MUL     NINE        ; gives location in table
        ADD     SI,AX       ;Add to address of table
        MOV     CX,09       ;Nine characters
        LEA     DI,DAYNAM   ;Address of destination
        REP MOVSB           ;Move 9 chars from table
```

14-3. (a) `ITEMNO    DB   '06 ,'10','14','21','24'`

(c) `ITPRICE   DW   9395,8225,9067,8580,1385`

14-4. A possible organization is into the following procedures:

Main Loop	*Call Subroutines*
B10READ	Display prompt, accept item number.
C10SRCH	Search table, display message if invalid item.
D10MOVE	Extract description & price from table.
E10CONV	Convert quantity from ASCII to binary.
F10CALC	Calculate value (quantity × price).
G10CONV	Convert value from binary to ASCII.
K10DISP	Display description & value on screen.

14-5.
```
SORTAB DB        5 DUP(9 DUP(?))
       LEA       SI,ITDESC       ;Initialize
       LEA       DI,SORTAB       ; table address
       MOV       CX,45           ; & no. of characters
       CLD                       ;Left to right
       REP MOVSB                 ;Move
```

The above routine moves the table. Refer to Figure 14-6 for sorting table entries.

15-1. 512.

15-3. In the directory, the first byte of file name is set to hex E5.

15-5. The first byte of the FAT contains hex F8.

15-6. (a) Positions 28-31 of the directory; (b) hex B4A, stored as 4AOB.

16-1. All the function calls involve INT 21H: (a) 16H; (c) 15H; (e) 14H.

16-2. (a) 4; (b) 108 (9 sectors × 3 tracks × 4 records/track); (c) one access per sector, or 27 in all.

16-3. Use Figure 16-1 as a guide for creating a disk file, and Figure 13-6 for conversion from ASCII to binary.

16-4. Use Figure 16-2 as a guide for reading the disk file, and Figure 13-6 for conversion from binary to ASCII.

16-5. (a) Block 0, record 44; (c) block 1, record 21.

16-6. Decimal 2652 is hex 0A5C, stored as 5C0A0000.

16-7. The function calls involve INT 21H: (a) 22H; (c) 28H.

16-8. FCBFLSZ contains the size of the file in bytes (number of records times length of records), and FCBRCSZ contains the length of records. Divide FCBFLSZ (four bytes in the DX:AX) by FCBRCSZ (two bytes).

16-9. Figure 16-4 provides an example of reading a block.

16-10. Chapter 13 shows how to convert ASCII numbers to binary.

16-11. You could use as guides Figure 16-3 for random reading and Figure 13-6 for conversion between ASCII and binary data.

17-1. 01 and 06.

17-3. (a)

```
MOV     AH,3CH          ;Request create
MOV     CX,00           ;Normal file
LEA     DX,PATH1        ;ASCIIZ string
INT     21H             ;Call DOS
JC      error           ;Exit if error
MOV     CUSTHAN,AX      ;Save handle
```

17-4. (a)

```
MOV     AH,3DH          ;Request open
MOV     AL,00           ;Read only
LEA     DX,PATH1        ;ASCIIZ string
INT     21H             ;Call DOS
JC      error           ;Exit if error
MOV     CUSTHAN,AX      ;Save handle
```

17-5. Where a program opens many files.

18-1. Use INT 13H and AH = 00.

18-2. Use INT 13H and AH = 01.

18-4.

```
MOV     AH,03           ;Request write
MOV     AL,03           ;3 sectors
LEA     BX,OUTDSK       ;Output area
MOV     CH,08           ;Track 08
MOV     CL,01           ;Sector 01
MOV     DH,00           ;Head #0
MOV     DL,01           ;Drive B
INT     13H
```

18-5. Status byte in the AH contains 00000011.

19-2. (a)

```
MOV     AH,05           ;Request print
MOV     DL,0CH          ;Form feed
INT     21H
```

(b)

```
        LEA     SI,NAMEFLD      ;Initialize name
        MOV     CX,length       ; and length
B20:
        MOV     AH,05           ;Request print
        MOV     DL,[SI]         ;Character from name
        INT     21H             ;Call DOS
        INC     SI              ;Next character in name
        LOOP    B20             ;Loop length times
```

(c) You could code line feed (hex 0A) in front of address. The solution is similar to (b). (e) Issue another form feed (hex 0C).

19-3.

```
HEADNG DB   13, 10, 15, 'Title', 12
```

19-5. You won't be able to use CX for looping five times because the loop that prints the name uses the CX. You could use the BX as follows:

```
        MOV         BX,05
C20:
        .
        .
        DEC         BX
        JNZ         C20
```

20-1. (a) .SALL.

20-2. (a)
```
MULTBY MACRO MULTPR,MULTCD
       MOV   AL,MULTCD
       MUL   MULTPR
       ENDM
```

20-3. To include the macro in pass 1, code the following:

```
IF1
  INCLUDE library-name
ENDIF
```

20-4. The macro definition could begin with:

```
BIPRINT MACRO PRTLINE,PRLEN
```

PRTLINE and PRLEN are dummy arguments for the address and length of the line to be printed. Refer to Chapter 19 for using BIOS INT 17H to print.

20-5. Note that you cannot use a conditional IF to test for a zero divisor. A conditional IF works only during assembly, whereas the test must occur during program execution. Code assembler instructions such as the following:

```
CMP  DIVISOR,00      ;Zero divisor?
JNZ  (bypass)        ;No - bypass
CALL (error message routine)
```

21-1. (a) EXTRN SUBPRO:FAR

21-2. (a) PUBLIC QTY,VALUE,PRICE

21-3. Use Figure 21-5 as a guide.

21-4. Use Figure 21-6 as a guide for passing parameters. However, this question involves pushing three variables onto the stack. The called program therefore has to access [BP+10] for the third entry (PRICE) in the stack. You can define your own standard for returning PRICE through the stack. Watch also for the pop-value in the RET operand.

21-5. This program involves material in Chapters 8 (screen I/O), 13 (conversion between ASCII and binary), 12 (binary multiplication), and 21 (linkage to subprograms). Be especially careful of the stack.

Index